**C++** and the Object-Oriented Paradigm

Paradigm

An IS Perspective

C++ and the Object-Oriented Paradigm

An IS Perspective

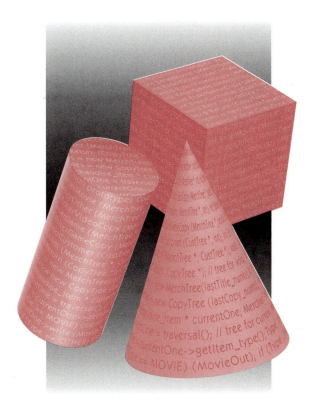

Jan L. Harrington

Marist College, Department of Computer Science
and Information Systems

John Wiley & Sons, Inc.

New York   Chichester   Brisbane   Toronto   Singapore

Acquisitions Editor: Beth Lang Golub
Marketing Manager: Leslie Hines
Production Coordinator: Jeanine Furino
Manufacturing Coordinator: Dorothy Sinclair
Designer: Dawn Stanley
Cover Designer: Laurie Ierardi
Compositor: Black Gryphon Ltd.

ISBN 0-471-10880-4

Printed in the United Stated of America

10 9 8 7 6 5 4 3 2 1

To the Instructor

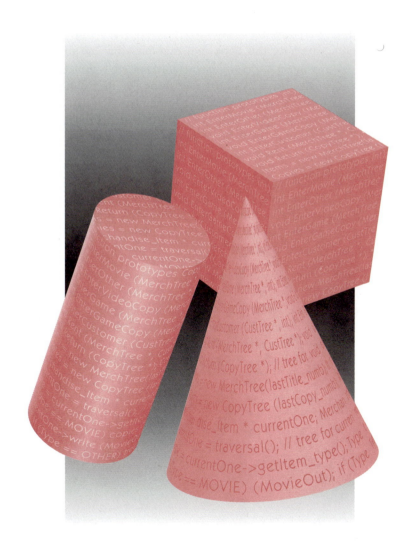

Peruse any current publication that contains job advertisements and you'll find that a significant proportion of those ads are looking for C++ application developers. Although many of today's legacy systems are supported by COBOL programs, much new development has migrated to object-oriented C++. If students majoring in IS are to be competitive when they graduate, they need some competence working with the object-oriented paradigm, and in particular, C++.

There are certainly many books written to teach C++. Why should you pick this one? There are four simple reasons:

- Because this book is written for students studying information systems, not for computer science students. If you are teaching in an MIS, CIS, or IS program, then you will find this book better focused on the specific needs of your students.

- Because this book uses examples that are meaningful to students whose careers will be in a business environment. Instead of computing the areas of graphic shapes or the velocity of an accelerating object, students will see examples such as computing interest on loans and managing the data for a small pharmacy. (The book also contains some "fun" program examples, just to keep things from getting too heavy.)

- Because this book looks at the broader impact of the object-oriented paradigm, rather than just teaching programming. The book begins with a look at the design of object-oriented applications. It finishes with chapters on object-oriented operating systems and object-oriented databases.

- Because this book builds on the programming knowledge your students already have. To use this book, students should be fluent in some structured programming language. Although it is true that those with backgrounds in Pascal, Modula-2, or C will have the easiest time making the transition to C++, students who have only programmed in COBOL will also be able to use this book successfully.

You will also find one other major difference between this text and many other C++ books. This book begins by teaching object-oriented concepts; it doesn't start with the structured elements of the C++ language. Your students already know about writing loops and if statements. Instead, it tries to ease the transition to the object-oriented model by focusing on the building blocks of object-oriented applications. The procedural parts of the language come *after* classes have been introduced.

Your students will find this book easy to read. It's written in an informal, conversational style rather than the formal language found in many computer science textbooks.

Coverage and Organization

One of the biggest issues in creating a book of this type is exactly how much of the language to cover. C++ is a very rich language; experience teaching the course for which this book is designed indicates that there simply isn't enough time in the semester to present every feature of the language. Rather than overwhelm students with more material than they can possibly absorb in one semester, this book covers the fundamentals of the language as it gives students a firm grounding in the object-oriented paradigm.

The book begins by giving students reasons for making the switch from structured to object-oriented programming. In Chapter 1 they look at a program written in C and one in C++ and get a chance to compare the structure and ease of maintenance. (Students don't have to know C to understand the example.) Chapter 2 then tackles the issues of designing object-oriented programs, beginning with a look at the software development life cycle to help students place the software development process in the overall development of an information system. Chapter 2 continues by introducing students to identifying classes and class hierarchies, reinforcing the view of a C++ program as code that manipulates objects.

Chapter 3 begins a student's introduction to the C++ language. In that chapter students learn to write simple class definitions. They are introduced to C++'s simple variable types and to function prototypes. The chapter finishes with a look at a simple function and at using static binding to create objects.

Many instructors have indicated that they would like I/O operations taught early in the course, rather than waiting until the end like many texts. Chapter 4 therefore presents stream I/O. Students learn to treat I/O in a generic fashion, regardless of the source or destination. Chapter 4 also represents a student's first exposure to using the ANSI C++ class libraries.

The procedural portion of C++ is covered in Chapters 5 and 6. Chapter 5 introduces the basic elements of the language; Chapter 6 focuses on arrays. Chapter 6 also introduces the idea of arrays of objects. Because so much business programming involves text processing, Chapter 7 covers string manipulation and string functions and reinforces array concepts by dealing with arrays of strings.

Chapter 8 introduces pointers. Although students who know Pascal, Modula-2, or C will have been introduced to pointers, many students find them difficult to understand and therefore shy away from their use. Chapter 8 therefore teaches pointer concepts from the beginning and includes many examples to show how pointers can be used to access objects and arrays of objects. Chapter 9 discusses the use of pointers to implement object-oriented data structures, including arrays, linked-lists, and binary trees. Students will learn how to create special classes that manage the data structures to hide the details of the data structures from programs using them. The chapter begins with arrays, continues with linked-lists, and ends with binary trees. Should you choose not to cover any of these topics, you can stop partially through the chapter.

Chapters 10 and 11 return to the object-oriented concepts of inheritance, overloading, and polymorphism. Students learn to create class hierarchies and use virtual functions to implement polymorphism. These chapters also reinforce and expand upon the data structures concepts introduced in Chapter 9. If you have chosen not to cover binary trees, you can easily skip the last section of Chapter 10, which deals with in-order traversal of a binary tree.

Appendix A gives students a broad view of how the object-oriented paradigm is used in computing beyond writing stand-alone programs. The first portion of the appendix looks at object-oriented databases, focusing on how the OOP programming model is easily extended to provide a data model. In the second half of the appendix, students learn how OOP concepts have been integrated into operating systems.

Exercises

There are three types of exercises found in this book. The first appears at the end of the first three and Appendix A. These are conceptual, pen-and-paper exercises that are designed to help students master the concepts of the object-oriented paradigm.

The remaining exercises require programming. The first type of programming exercise involves short, stand-alone programs, generally requiring less than three pages of code. These are truly "exercises," designed to help students master some specific element of C++ programming. Some involve simple business problems; others involve simple games to give the students something fun to program.

The second type of programming exercise involves developing a larger business application. There are several longer programs running throughout the exercises of the book, focusing on traditional business programs. These longer programs begin at the end of Chapter 7, after students have been introduced to strings. (It is very difficult to do meaningful business programs without handling text.) You might want to assign one of these to students as a final project. The longer programs are also suitable for teams of students. You can identify the longer programs by the "Long" icon that appears in the margin next to them. (The half moon with a dot under it is a fermata, musical notation for a note that is to be held longer than its assigned time value.)

Long

Support Materials

To help you teach your object-oriented C++ course, you will receive an instructor's manual and an accompanying disk. This disk contains the source code of the examples in this book. It has been formatted under MD-DOS because most people working on alternative platforms can read MS-DOS disks, while the reverse isn't generally true.

The programs have been tested using Turbo C++ for Windows and Visual C++ for Windows as well as Symantec C++ and CodeWarrior C++ for the Macintosh. (Symantec's Macintosh compiler doesn't support binary files; otherwise, the code is compatible.) They use only the ANSI libraries, purposely avoiding those that are specific to any one compiler. If you are working in another environment, you should only have to port the text files to an appropriately formatted disk and check the names of the header files. (Macintosh users will also need to strip the CR/LF characters from the beginning of each line. A global search and replace for the nonprinting character that appears as a box will do the trick.)

Acknowledgments

No book makes it into print without the work of a team of people. I would therefore like to take this opportunity to thank the following important individuals:

- Beth Golub, the Acquisitions Editor at Wiley who's been terrific support all through this project.
- Jeanine Furino, Production Editor, who shepherded this project smoothly through the production process.
- All of the reviewers:
  - Nabil Adams
  - Robert Brown
  - William Crouch
  - John Durham
  - Leonard Garrett
  - Mary Garrett
  - Gordon Howell
  - Jerzy Letkowski
  - Chuck Nelson
  - Steven Roehrig
  - Elmer Swartzmeyer
  - David Teagarden
  - Doreen Vorce
  - Bruce White

From this cast of thousands has sprung this book. Thanks everybody!

JLH

Contents

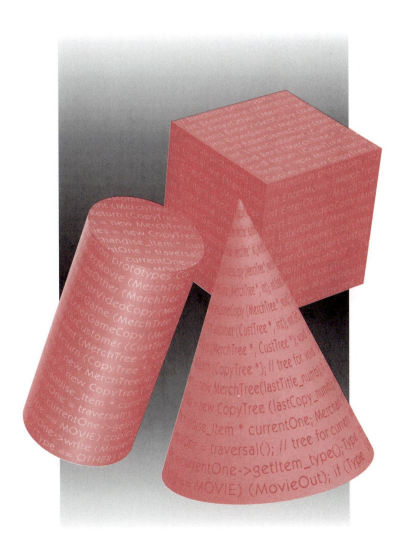

Chapter 5: Structured Elements of C++

Chapter 6: Arrays

Chapter 7: Strings

Chapter 8: Introducing Pointers

Chapter 9: Using Pointers

Chapter 10: Overloading

Chapter 11: Inheritance and Polymorphism

Appendix A: Beyond Programming

Appendix B: Program Listings

Glossary

Index

1

Introducing the Object-Oriented Paradigm

OBJECTIVES

In this chapter you will learn about:

- The advantages that object-oriented technology has over traditional ways of structuring application programs.
- The history of the object-oriented paradigm.
- The basic principles underlying object-oriented technology.

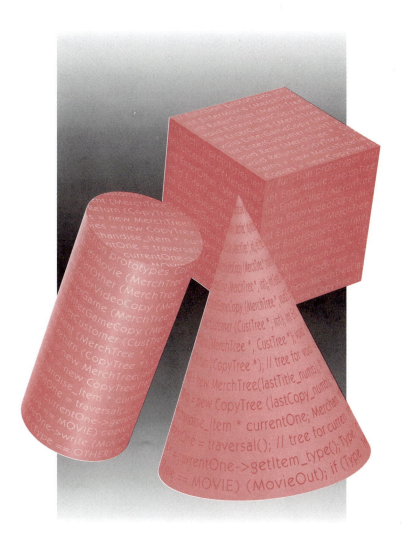

If you look at recent articles in computer journals and magazines, you'll notice an emphasis on something known as *object-oriented programming* (sometimes abbreviated *OOP*). Object-oriented programming is a method for developing and organizing application programs that is fundamentally different from *structured programming*, a technique that has formed the mainstay of good programming practices for more than 20 years.

Because object-oriented programming provides some significant advantages over structured programming, many businesses are developing new application programs using object-oriented methodologies. Object-oriented technology has also had an impact on systems analysis and design procedures, operating systems, and database management. As a whole, object-oriented technology represents a *paradigm* (a theoretical model that can be used as a pattern for some activity). The movement from structured techniques to object-oriented techniques is called a *paradigm shift* because it represents a major change in the methods used to design and develop business data processing applications.

The focus of this book is on designing and creating object-oriented application programs for business use. Although there are a number of languages that can be used to write object-oriented programs, C++ is the most widely used. In this book you will learn to use that language to write object-oriented applications. You will also be exposed to the impact of object-oriented techniques on the software development life cycle, on operating systems, and on database management.

As an introduction to the object-oriented paradigm, this chapter begins by examining the goals of business application programming. It then reviews a program written in a structured programming language. The example uses C, a language that shares many elements with C++. (Even if you don't know C, your familiarity with COBOL, Pascal, or Modula-2 will make it possible for you to follow the logic of the program.) You will read about the ways in which structured programming limits the effectiveness and efficiency of application programming. Then, you will see the same program rewritten in object-oriented C++. You will be introduced to the basic concepts behind its structure and see how those characteristics provide solutions to many of the limitations presented by structured programming.

Note

There are many similarities between C and C++, leading some people to view C++ as a superset of C. Although the two languages do have much syntax in common, they are really distinct languages.

Goals of Application Programming

When a business spends the money to develop its own application programs, it wants to get the most out of its investment by making development faster, cheaper, and as error free as possible. A business also wants to make its programs as easy to modify as possible. (As much as 80 percent of business programming activity involves maintenance of existing programs rather than writing new code.) Some of the techniques that a business might use to achieve these goals include the following:

- Make programs easy to understand by programmers who didn't write the programs. This can be achieved through clear, simple program structure and good documentation. Unfortunately, many businesses report delays of as long as two years between the time a program is requested by a user and the time the program is ready for use. There is often enormous pressure placed on application programmers to produce programs quickly. As a result, both structure and documentation are shortchanged in the rush to simply create working code.

- Create program code that can be reused. Using previously tested modules speeds up program development and makes programs more error free. As you will see, this is easier to do with an object-oriented program than with a structured program.

- Write code that separates data manipulation actions from the user interface. This makes it easier to move program code from one computing platform and/or operating system to another. It is not unusual to find a single business running several operating systems (for example, UNIX, Windows, OS/2, and/or the Macintosh operating system), each of which has its own graphic user interface.

Note

The programs that you see throughout this book use a line-oriented, text-based interface. Writing graphic user interface (GUI) code is specific to the operating system under which the program will run. Although you will read about some of the principles for organizing a user interface, covering a specific GUI is beyond the scope of this book.

Reviewing Structured Programming

Structured programming arose as an attempt to make the structure of application programs easier to develop and maintain. As you know, a structured program is made up of only three logical structures: simple sequence (executing one step after another, in order), iteration (repeating program steps), and selection (choosing between two actions based on the truth of a logical condition). More complex logical procedures are created by nesting the three structures within one another.

As an example of a structured program, take a look at a program that computes repayment tables for consumer loans, showing the interest paid, the payment made, and the principal remaining after the payment, as in Figure 1.1. The loan in Figure 1.1 is a fixed-payment loan (for example, an educational loan). The computations are based on the loan's principal, interest rate, and monthly payment. The program also handles a variable-payment loan (for example, a credit card). In that case, the computations are based on the loan's principal, interest rate, percentage of balance to be paid each month, the minimum monthly payment, and the minimum monthly interest charge.

Like most C programs, the Loans program defines the constants and data structures it uses in a *header file*. As you can see in Listing 1.1, the Loans program uses two data structures, one for each type of loan. (C structures are similar to records in Pascal, Modula-2, and COBOL.) The header file also contains definitions for constants used throughout the program. By giving constants names the program becomes easier to read and easier to modify. (A constant can be changed by modifying its definition in the header file, without needing to search through the program for every place the constant has been used.)

The Loans program appears in Listing 1.2. It is made up of a collection of *functions*. Each function is a self-contained module of code, filling the role of both procedures and functions in Pascal and Modula-2. (There is nothing truly

```
                                        REMAINING
                 PAYMENT   INTEREST  PRINCIPAL
                 -------   --------  ---------
         1        60.00      7.29      947.29
         2        60.00      6.91      894.20
         3        60.00      6.52      840.72
         4        60.00      6.13      786.85
         5        60.00      5.74      732.59
         6        60.00      5.34      677.93
         7        60.00      4.94      622.87
         8        60.00      4.54      567.41
         9        60.00      4.14      511.55
        10        60.00      3.73      455.28
        11        60.00      3.32      398.60
        12        60.00      2.91      341.51
        13        60.00      2.49      284.00
        14        60.00      2.07      226.07
        15        60.00      1.65      167.72
        16        60.00      1.22      108.94
        17        60.00      0.79       49.73
        18        50.10      0.36        0.00
```

Figure 1.1   A loan repayment table

Listing 1.1   Loans.h: Header file for first C loan program

/* Header file for first C version of loan program */
/* Loans1c.h */

```c
#define PAYMENT 0
#define INTEREST 1
#define PRINCIPAL 2
#define MAX_TERM 120
#define NUM_COLUMNS 3

struct Fixed_Payment
{
    float principal;
    float interest_rate;
    float payment;
};
```

Continued next page

Listing 1.1 (Continued) Loans.h: Header file for first C loan program

```
struct Variable_Payment
{
    float principal;
    float interest_rate;
    float payment_percent;
    float minimum_payment;
    float minimum_interest;
};
```

equivalent in COBOL, although subroutines can be used to provide similar functionality and program structure.) The header file is "included" in the program that uses it, meaning that the header file's contents are merged into program when the program is compiled.

Note

To C programmers: There are certainly ways in which the Loans program could be written to make it more compact. However, keep in mind that most people looking at this program don't know C and would therefore find some of C's tricks hard to follow.

Listing 1.2 Loans1.c: First C loan program

```
#include <stdio.h>
#include "Loans1c.h"

/* These are function prototypes, which define the functions used by the program */
int MainMenu ();
void Make_Fixed ();
void Make_Variable ();
void Show_Fixed (float payment_table[MAX_TERM][NUM_COLUMNS], struct
    Fixed_Payment *);
void Show_Variable (float payment_table[MAX_TERM][NUM_COLUMNS], struct
    Variable_Payment *);
void Display_Table (float payment_table[MAX_TERM][NUM_COLUMNS], int);

/* Execution begins with the function called main(); it needs no prototype*/
main()
{
    float payment_table[MAX_TERM][NUM_COLUMNS];  /* array to hold repayments */
    struct Fixed_Payment * fixed, fixed_temp;  /* variable for fixed-payment loan */
    struct Variable_Payment * variable, variable_temp;
        /* variable for a variable-payment loan */
```

Continued next page

Listing 1.2 (Continued) Loans1.c: First C loan program

```
    int choice = 0;
    fixed = &fixed_temp;        /* get pointer to fixed-payment loan storage */
    variable = &variable_temp;  /* get pointer to variable-payment loan storage */

    while (choice != 9)
    {
        choice = MainMenu();    /* display the menu and pick an option */
        switch (choice)         /* select action based on chosen option */
        {
            case 1:
                Make_Fixed (fixed);
                break;
            case 2:
                Show_Fixed (payment_table, fixed);
                break;
            case 3:
                Make_Variable (variable);
                break;
            case 4:
                Show_Variable (payment_table, variable);
                break;
            case 9:
                break;
            default:
                printf ("Unrecognized menu option. Please choose again.\n");
        }
    }
}


/* This function handles the program's single menu */
int MainMenu (void)
{
    int menu_choice;

    printf ("\n\n");           /* formatted output to screen */
    printf ("---- Loan Repayment Schedule Calculator ----\n\n");
    printf ("1. Create a fixed-payment loan\n");
    printf ("2. Display payment table for fixed-payment loan\n");
    printf ("3. Create a variable-payment loan\n");
    printf ("4. Display payment table for variable-payment loan\n");
    printf ("9. Quit\n\n");
    printf ("Choice: ");
    scanf ("%d",&menu_choice);  /* formatted input from keyboard */
    return menu_choice;         /* chosen option is sent back to calling function */
}
```

Continued next page

Listing I.2 (Continued) Loans I.c: First C loan program

```
/* This function gathers the data for a fixed-payment loan */
void Make_Fixed (struct Fixed_Payment * fptr)
{
    printf ("\nprincipal: ");
    scanf ("%f",&fptr->principal);
    printf ("\nInterest rate: ");
    scanf ("%f",&fptr->interest_rate);
    printf ("\nMonthly payment :");
    scanf ("%f",&fptr->payment);
}


/* This function assembles the data for the repayment of a fixed-payment loan */
void Show_Fixed (float payment_table[MAX_TERM][NUM_COLUMNS], struct
    Fixed_Payment * fptr)
{
    int i = 0;
    float monthly_interest;

    while (fptr->principal >= fptr->payment)
    {
        payment_table[i][PAYMENT] = fptr->payment;
        monthly_interest = fptr->principal * (fptr->interest_rate/12.0);
        payment_table[i][INTEREST] = monthly_interest;
        fptr->principal = fptr->principal - fptr->payment - monthly_interest;
        payment_table[i++][PRINCIPAL] = fptr->principal;
    }
    if (fptr->principal > 0.0)
    {
        payment_table[i][INTEREST] = fptr->principal * (fptr->interest_rate/
12.0);
        payment_table[i][PAYMENT] = fptr->principal +
payment_table[i][INTEREST];
        payment_table[i][PRINCIPAL] = 0.0;
    }
    Display_Table (payment_table,i);  /* call the function that displays the table */
}


/* This function gathers data for a variable-payment loan */
void Make_Variable (struct Variable_Payment * vptr)
{
    printf ("\nprincipal: ");
    scanf ("%f",&vptr->principal);
    printf ("\nInterest rate: ");
    scanf ("%f",&vptr->interest_rate);
```

Continued next page

Listing 1.2 (Continued) Loans1.c: First C loan program

```
    printf ("\nPayment Percentage: ");
    scanf ("%f",&vptr->payment_percent);
    printf ("\nMinimum monthly payment: ");
    scanf ("%f",&vptr->minimum_payment);
    printf ("\nMinimum monthly interest: ");
    scanf ("%f",&vptr->minimum_interest);
}


/* This function assembles the data for the repayment of a variable-payment loan */
void Show_Variable (float payment_table[MAX_TERM][NUM_COLUMNS],
    struct Variable_Payment * vptr)
{
    int i = 0;
    float interest, payment;

    while (vptr->principal >= vptr->minimum_payment)
    {
        interest = vptr->principal * (vptr->interest_rate/12.0);
        if (interest < vptr->minimum_interest) interest = vptr-
>minimum_interest;
        payment_table[i][INTEREST] = interest;
        vptr->principal = vptr->principal + interest;
        payment = vptr->principal * vptr->payment_percent;
        if (payment < vptr->minimum_payment) payment = vptr->minimum_payment;
        vptr->principal = vptr->principal - payment;
        payment_table[i][PRINCIPAL] = vptr->principal;
        payment_table[i++][PAYMENT] = payment;
    }
    if (i==0)
        payment_table[i][INTEREST] = 0;
    else
    {
        payment_table[i][INTEREST] = vptr->principal * (vptr->interest_rate/
12.0);
        if (payment_table[i][INTEREST] < vptr->minimum_interest)
            payment_table[i][INTEREST] = vptr->minimum_interest;
    }
    payment_table[i][PAYMENT] = vptr->principal * payment_table[i][INTEREST];
    payment_table[i][PRINCIPAL] = 0.0;
    Display_Table (payment_table, i);   /* call the function that displays the table */
}
```

Continued next page

Listing 1.2 (Continued) Loans1.c: First C loan program

```
/* This function displays the repayment table */
void Display_Table (float payment_table[MAX_TERM][NUM_COLUMNS], int
    num_payments)
{
    int i;

    printf ("                              REMAINING\n");
    printf ("     PAYMENT    INTEREST   PRINCIPAL\n");
    printf ("     -------    --------   ---------\n");
    for (i = 0; i <= num_payments; i++)
        printf ("%3d %10.2f%10.2f%10.2f\n",i, payment_table[i][PAYMENT],
            payment_table[i][INTEREST],payment_table[i][PRINCIPAL]);
    printf ("\n");
}
```

Data are passed into a function through its *parameter list*. The current convention for listing parameters includes both the parameter's data type and its name. For example, int num_payments defines an integer parameter named num_payments. Each function can return one value directly with the return statement. However, multiple values can be returned using other methods. (Don't worry about the details right now; you'll learn a great deal about functions and how values are returned throughout this book.)

Program execution begins with the function named main. (This is true of all C and C++ programs.) By convention, the other functions used by the program follow. (This is in direct contrast to Pascal and Modula-2, where procedures and functions are typically defined first.)

Main's first task is to define variables used by the program, including an array to hold the repayment table, one copy of the fixed-payment loan data structure, and one copy of the variable-payment loan data structure. Main also defines variables to hold pointers to the data structures. These will simplify access to the variables inside the structures.

The bulk of the main function contains a while loop that keeps the program going. This loop continues until the user chooses the Quit option from the menu. Inside the loop, the program calls the MainMenu function to display the menu and accept a choice from the user. The switch statement (similar to a case statement in Pascal or Modula-2 and GO TO/DEPENDING ON in COBOL) then dispatches actions based on the chosen menu option.

As you study the rest of the functions in this program, there are two structural characteristics you should notice. First, the data structures and the code that operates on them are separate; the data structures belong to the program as a whole, rather than being a part of the individual functions that operate on those structures. Second, input and output operations are combined with data manipulation operations. As you will see shortly, there are several reasons why these two characteristics present problems for the development and maintenance of the program.

Because so much business programming activity involves modifying code rather than writing new code, let's now look at what happens when someone tries to add a third type of loan (a mortgage loan) to the Loans program. First, a new data structure must be added to the data file (see Listing 1.3).

Listing 1.3 Loans2c.h: Header file for second C loan program

```
/* Header file for second C version of loan program */
/* Loans2c.h */

#define PAYMENT 0
#define INTEREST 1
#define PRINCIPAL 2
#define MAX_TERM 360
#define NUM_COLUMNS 3

struct Fixed_Payment
{
    float principal;
    float interest_rate;
    float payment;
};

struct Variable_Payment
{
    float principal;
    float interest_rate;
    float payment_percent;
    float minimum_payment;
    float minimum_interest;
};
```

Continued next page

Listing 1.3 (Continued) Loans2c.h: Header file for second C loan program

```
struct Mortgage
{
    float principal;
    float interest_rate;
    int num_periods;
    int periods_per_year;
    float payment;
};
```

The program must also include two new functions to handle the mortgage loan (Listing 1.4). In addition, the MainMenu function (Listing 1.5) and the switch statement that processes menu choices (Listing 1.6) must be modified. Notice at this point that the program is becoming increasingly complex. There are now six functions that handle the loans. However, those six represent really only two types of functions, one to perform input and another to perform the repayment calculations. Nonetheless, each function has its own name and its own parameter list.

Listing 1.4 Make_Mortgage: Functions to support mortgage loan computations

```
void Make_Mortgage (struct Mortgage * mortgage)
{
    printf ("\nPrincipal (0 to compute): ");
    scanf ("%f",&mortgage->principal);
    printf ("\nPayment (0 to compute): ");
    scanf ("%f",&mortgage->payment);
    printf ("\nYearly interest rate: ");
    scanf ("%f",&mortgage->interest_rate);
    printf ("\nTotal payment periods in loan: ");
    scanf ("%d",&mortgage->num_periods);
    printf ("\nPayment periods per year: ");
    scanf ("%d",&mortgage->periods_per_year);
}

void Show_Mortgage (float payment_table[MAX_TERM][NUM_COLUMNS], struct
    Mortgage * mptr)
{
    int i = 0;
    float period_interest_rate, PVIFA;

    period_interest_rate = mptr->interest_rate/mptr->periods_per_year;
```

Continued next page

Listing 1.4 (Continued) Make_Mortgage: Functions to support mortgage loan computations

```
/* PVIFA = present value interest factor */
    PVIFA=(1/period_interest_rate)-(1/(period_interest_rate*pow((double) 1+
        period_interest_rate,(double) mptr->num_periods)));
    if (mptr->payment == 0)
        mptr->payment = mptr->principal/PVIFA;
    else
        if (mptr->principal == 0)
            mptr->principal = mptr->payment * PVIFA;
        else
        {
            printf ("\nYou must enter either principal or payment.");
            return;
        }
    while (mptr->principal > 0.0)
    {
        payment_table[i][INTEREST] = mptr->principal * period_interest_rate;
        payment_table[i][PAYMENT] = mptr->payment;
        mptr->principal = mptr->principal - (mptr->payment -
payment_table[i][INTEREST]);
        payment_table[i++][PRINCIPAL] = mptr->principal;
    }
    Display_Table (payment_table, i-1);
}
```

Listing 1.5   MainMenu: The modified MainMenu function

```
int MainMenu (void)
{
    int menu_choice;

    printf ("\n\n");
    printf ("---- Loan Repayment Schedule Calculator ----\n\n");
    printf ("1. Create a fixed-payment loan\n");
    printf ("2. Display payment table for fixed-payment loan\n");
    printf ("3. Create a variable-payment loan\n");
    printf ("4. Display payment table for variable-payment loan\n");
    printf ("5. Create a mortgage loan\n");
    printf ("6. Display a payment table for a mortgage loan\n");
    printf ("9. Quit\n\n");
    printf ("Choice: ");
    scanf ("%d",&menu_choice);
    return menu_choice;
}
```

Listing 1.6   The modified switch statement

```
while (choice != 9)
{
    choice = MainMenu();
    switch (choice)
    {
        case 1:
            Make_Fixed (fixed);
            break;
        case 2:
            Show_Fixed (payment_table, fixed);
            break;
        case 3:
            Make_Variable (variable);
            break;
        case 4:
            Show_Variable (payment_table, variable);
            break;
        case 5:
            Make_Mortgage (mortgage);
            break;
        case 6:
            Show_Mortgage (payment_table, mortgage);
            break;
        case 9:
            break;
        default:
            printf ("Unrecognized menu option. Please choose again.\n");
    }
}
```

The Limitations of Structured Programming

Now that you've seen what happens when the Loans program must be modified, we can look at the limitations this type of structured program presents in terms of managing the application program development and maintenance process.

Program Complexity

As mentioned earlier, each function that processes loan data must be written specifically to handle a single type of loan. The names of the functions that perform some action on a loan are tailored to the type of loan (for example,

`Make_Fixed` versus `Make_Variable`). The program code that calls a function must therefore be different for each type of loan, even though the functions really only do two things (input data and compute repayment data).

Although this may not be a problem with a program that handles only two types of loans, as you have seen, the complexity of the logic of the program increases as the program is expanded to handle additional types of loans. Such complexity makes a program harder to understand. When we consider that the program is most likely to be modified by someone who didn't write the original code, the difficulty in understanding translates into added time for modifications to be made. To make matters worse, programs that are difficult to understand tend to become even more complex as they are modified. Debugging becomes more difficult, increasing the time it takes to debug as well as increasing the chances that some errors won't be found during the testing process.

A solution would be to present a consistent interface to the programmer for loan processing. Regardless of the type of loan the program is handling, the programmer should be able to call the functions that perform the actions on data in exactly the same way, without having to remember exactly what the function is called for each and every type of loan. Unfortunately, structured programming can't provide this capability because each individual function must have a unique name and calling sequence.

Software Reusability

Because data structures used by the loan calculations are a part of the program as a whole, rather than combined with the functions that perform the calculations, the program as written doesn't lend itself to segmentation so the loan repayment calculations can be reused by other programs. However, a programmer could certainly place the repayment calculations in separate files that could be compiled and then linked into another program. The code could therefore be reused.

Unfortunately, reusing the separately compiled functions is somewhat complex, primarily because the functions lack the consistent programmer interface discussed earlier. Programmers must keep track of different calling sequences for the different types of loans instead of working with a universal calling sequence. Although software reuse is certainly possible, the structured program makes reuse more difficult and time consuming than programmers would like.

Program Portability

Moving the loan program to a different computing platform, especially one that uses a GUI, requires significant changes to the body of the program. This occurs because the I/O code is intermingled with the code that performs the computations on data.

Previewing Object-Oriented Programming

The object-oriented paradigm was developed in 1969 by Dr. Kristin Nygaard, a Norwegian who was trying to write a computer program that described the movements of ships through a fjord. He found that the combination of the tides, the movements of the ships, and the shape of the coastline were difficult to deal with using structured programming. Instead, he looked at the items in the environment he was trying to model—ships, tides, and the fjord's coastline—and the actions each item was likely to take. Then he was able to handle the relationships between them.

The object-oriented technology we use today has evolved from Dr. Nygaard's original work on ships and fjords. The paradigm retains the concept of combining a description of the items in a data processing environment with the actions performed by those items. As you will see, this simplifies the programming environment, presents a consistent interface to the programmer, facilitates software reuse, and generally contributes to making application program development faster and more error free.

Note

There are many software development environments that support object-orientation. In fact, there are many different implementations of C++. In this book, you will learn ANSI C++. ANSI (the American National Standards Institute) has established standards for many computer and database languages. Virtually all C++ compilers support most of the ANSI standard. A compiler developer may also have added special features to make programming easier or to support a graphic user interface.

Basic Object-Oriented Concepts

The object-oriented paradigm exists independent of any specific development environment. Nonetheless, there are some basic concepts that are common to all implementations, including objects, classes, and inheritance. In this section you will be introduced to those basic concepts and get your first look at how they are implemented in C++.

Objects

At the heart of the object-oriented paradigm is the *object*, an entity in the data processing environment that has data that describe it and actions that it can perform. An object can be something that has a physical existence, such as a boat, product, or computer. It can also be an event (for example, the sale of a product, a professional conference, or a business trip), a place, or even a part of a program's user interface (for example, a menu or a window).

Any given object-oriented program can handle many objects. For example, a program that handles the inventory for a retail store uses one object for each product carried by the store. The program manipulates the same data for each object, including the product number, product description, retail price, number of items in stock, and the reorder point.

Each object also knows how to perform actions with its own data. The product object in the inventory program, for example, knows how to create itself and set initial values for all its variables, how to modify its data, and how to evaluate whether enough items are in stock to satisfy a purchase request. The important thing to recognize is that an object consists of *both* the data that describe it and the actions it can perform.

Objects created from classes respond to *messages* they receive from a program or other objects. A message includes an identifier for the group of actions the object is to perform along with the data the object needs to do its work. Messages therefore constitute an object's window to the outside world.

Classes

The template from which objects are created is known as a *class*. A class contains declarations of the data that describe an object along with descriptions of the actions an object knows how to perform. These actions are known as *methods* or *member functions*. (The latter term is most commonly used with C++.)

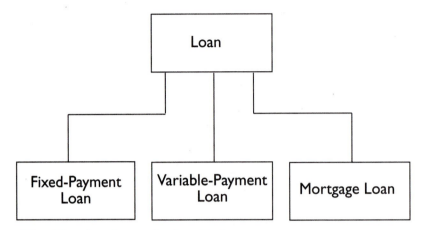

Figure 1.2   The class hierarchy for the Loans program

Note

> One of the great ironies of object-oriented programming is that member functions must be written using structured programming techniques. In fact, it is possible to write ordinary structured programs using C++, without tapping any of the language's object-oriented capabilities.

Classes are often related in a hierarchy that moves from general to specific. For example, the diagram in Figure 1.2 shows the class hierarchy for the object-oriented version of the Loans program. The program begins with a generic type of object known as a Loan. The Loan object has two values that describe it: the loan principal and the interest rate. These are values that are common to all three types of loans. However, the rest of the data that describe a loan are specific to the type of loan.

The specific types of loans therefore share the values defined in the generic Loan object, but add values of their own that distinguish one type of loan from another. The sharing of the characteristics of a generic class by other classes is known as inheritance. In other words, the Fixed-Payment Loan, Variable-Payment Loan, and Mortgage Loan classes inherit the principal and interest rate from the Loan class. They needn't redefine these pieces of data; they only need to add values that give them their individual characteristics.

The Fixed-Payment Loan, Variable-Payment Loan, and Mortgage Loan classes are known as derived classes. The class from which they are derived—Loan—is known as a base class.

Note

Member functions can also be inherited. However, the situation is a bit more involved than with data. You will learn much more about inheritance throughout this book.

Class Variables

Like most object-oriented programs, the object-oriented version of the Loans program declares its classes in a header file. In Listing 1.7 you can see the header file for the first version of the program, which handles just fixed- and variable-payment loans. Notice that the Loan class defines two variables (`principal` and `interest_rate`) and contains prototypes for two functions.

Listing 1.7   Loans.h: Header file for the first C++ loan program

```
#define PAYMENT 0   // description of payment table that must be passed in
#define INTEREST 1
#define PRINCIPAL 2
#define MAX_TERM 120
#define NUM_COLUMNS 3

class Loan   // Generic Loan class from which specific classes are derived
{
    protected:
        float principal;
        float interest_rate;

    public:
        Loan (float float);
        virtual int CreatePaymentTable (float);

};

class Fixed_Payment : public Loan
{
    private:
        float payment;
```

Continued next page

Listing 1.7 (Continued)   Loans.h: Header file for the first C++ loan program

```
    public:
        Fixed_Payment (float i_principal, float i_interest_rate, float
    i_payment);
        int CreatePaymentTable (float payment_table[MAX_TERM][NUM_COLUMNS]);
};

class Variable_Payment : public Loan
{
    private:
```

/* percentage of principal to be paid each month */
```
        float payment_percent;
```

/* minimum payment to be used when principal gets low */
```
        float minimum_payment;

        float minimum_interest;    /* minimum interest assessed */
```

```
    public:
        Variable_Payment(float i_principal, float i_interest_rate,);
            float i_payment_percent, float i_minimum_payment,
                float i_minimum_interest);
        int CreatePaymentTable (float payment_table[MAX_TERM][NUM_COLUMNS]);
};
```

Note

"Declaring" a class is not the same as "defining" a class. When you declare a class, you are setting up a template from which objects can be created. Then, objects can be defined, based on the pattern provided by the declaration. C++ makes this distinction so that the declaration of a class remains independent of any objects that might be created from it. This makes it possible to use the same class declaration in many programs, under many different circumstances.

The variables in the base class have been labeled as `protected`. They are available to derived classes, but not to other classes or programs. The derived classes have labeled their variables as `private`; they are inaccessible outside the class. This technique of restricting variables to classes is known as information hiding. Because information is hidden in this way, objects must use messages to interact with other objects and programs.

Member Functions

The function named Loan is a *constructor*. This is a special function that always has the same name as the class; it is executed automatically whenever an object is created from the class. The second function—CreatePaymentTable—performs the computations necessary to load the repayment table array.

Notice that the remaining two classes—Variable_Payment and Fixed_Payment—don't include the data from the Loan class. Instead, they simply add the data that are specific to the loan. Both Variable_Payment and Fixed_Payment have their own constructors (member functions with the same name as the class). Although each constructor has a different name, keep in mind that the programmer never has to call the constructor; creating an object executes the constructor without a specific request from a program.

Each derived class also contains a prototype for a CreatePayment-Table function. Although these functions have the same name, they will act in different ways, based on the class in which they are defined. The ability to redefine the same function so that it acts differently in different derived classes is known as *polymorphism*. As you will see shortly, this presents a consistent interface to the programmer, making it easier to write and maintain the program that uses these classes.

The member functions are defined in a separate file (Loans.cpp in Listing 1.8). Notice that there is no function to create a payment table for the Loan class. This is intentional. No objects are ever created from Loan; it is merely used as a base class from which other classes are derived.

Note

There is no rule that says member functions have to be in a separate file from their class's definition. However, by convention executable code is placed in its own file or files, while definitions of data structures are placed in header files. For long programs, each class may be placed in its own header file; the member functions for each class are also placed in separate files.

Listing 1.8   Loans.cpp: Member functions for the first version of the C++ loan program

```
#include "Loans.h"
#include <iostream.h>
```

// Constructor for the base class Loan
```
Loan::Loan (float i_principal, float i_interest_rate)
{
    principal = i_principal;
    interest_rate = i_interest_rate;
}
```

// Constructor for the Fixed_Payment class
```
Fixed_Payment::Fixed_Payment(float i_principal, float i_interest_rate,float
    i_payment)
{
    Loan::Loan (i_principal,i_interest_rate);  // Call the base class constructor
    payment = i_payment;
}
```

// Function to create the repayment table for the Fixed_Payment class
```
int Fixed_Payment::CreatePaymentTable (float
    payment_table[MAX_TERM][NUM_COLUMNS])
{
    int i = 0;
    float monthly_interest;

    while (principal >= payment)
    {
        payment_table[i][PAYMENT] = payment;
        monthly_interest = principal * (interest_rate/12.0);
        payment_table[i][INTEREST] = monthly_interest;
        principal = principal - (payment - monthly_interest);
        payment_table[i++][PRINCIPAL] = principal;
    }
    if (principal > 0.0)
    {
        payment_table[i][INTEREST] = principal * (interest_rate/12.0);
        payment_table[i][PAYMENT] = principal + payment_table[i][INTEREST];
        payment_table[i][PRINCIPAL] = 0.0;
    }
    return i;
}
```

Continued next page

Listing 1.8 (Continued) Loans.cpp: Member functions for the first version of the C++ loan program

```cpp
// Constructor for the Variable_Payment class
Variable_Payment::Variable_Payment(float i_principal, float i_interest_rate,)
    float i_payment_percent, float i_minimum_payment, float i_minimum_interest
{
    Loan::Loan (i_principal, i_interest_rate);  // Call the base class constructor
    payment_percent = i_payment_percent;
    minimum_payment = i_minimum_payment;
    minimum_interest = i_minimum_interest;
}


// Function to create the repayment table for the Variable_Payment class */
int Variable_Payment::CreatePaymentTable (float
    payment_table[MAX_TERM][NUM_COLUMNS])
{
    int i = 0;
    float interest, payment;

    while (principal >= minimum_payment)
    {
        interest = principal * (interest_rate/12.0);
        if (interest < minimum_interest) interest = minimum_interest;
        payment_table[i][INTEREST] = interest;
        principal = principal + interest;
        payment = principal * payment_percent;
        if (payment < minimum_payment) payment = minimum_payment;
        principal = principal - payment;
        payment_table[i][PRINCIPAL] = principal;
        payment_table[i++][PAYMENT] = payment;
    }
    if (i == 0)
        payment_table[i][INTEREST] = 0;
    else
    {
        payment_table[i][INTEREST] = principal * (interest_rate/12.0);
        if (payment_table[i][INTEREST] < minimum_interest)
            payment_table[i][INTEREST] = minimum_interest;
    }
    payment_table[i][PAYMENT] = principal + payment_table[i][INTEREST];
    payment_table[i][PRINCIPAL] = 0.0;
    return i;
}
```

The Main Program

The program that uses the classes and member functions appears in Listing 1.9. There are several important differences between this program and the structured program you originally saw in Listing 1.2. First, the program contains code for input and output, but doesn't have code for processing the loans; that code is part of the class definitions that you saw in the Loans.cpp file. The major benefit of this arrangement is that you can change the interface without affecting the code that performs computations.

Listing 1.9 main.cpp: Main program for the first C++ version of the loan program

```
#include <iostream.h>
#include <iomanip.h>

#define PAYMENT 0    // description of payment table
#define INTEREST 1
#define PRINCIPAL 2
#define MAX_TERM 120
#define NUM_COLUMNS 3

// Function prototypes
int MainMenu (void);
Fixed_Payment * Make_Fixed ();
Variable_Payment * Make_Variable ();
void Display_Table (float payment_table[MAX_TERM][NUM_COLUMNS], int);

void main(void)
{
    int choice = 0, num_payments = 0;
    Fixed_Payment * fixed;    // Pointer variable for a Fixed_Payment object
    Variable_Payment * variable;    // Pointer variable for a Variable_Payment object
    float payment_table[MAX_TERM][NUM_COLUMNS];    // Repayment table array

    while (choice != 9)
    {
        choice = MainMenu();
        switch (choice)
        {
            case 1:
                fixed = Make_Fixed ();
                break;
```

Continued next page

Listing 1.9 (Continued) main.cpp: Main program for the first C++ version of the loan program

```
            case 2:
```

// Execute the function that creates the repayment table for a Fixed_Payment object
```
                num_payments = fixed->CreatePaymentTable (payment_table);
```

// Run the local function that displays the repayment table
```
                Display_Table (payment_table, num_payments);
                break;
            case 3:
                variable = Make_Variable ();
                break;
            case 4:
```

// Execute the function that creates the repayment table for a Variable_Payment object
```
                num_payments = variable->CreatePaymentTable (payment_table);
```

// Run the local function that displays the repayment table
```
                Display_Table (payment_table, num_payments);
                break;
            case 9:
                break;
            default:
                cout << "Unrecognized menu option. Please choose again." <<
    endl;
        }
    }
}

int MainMenu (void)
{
    int menu_choice;

    cout << "---- Loan Repayment Schedule Calculator ----\n\n";
    cout << "1. Create a fixed-payment loan" << endl;
    cout << "2. Display payment table for fixed-payment loan" << endl;
    cout << "3. Create a variable-payment loan" << endl;
    cout << "4. Display payment table for variable-payment loan" << endl;
    cout << "9. Quit" << endl << endl;
    cout << "Choice: ";
    cin >> menu_choice;
    return menu_choice;
}
```

Continued next page

Listing 1.9 (Continued) main.cpp: Main program for the first C++ version of the loan program

```
Fixed_Payment * Make_Fixed (void)
{
    float i_principal, i_interest_rate, i_payment;
    Fixed_Payment * objptr;

// Gather data for Fixed_Payment loan
    cout << "\nPrincipal: ";
    cin >> i_principal;
    cout << "\nInterest rate: ";
    cin >> i_interest_rate;
    cout << "\nMonthly payment: ";
    cin >> i_payment;

// Create a Fixed_Payment object and run the constructor
    objptr = new Fixed_Payment (i_principal, i_interest_rate, i_payment);
    return objptr;
}

Variable_Payment * Make_Variable ()
{
    float i_principal, i_interest_rate, i_payment_percent, i_minimum_payment,
        i_minimum_interest;
    Variable_Payment * objptr;

// Gather data for a Variable_Payment loan
    cout << "\nPrincipal: ";
    cin >> i_principal;
    cout << "\nInterest rate: ";
    cin >> i_interest_rate;
    cout << "\nPayment Percentage: ";
    cin >> i_payment_percent;
    cout << "\nMinimum monthly payment: ";
    cin >> i_minimum_payment;
    cout << "\nMinimum monthly interest: ";
    cin >> i_minimum_interest;

// Create a Variable_Payment object and run the constructor
    objptr = new Variable_Payment (i_principal, i_interest_rate,
    i_payment_percent,
        i_minimum_payment, i_minimum_interest);
    return objptr;
}
```

Continued next page

Listing 1.9 (Continued) main.cpp: Main program for the first C++ version of the loan program

```
// Display the repayment table; this is included in the main program because it
// is totally I/O and therefore dependent on the computing platform.
void Display_Table (float payment_table[MAX_TERM][NUM_COLUMNS],int
    num_payments)
{
    cout << "                              REMAINING" << endl;
    cout << "      PAYMENT " << "INTEREST" << "PRINCIPAL" << endl;
    cout << "      ------- " << "---------" << "---------" << endl;
    for (int i = 0; i <= num_payments; i++)
    {
        cout << setiosflags(ios::showpoint | ios::fixed | ios::right);
        cout << setw(3) << i+1
            << setw(10) << setprecision(2) << payment_table[i][PAYMENT]
            << setw(10) << setprecision(2) <<payment_table[i][INTEREST]
            << setw(10) << setprecision (2) <<payment_table[i][PRINCIPAL] <<
    endl;
    }
    cout << endl;
}
```

Second, `main.cpp` is considerably less complex than the structured version of the program. Although the C++ functions to create objects look very much like the C functions to initialize the structures that contain loan data, the C++ program doesn't need separate functions to create repayment tables. Instead, the program calls the member functions that are part of the objects. The `main.cpp` function is therefore easier to understand than `Loans.c`. This will cut down on the time and effort required for someone who didn't write the initial program to make modifications. It will also help keep the program's logic simple and clean as the program changes over time.

Third, the separation of the member functions from the main program makes it easier to reuse the classes. The `Loans.cpp` file can be compiled and stored in a program library. A programmer who wants to use the loan repayment computations then only needs to know the data required by each class and the structure of the array used to hold the repayment table to incorporate the computations in his or her program.

Finally, the programmer handles each class in exactly the same way. For example, a new object, regardless of type, is created with the syntax

```
pointer_variable = new Object_Name (parameter_list)
```

The new operator allocates a block of memory for the object, runs the constructor, and returns the main memory address of the block of memory (a *pointer*). The program can then use this pointer to reference the object.

Note

If your programming background is in C, Pascal, or Modula-2, then you've been introduced to pointers, although you probably aren't thrilled about using them. If your programming background is in COBOL, then it's likely that you've never used pointers. However, you can't write good programs in C++ without using pointers in some way. You will therefore find a lot of emphasis on pointers throughout this book.

When the program wants to execute a member function other than the constructor, it uses the pointer to the object's location in memory to indicate the specific object with which it wants to work. For example, in main.cpp, the pointer variable fixed contains a pointer to a fixed-payment loan; the pointer variable variable contains a pointer to a variable-payment loan. The statements to create the repayment table are therefore

```
num_payments=fixed->CreatePaymentTable(payment_table)
num_payments=variable->CreatePaymentTable(payment_table)
```

The important thing to recognize is that the functions are called in exactly the same way. In other words, the programmer has to deal with only one method for performing a given action, even though the entity on which the action is performed is slightly different. By providing the programmer with a consistent interface in this way, object-oriented programming simplifies and speeds up writing code and debugging.

Object-oriented programming also makes modifying programs easier. When the time comes to add mortgage loans to the program, the first change is to add a new derived class to the header file (see Listing 1.10). Then, the member functions for that class must be written, in this case stored in the Loan.cpp file (Listing 1.11).

The final modifications are made to main.cpp. Because the object-oriented program is simpler than the structured program, adding support for a new type of loan is also simpler than modifying the C program. The modifications include changing the main menu to include two new options, just as with the C program (Listing 1.5), creating a function to gather the data

Listing 1.10   The class definition for a mortgage loan

```
const PAYMENT = 0;      /* description of payment table that must be passed in */
class Mortgage : public Loan
{
    private:
        int num_periods;
        int periods_per_year;
        float payment;

    public:
        Mortgage(int num_periods, int periods_per_year, float principal,
            float interest_rate, float payment);
        int CreatePaymentTable (float payment_table[MAX_TERM][NUM_COLUMNS]);
};
```

Listing 1.11   Member functions for the Mortgage class

```
Mortgage::Mortgage(int num_periods, int periods_per_year, float principal,
        float interest_rate, float payment);
{
    Loan::Loan(i_principal, i_interest_rate);
    num_periods = 0;
    periods_per_year = 0;
    payment = 0;
}

int Mortgage::CreatePaymentTable (float payment_table[MAX_TERM][NUM_COLUMNS])
{
    int i = 0;
    float period_interest_rate, PVIFA;

    period_interest_rate = interest_rate/periods_per_year;
    PVIFA = (1/period_interest_rate) - (1/(period_interest_rate * pow((double)
    1 + period_interest_rate,(double) num_periods)));
    if (payment == 0)
        payment = principal/PVIFA;
    else
        if (principal == 0)
            principal = payment * PVIFA;
        else
        {
            cout << "\nYou must enter either principal or payment.";
            return (0);
        }
```

Continued next page

Listing 1.11 (Continued) Member functions for the Mortgage class

```
    while (principal > 0.0)
    {
        payment_table[i][INTEREST] = principal * period_interest_rate;
        payment_table[i][PAYMENT] = payment;
        principal = principal - (payment - payment_table[i][INTEREST]);
        payment_table[i++][PRINCIPAL] = principal;
    }
    return i-1;
}
```

for the mortgage loan object (Listing 1.12), and finally adding code to the `switch` statement that supports both creating the new object and creating its repayment table (Listing 1.13).

Listing 1.12 Make_Mortgage: The function to gather data for a mortgage loan and create the object

```
Mortgage * Make_Mortgage ()
{
    int i_num_periods, i_periods_per_year;
    float i_principal, i_interest_rate, i_payment;
    Mortgage * objptr;

    cout << "\nPrincipal (0 to compute): ";
    cin >> i_principal;
    cout << "Payment: (0 to compute) ";
    cin >> i_payment;
    cout << "Yearly interest rate: ";
    cin >> i_interest_rate;
    cout << "Total payment periods in loan: ";
    cin >> i_num_periods;
    cout << "Payment periods per year: ";
    cin >> i_periods_per_year;
    objptr = new Mortgage
    (i_num_periods,i_periods_per_year,i_principal,i_interest_rate,
        i_payment);
    return objptr;
}
```

Listing 1.13   Adding support for mortgage loans to the object-oriented version of the loan repayment program

```
while (choice != 9)
{
    choice = MainMenu();
    switch (choice)
    {
        case 1:
            fixed = Make_Fixed ();
            break;
        case 2:
            num_payments = fixed->CreatePaymentTable (payment_table);
            Display_Table (payment_table, num_payments);
            break;
        case 3:
            variable = Make_Variable ();
            break;
        case 4:
            num_payments = variable->CreatePaymentTable (payment_table);
            Display_Table (payment_table, num_payments);
            break;
        case 5:
            mortgage = Make_Mortgage();
            break;
        case 6:
            num_payments = mortgage->CreatePaymentTable (payment_table);
            Display_Table (payment_table, num_payments);
            break;
        case 9:
            break;
        default:
            cout << "Unrecognized menu option. Please choose again." <<
endl;
    }
}
```

The important thing to notice when looking at Listing 1.13 is that the repayment table for the mortgage loan is created in exactly the same way as the repayment tables for the first two types of loans. This is a much easier modification for the programmer because the coding remains consistent. The program also remains simpler, even as functionality is added.

Summary

In this chapter you have read about some of the goals of business application program development, including the following:

- Programs should be developed as quickly and cheaply as possible.
- Programs should be as error free as possible.
- Programs should be easy to modify by programmers who didn't originally write the program.
- As much code as possible should be reusable.
- Data manipulation should be separate from I/O code to facilitate porting programs to different hardware and operating system platforms.

Prior to the widespread use of object-oriented programming, structured programming was considered to be the best way of organizing an application program to meet the preceding goals. However, structured programs present the following limitations to the application development process:

- Programs that handle many versions of the same action become unnecessarily complex; the programmer must perform every action individually, regardless of the similarity of the action to others in the program. This complexity tends to increase as programs are modified over time, leading to increased maintenance time and more difficult debugging.
- Software reuse, although possible, is difficult because there is no consistent interface for the programmer.
- Program portability is difficult because I/O code is intertwined with code that manipulates data.

Object-oriented programming attempts to remove these limitations. In the object-oriented paradigm, entities in the program environment are defined as objects. Objects have data that describe them and member functions that define what the objects know how to do.

The templates from which objects are created are called classes. Classes can be arranged in a hierarchy that moves from the general to the specific. General classes (base classes) share their variables and member functions with more specific classes created from them (derived classes); this is known as inheritance.

Related derived classes that perform similar actions in slightly different ways present a consistent interface to the programmer. The programmer sends the same message to the class. The class acts on that message according to the definition of the member function. The ability for different classes to act in different ways to the same message is known as polymorphism.

The internals of a class are hidden from the program that uses it. This reduces program complexity. Information hiding also facilitates software reuse. In addition, object-oriented programs separate I/O from data manipulation code, making it much easier to move software from one computing platform to another.

Exercises

1. Think about the world in which you live. List at least five examples of how you view your environment in terms of objects.

2. To some extent, you can imitate object-orientation in a structured programming language such as C, Pascal, or COBOL. Pick a non-OOP language with which you are familiar and explain how this might be done. What would be the drawbacks to actual use of such a "simulated OOP" system?

3. On a farm, when people plowed with a horse or other draft animal, the animal had behaviors of its own, much as does an object in an object-oriented program. When tractors became available, farmers had mechanical draft animals that couldn't learn behaviors in the same way as live draft animals. How has this change affected what the farmer has to do? What does this tell you about the relationship between objects and the programs that use them?

4. When an executive assigns people to tasks on a project team or committee, he or she often makes those assignments based on knowledge of the capabilities of the people being assigned. However, in some cases, it isn't

possible to know the capabilities of people who will be making up a project team or committee.

- How does familiarity with the capabilities of the people in question make task assignment and supervision easier in large projects?
- What might a manager do if he or she doesn't have good information about the capabilities of the people he or she is assigning to a project?
- Draw an analogy between the answers you have just written and the idea of classes and member functions.

5. As you read in this chapter, one of the major reasons for object-oriented development is the ability to reuse software developed in earlier projects. To implement software reuse, you must keep track of reusable code in some way. Outline a method for keeping track of reusable software:

- What data about reusable software should be collected?
- How will you ensure that the code is adequately debugged?
- How will you add, modify, or delete software in the collection?
- How will you make reusable code available to your organization?
- Compare these answers to read in this chapter about C++.

6. Third-generation high-level structured programming languages such as COBOL or Pascal tend to run into trouble on very large projects. List the major types of and/or reasons for this trouble. In each case, identify one or more features of object-oriented programming that might alleviate the problem.

7. Object-oriented programming systems tend to be thought of as a major tool for coping with extremely large systems development projects. Do you think there will eventually emerge a category of projects too large or too complex even for OOP? What would be the characteristics of such projects? What measures would be needed to cope with them?

8. Are classes themselves objects? Why or why not? If they are objects, what special characteristics should or do they have?

2 Designing Object-Oriented Applications

OBJECTIVES

As you read this chapter you will learn about:
- The way in which software development fits into the systems development life cycle.
- The process for designing an object-oriented application, including identifying classes and class hierarchies.

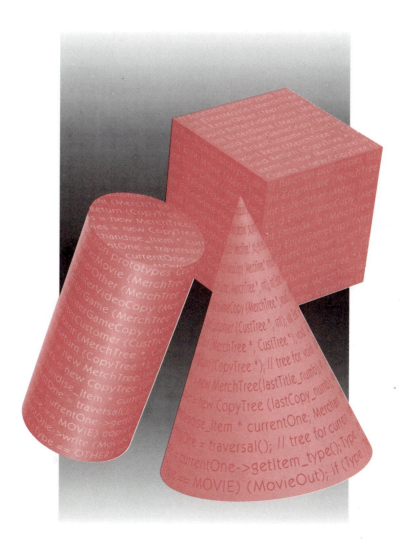

It's very tempting to dive right into a new programming language, to start programming right away. However, in most cases that's a big mistake. Experience has shown that successful application development projects are carefully planned before they are started. The development team pays special attention to the needs of the users and follows a set of procedures—the *software development life cycle*—that has been shown to provide a solid framework for the development process.

This chapter begins by reviewing the software development life cycle. It then turns to the specific issues of object-oriented applications, in particular the very difficult issue of figuring out exactly what a class is and how classes are related.

The Software Development Life Cycle

If you have taken a systems analysis and design course, then you are probably familiar with the *system development life cycle*, the process commonly used to design and implement information systems. Although there are many ways to represent its steps, the systems development life cycle generally includes the following phases:

- Analyzing a business environment to determine user and organizational needs.
- Developing alternative solutions to meet those needs.
- Evaluating and choosing an alternative.
- Designing a system to meet the specifications of the chosen alternative.
- Developing the system.
- Putting the system into everyday use.

The software development life cycle is a subset of the system development life cycle, focusing on the creation of software. It fits inside the system design and implementation phases of the system development life cycle and includes the following activities:

- Determining user needs. For programs that are part of a systems development project, this has already been performed during the analysis phase of the system development life cycle. However, if the program is being added to a system already in use, the programming team will need to determine exactly what the users need the program to do before proceeding any further.

- Designing the program. This takes place during the detailed system design phase of the system development life cycle.
- Writing the program. This takes place during the development phase of the system development life cycle.
- Testing the program. This also takes place during the development phase of the system development life cycle.

Determining User Needs

When a program is part of a major systems development project, basic user needs are determined during the needs assessment phase of the systems development life cycle. However, once a system has been released by the developers for everyday use, it is not unusual for users to realize that they need programs to perform added functions. In that case, an information systems manager may assign the development of a specific program to a programmer (or team of programmers), who is then responsible for the entire software development process.

How do you find out what a user wants a program to do? The most obvious answer is to ask the user. However, that's not as easy as it sounds. Users often have trouble expressing what they need. To make matters worse, what you hear the user saying may not be what the user thinks he or she said. (Remember the "telephone game"?) There are, however, some things you can do to increase the effectiveness of the communication between you and someone for whom you will be writing a program:

- Ask the user to show you, on paper, the output that he or she would like to have. For many people, *showing* what they want is easier than telling.
- Ask the user to demonstrate how he or she intends to use the program. This is another technique that can help people who have trouble verbalizing their needs.
- Repeat back to the user what you thought the user said. Let the user indicate whether what you heard is what he or she meant. This gives you a chance to clear up any misunderstandings in communication.

- After the interview with the user is over, write down what you think the user is asking the program to do. Let the user review the document. This is a further check that you have understood what the user wants (not necessarily what the user said).

A small word of caution is in order at this point. Even if you understand exactly what a user wants, you may not always be able to meet those needs. Some programs are simply infeasible. In other words, it may be that the effort to write and debug the program will take more organizational resources than the benefits of the program warrant. It may also be that running the program will tie up computing resources disproportionate to the benefit of the output provided by the program.

In most cases, if a programmer or programming team leader (in the case of a team effort) believes a programming assignment to be infeasible, he or she brings those concerns to the attention of the person who originally assigned the program development task. The manager can then reevaluate the user's request for the program and decide whether to go ahead with the project.

Designing the Program

Program design is performed either by the single programmer assigned to write a program or by members of a programming team. In the case of a team project, the entire team often works together to create a high-level design that defines the major functions the program should perform. Portions of the design are then assigned to individual programmers who flesh out the detail.

This process is known as *top-down design* because the overall structure of the program is designed first and the details are filled in later. In the case of an object-oriented program, top-down design means identifying the major functions the program must perform and the objects on which the program will act. Designing the member functions and the specific actions they must perform are part of the refining process.

The major alternative to top-down design is *bottom-up design*. The bottom-up process begins by identifying functional modules that a program will use and then assembling those modules into a complete program. As you become more familiar with the object-oriented paradigm, you will see that bottom-up design isn't well suited to that model. For example, it is difficult to define member functions when you haven't first defined the type of object the function will manipulate.

Writing the Program

Writing the program is the process of taking the program design and turning it into executable code. Assuming the program design has been completed, there is no specific order in which portions of the program should be written, although at least a minimal `main` function is usually among the first written so that other functions can be tested immediately.

Writing a program often requires more than simply writing code. Keep in mind that business software is often modified by programmers who didn't write the program. This means that the maintenance programmer must spend time figuring out the logic of the program before any modifications can be made. If a program is poorly structured and/or poorly documented, then understanding the code can take longer than rewriting the program from scratch would take.

To make programs easier to modify, many IS departments have developed programming standards. Typical standards cover the following areas:

- Naming conventions: Naming conventions govern the naming of functions, variables, and constants. For example, a naming standard might indicate that the names of all constants should be in upper-case letters and that array index variables should be named $xidxn$ and $yidxn$, where n is a number used to distinguish one array from another. By naming items consistently throughout all programs, programmers know what to expect when reading a program they didn't write.

- Documentation standards: Although it takes time and effort to add comment statements to programs, they are probably the most valuable type of documentation that can be provided for a program. Documentation standards usually specify the minimal places in a program that should be commented. For example, a documentation standard might indicate that every function should include a statement of the purpose of the function and that it should include a data dictionary (a statement of the purpose of every variable and constant used in the function).

- Physical layout: The physical layout of the code in a program's source file can seriously affect the program's readability. Programming standards therefore often cover issues such as placement of portions of code in separate files and the indentation of related blocks of code.

Software Testing

Software testing is the process through which software developers ensure that a program is as error free as possible. When creating a software testing scheme, programmers must decide who will do the testing and exactly what will be tested. Because poorly debugged software is a common cause of inaccurate data, it is vitally important that software testing plans be comprehensive.

Who Should Test Software

When a programmer writes a program, he or she runs the program to find out if it is working properly. A programmer usually catches many of a program's bugs during this self-testing process. However, should the programmer be the only person to test the software? Who should make the determination that the program is ready to be turned over to the users? As surprising as it may seem, the answer is "not the programmer."

Note

A program that compiles successfully doesn't necessarily "work." To be considered a working program, a program must meet the specifications set down in its design, must run without crashing, and must produce accurate results.

Most programmers unconsciously tend to run their programs in such a way that, once the major bugs have been eliminated, the program works. Programmers know the program intimately and understand how it should be used. Unfortunately, users can't read the programmers' minds and often do things with a program that a programmer didn't anticipate. It is therefore essential that software be tested by people who didn't write it. In particular, users should be involved in the testing process.

Commercial software developers send copies of software under development to external users for testing. This "beta test" phase lets people who use the program in their daily activities test it in a realistic manner, using real data in a real business setting. Programs written for in-house use should also be tested by users.

Note

There are a number of stories floating around the computer industry about user misunderstandings of software. One of the oldest concerns a user calling a technical support line. The user said to the technical support specialist: "It says on the screen to press any key to continue. Where's the 'any' key?" This is exactly the type of software problem that user testing is designed to catch.

What Should Be Tested and the Testing Plan

How a program is tested is just as important as who does the testing. To be effective, testing should be based on some testing plan that answers the questions:

- What should be tested?
- What data should be used?
- How should testing organized?

The detail with which the testing plan is specified often varies with who is doing the testing. Testing done by programmers is usually clearly laid out. In some organizations, programmers use a checklist of features that are to be tested along with specifications of the test data they are to use. In particular, programmers want to test extreme values (very high and very low values), situations where the program has very little data, and situations where the program is using large amounts of data. They also want to see what happens when someone enters unacceptable values or when file operations fail as a test of the program's error-handling routines.

When a program is sent to users for testing, instructions are considerably more vague. The intent of outside testing is so let someone who doesn't know the internals of the program use the program naturally. This is often the best way to identify features that don't work as a user expects, that a user finds hard to understand, or that simply don't work at all. Whenever a user finds a problem, he or she fills out a form explaining the problem, which is then transmitted to the programmers for action.

Note

You can put a professional programmer's testing methods to work on your own programs. When you test programs written for this class, be sure to test extreme values; test for bad input data and failure of file operations. (You will see examples of code to handle bad data and file problems throughout this book.) If your instructor allows it, you may also want to let someone else run your program to see if any errors arise that you hadn't anticipated.

Deciding When the Program Is Ready

One of the toughest decisions in any software development project is deciding when the program is ready to be released to users for everyday use. Typically, this occurs when programmers have fixed most or all of the problems identified during the testing phase. In most cases, errors are documented and checked off as they are fixed. When only a few minor errors remain, a programming team leader or software development manager makes the decision whether the program can be released with those errors. The manager weighs the benefits of getting the program to the users quickly against the cost of releasing software containing known bugs.

Designing Object-Oriented Programs

Like any other program, the design of an object-oriented program takes place during the design phase of the software development life cycle. Designing an object-oriented program means using the needs of the users and knowledge of the environment that the program will serve to create a structure for the program. However, designing an object-oriented program is unique in that it means looking at the program in terms of the objects it will manipulate. In fact, probably the most difficult part of creating object-oriented software is identifying the classes needed by the software and the way in which those classes interact. Once you've defined a program's class hierarchy, writing the class declarations in C++ is relatively easy.

Unfortunately, there aren't any simple rules for determining what the classes should be for any given program; identifying classes can be as much of an art as a science. The process is somewhat imprecise because there is often more than one way to design an object-oriented program. Choosing between alternative designs involves weighing the advantages and disadvantages of each; it's not unusual for there to be no clear-cut best design. To make the process a bit easier, let's start by looking at some examples. Once you understand the examples, we'll generalize some guidelines you can use when you approach your own programs.

The Office Supply Inventory

Hard times have hit the major international management consulting firm of Rye Associates Inc. Top management has ordered financial cutbacks in every aspect of the organization, including the purchasing of office supplies. Instead of simply ordering whatever anyone needs, office managers have been instructed to keep detailed records of office supply levels. In other words, corporate management wants to know the state of the current office supply inventory at any given time. It also wants office managers to reorder only when levels drop below a predetermined reorder point.

Although many office managers see the demand to keep track of office supplies as a major burden, the head of Information Systems has come up with a relatively simple solution. She asks one of the C++ programmers to create a program that tracks current inventory levels of office supplies. At the end of each month, one of the department secretaries will take a physical inventory of all the office supplies. (The monthly physical inventory is a lot simpler than trying to capture data every time someone takes something out of the supply cabinet.) These data will be entered into the program, which will then print out a summary of the inventory. By comparing summaries from many months, the IS manager can get a good picture of how supplies are being used.

The program will also generate a monthly order list. All supplies for which the current stock level has dropped below the reorder point will be placed on that list, which can then be sent directly to Purchasing.

In this case, the needs of the user (the IS manager) have been well specified. The first task facing the C++ programmer therefore is deciding what classes to use in the program. The office supply inventory program actually deals with only one thing: the office supplies that make up the inventory. However, just what is the class?

The class is a type of office supply, in this particular instance called Inventory Item. From that class the program will create one object for each type of supply used by the IS department, such as floppy disks, black fine-line pens, or Post-It notes. The class might be diagrammed as in Figure 2.1. Each item is described by an item number, a text description of the item, the number on hand as of the most recent physical inventory, and the reorder point.

Figure 2.1 The Inventory Item class and the data that describe it

One of the most common mistakes made by people just starting to work with object-oriented concepts is to look at the entire inventory, rather than the inventory item, as the class. Keep in mind, however, that a class is a template from which you stamp out objects. Each object represents one real-world occurrence, or *instance*, of the class. If the inventory were the class, then each object would represent a separate inventory (the contents of a separate supply cabinet, if you will). This is clearly not what the C++ programmer is trying to represent. In this example, the inventory is actually the collection of all the objects created from the Inventory Item class.

Note

Because an object represents an instance of a class, the verb *instantiate* is often used to refer to the process of creating an object from a class.

The C++ programmer must also define the actions that the Inventory Item class will perform. Given the requirements defined by the IS manager, the programmer comes up with the following list:

- Create a new inventory item.
- Modify the data describing an inventory item.
- Delete an item from the inventory.
- Check to see if the item needs to be reordered.
- Return information about the item's current stock level.
- Return information about the item's description.

This list illustrates one very important characteristic of member functions. Each member function acts on only one object at a time. Therefore, there is no member function to print a report of items that needs to be reordered. Instead, there is a function that checks a single object to see if it needs to be reordered.

Catalog #
Item Name
Manufacturer
Unit
Shipping Weight
Quant & Price
Type
Size
Color
Lined/Unlied
Material
Finish
Seat Fabric
Drawers

Supply Item

Figure 2.2   A class to handle an office supply company's merchandise

The main program that uses this class will need to process each object separately, running the member function that checks the reorder point against the stock level for every item in the inventory.

The last two member functions send data from the object back to the program manipulating the object. These are used by the monthly inventory summary report. They are necessary because an object's data are hidden from the program using the object (information hiding). The inventory program, however, needs the item description and stock level for the monthly inventory summary report.

The Office Supply Company

One of the companies from which Rye Associates purchases office supplies is Country-Wide Supplies. Country-Wide uses an object-oriented C++ program to keep track of the supplies in its catalog. The program manages information about all available merchandise items, including their price, shipping weight, and other descriptive characteristics.

As you might expect, the underlying class in Country-Wide's program is the office supply item. The entire program could therefore be based on a single class like that in Figure 2.2. The problem with this design, however, is that the descriptive characteristics that are stored about the items vary, depending on the general type of the item; every type of product doesn't have values for every data item. For example, paper products are described by their size and color, while writing products are described by type of tip, size of tip, and color.

Your first thought may be that Country-Wide can simply leave data items that don't apply to any given type of merchandise without values. Although such a solution will certainly work, it isn't very efficient in terms of storage space. Whenever an object is created, space is allocated in main memory for the entire object. That means that even if no values are assigned to some data items, those data items still consume storage. The unnecessary storage may also consume extra disk space when the object is transferred to external storage.

The fact that there are many variations on one type of object suggests that Country-Wide is dealing with some generic properties of an item (the price and shipping weight, for example) along with other properties that apply to more specific types of items. Such a situation can be handled through inheritance. A portion of a possible class hierarchy for Country-Wide appears in Figure 2.3. (Because an office supply company typically handles so many types of products, showing the entire class hierarchy in one drawing isn't particularly practical!) Notice that the hierarchy begins with the base class—Supply Item— and is then made more specific with derived classes. For this example, there are three derived classes on the second level of the hierarchy—Writing Instrument (pens and pencils), Paper Product, and Furniture. The Furniture class has two derived classes—Chair and Desk.

Only the four classes with black circles in their boxes in Figure 2.3 (Writing Instrument, Paper Product, Chair, and Desk) are actually used to create objects. When an object is created, it receives its own data along with the data of its base class. For example, a Writing Instrument object inherits all the data that are defined as part of the Supply Item class.

The Furniture class also inherits the data defined as part of the Supply Item class. The Desk class therefore inherits not only the data defined as part of the Furniture class, but also the data that the Furniture class inherited from the Supply Item class.

The major advantage to using the design in Figure 2.3 is that no storage space is wasted when objects are created: Every data item is used for every object. However, in this particular example, using the class hierarchy instead of a single class can make the objects harder to use. For example, if the program using this class hierarchy needs to display or print every product carried by Country-Wide, then the program must use separate code for each class; the

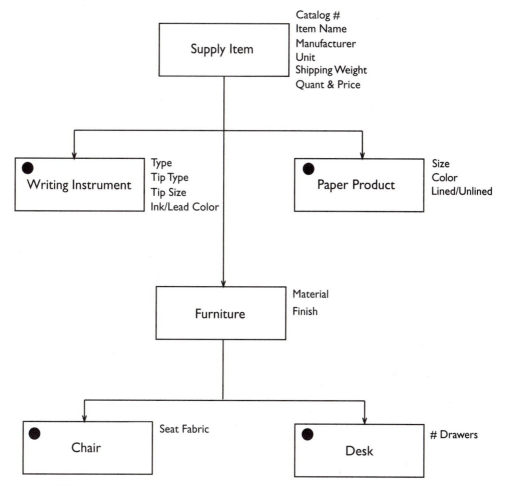

Figure 2.3 A portion of the class hierarchy for an office supply company

output will be inaccurate if the programmer happens to forget about a class. If the coding is based on a single class, the programmer only has to write code that processes one class and runs no risk of missing any objects.

Which design is better: one class or a class hierarchy? The answer is "it depends." The best design depends in large measure on how the class or classes will be used. If the program is intended for telephone salespeople who answer questions about specific products or types of products, then the class hierarchy is probably the best choice. It is the most efficient in terms of storage, allowing more objects to reside in main memory, speeding up the program. However, if the program is designed for more general use, including a need to provide a listing of every product, then the single-class design is probably best. Although it may waste a bit of storage and its performance may suffer when objects must be loaded from disk during execution, it simplifies access to the merchandise as a whole.

The Corner Pharmacy

The Corner Pharmacy is a full-service drug store owned and operated by George and Gladys Bellows. It has been in the Bellows family for three generations and currently isn't part of any national chain. As well as containing a pharmacy, the store sells cosmetics, personal care items, and other merchandise typically found in a drug store. Both Mr. and Mrs. Bellows are registered pharmacists; the store employs two other pharmacists as well as a ten-person sales staff.

The Bellows are concerned that their business is suffering because they aren't managing their prescriptions on a computer like drug stores that belong to national chains. Among other things, the national chains advertise being able to check for drug interactions. The Bellows are therefore going to have someone write a program that will handle prescriptions.

Note

The Bellows did look at existing pharmacy management software packages. However, they discovered that those packages were designed for much larger stores and provided functions the Bellows didn't need. The cost of having custom programming done to exactly match the Bellows's specifications was less than purchasing a ready-made package with capabilities that would never be used.

As you know, the first step in the process is to analyze the needs of the users of the program. The Bellows sat down with the programmer and identified three major things about which they needed to store data: customers, drugs, and prescriptions. They stated that it is vital that data about drug interactions be part of the program. The Bellows also emphasized that there is a slight difference in the handling of prescriptions for controlled and noncontrolled substances.

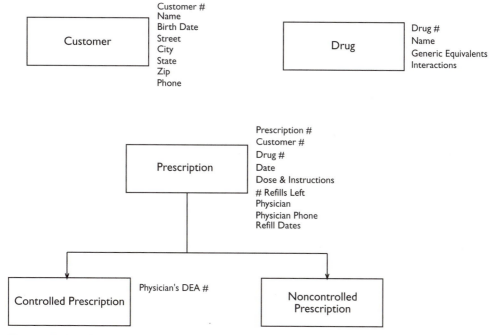

Figure 2.4   Classes to manage a pharmacy's prescriptions

After listening carefully to the Bellows's description of the data the program needs to store and what it needs to do, the programmer produced the classes shown in Figure 2.4. There are three stand-alone classes (Customer, Drug, and Prescription). The Prescription class also has two derived classes, one for a prescription of a controlled substance and the other for a noncontrolled substance.

There is certainly a relationship between the three stand-alone classes. Each prescription is for one customer and one drug. Why, then, isn't Prescription a derived class of Customer and Drug? If the classes were designed in that way, the class hierarchy would look like Figure 2.5. (Deriving a class from more than one base class is known as *multiple inheritance*.)

This design may initially seem very intuitive, especially if you've taken a data management course and are familiar with the design of relational databases. However, keep in mind that with inheritance, the derived class inherits all the data items of the base class. In other words, every time a Prescription

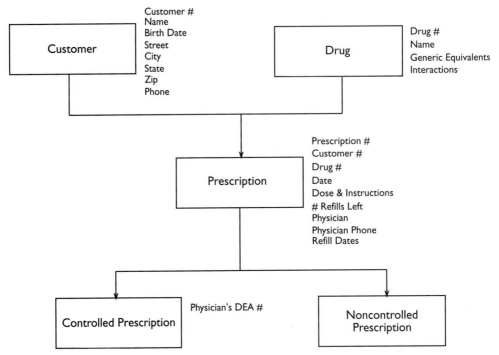

Figure 2.5   Attempting to use inheritance in the prescription class hierarchy

object was created, it would include *all* the customer data as well as *all* the drug data. Inheritance isn't a logical relationship between classes; it's a migration of class data and functions down a hierarchy.

There is one primary reason why, in this particular example, inheritance isn't appropriate. Consider first how these classes might be used. An object is created from each Customer class for every person for whom a prescription is filled; an object is created from the Drug class for every drug carried by the pharmacy. (Note that drugs include nonprescription substances because over-the-counter medications can interact with prescription drugs.)

When a prescription is filled for the first time, an object is created from the Prescription class. Although the Prescription object inherits all the data from the Customer and Drug classes, it's unlikely that customer data (other than the Customer #) and drug data (other than the Drug #) would be repeated. Repeating the data introduces a lot of unnecessary duplication into the program. The duplicated data don't take up any extra room—the space for the inherited data items is allocated regardless of whether values are entered—but this type of duplication introduces a major risk of inaccurate data. How can you guarantee that each time a customer's name and address are entered they are entered in exactly the same way, every time? How can you guarantee that each time the generic equivalents of a drug and the drugs with which a drug interacts are entered in exactly the same way, every time? In addition, would a pharmacist want to take the time to reenter all the drug information each time he or she fills a new prescription?

Given that the bulk of the data from the base classes aren't going to be repeated in the derived class, inheritance isn't appropriate in this case. Instead, the Customer, Drug, Controlled Prescription, and Noncontrolled Prescription classes will be managed as stand-alone classes. The application program that manipulates objects created from these classes will use the Customer # and Drug # to search Customer and Drug objects to locate objects related to any given prescription.

Note

You'll read more about class hierarchies and identifying exactly when inheritance is appropriate in Chapter 10.

Classes and the User Interface

In Chapter 1, you read about the advantages of keeping I/O operations separate from actions performed on objects. One of the ironies of doing so is that elements of the user interface, which usually include I/O, are often implemented as objects. This is particularly true for graphic user interfaces.

As an example, consider the four types of windows in Figure 2.6. Although all are rectangular and approximately the same size, they have different characteristics. The document window at the top left of Figure 2.6 has scroll bars, a title bar, a close box, a size box, and a zoom box. The shadowed window to its right and the alert window below have none of those characteristics but instead have distinctive borders. The round-cornered window at the lower right has a title bar and close box, but no scroll bars, grow box, or zoom box; its title bar is also rather different from the title bar of the document window.

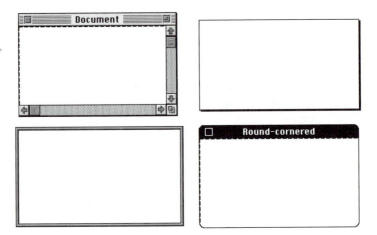

Figure 2.6   Sample window types

Because these windows are variations of a generic rectangular window, they lend themselves to a class hierarchy like that in Figure 2.7. The base class, Window, includes a unique ID number for a window along with the coordinates of the window's position on the screen. These coordinates also represent the window's size.

There is one derived class for each type of window in Figure 2.6. The Document class includes data that describe all the possible types of elements that a programmer might choose to include in a window; the same is true for the Round-cornered class. However, the Shadow and Alert classes don't have any data other than what they inherit from the base class.

Why, then, are the Shadow and Alert classes necessary? The answer lies in the member functions. In particular, each class has a member function that draws the window on the screen. The way in which that function acts varies among the four types of windows because each type of window looks different. Even though the Alert and Round-cornered classes don't add any data to that of the base class, the way in which they respond to a "draw yourself" message is different.

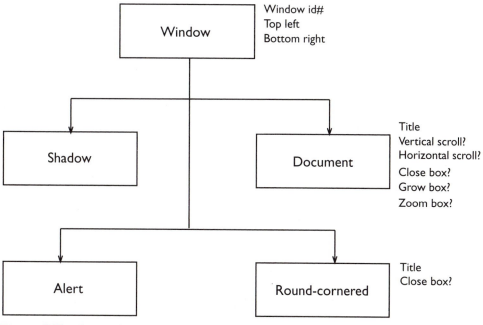

Figure 2.7 A window class hierarchy

 Note Window classes typically also include pointers to objects that describe the contents of the windows. For example, a Document window might contain a pointer to text that has been entered; an Alert window contains pointers to the buttons that appear in the window.

Some Guidelines for Defining Classes, Class Hierarchies, and Member Functions

As you've read through the preceding examples, several general principles have emerged for defining classes, class hierarchies, and member functions. When defining classes, you should pay attention to the following guidelines:

- Choose classes to represent the most specific entities in the data processing environment. When representing an inventory of items, for example, choose classes for the items in the inventory, rather than the inventory itself.
- Consider inheritance when you have similar types of items that share some data, but have data specific to a given item type. Create a base class that contains the common data and use derived classes to represent the item-specific data.
- Consider inheritance when you have similar types of items that react differently to the same message.
- After identifying classes that will store program data, consider classes that will be used to manage the user interface.

When deciding what member functions to define for a class, consider the following:

- Each class needs at least one function that is run when the object is created (a constructor). You may also want to include a destructor that will be run when the object is destroyed.
- A member function acts on just one specific object rather than on all objects of the same class. Therefore, a member function must represent an action appropriate for a single object. If all objects of the same class need to be processed, then it is the responsibility of the program manipulating the objects or a class specifically designed to handle multiple objects of another type to do so. (You will be introduced to classes that manipulate groups of objects of other classes beginning in Chapter 9.)
- Because the data that describe an object are hidden from the program manipulating the object, classes often need member functions that return data values to the program manipulating the object.

Summary

This chapter has looked at the software development life cycle, a sequence of steps that helps lead to a successful software development project. It has also discussed the design of object-oriented programs, including identifying the major objects and member functions needed by a program.

Software development is one portion of the systems development life cycle, which can be described as consisting of the following steps:

- Analyzing a business environment to determine user and organizational needs.
- Developing alternative solutions to meet those needs.
- Evaluating and choosing an alternative.
- Designing a system to meet the specifications of the chosen alternative.
- Developing the system.
- Putting the system into everyday use.

The software development life cycle, which occurs during the third and fourth steps of the systems development life cycle, breaks the process into four activities:

- Determine user needs.
- Design the program.
- Write the program.
- Test the program.

Identifying the major classes that form the basic structure of an object-oriented program relies on the program designer's knowledge of the environment that the program will model. The designer creates classes for each entity about which the program will store data. He or she also designs classes for appropriate sections of the program's user interface.

Exercises

Draw a diagram like those used in this chapter to describe the classes you would create for the programs described below. On a separate page, list the member functions you would need for each class.

1. A program that would manage a student's calendar, including class schedule, reading assignments, assignments to hand in, and exam schedules. The program should also track school holidays.

2. A program that keeps track of grades a student receives during the semester, identified by course, type of graded item, and the weight of that item in the overall course grade.

3. A program that helps someone building a house pick the options for that house, including siding material and color, inside wall covering and color/pattern, and floor coverings for each room.

4. A program that manages a video store, including the movies in inventory, the people who rent them (the customers), and the actual rentals of those items.

5. A program that a salesperson could use to manage his or her contacts with customers, including when each contact was made, the substance of the contact, and how the contact should be followed up.

6. A program that a student could use to manage a bibliography for a term paper, including sources of research material, quotations taken from the research, and data to be used in writing the paper.

7. A program to manage a Human Resources department (formerly called "Personnel"), including employees, their job history with the company, and their dependents.

8. A program that a hobby shop could use to control its inventory. The program should tack items in inventory along with the sales of those items. (*Hint:* Don't forget about the people making purchases.)

9. A program to manage the service department of an automobile dealership. The program should handle cars and their owners, service appointments, and work done during those appointments.

10. A program to handle accounts payable (money a company owes). The program should track the vendors to whom money is owed, the statements that are received from those vendors, and payments made. When developing your classes, consider the effect of writing checks on a company's bank account.

3

Classes

OBJECTIVES

As you read this chapter, you will learn about:
- Defining the variables that hold a class's data.
- Function return values and parameter lists.
- Writing prototypes for member functions.
- Writing some simple member functions.
- One way to create objects from classes.

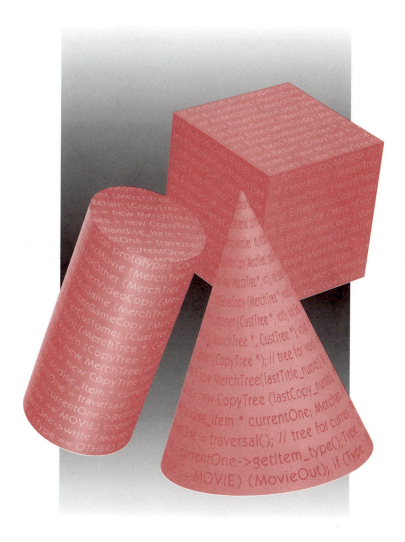

As you know, the basic building block of an object-oriented program is its class hierarchy. Typically, the first step in writing such a program is defining the classes from which the program's objects will be created. This chapter therefore begins your study of the C++ language by examining how classes are written. The concepts you learn here—defining variables and writing prototypes for member functions—are also used in writing the program that manipulates the objects created from your classes.

Sources for Classes

In most cases, classes come from one of two sources. Either you use a previously defined class from a *class library* or you write the class yourself as part of your program. A class library is a collection of classes and their member functions that have been compiled for use by many programs. In most cases, class libraries and their accompanying header files are shipped along with C++ compilers and are specific to the computing platform for which the compiler generates programs.

Starting with Chapter 4, you will be making extensive use of the class library that supports simple screen, keyboard, file, and printer I/O. If you are developing software for a graphic user interface, classes that define and manipulate elements of the interface—windows, menus, and so on—will be provided in class libraries. You may also encounter class libraries of graphics routines and text-handling routines.

Almost every object-oriented program you write will need to use classes that aren't supplied in a class library. These classes can, however, be placed in a custom class library, should you choose to make your classes available for easy reuse. The way in which you create compiled class libraries from code you write yourself depends on the compiler with which you are working.

The Class Declaration Format

Classes are declared using the following format:

```
class class_name
{
    private | protected | public:
        variable definitions

    private | public:
        member function prototypes
};
```

The preceding general syntax is expressed in a format used frequently in computer documentation. Any part of the syntax that appears in regular type (for example, `class`) represents a part of the syntax that you should use exactly as it appears. Any part that appears in italics (for example, *class_name*) is a description of something that you must add, something that is determined by exactly what you are doing. In the example above, you must choose and enter a class name.

When you see items separated by a vertical bar (|), that means you must choose one option from among those listed. For example, in the class declaration syntax, you must choose one of `private`, `protected`, or `public`. Because these appear in regular type, it means you choose one and use it exactly as it appears.

Any class declaration begins with the keyword `class`, followed by the name of the class. Class names can include letters, numbers, and underscores and must not be the same as any C++ keyword. The body of the class definition is surrounded by braces (`{` and `}`) and ends with a semicolon. As you will see, C++ uses braces for grouping in many circumstances; the semicolon is used to indicate the end of a statement.

Note

Unlike many other programming languages, C++ is case sensitive. In other words, `Class` is not the same as `class`. All keywords use only lowercase letters. If you want to be sure that a class name doesn't conflict with a keyword, use at least one capital letter.

The body of the class declaration—the part found within the braces—has two sections, one containing the variable declarations and the other containing the member function prototypes. The declarations are preceded by a keyword that indicates the accessibility of the variable or function; you will learn more about these keywords shortly.

```
class Product  ◄──────────  class name
{
    private:  ◄──── Access for variables          Variable declarations
        int prod_numb;
        char prod_name[26]; prod_desc[81];
        float prod_price, numb_on_hand;
    public:  ◄──────── Access for functions
        Product(int, char[], char[], float, float);
        void viewProduct();
        float getPrice();
        void updateOnHand (int);          Function prototypes
};
```

Figure 3.1   A sample class declaration

Note

To be completely accurate, it is possible to include the body of member functions within the class declaration. Such functions are known as *inline functions*. When a compiler encounters a call to an inline function, it substitutes the entire body of the function for the call. In other words, inline functions act as macros. The result is code that is duplicated each time the program calls the function. You should therefore get into the habit of defining member functions outside the class declaration, restricting the use of inline functions to very short functions that aren't called frequently.

As a very first example, consider the class declaration in Figure 3.1. This class is named Product. It contains private variables (variables whose contents are accessible only to member functions) for a product number, product name, product description, product price, and the product on hand. The member functions are all public, meaning that they can be called by any other function, even those outside the class. The functions initialize an object's data, format a display of all data about a product, send the product price back to a calling function, and update the number of items on hand.

Classes and Header Files

Classes and definitions of constants used by the member functions in those classes are typically placed in header files. By convention, a header file is stored with a file name extension of .h.

To gain access to the contents of a header file, a file that defines functions that use a header file *includes* the header file using a *compiler directive*. A compiler directive is an instruction to the compiler that is processed during compilation. Compiler directives begin with a pound sign (#).

The directive to merge the contents of a header file into a file containing function source code is

```
#include file_name
```

Most compilers support two slightly different versions of this directive. The first instructs the compiler to look for the header file in a disk directory that has been designated as the repository for header files. For example, if you want to use the class library that supports the I/O you will learn about in Chapter 4, the command is written

```
#include <streamio.h>
```

Notice that the name of the header file is surrounded by the less than and greater than symbols. However, if the header file is in a different directory, you surround its path name with double quotes, as in

```
#include "/my.headers/custom.h"
```

Note

Although the C++ discussed in this book adheres to the ANSI standard, C++ compilers do differ. In particular, the names given to the header files that support the libraries shipped with the compiler may not be the same. The header file names used in this book are those typically used with the MS-DOS and Macintosh operating systems. Therefore, if you are working on a different platform, check your compiler's documentation to verify header file names.

Defining Constants

Most programs include constants of some type. You use constants to represent the dimensions of an array, or to represent the values true and false. In general, a constant is a value that doesn't change during a program run. However, in C++ we need to be a bit more precise about the definition.

Some programmers place *literal values* in a program. Literals are values such as 1, 195, *c*, or *This is a test* that appear directly in the code. Such values aren't stored in main memory like a variable, but instead are translated into the source code when the program is compiled.

Good C++ programming attempts to avoid using any meaningful literal values in the body of a program. Instead, the literals are represented by words. There are two major benefits to doing this. First, the program is easier to read. For example, if you see the word TRUE, you know exactly what it means. However, if you see the number 1, you can't be instantly sure what role that literal value is playing in the program.

Second, assigning words to literals makes the program easier to modify. Definitions are typically placed at the beginning of a header file. If you decide to change the dimension of an array, for example, you simply change the value associated with the name MAX_ARRAY_SIZE in the header file, rather than hunting through the source code for every place the array is used.

C++ provides two ways of giving literals names, one inherited from C and the other unique to C++. There are some distinct advantages to using the C++ version.

The #define Directive

The #define directive, which C++ inherited from C, creates a macro whose contents are substituted in the code, just as if you had typed the literal directly into program statements. For example, many programs use the macros

```
#define TRUE 1
#define FALSE 0
```

(As far as C++ is concerned, anything with a value of zero is false; anything nonzero is true.) Notice that the directive is followed by the name of the macro and then by the macro's definition.

Note

By convention, the names of constants are all uppercase letters.

Note

Throughout this book you'll find many more programming styles to which C++ programs adhere "by convention." No one enforces these styles, but because they are so widely used they make reading and understanding programs much easier. You will therefore be a better C++ programmer if you adhere to common programming style practices.

Because the value of the macro generated by the #define directive is inserted directly into the code when a program is compiled, the #define directive can be responsible for unnecessary repeated code. However, when #define is used to put a name on a literal, the values are typically short. This is therefore a minor drawback.

However, a larger problem arises if you happen to be working with a debugger: There is no way to watch the contents of a literal because it isn't assigned to a memory location like a variable. The value of a macro is physically placed in the code, just as if you had typed the literal from the keyboard. The word you used in your source code doesn't become a part of the compiled program. You can avoid this problem, and the issue of unnecessary repeated code, by using the C++ method for defining constants.

The const Statement

The C++ const statement defines a *constant*—a variable whose contents can't be changed. This means that when the program is compiled, space is set aside for the constant, just as space is set aside to hold the value of a variable. Wherever the constant is used in the program, the compiler inserts a reference to the constant's storage location. In some cases, this can use less space than macro substitution. More importantly, however, because the constant is actually placed in a storage location, it can be watched by a debugger. This can be extremely useful if a program is suspected of corrupting main storage in some way.

The const statement looks much like an assignment statement. For example, to define maximum array dimensions you might use

```
const MAX_ROWS = 100;
const MAX_COLUMNS = 3;
```

Notice that the keyword const is followed by the name of the constant, an equals sign, and the value of the constant. The statement is terminated by a semicolon.

Note

Compiler directives don't end with semicolons because they aren't C++ statements.

Although it is generally better to use const with a C++ program, many of the function libraries you will be using (for example, the string processing libraries) come from C; you will therefore also see some use of #define.

Variables

As in any other high-level language, C++ variables are labels that reference a storage location for data. All variables must be declared before they are used, regardless of whether they are part of a class definition or part of a program that manipulates objects. A variable declaration has the format

```
variable_type variable_name;
```

You can name a variable just about anything you want—using a combination of letters, numbers, and underscores (beginning with a letter or underscore)—as long as the name isn't the same as a C++ keyword.

To make programs easier to read, be sure to use meaningful variable names. In other words, stay away from variables such as xy, aa, or g1. Use variable names like interest_rate or CurrentBalance, which convey the meaning of the value the variable holds.

Note

Although variables must be declared before they are used, they don't have to be initialized. In other words, it is perfectly OK with a C++ compiler if you use a variable on the right side of an assignment operator without giving that variable a value. Doing so, however, can be risky, because there is no guarantee what initial value the storage location labeled by that variable will have; don't count on variables being initialized automatically when a program is run.

Most C++ compilers provide seven simple variable types, which you can then use to build data structures tailored to a specific program. In this section you will read about those seven simple variable types along with enumerated variables. You will also be introduced to defining your own variable types.

Simple Variable Types

The seven simple variable types handle integer, floating point, and character data. The amount of data stored in integer and floating point variables will vary, depending on the C++ compiler you are using.

Integer Data Types

The basic integer variable is int. On most PC systems, an int variable is given 16 bits of storage, holding values from -32,768 to 32,767. However, on larger systems int may allocate 32 bits of storage (-2,147,483,648 to 2,147,483,647). The best way to be sure what you're getting with an int is to check your compiler's documentation.

Most C++ compilers provide a short integer. If the default integer size is 16 bits, then short is also usually 16 bits. However, if the default integer size is 32 bits, then short provides a 16-bit integer, which can be used to save space when you are certain that the values being stored won't exceed the range of a 16-bit storage location.

By the same token, most C++ compilers provide a long integer. If the default integer size is 16 bits, then long typically provides a 32-bit storage location. If the default integer size is 32 bits, long may set aside 32 or 64 bits, depending on the compiler and the computing platform.

You can double the range of an int if you can live with only positive values by using the unsigned integer variable type. A 16-bit unsigned integer handles the range 0 to 65,535; a 32-bit unsigned integer handles the range 0 to 4,294,967,295.

The Inventory Item class, used in the office supply inventory application you read about in Chapter 2, uses integer variables to store the number of items on hand as the reorder point. Because these quantities are always relatively small, int variables will do; if the default integer is 32 bits, the programmer might choose to use short instead. The variable definitions look like:

```
int NumbOnHand, ReorderPoint;
short NumbOnHand, ReorderPoint;
```

Notice that in both these examples, more than one variable has been placed in the same statement, separated by commas.

Note

When writing a program that manipulates objects, you can perform some variable initialization as part of the variable declarations. Because class definitions do not allow this type of initialization, the discussion of how to do so appears in Chapter 5.

Floating Point Data Types

Floating point variables store data with fractional portions, very large values, and very small values. Most C++ compilers support single-precision floating point values (`float`) and double-precision floating point values (`double`). The range provided by floating point variables depends on the type of computer you are using, although it is much larger than that provided by even a long integer.

The drawback to floating point storage is that it uses more space than integers (5 to 10 bytes for floating point versus typically 2 bytes for integers). However, if you need to store numbers with fractional portions or numbers that are outside the integer range, use a floating point variable.

Country-Wide Supplies, the office supply company to which you were introduced in Chapter 2, uses a floating point variable to store the shipping weight of its merchandise in pounds and fractions of pounds:

```
float ShippingWeight;
```

Floating point variables could also be used to store prices (dollars and cents), the distance to the nearest habitable planet (light years), or the number of grains of sand in a bucket. (Even the largest floating point variable doesn't have enough range to store the number of sands on a beach!)

```
float Price;
double NearestPlanet, GrainsOfSand;
```

Character Data

The basic building block for handling character data is the `char` variable, which holds one ASCII code. A `char` variable therefore occupies one byte of storage. Character variables, for example, are often used to hold data such as single-letter codes (for example, *s*, *m*, or *l* for sizes):

```
char T_ShirtSize;
```

As you will see in Chapter 4, `char` variables are also used in programs to accept single-letter input from the keyboard. However, in business programs most character data are part of strings. C++ does not have a string variable type; instead, strings are handled as arrays of characters. (Strings are discussed in depth in Chapter 6.)

Creating Your Own Variable Types

One of the things that makes C++ a very flexible language is the ability to create your own variable types. As you will see in Chapter 6, this can greatly simplify working with arrays and strings. It can also help make a program easier to understand. At this point, you will be introduced to two mechanisms for defining custom data types: the `typedef` and `enum` statements. You will see many uses for them (especially `typedef`) throughout this book.

Using typedef

The `typedef` statement assigns a new variable type name to any existing C++ variable type. For example, the statement

```
typedef int BOOLEAN;
```

creates a new variable type named `BOOLEAN` that holds an integer value. The new variable type can then be used to define variables for use in a class definition or program. You might, for example, use the `BOOLEAN` variable type to hold flags used by a program:

```
BOOLEAN More, Finished, Done;
```

It might not be immediately clear why defining the BOOLEAN variable type is any better than simply declaring the three variables as int. However, declaring them as BOOLEAN makes the way in which the variables will be used very clear; the program will therefore be easier to understand.

Enumerated Variables

An enumerated variable is a special integer variable type that can help make a program easier to understand. When you declare an enumerated variable type, you provide a list of the permissible values for variables of that type. The list typically contains words that represent the values. For example, you might set up an enumerated variable type to hold sizes of the merchandise you sell:

```
enum Sizes {SMALL, MEDIUM, LARGE, X_LARGE};
```

The C++ compiler numbers the values surrounded by braces, beginning with zero. In this particular example, SMALL is 0, MEDIUM is 1, and so on.

Once the variable type has been defined, you can use it to declare variables:

```
enum Sizes T_ShirtSizes;
enum Sizes DressSizes;
```

Variable Accessibility

The variables in a class are assigned one of three *access modes* (public, private, or protected) that determine the access that functions have to the class's variables. If a variable is made public, then any function can access that variable. In most cases, public variables are not used because doing so violates the concept of information hiding.

The only part of a class that should be made public is the part that forms its interface to the outside world. In other words, the outside world (functions that use this class) needs to know how to access the class's member functions, but doesn't need to know how the class does its work. By hiding the details of how a member function performs its actions, the class remains independent of functions that call it. This means that the function is easier to modify. As long as a change in variable name or type doesn't affect a function's parameter list, the change can be made without requiring a change in functions that use the modified code.

Private variables are accessible only to functions that are members of the class to which the variables belong. If no other classes are derived from the class, then variables are typically private. However, if the class has derived classes, then those classes usually need access to the base class's variables. In that case, use protected access, which gives derived functions access to their base class's variables but restricts access by other functions.

Note

If necessary you can override private or protected access by declaring a class a *friend* to another class. Friend classes get access to the variables and functions of the class to which they are designated as friends. You will learn more about friend classes in Chapter 8.

Sample Class Declarations

To put this all together, let's look at the beginnings of some class declarations. At this point, the declarations will be incomplete because the prototypes of their member functions will be missing.

Currency Conversion

Because today's business world has such an international focus, many companies need a way to quickly convert between local currency and the currency of a country with which they are doing business. The basis for a C++ program to perform such conversions is a class called `Converter`:

```
class Converter
{
    private:
        float ConversionFactor;
        char Method;

    member function prototypes go here
};
```

The `ConversionFactor` variable holds the value by which local currency multiplied or divided to do the conversion. The `Method` variable determines whether the operation performed is multiplication or division.

Marketing Survey Analysis

The Andrews Show Company has conducted a large marketing survey to track the types of shoes people own and how many pairs they purchase each year. The survey is anonymous; respondents are identified only by a number. The survey also records a respondent's age and gender, along with shoe ownership and purchasing habits for four types of footwear.

The program that analyzes the survey data uses a class named `OneSurvey` to represent a single survey completed by one person. The class includes the following variables:

```
class OneSurvey
{
    private:
        int Survey_numb;
        char Gender;
        int Age, AthleticOwned, AthleticBought,
            DressOwned, DressBought, BootsOwned,
            BootsBought, SandalsOwned, SandalsBought;

    member function prototypes go here
};
```

The header file in which this class is defined contains two constants used to make it easier to manage sorting of an array of survey objects:

```
const SWAP_MADE = 1;
const NO_SWAP = 0;
```

The Hi/Lo Game

One of the first games written for personal computers was a "hi/lo" guessing game. The computer generates a random number between 0 and 100. The user then has seven tries to guess the number. Each time the user guesses, the computer lets the user know whether the guess was above or below the correct answer.

The object-oriented version of the hi/lo game uses one class to represent a game. It needs only two variables: the correct answer and the current guess made by the user:

```
class Game
{
    private:
        int answer, guess;

    member function prototypes go here
};
```

Member Function Prototypes

As you know, the actions performed by an object are defined using C++ functions. A class declaration must contain prototypes for all member functions or, in the case of very short functions (no more than a few lines of code), the body of the function itself.

A function prototype provides a template for the way in which a function is called. It has the general format:

```
return_value_type Function_Name (parameter list);
```

For example, the prototype for a function to determine whether an office supply item needs to be reordered might be written like:

```
BOOLEAN ReorderDecision (void);
```

The function uses the `return` statement to send back one value of type `BOOLEAN`. (Remember that `BOOLEAN` is a data type created earlier in this chapter with the `typedef` statement to hold a yes/no or true/false value.) Only one value can be returned in this manner; its type always appears first in the prototype. The name of this function is `ReorderDecision`. Because the function has no parameters (in other words, it gets no data from the function that calls it), `void` is used as a placeholder for the parameter list; `void` is also used in place of a return data type when a function returns no value.

Note

It is also perfectly acceptable to leave the parentheses that hold a parameter list empty—( )—when there are no input parameters.

Parameters and Parameter Lists

A *formal parameter* is a value that is passed into a function when the function is called by another function. These are the values the function needs to perform its operations. By default, C++ parameters are input values only; if the value is modified in the function, that modification is not returned to the calling function. This is known as a *pass by value*.

Note

The alternative to pass by value is *pass by reference*, which returns a modified value to the calling function. Pass by reference requires the use of main memory addresses. We will therefore defer discussion of it until Chapter 9.

A function prototype's parameter list must contain the data types of the function's formal parameters. For example, a member function that performs currency conversion for the Converter class must receive the value of the money to be converted. Because money usually involves a fractional portion, the parameter should have a data type of float. In its simplest form, the function prototype could be written:

```
float ConvertMoney (float);
```

Notice that the data type of the input value (float) is placed inside the parentheses. The float that precedes the name of the function is, of course, the data type of the value returned by the function.

When a function requires more than one input value, separate their data types in the parameter list with commas. For example, the SupplyItem class that supports Country-Wide Supplies' program includes a function to change the price of an item. Because there are many prices for one item, depending on the quantity of the item being purchased, the function must receive not only the new price, but also the quantity to which that price applies. The function prototype might therefore be written:

```
void ChangePrice (float, float);
```

Note that because prices and the quantities to which they apply are stored in a two-dimensional array, the data type of both parameters must be the same. In this case, because the price of an item represents currency, the array has been defined to hold float values.

There is one drawback to the prototype you have just seen. Because both parameters are of the same data type, someone looking at the prototype can't tell which represents the price and which represents the quantity. A prototype can, however, include variable names. The `ChangePrice` prototype could also be written:

```
void ChangePrice (float new_price, float quantity);
```

In this example, the parameter list contains the names of the variables that will be used in the function. The notation is like that for defining a variable: The variable's data type is followed by the variable name.

You can always include variable names in a prototype's parameter list along with the data types of the parameters. However, by convention they are not used unless absolutely required. As you will see in Chapter 6, for example, you will need to use a variable name when passing a two-dimensional array as a parameter.

Function Access Modes

Like a class's variables, member functions have access modes. If a member function is public, it can be called by any other function; if a member function is private, it can be called only by other member functions of the same class. (The protected access mode does not apply to member functions.)

A public member function is accessible to any other function, inside or outside the class. In most cases, member functions are public. However, you may occasionally need to write utility functions that are shared by member functions of a single class but that shouldn't be used by functions outside the class. Such functions have private access.

Note

You can give any class access to the member functions of another class by declaring the functions in the other class as *friend functions* to the class to which you want to give access. You will learn about declaring and using friend functions in Chapter 10.

Revisiting the Sample Classes

You have now seen all the elements of a class definition that are typically stored in a header file. To tie it all together, let's look at some class definitions that include member function prototypes.

As you look at these classes, remember that each has a constructor, a member function that has the same name as the class. A constructor, which is run automatically whenever an object is created from a class, has no return data type. Constructors, however, can have input parameters. Whether you use them depends on the way in which a program creates and references objects. You will learn more about this toward the end of this chapter.

Currency Conversion

The `Converter` class for the currency conversion program (Listing 3.1) needs five member functions. The first (`Converter`) is the constructor. The `Mod-Conversion` function takes data from the program using an object of this class and puts those values into an object. It can be used to initialize an object or modify an object. A currency conversion is performed by the `DoConversion` function. The `GetFactor` and `GetMethod` functions are used to send the contents of the private variables to a program using the class. As you will see in Chapter 4, these are used when writing the contents of objects to a file.

Listing 3.1   convert.h: Header file for the currency converter program

```
class Converter
{
    private:
        float ConversionFactor;
        char Method;

    public:
        Converter (void);
        void ModConversion (float, char);
        float DoConversion (float);
        float GetFactor (void);
        char GetMethod (void);
};
```

Marketing Survey Analysis

The OneSurvey class (Listing 3.2) that forms the basis of the shoe company's marketing research efforts is used in a different way than the Converter class. The Converter class acts on its data to perform a mathematical operation. However, the OneSurvey class is primarily a storage device for the results of a survey. The actual data analysis is performed on groups of data, working with many objects created from the OneSurvey class.

The role of the OneSurvey class is to make individual values available to the program that uses objects created from the class. Therefore, the member functions consist primarily of functions that return individual values to the calling program. You will see how to write this type of function later in this chapter. The copy function is used to copy data from one object to another. It is used when sorting an array of survey objects. (Arrays of objects are discussed in Chapter 6.)

Listing 3.2   survey.h: Header file for the marketing survey program

```
const SWAP_MADE = 1;
const NO_SWAP = 0;

class OneSurvey
{
    private:
        int Survey_numb;
        char Gender;
        int Age, AthleticOwned, AthleticBought, DressOwned, DressBought,
            BootsOwned,BootsBought, SandalsOwned, SandalsBought;

    public:
        OneSurvey(); // constructor
            int, int, int, int, int);
        char GetGender (void);
        int GetAge (void);
        int GetAthleticOwned (void);
        int GetAthleticBought (void);
        int GetDressOwned (void);
        int GetDressBought (void);
        int GetBootsOwned (void);
        int GetBootsBought (void);
        int GetSandalsOwned (void);
        int GetSandalsBought (void);
```

Continued next page

Listing 3.2 (Continued) survey.h: Header file for the marketing survey

```
// The copy function copies one object into another. It is used when sorting an array
// of survey objects. You will see how it is used in Chapter 6.
        void copy (OneSurvey);
};
```

The Hi/Lo Game

The hi/lo game (Listing 3.3) has three member functions: a constructor, a function to determine whether a guess is above or below the correct answer (evaluateGuess), and a function to send the correct answer back to the program running the game (GetAnswer).

Listing 3.3   game.h: Header file for the hi/lo game program

```
class Game
{
    private:
        int answer, guess;

    public:
        Game (void);
        int evaluateGuess (int);
        int GetAnswer (void);
};
```

A First Look at Member Functions

Much of what you read about in the rest of this book deals with writing functions. With very few exceptions, member functions are just like the functions that make up the programs that manipulate classes. In this section you will be introduced to the structure of functions and look at how one type of simple function is written.

By convention, member functions are placed in files with a .cp or .cpp extension. If relatively short, you can place all member functions for one class in the same file. However, if a function runs more than two pages of code, it should probably be stored in its own file.

Because the functions that make up a C++ program are typically stored in at least two files (one for a class's member functions and one for the program that uses objects created from the class) and because C++ programs use functions stored in precompiled libraries, the program must be linked into one run-time module for execution.

The way in which you let a compiler know which source files make up one program varies from one compiler to another. Many microcomputer compilers, for example, use a *project file*, a special file that simply lists the source files for one program. The linking process is performed automatically after source files have been compiled. Other compilers require a *make file*, a file that lists source files that are to be compiled along with the object code files and function libraries that are to be linked. Because the linking process is very compiler-dependent, you should consult the documentation that comes with your compiler to find out exactly what you need to do to link a program before running it.

Regardless of whether you use a project file or a make file, you must create a new one for every program you prepare. Each project or make file is specific to one given program. For example, a project file for the survey analysis program might contain:

```
survey.cpp
main.cpp
```

The `survey.cpp` file contains the member functions; the `main.cpp` file contains the `main` function. Notice that the header file (in this case, `survey.h`) isn't part of the project file. This is because the contents of the header file are included in both `survey.cpp` and `main.cpp` when the program is compiled.

Function Structure

All functions have the same basic structure:

```
returnType FunctionName (parameterList…)
{
    body of function goes here
}
```

Notice that this is similar to the structure of a class. However, there is no semi-colon after the closing brace.

If a function is a member function, then its header must also include the name of the class to which it belongs:

```
returnType className::FunctionName (parameterList…)
```

The class name is followed by the *scope resolution operator.* When you write member functions, don't forget that the return data type precedes the class name.

A function's parameter list is slightly different from that used in the function's prototype: variable names *must* be included for each parameter, along with the parameter's data type. This declares the variables that will be passed into the function; the variables don't need to be redeclared within the function.

The variables in a function's parameter list must match the parameters in the function's prototype. There must be the same number of parameters; they must also have the same data types. For example, the `DoConversion` function that belongs to the `Converter` class has the following structure:

```
float DoConversion (float Dollars)
{
    body of function goes here
}
```

Functions That Return Private Data

The simplest member functions are those that send the value of a private variable back to the program calling the function. In most cases, you will write one "get" function for each class variable whose value is likely to be output by a program manipulating objects created from the class.

Such functions often have names that begin with `Get`, like those that are part of the `OneSurvey` class. Each "get" function has only one statement in its body: `return`. The return statement sends one value back to the program that called the function and terminates execution of the function. For example, the `GetAge` function is written:

```
int OneSurvey::GetAge (void)
{
    return Age;
}
```

The double colon (: :) in the first line of the function is the *scope resolution operator*. It separates the name of the class to which the function belongs from the name of the function. The purpose of the scope resolution operator is to tell the compiler the class to which a function belongs. This makes it possible for many classes to have functions with the same name and parameter list; the preceding class name and scope resolution operator let the compiler tell the functions apart.

A compiler interprets functions that are declared without a class name and scope resolution operator as functions that aren't part of a class, but are instead part of the main program. One of the most common errors C++ programmers encounter is leaving off the class name and scope resolution operator. If you do so, the compiler will tell you that the variables in the function haven't been declared. This occurs because the compiler doesn't know that it should be looking in a specific class declaration for variable declarations.

Defining Objects

There are two methods for creating objects from classes. One lets you handle objects much like variables; the other gives you a pointer to the main memory allocated to the object. Although we'll defer a discussion of pointers until Chapter 7, it's important that you understand the difference between the two methods and the criteria for deciding when to use each method.

Static Versus Dynamic Binding

When an object is created, space is set aside to hold the object's data, and the member functions of the class from which the class was created are linked to the object. This object to function linking is known as *binding*. The difference between the two methods for creating objects has to do with when binding actually occurs. Binding can be performed when a program is compiled (*static binding*). The space set aside for the objects remains allocated, and the binding remains intact while the program is running. Static binding is therefore most appropriate for objects that are needed throughout the entire run of the program. To get static binding, you define objects as if they were variables.

Alternatively, you can allocate space for objects and bind objects to member functions while the program is running (*dynamic binding*). The benefit of dynamic binding is that you can create and destroy objects as needed, providing more efficient use of memory. It is therefore appropriate for objects that are used temporarily or for large programs that must continually free memory to continue operation. To get dynamic binding, you obtain a pointer to the object's place in memory with the `new` operator.

Defining Objects Using Static Binding

To allocate space for an object as you would a variable, resulting in static binding, you define a variable whose data type is the class from which you want to create an object. For example, to create objects for the currency converter program, you could use the statement:

```
Converter Germany, Great_Britain, France;
```

Space is allocated for three objects—one to convert German currency, one to convert the currency of Great Britain, and one to convert French currency.

Summary

In this chapter you learned how classes are defined. A class declaration consists of two components: the variables that hold a class's data and the member functions that perform actions on objects created from the class.

Each variable and member function is assigned an access mode. Private access, generally used for variables, means that only functions that are members of the class can access those variables. When inheritance is involved, variables are often Protected, providing access to member functions of the class and any derived classes. Public access, used primarily for functions, lets any function call the function; a public variable can be accessed by any function. Private member functions are accessible only to other member functions in the class. Protected access doesn't apply to member functions.

Variables are declared by giving a data type and a name. They may use any of C++'s simple data types—`int`, `long`, `short`, `float`, `double`, `char`—or they may use custom data types defined by the programmer using `typedef` or `enum`.

Member functions are most often declared by including just their prototypes. A function prototype includes the function's return value type, the function's name, and its parameter list. The body of short functions (inline functions) may be included in the class declaration.

A prototype's parameter list includes the data types of the values that will be passed into the function. Variable names aren't required for simple data types, but may be required for some complex data types, such as two-dimensional arrays.

Each class has at least one special member function called a constructor. A constructor, which has the same name as the class, is run automatically whenever an object is created from the class. A class may also have a destructor, a member function that is run automatically when an object created from the class is destroyed. The name of a destructor is a tilde (~) followed by the name of the class.

Objects can be created from a class in two ways. Using static binding, objects are declared just like variables; instead of the data type, the declaration uses the class name. Space in memory for the object is allocated when the program is compiled. The alternative—dynamic binding—allocates space for an object when the program is running. Dynamic binding provides a pointer to the location of an object in memory. The major advantage of dynamic binding is that it allows dynamic memory management; unneeded objects can be removed from memory, freeing up space under low-memory conditions.

Exercises

Write declarations for the classes described below. Be sure to use meaningful variable names and to add comments where necessary. (You'll be writing code to manipulate these classes throughout this book. Some classes will also be modified to add text data once you have learned to manipulate strings. You should therefore document your classes so that you can remember the meaning of each variable, even if you haven't worked with the class for some time.)

1. A picture frame: Write a class declaration for an order for the custom framing of a picture. Include the following variables:

   - Job ticket number (a unique number assigned to each order)
   - The width of the frame in inches
   - The length of the frame in inches
   - The price of the frame per running inch
   - The price of mounting the picture
   - The price of glass
   - The price of labor

The member functions for this class should include:

- A constructor
- A function to place data into an object
- A function to compute the cost of framing (including the frame, glass, mounting, and labor)
- Functions to return each variable in the class

2. An oil storage tank: Write a declaration for a class that describes a tank in an oil tank farm. Include the following variables:

- Tank #
- Capacity in gallons
- Current number of gallons of oil in the tank

The member functions for this class should include:

- A constructor
- A function to place data into an object
- A function to compute how full the tank is expressed as a percentage of the capacity
- A function to compute the available space in the tank expressed as a percentage of the capacity
- Functions to return each variable in the class

3. A paycheck: Write a class declaration for a paycheck. Include the following variables:

- Check #
- ID# of employee receiving the check
- Date of check (stored as six digits: MMDDYY)
- Net pay (amount of pay before deductions)
- Federal tax amount
- State tax amount
- Social Security tax amount
- Gross pay (amount of pay after deductions)

The member functions for this class should include:

- A constructor
- A function to place all data except the gross pay into an object
- A function to compute the gross pay
- Functions to return each variable in the class

4. Service performed on an automobile: Write a class declaration for one type of service (for example, a tuneup) performed on a car. This class will become part of a program that manages the service department of an automobile dealership. Include the following variables:

- The car's vehicle ID # (VIN)
- The date the service was performed (stored as six digits: MMDDYY)
- The service code (a three-digit code that identifies the type of service)
- The number of hours of labor used to perform the service
- The cost of parts and other supplies used to perform the service
- The total cost of the service

The member functions for this class should include:

- A constructor
- A function to place all data except the total cost into an object
- A function to compute the total cost of the service
- Functions to return each variable in the class

5. A check generated by an accounts payable system: Write a class for a check used to pay a bill owed by a company. This class will become part of an accounts payable program. Include the following variables:

- Check #
- Bank account # from which the check is drawn
- ID# of the payee
- Date of check (stored as six digits: MMDDYY)
- Amount of the check

The member functions for this class should include:

- A constructor
- A function to place all data into an object
- A function to deduct the amount of the check from the correct bank account
- A function to deduct the amount of the check from the balance due to the payee
- Functions to return each variable in the class

6. A statement or payable invoice received from an organization or person to which a company owes money: Write a class for a statement or invoice. This class will become part of an accounts payable program. Include the following variables:

    - ID# of the organization or person from which the statement or invoice was received
    - Invoice or statement #
    - Date statement or invoice was received (stored as six digits: MMD-DYY)
    - Amount of the statement or invoice
    - Account code to which the amount of the invoice should be posted

    The member functions for this class should include:

    - A constructor
    - A function to place all data into an object
    - A function to post the amount of the statement or invoice to the correct account
    - A function to add the amount of the statement or invoice to the balance due the organization or person from which the invoice or statement was received
    - Functions to return each variable in the class

4

Stream I/O

OBJECTIVES

In this chapter you will read about:
- Viewing I/O as a stream of characters.
- Working with the default I/O streams.
- Using the I/O stream classes.
- Using stream I/O with files.
- Assigning input data to variables.
- Initializing objects.

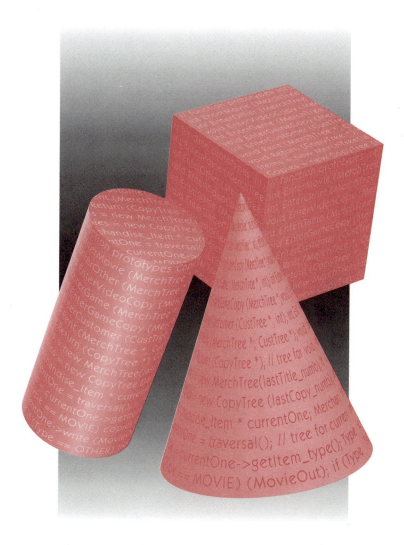

C++ supports several kinds of I/O. The easiest to use and the most universal is *stream I/O*. Stream I/O views input and output as a simple stream of characters coming from or going to a source or destination, including screen, keyboard, printer, or file. In this chapter you will learn to use stream I/O to create text-based screen displays, to accept keyboard input, to write to and read from files, and to create text-based printed output. You will also learn how to use C++'s assignment operator to take the data a program receives from an I/O stream and initialize variables and objects. As you do this, you will learn how to write more member functions.

Stream I/O is provided by an intertwined class hierarchy that includes the base class `ios`, the `iostream` class (provides default streams for screen and keyboard I/O), and the file management classes `ifstream` (supports file input) and `ofstream` (supports file output). As you can see in Figure 4.1, the hierarchy includes a number of interlinked classes. When you look at the illustration, keep in mind that the arrows show the direction of the inheritance. In this case (just to make it all fit in one diagram) the inheritance isn't linear from top to bottom: `fstream` is derived from `iostream`, which is below it in the drawing, as well as from `fstreambase`, which is above it.

Note

Because ANSI C++ views printing as writing to a file that happens to be a printer, there are no specific classes that support printing.

The Default I/O Streams

When you run a C++ program, three I/O streams are created automatically from the `iostream` class: `cin` (for keyboard input), `cout` (for screen output), and `cerr` (for error output, usually directed to the screen). To use them, you only need to be sure to include the class's header file in your main program. (This file is usually named `iostream.h` or `streamio.h`; check your compiler's documentation to be sure.)

Introducing cin and cout

In Listing 4.1 you will find a very simple program that uses the `cin` and `cout` streams. This program contains just one function—`main`—where execution of a C++ program always begins. By default, `main` has a return type of `int`.

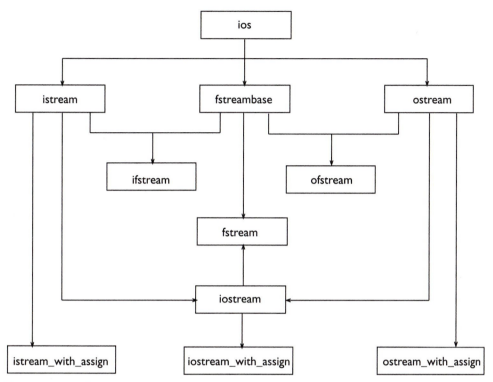

Figure 4.1   The ios class hierarchy

However, because a program's return value isn't commonly used by an operating system, many C++ programs are written giving main a return type of void. In addition, main usually doesn't take any input parameters.

Listing 4.1   Age.cpp: A program to capture someone's age and display it on the screen

```
#include <iostream.h>

void main()
{
    int Age;
    cout << "What is your age? ";
    cin >> Age;
    cout << "John/Jane, you are " << Age << " years old.";
}
```

The body of the program is sandwiched within braces ({ and }). C++ uses braces for grouping, much in the way Pascal uses `begin` and `end` and COBOL uses paragraph headers. Every function begins with an opening brace and ends with a closing brace. Other pairs of braces, for grouping constructs such as the body of loops, are nested within the braces that group the function. As with parentheses and features of other languages that define groups of statements, braces must be balanced. In other words, there must be a closing brace for every opening brace.

The program in Listing 4.1 contains three stream I/O statements. Running the program produces something like the following:

```
What is your age? 19
John/Jane, you are 19 years old.
```

Using cout

The first executable statement in the Age program uses `cout` to display the "What is your age?" prompt on the screen. The statement begins with the name of the stream (`cout`) followed by `<<`, the *stream insertion operator*. The stream insertion operator puts a value into a stream so that it can be sent to the stream's destination. In this example, the value being inserted is a literal string, surrounded by double quotes.

Note

In many programming languages, it doesn't matter whether you surround literal strings with double or single quotes, as long as they match at either end of the string. However, C++ uses single quotes for individual characters (those stored in a `char` variable) and double quotes for strings. Placing double quotes around a single character requests a different type of storage than placing the same character in single quotes. You will learn more about this in Chapter 6.

The third executable statement in Listing 4.1 also uses the `cout` stream. It inserts three values into the stream, one after the other. The first is a literal string, the second a variable, and the third another literal string. Each individual value sent to the stream is prefaced by its own stream insertion operator. When you place a variable in a `cout` stream, `cout` displays the contents of the variable.

The behavior of cout varies slightly from one compiler to another. Some compilers automatically begin a new line of output with each use of cout; others begin output exactly where the previous screen display ended. If your compiler doesn't automatically begin a new line, there are two ways to do so. First, you can insert an endl at the end of an output stream, as in:

```
cout << "This is a test" << endl;
cout << "This one starts on a new line";
```

Alternatively, you can use an *escape character* (a value that sends formatting information to an output device). The new line escape character is \n:

```
cout << "This is a test";
cout << "\nThis one starts on a new line";
```

The backslash (\) alerts the I/O stream that what follows is a formatting code rather than a value to be displayed. In the preceding example, the \n could be placed at the end of the first string or the beginning of the second.

Note

If your compiler automatically inserts a new line with each use of cout, using endl or \n will insert an extra line in the output.

Using cin

The second executable statement in Listing 4.1 uses cin to accept a value from the keyboard. The statement begins with the name of the stream (cin), followed by >>, the *stream extraction operator*. The stream extraction operator takes a value from a stream and places it into the variable whose name follows the operator.

The cin stream can handle more than one input value. For example, if you have one integer variable—Age—and one character variable—Gender—the following statement will accept both values:

```
cin >> Age >> Gender
```

The values are separated by a space, a tab, or the Enter key. The drawback to this is that you can't use cin to enter a string of text because cin sees each word as a separate value. As you will see in Chapter 6, string input requires the use of a special function from the C++ libraries.

The cin stream does virtually no data type checking. It won't warn you, for example, if you enter a floating point value instead of an integer for a person's age. The value will simply be truncated to an integer when it is stored. C++ also won't warn you if you enter a character instead of an integer; the character is simply translated to an integer value.

Note

C++ is said to have *weak data typing* because it does very little checking of the type of data you place in a variable. This is in direct contrast to strongly typed languages such as Modula-2 and Pascal.

The cin stream has one little "gotcha" of which you should be aware: it will wait forever for a value. This means that you can't use cin if you want the user to be able to press Enter without entering a value to signal the end of input. In Chapter 6, however, you will be introduced to some iostream member functions you can use when you need to be able to trap for no input.

A Simple Text Menu Function

You can combine cin and cout to provide a simple text menu for controlling a program. Although you will be introduced to a more flexible, object-oriented method for handling menus once you've learned to handle arrays of strings, this technique can make your programs easy to use with knowledge you already have.

The currency converter program, which you will see in its entirety in Chapter 5, contains a function that is called by its main function to produce a three-option menu (Listing 4.2). This function returns an integer value (the number of the option chosen by the user) and takes no input parameters. Notice that the only difference between this function—which isn't attached to a class—and a member function is that there is no class name or scope resolution operator.

The function defines one variable for its own use to hold the value chosen by the user (choice). It then displays the menu and waits for the user to enter something. The function ends by returning the value entered to the calling function.

The currency converter's main function, which uses the Menu function, calls it by assigning its return value to an integer variable:

```
option = Menu();
```

Listing 4.2   Menu: A function to provide a simple text menu

```
int Menu ()
{
    int choice;

    cout << "\n\nPick a menu option:" << endl;
    cout << "  1. Set conversion rate" << endl;
    cout << "  2. Do a conversion" << endl;
    cout << "  9. Quit" << endl;
    cout << "\nWhich one? ";
    cin >> choice;
    return choice;
}
```

There are two things to keep in mind about this statement. First, `option` must be declared in the `main` function as an integer variable. Second, C++ uses an equals sign as its *assignment operator*. This is the same as the COBOL assignment operator, but different from that used by Pascal or Modula-2.

Note

Yes, it takes a bit of extra time and coding to create understandable menus for your programs. However, a program is only as good as its usability. You should therefore always be thinking about the interface your program presents to the user and how you can make the interface as easy to use as possible.

Grabbing a Single Character

There is one small drawback to the menu function in Listing 4.2: The user must press Enter after typing menu selection. Since the menu choice is a single number, why not simply have the computer grab whatever the user enters without requiring Enter? There are at least two ways to do this, one of which uses a `cin` member function and the other which uses a function from the standard ANSI C libraries.

Using a cin Member Function

The `cin` stream is actually an object created from the `iostream` class. It therefore can use any of the member functions defined for its class. One of those functions is `get()`, which returns a single character. The `get()` function is called like any other member function. For example, the line

```
cin >> choice;
```

could be replaced with

```
choice = cin.get();
```

In both cases, the character that the user types appears on the screen. The difference between the two is that the first requires a press of the Enter key to transmit the keyboard input to the `cin` stream; the second takes a single character without waiting for the Enter key.

Because the `get()` function returns a value just like any other function, the last two executable statements of Listing 4.2 (the `cin` and the `return`) could actually be replaced by just one statement:

```
return cin.get();
```

Combining the two statements into one avoids using a storage location for the menu choice. It also avoids taking the time to write the result of the `get()` function to a storage location in main memory and then retrieve that value to return it to the calling function. The program therefore uses just a little bit less memory and runs just a little bit faster.

Using a Function from a Library

As you have read, a C++ compiler is accompanied by libraries of functions that handle I/O, string manipulation, mathematics, graphics, and so on. Some of these are actually C libraries. For example, `stdio` provides support for formatted C I/O. (C cannot use stream I/O.) Although most C++ programs don't need to use the formatted I/O portion of `stdio`, they often make use of a function within the `stdio` library that grabs a single character from the keyboard input buffer: `getchar()`. This function differs from `cin.get()` because it doesn't echo the character typed to the screen. In other words, the user doesn't see what he or she has typed.

To use the `getchar()` function, you must include the header file `stdio.h` in your source code file. You can then use it to store a single character in a variable:

```
choice = getchar();
```

You could also use it directly in another statement that requires a value, such as the `return` statement in the menu function:

```
return getchar();
```

Because `getchar()` doesn't echo the typed character to the screen, it isn't as appropriate for making a menu choice as `cin.get()`. However, it is very handy for a "hit any key to continue" situation:

```
cout << "Hit any key to continue: ";
getchar();
```

Notice in this case that the result of the call to `getchar()` isn't assigned to a variable. This is because the value isn't used. Where does the typed character go? Initially, it goes into the keyboard input buffer. Eventually, as more I/O occurs, it is deleted from the buffer and disappears.

Note

Many C++ programmers prefer to avoid combining C-style I/O with C++ stream I/O. If you do want to keep your I/O to C++ I/O only, then use `cin.get()` rather than `getchar()`.

Formatting cout Displays

By default, `cout` displays one value after the other, without any formatting or special spacing. The `ios` class hierarchy, however, provides some functions that can help format stream output. To gain access to these *manipulators*, include the header file `iomanip.h` in the program that uses them.

The currency converter program uses manipulators to display the result of a currency conversion. Because the results are currency, the floating point values should be displayed with two digits to the right of the decimal point, even if the values are zero. These settings are placed with the following statement:

```
cout << setiosflags (ios::showpoint | ios::fixed)
    << setprecision(2);
```

There are two functions in this statement. The second, `setprecision`, is the easiest to use. It takes one input parameter: the number of digits that should appear to the right of the decimal point. Like other manipulators, it stays in effect until `cout` encounters another call to the function.

There are two other manipulators similar to `setprecision` that you might find useful: `setwidth` and `setfill`. The `setwidth` function sets the width of the field in which a value is displayed. It takes one parameter—the width of the field, which is often entered as a constant. If the value contains fewer characters than the field, it is right justified in the field. If the value is larger than the field, it is truncated. Unlike other manipulators, the width setting returns to the default after each stream insertion. In other words, if you use

```
cout << setwidth(10) << Number1 << Number2;
```

only `Number1` will appear in a field 10 characters wide; `Number2` takes up just enough space to display its value. If you want both values in 10-character-wide fields, you must use

```
cout << setwidth(10) << Number1 << setwidth(10) << Number2;
```

The `setfill` function determines what character will appear in the empty space surrounding a value that doesn't fill the entire width of its field. The default fill character is a space. However, you can set it to any character. For example, you might want to use asterisks as leading characters for currency values. Assuming that you have the value 156.895 stored in a floating point variable. the statement

```
cout << setprecision(2) << setwidth(10) << setfill('*')
    << Float_Number;
```

produces the output value `****156.89`.

Using ios Flags

The `setiosflags` manipulator, which provides formatting for numbers and characters, takes one input parameter that is a 32-bit binary value. Each bit in the parameter is a flag indicating which I/O characteristics should be set. The parameter list of `setiosflags` therefore contains a logical OR operation—indicated by the *bit-wise OR operator* (|)—that sets the appropriate bits.

To see how this works, let's first review the logical OR operation. OR works on one pair of bits at a time, using the truth table in Figure 4.2. This table can be summarized in the following way:

```
a | 1 = 1
a | 0 = a
```

```
OR │ 0   1
───┼──────
 0 │ 0   1

 1 │ 1   1
```

Figure 4.2   The truth table for the logical OR operation

In other words, if you OR a bit with 0, you preserve the value of the bit. If you OR a bit with 1, you set the bit to 1, regardless of the bit's original value. This means that if you want to set one bit in a storage location, you OR the current contents of the location with a value that contains a 1 in the position of the bit you want to set and 0s in all other positions.

Now let's look at the bit positions for some of the specific flags and see how the OR works to set the appropriate bits. Because the high-order 16 bits (bits 16 through 31) of the 32-bit value currently aren't used, we'll be looking at just the low-order 16 bits (bits 0 through 15).

The example from the currency converter program uses the showpoint flag to force the display of a decimal point. It has the binary value 0000 0001 0000 0000. The fixed flag ensures that a floating point value will appear as in fixed point rather than scientific notation. It has the binary value 1000 0000 0000 0000. The OR operation works on each pair of bits in the following manner:

```
    0000 0001 0000 0000  showpoint
│   1000 0000 0000 0000  fixed
    1000 0001 0000 0000  Final value sent to setiosflags
```

The result now has a bit set in the correct position for each of the two flags that should be transmitted to the setiosflags manipulator.

The ios flags are defined as an enumerated variable in the ios class. To reference them, you must use the scope resolution operator to indicate the class from which they come. The showpoint flag is therefore written:

```
ios::showpoint
```

It is placed inside the setiosflags's parameter list. Other flags are added to the parameter list with the bit-wise OR operator. A summary of the ios flag you might find useful can be found in Table 4.1.

Table 4.1   Flags for the setiosflags function

Flag	Function
left	Left justify output in its field.
right	Right justify output in its field
dec	Display numeric output in base 10
oct	Display numeric output in octal (base 8)
hex	Display numeric output in hexadecimal (base 16)
showbase	Show the base in which a number is displayed
showpoint	Display a decimal point for a floating point number
uppercase	Display all letters in uppercase
showpos	Display a plus sign (+) in front of positive numbers
scientific	Display floating point numbers in scientific notation
fixed	Display floating point numbers in fixed point notation

Resetting the ios Flags

The ios flags stay in effect for a given stream until the stream is closed or until they are explicitly reset with resetiosflags. For example, to turn off the showpoint and fixed formatters, you would use:

```
cout << resetiosflags(ios::showpoint | ios::fixed);
```

C++ also provides a *bit-wise AND operator* (&). The bit-wise AND operator performs a logical AND operation on pairs of bits in two storage locations.

Note

Putting Data into Objects

When you use static binding to create objects, you typically don't have data for the objects at the time memory is allocated for the objects. This means that all a constructor can do is initialize the objects; you need member functions to place data into objects' variables. In this section you will see how to write constructors that initialize objects and member functions that put data into objects. You will also see how to call those member functions from the program that is manipulating the objects.

The sample program for this section is a "bucket management" program. It keeps track of our buckets, storing data about their capacity and how many holes they have. The class declaration—stored in bucket.h—appears in Listing 4.3.

Listing 4.3   bucket.h: Header file for the bucket management program

```
class Bucket
{
    private:
        int numbHoles;
        float capacity;

    public:
        Bucket(void);
        void InitBucket (int, float);
        int GetnumbHoles (void);
        float Getcapacity (void);
};
```

Constructors That Initialize Objects

A constructor that simply initializes an object's variables, without inserting any real data, uses the C++ assignment operator to place a zero into numeric variables or a null into a character variable. For example, the constructor for the Bucket class (Listing 4.4) assigns zero to both numeric variables.

Listing 4.4   The constructor for the Bucket class

```
Bucket::Bucket()
{
    numbHoles = 0;
    capacity = 0.0;
}
```

The constructor for the `Converter` class (Listing 4.5) used by the currency conversion program is very similar. Notice, however, that because it uses a character variable, initialization is slightly different. The `Method` variable is assigned a null (two single quotes typed next to each other.)

Listing 4.5   The constructor for the Converter class

```
Converter::Converter()
{
    ConversionFactor = 0.0;
    Method = '';
}
```

Note

The constructors that you have seen so far don't take any input parameters. This is because they are designed for use with static binding, where objects are created when a program begins its run, before the program has a chance to collect any data for an object. However, when you create objects for dynamic binding, the program can collect data that can be passed to a constructor. You will therefore see examples of constructors that have input parameters beginning in Chapter 8.

Member Functions That Put Data into Objects

The Bucket program uses static binding to create objects. Because data aren't available when the objects are created at the start of program execution, the class must contain a member function that puts data into the object. This function (`InitBucket` in Listing 4.6) receives data through its parameter list. It then assigns the values in the input variables to the object's variables.

Listing 4.6   InitBuck: A function to place data into a Bucket object

```
void Bucket::InitBucket (int Holes, float Gallons)
{
    numbHoles = Holes;
    capacity = Gallons;
}
```

```
How many holes in bucket #1? 5
How many gallons does bucket #1 hold? 4.5
How many holes in bucket #2? 10
How many gallons does bucket #2 hold? 12
How many holes in bucket #3? 99
How many gallons does bucket #3 hold? 2.5


Bucket #1 holds 4.50 gallons and has 5 holes.
Bucket #2 holds 12.00 gallons and has 10 holes.
Bucket #3 holds 2.50 gallons and has 99 holes.
```

Figure 4.3   Output of the Bucket program

You may be thinking that it would be simpler to put `cout` and `cin` statements in the `InitBucket` member function. You could then collect the data right into the object's variables. There is nothing to prevent you from doing so. However, keep in mind that one of the goals of object-oriented programming is to separate the user interface from data manipulation to provide more flexible and sharable code. The only classes whose functions should contain I/O statements are those that support the user interface (for example, classes that provide menus and windows) and in some cases, those that provide file I/O.

Calling Member Functions Using Static Binding

The program that manipulates `Bucket` objects can be found in Listing 4.7; running it produces output something like Figure 4.3. This program defines three `Bucket` objects (`Bucket1`, `Bucket2`, `Bucket3`). It then asks the user to enter the number of holes and the capacity of each bucket. When it has the data for one bucket, it calls the `InitBucket` member function to place the data collected by the program into the object.

To call a member function using static binding, you use syntax with the following general format:

```
Variable_to_hold_return_value =
    Object_name.Member_function(parameter list);
```

Listing 4.7   A program to manipulate Bucket objects

```
#include <iostream.h>
#include <iomanip.h>
#include "bucket.h"

void main()
{
    Bucket Bucket1, Bucket2, Bucket3; // Define three buckets

    int iHoles; // Input variable for the number of holes
    float iGallons; // Input variable for the capacity of a bucket

    cout << "How many holes in bucket #1? ";
    cin >> iHoles;
    cout << "How many gallons does bucket #1 hold? ";
    cin >> iGallons;
    Bucket1.InitBucket (iHoles, iGallons);

    cout << "How many holes in bucket #2? ";
    cin >> iHoles;
    cout << "How many gallons does bucket #2 hold? ";
    cin >> iGallons;
    Bucket2.InitBucket (iHoles, iGallons);

    cout << "How many holes in bucket #3? ";
    cin >> iHoles;
    cout << "How many gallons does bucket #3 hold? ";
    cin >> iGallons;
    Bucket3.InitBucket (iHoles, iGallons);

    cout << setprecision(2) << setiosflags (ios::fixed | ios::showpoint)
        << endl << endl;
    cout << "Bucket #1 holds " << Bucket1.Getcapacity() << " gallons and has "
        << Bucket1.GetnumbHoles() << " holes." << endl;
    cout << "Bucket #2 holds " << Bucket2.Getcapacity() << " gallons and has "
        << Bucket2.GetnumbHoles() << " holes." << endl;
    cout << "Bucket #3 holds " << Bucket3.Getcapacity() << " gallons and has "
        << Bucket3.GetnumbHoles() << " holes." << endl;
}
```

For example, the Bucket program calls the InitBucket function for Bucket1 with:

```
Bucket1.InitBucket(iHoles, iGallons);
```

There is no variable to hold a return value because the `InitBucket` function doesn't return a value using the `return` statement.

Notice that the parameter list in the member function call contains just the names of the variables holding the values that are to be sent to the member function; data types aren't used. The parameters are mapped to the member function's parameter list in order. In this particular example, the contents of the `iHoles` variable are sent to the `Holes` variable; the contents of the `iGallons` variable are sent to the `Gallons` variable. Parameters in the function call must match the data types of the parameters in the first line of the function. However, parameters in the call don't need to have the same variable names as parameters in the function.

Member Functions and cout

If you look carefully at the last three statements in Listing 4.7, you'll notice that the `cout` statements contain calls to member functions of `Bucket` objects. These member functions, which appear in Listing 4.8, return the values stored in a `Bucket` object's private variables.

Listing 4.8   GetnumHoles and Getcapacity: Functions to return private data from a Bucket object

```
int Bucket::GetnumbHoles ()
{
    return numbHoles;
}

float Bucket::Getcapacity ()
{
    return capacity;
}
```

The way in which these functions are embedded in the `cout` seems to be in direct contrast to the way in which member functions that return values are called: There's no variable to hold the return value and no assignment operator. Actually, the return value does come back to the calling program. Rather than being assigned to a variable, it is inserted into the `cout` stream. In general, `cout` can evaluate expressions and display the result of the expression.

You certainly could assign values to variables and use those variables in the cout:

```
iHoles = Bucket1.GetnumbHoles();
iGallons = Bucket1.Getcapacity();
cout << "Bucket #1 holds " << iHoles << " gallons and has "
    << iGallons << " holes." << endl;
```

However, if you're not going to use the values other than for output, there's really no reason to ask the computer to store the values in main memory and then retrieve them for display. Your code will be shorter and the program will execute faster if you simply place the function calls in the cout, without first storing the values in memory.

Files and Stream I/O

C++ supports two types of files: text and binary. Text files store data as ASCII codes that are grouped into lines ending with a "new line" character. Values within a line are separated by spaces. Text files can be used for data storage or to create images of printed output that can be sent to a printer later. However, because values are separated by spaces, reading text files that contain string data can become a bit complicated. This section therefore looks at handling files of simple variable types; we'll revisit text files in Chapter 6 once you've learned to handle arrays and strings.

Binary files store streams of bits, without any attention to ASCII codes or separating spaces. They are convenient for storing objects. However, using binary files requires using the address of a storage location. We will therefore defer a discussion of them until Chapter 7.

To open a file for reading, you create an object (a stream) of the ifstream class; to open a file for writing, you create an object of the ofstream class. You can then use the names of the streams you created with the stream insertion and extraction operators.

Opening a File for Reading

The currency converter program uses a file named "Data" to store the data from its objects. To open the file for reading at the start of every program run, the program includes the statement

```
ifstream Read_File ("Data");
```

Notice that this looks very similar to other statements you have seen that create objects for static binding. The ifstream object is named Read_File. It is associated with a file whose path name is inside the parameter list. This parameter is passed to the class's constructor, which uses it to locate and open the file.

If the file name is entered as a constant, as it is in the preceding example, it must be surrounded by double quotes to make it a string. You may, however, wish to ask a user to enter a file name. In that case, the file name would be stored in a variable that contains a string.

Opening a File for Writing

The currency converter program rewrites the Data file each time the program ends. It therefore opens the file for writing with the statement

```
ofstream Write_File ("Data");
```

When opened in this way, an existing file is truncated to length zero. This means that opening the file destroys all its previous contents; you must rewrite the entire file to preserve its contents. If the file doesn't exist, it is created.

The alternative to truncating an existing file on opening is to open the file for appending. In that case, anything you write to the file is added on the end. To open in append mode, you simply insert the appropriate ios flag into the parameter list:

```
ofstream Write_File ("Data", ios::app);
```

Controlling File Replacement

If you want to open a file only when a file doesn't exist, you can use the ios flag noreplace to prevent opening an existing file. In that case, the statement to open the file is written:

```
ofstream Write_File ("Data", ios::noreplace);
```

Controlling File Creation

In some cases, you may want to open a file for writing only if a file already exists; if a file doesn't exist, you *don't* want to create a new one. To prevent a new file from being created, place the nocreate flag into the file object's parameter list, as in:

```
ofstream Write_File ("Data", ios::nocreate);
```

After opening a file using the `noreplace` or `nocreate` flags, you need to check to see if the file has been opened. You will find out how to do so in Chapter 5.

Writing to a Text File

Writing the contents of simple variables to a text file is just like writing them to the screen using the `cout` stream. As you can see in Listing 4.9, the stream insertion operator is used to send the values returned by "get" functions to the `Write_File` stream. The file stream automatically places a space after each value as it is written to the file.

Listing 4.9   Writing data from simple variables for storage in a text file

```
Write_File << England.GetFactor() << England.GetMethod();
Write_File << France.GetFactor() << France.GetMethod();
Write_File << Japan.GetFactor() << Japan.GetMethod();
```

Reading from a Text File

Reading numeric and character data from a text file is just like reading values from the keyboard using the `cin` stream. In Listing 4.10, for example, the stream extraction operator is used to take two values from the `Read_File` stream and store them in program variables. The values in these variables are then used as parameters in a call to a function that initializes an object.

Listing 4.10   Reading data for storage in simple variables from a text file

```
Read_File >> Factor >> How; // Read two values from the text file
England.ModConversion (Factor, How); // Call member function to initialize object
Read_File >> Factor >> How;
France.ModConversion (Factor, How);
Read_File >> Factor >> How;
Japan.ModConversion (Factor, How);
```

Closing Files

The currency converter program reads from and writes to the same file. However, the same file can't be open for reading and writing at the same time. (If this seems a bit odd, consider what would happen if you opened a file for reading and then immediately opened it for writing in truncate mode.) The Data file must therefore be closed after it is read, before it is opened for writing.

Files are closed automatically when the function in which the file's object was created ends. That means that you don't have to worry about closing files at the end of a program. However, as in the case mentioned in the previous paragraph, there are times when you need to close a file explicitly. To do so, you use the ifstream or ofstream member function close(), calling it just as you would any other member function. For example, the stream Read_File is closed with the statement

```
Read_File.close();
```

Printing to PC Printers

The way in which you create printed output from a program varies a great deal depending on the type of computer and its operating system. Macintosh printing, for example, requires calls to routines in the ToolBox and is therefore outside standard functions of the C++ language. On the other hand, most MS-DOS C++ compilers support predefined "file names" for printers connected directly to a single computer: PRN, LTP1, and LPT2. These streams actually represent ports on a PC. They are associated with specific physical ports in the system's CONFIG.SYS file. You might, for example, map PRN to a parallel port and LPT1 and LPT2 to serial ports.

Note

Although some PC compilers provide extensions to the C++ language to support sophisticated printing, the printing described in this section is limited to the characters in the MS-DOS character set. It is suited for printers that print one character at a time (for example, dot-matrix printers).

To print directly to a PC printer, you open an output stream to the port to which the printer is connected. For example, assuming that PRN is the parallel port, you can open a stream to a dot-matrix printer with:

```
ofstream printer ("PRN");
```

This statement creates a stream named `printer` that can then be used just like any other I/O stream.

To write to the printer, you insert data into the `printer` I/O stream. For example, the program in Listing 4.11 asks the user for the number of buckets purchased along with the total cost of the buckets. The prompts for input appear on the computer's screen. However, the output is sent to a printer rather than back to the monitor.

Listing 4.11   Printing to a PC printer

```
#include <streamio.h>

void main (void)
{
    int numbBuckets;
    float price;

    ofstream printer ("PRN"); // Opens a stream to the printer

    cout << "How many bucket did you buy?";
    cin >> numbBuckets;
    cout << "How much did they cost?";
    cin >> price;

// You can use manipulators to format printed output just as you can file output or
// output to the screen
    printer << setprecision(2) << setiosflags (ios::fixed | ios::showpoint);
    printer << "You spent " << price << " on ";
    printer << resetiosflags (ios::fixed | ios::showpoint);
    printer << numbBuckets << ". How could you?";
}
```

Printing Alternatives

If your compiler doesn't support PRN, LPT1, LPT2, there is still an easy way to create text-only printed output. The process involves using a text file as a substitute for the printer. Once the text file exists, you can print it. To use a text file as a substitute for a printer:

1. Open a text file as an output stream.
2. Write output to the file as if you were writing to the printer.
3. Exit the program that created the file.

4. If you are working in an MS-DOS environment, use the `PRINT` command to print the text file. In a UNIX environment, use the `lp` command or your system's equivalent. On a Macintosh, open the file with a text editor or word processor and set the font to Monaco or Courier (or any mono-spaced font). Then print the file.

Summary

C++ views input and output as a stream of characters. Streams can accept input from a file or from the keyboard; streams can send output to a computer screen, to a file, or directly to a printer. Stream I/O is performed in the same manner, regardless of the source or destination of the data being transferred.

C++ supports two default I/O streams: `cin` for keyboard input and `cout` for screen output. Keyboard input is extracted from the `cin` stream with the stream extraction operator (>>) and stored in program variables. Output is inserted into the `cout` stream with the stream insertion operator (<<) and displayed on the screen. Data for the `cout` stream may be stored in program variables or can be inserted as constants.

The `cout` stream can be formatted using manipulators. Manipulators set characteristics such as the width of the field in which data appear, the base in which numbers are displayed, whether a decimal point appears, and the character that fills empty space left in a print field.

Stream output is often used to accept data that are then passed to a member function that assigns values to an object. This technique is particularly useful for objects created using static binding because data are usually not available when the objects are created.

There are two types of C++ files. Text files store data as streams of individual ASCII codes, separating values with spaces. Binary files store streams of bits, without regard to ASCII codes and without spaces separating values.

To read from or write to a text file, a C++ program opens an I/O stream to the file. Data are then written to an output file's stream using the stream insertion operator; data can be read from an input file's stream using the stream extraction operator. Text file I/O streams can also be formatted using manipulators.

MS-DOS C++ compilers typically support default file names for direct output to printers. However, these are suitable only for one-character-at-a-time output. More sophisticated printing on most platforms is supported by extensions that aren't a part of the standard C++ language.

```
*****************************************************
*               Some State Lottery              *
*                  10/15/96                     *
*                                               *
*            4  9  10  11  12  29               *
*                                               *
*****************************************************
```

Figure 4.4 A sample lottery ticket

Exercises

1. Write and test a program that lets a person pick six numbers for playing a biweekly state lottery. Accept the six numbers from the keyboard. (*Hint*: The single class for this program is the lottery ticket. You will need to create just one object from the class.) Print the lottery ticket to the screen and printer. (If you don't have direct printing capabilities, "print" to a file.) The lottery ticket might look something like Figure 4.4.

2. Write and test a program that prints sales flyers for a grocery store. Create a class for a grocery store product, including the regular price and the sale price of the object. Create objects for ground beef, milk, yogurt, and lettuce. Ask the user to enter the regular and sale prices for each item, storing the data in the appropriate objects. Then, use the objects to print the sales flyer. It might look something like Figure 4.5.

3. Write and test a program that stores emergency phone numbers. In this case, the class is a phone number. Its single variable is a phone number, stored as an integer. Create objects for police, fire, and ambulance. Include the following capabilities in your program:

    -   Accept data for each object from the user.
    -   Store the data in a file each time the program ends.
    -   Read stored data from the file each time the program begins. Display the data for the user immediately after reading it.

```
                Jones' Corner Grocery

                    SALE PRICES
             Week of 10/10/96 - 10/16/96


                 REGULAR PRICE      SALE PRICE
Ground Beef        $1.79/lb         $1.09/lb
2% Milk             1.75/gal         .99/gal
Plain Yogurt         .79 each        .49 each
Lettuce              .99/head        .49/head
```

Figure 4.5   A sample grocery store sales flyer

4. Write and test a program for a college admissions office. The class on which this program is based is an academic year. Include the following variables, all of which are integers:

    • Academic year
    • Number of people who asked for information about admission to the college
    • Number of people who applied for admission
    • Number of people who were accepted
    • Number of those accepted who actually attended

    Create the following member functions:

    • A constructor
    • An initialization function that accepts data from the calling functions and places them in an object
    • Functions that return each class variable to a calling function

    The program should create four objects, one for each of the past four years, and do the following:

    • Read current data values from a file when the program begins
    • Write data values to a file when the program ends

- Give the user the opportunity to change the data in all objects (excluding the year, of course)
- Prepare a nicely formatted report showing all the data

5. Write and test a program that a teacher might use to store student grades. The class for this program is a student. It has the following variables:

- Student number (integer)
- Percentage grade on midterm exam (floating point)
- Percentage grade on final exam (floating point)
- Percentage grade for class participation (floating point)
- Percentage grade for assignment 1 (floating point)
- Percentage grade for assignment 2 (floating point)
- Percentage grade for assignment 3 (floating point)
- Percentage grade for assignment 4 (floating point)

For this exercise, it will be up to you to decide what member functions you need. The program should do the following:

- Create and manipulate five objects (it's a very small class)
- Store data in a data file
- Read data into main memory so it can be manipulated while the program is running
- Give the user the opportunity to change data in each object. (*Hint:* Present the current data values with cout; then let the user input a value.)
- Present a nicely formatted report that shows the current grades for each student.

6. Write and test a program that manages data about the distance driven by cars in a corporation's fleet. For each car, the program should store its vehicle identification number (VIN) and the number of miles driven each day in a seven-day period. The data should be stored in a text file. Write the program to handle five cars. Allow the user to enter data for each day and then display the data in a nicely formatted report. It is up to you to decide how the class for this program should appear. You should also determine the member functions that are required.

7. In many medical practices, the diagnoses that are determined for a patient are coded using numeric codes. Write and test a program that handles data about a diagnosis made for a patient. The program should handle a patient number, a diagnosis code, and a date (stored as a six-digit integer). Each run of the program corresponds to the diagnoses for one patient (up to five per patient). Allow the user to enter the patient number and date only once. Then collect the five diagnosis codes. After you've initialized objects, display a report that summarizes what the user has entered. Make your own choices about the structure of the class and its member functions.

8. Consider the program you wrote for Exercise 7. Assume that you store the data collected by a program run in a text file and read that data back into the program each time the program begins. If you append data to the file, rather than overwriting it each time, what is the effect of doing this on the objects in the program? This being the case, what would you have to do to modify the program so it could handle multiple sets of objects? Can you do this effectively, knowing as much about C++ as you do at this point? Why or why not?

5

Structured Elements of C++

OBJECTIVES

In this chapter you will learn about:

- The details of C++ variables, including storage options and scope.
- The operators used to construct C++ statements.
- C++ selection statements.
- C++ iteration statements.
- Generalized procedures for working with functions.

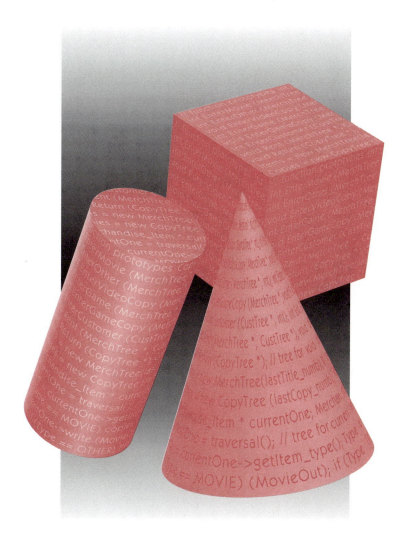

Although the high-level structure of an object-oriented program is based on the classes the program manipulates, ironically the member functions that define what objects created from classes can do are written using structured programming techniques. To write an executable C++ program, you must therefore know the syntax of C++'s structured elements as well as its object-oriented capabilities. This chapter introduces you to C++'s structured elements, including selection and iteration. You'll also read more about C++ variables, operators, functions that aren't member functions, and passing values into functions.

Variables Revisited

One of the things that makes C++ so popular for software development is that it provides more control over memory use than other high-level languages. For example, to some extent you can control where a variable is placed and how long the variable remains in main memory by changing its *storage class*. You can also control how long a variable remains in memory by the place in the program where the variable is declared (the *scope* of a variable). This section looks at these two important aspects of C++ variables, which together give you some control over memory use. It also discusses initializing variables when they are declared.

The Scope of a Variable

If your programming experience includes COBOL, then you have been required to declare all your variables at the beginning of a program. If you are familiar with Pascal, then you are used to declaring variables in a procedure's var section. However, C++ doesn't limit you to any single place for declaring variables used by functions. You can declare a variable just about anywhere, as long as the declaration appears before you use the variable. However, the portion of a program that can recognize and use a variable depends on where the variable has been declared. The extent to which a variable can be seen by parts of a program is known as its scope.

A variable's scope is limited to the innermost set of braces ({ and }) within which it is declared. As an example, consider the program framework in Figure 5.1. This small sample contains a main function and a function called by main named processData. The integer variable numbBuckets is visible to and can be used by any part of the main function. However, the integer variable numbHoles that is declared inside the braces nested within main is

```
void main (void)
{
    int numbBuckets;          ←——— Accessible to the
                                      entire main
                                      function
    {
        int numbHoles;        ←
    }                               Accessible only
                                    within the inner
                                    braces
}

void processData();
{                                  Local to function
    float numbHoles;          ←
}
```

Figure 5.1   The scope of variables

visible and can be used only within those braces. Whether numbHoles
remains in main memory when the program exits the inner braces depends on
the variable's storage class (discussed in the next section).

The numbHoles variable declared in the processData function is
accessible only to that function because it is declared within the function. It is
said to be *local* to the function. In fact, any variable defined inside a function is
a local variable. Although the variable in processData has the same name as
a variable in main, there is no conflict. The two variables do not overlap in
their scope. They can therefore coexist in the same program, with either the
same or different data types.

A Word About Global Variables

In COBOL, all variables are *global.* In other words, any variable declared in the
DATA SECTION is accessible to the entire program. Pascal and Modula-2 also
support global variables (variables declared in the var section that is outside
any procedures). C++ global variables are variables declared outside any func-

tion. However, *although C++ does support global variables, you should use them sparingly in an application program.* In most cases, only `const` variables are global.

The use of global variables in a C++ program presents several problems, including the following:

- Global variables may conflict with local variables that are inadvertently given the same names, leading to unanticipated program behavior.
- Global variables make functions harder to debug and modify because the variable definitions aren't stored with the functions. The greater the number of files in which a program's source code is stored, the more confusion global variables introduce into debugging and program maintenance. In fact, in large programs identifying the mere presence of global variables can be very difficult because there is no easy way to know where they might be declared.

Variable Storage Classes

A variable storage class is a category to which a variable belongs that instructs C++ how to place the variable in memory and how to keep the variable in storage. When reading about storage classes, don't forget that you can declare a C++ variable just about anywhere in a program.

There are three storage classes:

- `auto`: Automatic variables (the default storage class) are allocated space as soon as C++ encounters a declaration for the variable. An automatic variable stays in main memory until the program exits the function or portion of a function (defined by nested braces) in which the variable was defined.
- `static`: A static variable, which is allocated space in memory as soon as C++ encounters a declaration for the variable, stays in main memory as long as the program is running. If you want to preserve the value of a variable between multiple calls to the same function (for example, to keep a running total), then use a static variable. As you will see in Chapter 6, arrays that are initialized when they are declared *must* be static.

- `register`: A register variable is kept in a CPU register whenever possible. Because it takes less time to access data that is already in the CPU than it does to load data from main memory into the CPU, access to register variables is faster than access to automatic or static variables. However, CPUs have a limited number of registers, only a few of which will be available for variable storage at any given time. If the computer needs a register occupied by a register variable, it moves that variable to main memory. You should therefore use register variables sparingly.

Initializing Variables

Unlike languages such as Pascal and Modula-2, C++ does not require you to initialize a variable before it is used. In other words, you can use a C++ variable on the right side of an assignment operator without first assigning the variable a value. However, using an uninitialized variable is a very risky business. C++ doesn't necessarily automatically initialize storage locations when a program is launched. Some storage locations assigned to variables may still contain the values they had before the program was loaded into main memory. In other words, you can never count on the initial values given to a variable unless you explicitly initialize them. It is therefore good programming practice to always initialize variables.

There are three ways to initialize a variable:

- Assign the variable a value across an assignment operator, as in `counter = 0;`
- Assign the variable a value using an input statement such as `cin`.
- Assign the variable a value when it is declared.

Initialization When Declaring Variables

To initialize a variable when you declare the variable, use an assignment operator and the value to be given to the variable as a part of the declaration. For example, the following statement initializes a counter to zero:

```
int counter = 0;
```

C++ recognizes this as a variable declaration rather than an assignment statement because it begins with a data type instead of a variable name.

What about variables that are initialized in their declarations in functions other than the `main` function? `Auto` variables are destroyed when their function terminates. Because the computer reallocates space for the variables whenever the function is called, the variables are initialized whenever the function is called.

However, `static` variables are not reinitialized each time their functions are called. They are initialized once, when the function is called the first time and space is allocated in main memory for the variable. Then, they remain in main memory, with their values intact, until the program ends. The only way to reinitialize a `static` variable is to use an assignment statement.

C++ Operators

Like any high-level programming language, C++ provides operators that manipulate numeric and character values. As you will see in the following sections, many arithmetic operators are similar to what you have used in other high-level languages. However, some arithmetic operators are not found in languages other than C. The syntax of the logical operators is also unique to C and C++, although the functions that the operators perform are not.

Arithmetic Operators

The C++ arithmetic operators are summarized in Table 5.1 in order of precedence. These operators can be used in an assignment statement to place the result of an operation into a variable. For example, the statement

```
average = sum/numbItems;
```

takes the value stored in `sum`, divides it by the value stored in `numbItems`, and stores the result in `average`.

Expressions created using arithmetic operators can also be placed in any statement that expects a value. For example, the following are legal C++ statements:

```
cout << "The average is " << sum/numbItems;
return sum/numbItems;
```

Table 5.1   The C++ Arithmetic Operators, listed in order of precedence

Operator	Function
+	Positive
-	Negative
++i	Preincrement i
--i	Predecrement i[a]
*	Multiplication
/	Division[b]
%	Modulo
+	Addition
-	Subtraction
i++	Postincrement i
i--	Postdecrement i[c]

a. Preincrement and predecrement have the same precedence.
b. Multiplication and division have the same precedence.
c. Postincrement and postdecrement have the same precedence.

Embedding arithmetic expressions in other statements saves both storage space and execution time when you don't need to use the result of the arithmetic expression again in the function in which the expression appears. However, if the result is to be used more than once, then it is more efficient to store it in a variable rather than recomputing the value each time it is needed.

C++ uses its rules of precedence to decide the order in which expressions are evaluated. As with other high-level languages, when an expression contains more than one operator of the same precedence, evaluation proceeds from left to right. You can also override the default precedence with parentheses.

The Increment and Decrement Operators

C++ has two arithmetic operators—increment and decrement—that aren't found in languages such as COBOL, Pascal, or Modula-2. The increment operator increases a value by one; the decrement operator decreases the operator by one. When the increment or decrement occurs depends on whether the operator precedes or follows the variable whose value is being modified.

To see how the increment and decrement operators work, consider the examples in Table 5.2. In each case, `idx` begins with a value of 10; `sum` contains 100. Notice that when the operator is placed before a variable, the increment occurs before any other operation is performed in the expression; when the operator follows a variable, the increment or decrement occurs after all other operations have been performed.

Table 5.2   The effect of the increment and decrement operators

Statement	Action	Result
`sum = sum + (++idx)`[a]`;`	(Preincrement) Increment `idx`. Add `idx` to `sum`.	`idx = 11` `sum = 111`
`sum = sum + idx++;`	(Postincrement) Add `idx` to `sum`. Increment `idx`.	`idx = 11` `sum = 110`
`sum = sum + (--idx)`[b]`;`	(Predecrement) Decrement `idx`. Add `idx` to `sum`.	`idx = 9` `sum = 109`
`sum = sum + idx--;`	(Postdecrement) Add `idx` to `sum`. Decrement `idx`.	`idx = 9` `sum = 110`

a.   The parentheses have been inserted to make it clear to the C++ compiler that the statement includes an addition operator and a preincrement operator rather than any other combination of operators.

b.   As with the parentheses surrounding the preincrement operator, those surrounding the predecrement operator are present simply to separate the addition operator form the predecrement operator.

The increment and decrement operators are handy for loop index variables. Instead of writing `index = index + 1`, you can simply use `index++`. As you will see in Chapter 6, this can eliminate a line of code when you are stepping through the elements in an array.

Performing Exponentiation

There is one obvious omission from Table 5.1: There is no operator that performs exponentiation (raising a value to a power). If you need to compute the square of a number, you can always use a statement such as

```
square = number * number;
```

However, trying to perform other exponentiation can be clumsy and difficult. The answer is to use a library function that performs the operation.

Math functions are part of the math library; prototypes are in math.h. Exponentiation is performed with the pow function, which computes x^y:

```
double pow(double x, double y)
```

This function takes two parameters, both double-precision floating point numbers. It returns a double-precision floating point value. As you will see shortly, if you give the function integer or single-precision floating point values, C++ converts them to double-precision floating point.

The pow function is very flexible: It can accept fractional and negative powers as well as positive, integer powers. For example, you might use it to compute $109.15^{-.55}$:

```
double result = 0.0;
double base = 109.15;
double power = -0.55;
result = pow (base, power);
```

Logical Operators

The C++ logical operators are summarized in Table 5.3. As you can see, there are significant differences between these operators and those used in many other high-level languages. For example, while many languages use the word NOT for the inversion operator, C++ uses an exclamation point (!). By the same token, C++ uses != for the not equals operator rather than the more common <>.

Table 5.3   The C++ Logical Operators

Operator	Function
||	OR
&&	AND
!	NOT
|	Bit-wise OR
&	Bit-wise AND
==	Equal to
!=	Not equal to
<	Less than
<=	Less than or equal to
>	Greater than
>=	Greater than or equal to

In Chapter 4 you were introduced to the bit-wise OR operator (|), which let you set bits for formatting stream output. Notice that the logical OR operator is two straight lines typed next to one another (| |). One of the most common errors a C++ programmer can make is to forget to use *two* lines in a logical expression. For example, suppose you want to construct a logical expression that should be true if either of two conditions is true:

```
Ants > Bats OR Cats < Dogs
```

The correct way to write this statement in C++ is

```
Ants > Bats || Cats < Dogs;
```

What happens, however, if you inadvertently write

```
Ants > Bats | Cats < Dogs;
```

C++ first evaluates the two simple expressions. If `Ants > Bats` is true, the result is 1; otherwise the result is 0. If `Cats < Dogs` is true, the result is 1; otherwise the result is 0. C++ then takes the result of the two simple expressions and performs a bit-wise OR. If the final result is 0, the expression is false; if the final result is nonzero, the result is true. This will not necessarily be the same result as that from the expression using the logical OR. You must therefore be very careful to use the doubled operator when constructing a logical expression.

The same situation exists with the equal to operator and the AND operator. Notice that the logical equal to operator is *two* equal signs (==); the assignment operator is one. The logical AND operator is *two* ampersands (&&); the bit-wise AND operator is one. The reason it is so easy to make mistakes with these operators is because logical expressions with the single operators are legal in C++. For example, the expression

```
if (Cats = Dogs)
```

will be accepted by a C++ compiler. To evaluate the expression, C++ assigns the value of `Dogs` to `Cats` and then checks to see if the value in `Cats` is zero or nonzero. A nonzero value returns a result of true; a zero value returns a result of false.

Assignment Statement Shorthand

Assignment statements often store their results in one of the storage locations used in the expression on the right side of the assignment operator. For example, a program might accumulate a sum with

```
sum = sum + newNumb;
```

C++ provides a shorthand for this type of assignment. The preceding statement can be written

```
sum += newNumb;
```

In this notation, notice that the arithmetic operator precedes the assignment operator. The assignment statement shorthand operators are summarized in Table 5.4.

Table 5.4   Assignment statement shorthand

Shorthand	Equivalence
`sum += newNumb;`	`sum = sum + newNumb;`
`sum -= newNumb;`	`sum = sum - newNumb;`
`sum *= newNumb;`	`sum = sum * newNumb;`
`sum /= newNumb;`	`sum = sum / newNumb;`
`sum %= newNumb;`	`sum = sum % newNumb;`

Assignment, Data Type Conversion, and Typecasting

Unlike languages such as Pascal and Modula-2, C++ doesn't have separate operators for integer and floating point division. The type of division that C++ performs depends on the data types of the values that are part of the expression. C++ performs conversions of values as needed. In fact, C++ tries to evaluate any expression it encounters, converting data types whenever it can. This is in direct contrast to other languages, which won't compile expressions containing mismatched data types.

In this section you will be introduced to some of the rules C++ uses when converting data types. You will also read about a technique for forcing values to assume a specific data type.

Data Type Conversion Behavior

Consider the short C++ program in Listing 5.1. What output will the program produce when `value1` is 10.0 and `value2` is 20? If you simply do the arithmetic, you come up with 0.5. However, running the program actually displays zero. Why? Because C++ is converting the data type of the result as it passes across the assignment operator.

The actual conversions that occur when expressions contain more than one data type depend on exactly which data types are involved. In practice, C++ converts as necessary to complete the operation on the right side of an assignment operator and converts again, if necessary, when sending that result to its final destination. When converting numeric data before performing arithmetic operations, C++ converts to the data type in the expression that has the most range and precision. In Listing 5.1, for example, the integer value

Listing 5.1 mathTest.cpp: A program to demonstrate automatic data type conversions

```
void main (void)
{
    float value1;
    int result, value2;

    cout << "Enter the first value: ";
    cin >> value1;
    cout << "Enter the second value: ";
    cin >> value2;
    result = value1/value2;
    cout << result;
}
```

value2 is converted to a floating point value before the division is performed. The result is therefore 0.5. However, when the 0.5 is passed across the assignment operator, it is truncated to an integer because the variable result is an integer, producing the value zero.

There is a hierarchy of data types that determines how numeric conversions occur:

```
double
float
long
int
short
```

When an expression contains more than one type of data, data types lower in the list are converted to match whichever data type is highest in the list.

C++ also converts character data. When char data is used in an expression with integers, C++ converts the characters to integer, handling the ASCII codes as if they were numeric values. As you will see later in this chapter, this comes in handy when you want to use a character in a switch (case) construct.

Although C++ tries automatically to convert data types wherever possible, under some circumstances conversion isn't possible. In particular, variables that hold pointers (addresses in main memory) can't be converted to an arithmetic data type. When a C++ compiler encounters a conversion it cannot make, it generates a compiler error. This is often a hint that you are using a variable in a way that you didn't intend. For example, you might be telling C++ to use a main memory address instead of the value that is stored at that address.

Typecasting

Typecasting is a way of explicitly forcing C++ to covert a value to a specific data type. To perform typecasting, you precede a variable with the data type you want the variable to take. The typecasted data type is surrounded by parentheses.

You can, for example, use typecasting to force C++ to perform integer division, even if one of the values in the expression is stored in a floating point variable:

```
float value1 = 20.16;
int value2 = 5, result;
result = (int) value1 / value2;
```

To evaluate the assignment statement, C++ first converts `value1` to an integer, truncating any digits to the right of the decimal point. It then performs an integer division.

Selection

As you would expect, C++ supports selection. Like other high-level languages, it provides an `if` statement. C++ also provides is own version of the `case` statement: `switch`. This section looks at the syntax for both of these structures.

Using the if Statement

The C++ `if` statement has the following general syntax:

```
if (logical expression)
    statement(s) to execute if true;
else
    statement(s) to execute if false;
```

The `else` portion of the statement, of course, is optional. If either `if` or `else` are followed by more than one statement, the statements must be surrounded by braces.

One of the currency converter program's member functions uses the following if statement to determine which of two arithmetic operations to use to perform a conversion:

```
if (Method == 'm' || Method == 'M')
    return ConversionFactor * Dollars;
else
    return Dollars / ConversionFactor;
```

Notice that there is a semicolon after the statement following if, as well as one after the statement following else.

As you would expect, if statements can be nested. For example, the hi/low game program uses the following if structure to evaluate a guess:

```
if (guess == answer)
    return EQ;
else
    if (guess < answer)
        return LO;
    else
        return HI;
```

Because the if statement nested after the else is a single statement, no braces are required around it.

Checking the Result of File Operations

One of the characteristics of a well-written program is error trapping. Error trapping insulates the user from his or her mistakes and in many cases can prevent a program from crashing. In particular, a good program checks the result of file I/O operations. If a program doesn't catch a problem with opening a file, for example, any attempt to read from or write to the file will usually cause the program to crash.

The ios class provides several member functions that you can use in conjunction with an if statement to monitor the success of file operations. Assuming that you've created a file stream named myStream, the ways in which you can check the result of a file operation are summarized in Table 5.5. The first four expressions are used to check the result of operations such as opening a file. For example, the concurrency converter program checks to see if a file has been opened successfully before attempting to read from the file:

Table 5.5   Checking the result of file I/O operations

C++ statements	Purpose
`if (myStream)`	File operation was successful; no errors occurred
`if (myStream.good)`	File operation was successful; no errors occurred
`if (!myStream)`	File operation was unsuccessful; some error occurred
`if (myStream.bad)`	File operation was unsuccessful; some error occurred
`if (myStream.eof)`	End of file encountered

```
if (Read_File)
{
    Read_File >> Factor >> How;
    England.ModConversion (Factor, How);
    Read_File >> Factor >> How;
    France.ModConversion (Factor, How);
    Read_File >> Factor >> How;
    Japan.ModConversion (Factor, How);
    Read_File.close();
}
```

If the file wasn't opened successfully (in other words, `if (Read_File)` was false), the program could either do nothing—as it does in this case—or use an `else` to display an error message for the user.

Note

The end of file indicator is often used when a program is processing one line or record in a file at a time. You will see how to do this later in this chapter.

When any stream error condition occurs, C++ sets an error flag that indicates exactly which error conditions have arisen. You can check the value of the error flag with the `rdstate` function:

```
int errorFlag;
ofstream myStream;
  :
  :
errorFlag = myStream.rdstate();
```

The value returned by rdstate uses the first three bits to indicate specific error conditions. If a bit has a value of 1, then the associated error condition has occurred. The way in which these flags are interpreted can be found in Table 5.6.

Table 5.6   Stream error bits

Flags set	Value
eofbit	1
failbit	2
badbit	4
eofbit failbit	3
eofbit badbit	5
failbit badbit	6
eofbit failbit badbit	7

Once a stream's error flag has been set (in other words, rdstate returns anything other than zero), anything a program attempts to do with the stream will fail. The solution is to clear the error flag with the clear function:

```
myStream.clear();
```

Keep in mind that clearing the a stream's error flag only resets the error state. It doesn't solve any problems that might have occurred. If some error other than an end-of-file occurred, then attempting to use the stream again after clearing the error flag may simply trigger the error again.

Using the switch Statement

Although if statements can be nested without limit, deeply nested ifs are difficult to debug and modify. When a program needs to evaluate many possible values for a single variable (for example, deciding what to do based on an option in a menu), it is cleaner to use a switch statement. In fact, if you need to take actions based on more than two values of the same variable, you should use a switch rather than an if.

The switch statement (the C++ equivalent of the Pascal and Modula-2 case statement) takes action based on the value of an integer variable. It has the following general syntax:

```
switch (integer_variable)
{
    case integer_value1:
        statements to execute
        break;
    case integer_value2:
    case integer_value3:
        statements to execute
        break;
    :
    :
    default:
        statements to execute if no case is matched
}
```

There are several syntax details to which you need to pay attention when writing a switch structure:

- The entire body of the switch is surrounded in a single set of braces.
- Each case is associated with one integer value. However, multiple case statements can be associated with the same set of actions, as occurs with integer_value2 and integer_value3 in the preceding general syntax.

- The integer value can be an integer variable, an integer constant, a character variable, or a character constant. When the value is a character, C++ automatically typecasts it into an integer.
- Each case is followed by the statements that are to be executed when the value in the switch variable matches the value following case.
- The break statement at the end of a group of executable statements causes the switch to branch to the statement below the closing brace. Although not required as far as a compiler's syntax checking is concerned, a break prevents C++ from evaluating any other case statements within the switch.

Note

The break statement causes C++ to immediately jump out of the innermost set of braces in which it is contained. As you will see shortly, break can also be used to exit from a loop.

- The statements following default are executed if the value in the switch variable matches none of the preceding case values. A default statement is optional. If no default is present and the value in the switch variable doesn't match any case values, the switch statement simply does nothing.

The Currency Converter Program

To see how selection, and in particular switch statements, are used in a C++ program, let's take a look at the entire currency converter program. As you saw originally in Chapter 3, the header file (converter.h in Listing 5.2) contains a definition for the Converter class. Objects created from this class contain data about the conversion factor and the method that should be used to perform a conversion (multiplication or division).

The class definition also contains five member functions, all of which use techniques you have seen previously. The code for these functions is stored in the file converter.cpp (Listing 5.3):

- Converter (the constructor): Uses assignment to initialize an object's variables.

Listing 5.2   converter.h: Header file for the currency converter program

```
class Converter
{
    private:
        float ConversionFactor;
        char Method;

    public:
        Converter (void);
        void ModConversion (float, char);
        float DoConversion (float);
        float GetFactor (void);
        char GetMethod (void);
};
```

- `ModConversion`: Uses assignment to place values into an object's variables. This function can be used to set values for a new object or to modify existing values.
- `DoConversion`: Based on the value in the `Method` variable, converts U.S. dollars into a foreign currency. This function contains an `if` statement to choose the correct conversion algorithm and arithmetic operations to perform the conversion.
- `GetFactor`: Returns the value in the conversion factor variable.
- `GetMethod`: Returns the value in the conversion method variable.

Listing 5.3   converter.cpp: Member functions for the currency converter program

```
#include "converter.h"

Converter::Converter()
{
    ConversionFactor = 0.0;
    Method = '';
}

void Converter::ModConversion (float iFactor, char How)
{
    ConversionFactor = iFactor;
    Method = How;
}
```

Continued next page

Listing 5.3 (Continued) converter.cpp: Member functions for the currency converter program

```
float Converter::DoConversion (float Dollars)
{
```
// This simple selection statement chooses a conversion algorithm based on data
// stored in the object.
```
    if (Method == 'm' || Method == 'M')
        return ConversionFactor * Dollars;
    else
        return Dollars / ConversionFactor;
}

float Converter::GetFactor ()
{
    return ConversionFactor;
}

char Converter::GetMethod ()
{
    return Method;
}
```

The program that manipulates Converter objects can be found in Listing 5.4. It uses a switch structure to organize the actions to be taken for each menu option. There are two major advantages to using the switch rather than nested if statements. First, the code is easier to understand. Second, it is easier to modify. Adding a new menu option requires simply adding another case to the switch, along with statements that are to be executed when the new menu option is chosen.

Listing 5.4   main.cpp: Main program for the currency converter program

```
#include <iostream.h>
#include <fstream.h>
#include <iomanip.h>
#include "converter.h"

void main()
{
    Converter England, France, Japan;

    int Menu (void);
```

Continued next page

Listing 5.4 (Continued) main.cpp: Main program for the currency converter program

```cpp
ifstream Read_File ("Data");
int option = 0;
char country, How;
float Factor, Dollars, Amount;
```

// This selection verifies that the input file has been opened successfully.

```cpp
if (Read_File)
{
    Read_File >> Factor >> How;
    England.ModConversion (Factor, How);
    Read_File >> Factor >> How;
    France.ModConversion (Factor, How);
    Read_File >> Factor >> How;
    Japan.ModConversion (Factor, How);
    Read_File.close();
}
```

// If the input file wasn't opened successfully, it's likely the file didn't exist. In that case,
// the program does nothing. Alternatively, it could have displayed a message to the user.

// This loop continues the program until the user chooses Quit from the menu.
// You will learn how to write loops in the next section of this chapter.

```cpp
while (option != 9)
{
    option = Menu();
    switch (option)
    {
        case 1:
            cout << "Country ( E)ngland, F)rance, or J)apan ): ";
            cin >> country;
            cout << "Conversion factor: ";
            cin >> Factor;
            cout << "Method ( M)ultiply or D)ivide): ";
            cin >> How;
```

// This nested switch is executed only if the outer switch detects a 1 for the menu option

```cpp
            switch (country)
            {
```

// Multiple cases next to one another, without intervening body statements, are related to the
// same body statements. In this example, this technique is used to trap both upper- and
// lowercase characters.

```cpp
                case 'e':
                case 'E':
                    England.ModConversion (Factor, How);
                    break;
```

Continued next page

Listing 5.4 (Continued) main.cpp: Main program for the currency converter program

```cpp
                case 'f':
                case 'F':
                    France.ModConversion (Factor, How);
                    break;
                case 'j':
                case 'J':
                    Japan.ModConversion (Factor, How);
                    break;
                default:
                    cout << "You've entered a country I can't handle.";
            }
            break;
        case 2:
            cout << "Country: ( E)ngland, F)rance, or J)apan )";
            cin >> country;
            cout << "\nDollar amount to be converted? ";
            cin >> Dollars;
            cout << setiosflags (ios::showpoint | ios::fixed) <<
                setprecision(2);
```

// This nested switch is executed only if the outer switch detects a 2 for the menu option

```cpp
            switch (country)
            {
                case 'e':
                case 'E':
                    Amount = England.DoConversion (Dollars);
                    cout << "\n" << Dollars << " Dollars = " << Amount <<
                        " Pounds." << endl;
                    break;
                case 'f':
                case 'F':
                    Amount = France.DoConversion (Dollars);
                    cout << "\n" << Dollars << " Dollars = " << Amount <<
                        " Francs." << endl;
                    break;
                case 'j':
                case 'J':
                    Amount = Japan.DoConversion (Dollars);
                    cout << "\n" << Dollars << " Dollars = " << Amount <<
                        " Yen." << endl;
                    break;
                default:
                    cout << "\nYou've entered a country I can't handle.";
            }
            break;
```

Continued next page

Listing 5.4 (Continued) main.cpp: Main program for the currency converter program

```cpp
        case 9:
            ofstream Write_File ("Data");
            if (Write_File)
            {
                Write_File << England.GetFactor() << England.GetMethod();
                Write_File << France.GetFactor() << France.GetMethod();
                Write_File << Japan.GetFactor() << Japan.GetMethod();
            }
            break;
        default:
            cout << "You've entered an unavailable option.";
        }
    }
}

int Menu ()
{
    int choice;

    cout << "\n\nPick a menu option:" << endl;
    cout << "  1. Set conversion rate" << endl;
    cout << "  2. Do a conversion" << endl;
    cout << "  9. Quit" << endl;
    cout << "\nWhich one? ";
    cin >> choice;
    return choice;
}
```

As you study the program, notice that the `default` option in this `switch` provides an error message for the user, indicating that he or she has picked a value not in the menu. Notice also that the code following two of the `case` statements (1 and 2) includes an embedded `switch`. This is perfectly legal: A `case` can be followed by any executable statement. The inner `switch` structures look for character constants rather than integer constants. Keep in mind that C++ automatically typecasts the character constant to an integer, making its evaluation of the value based on its ASCII code.

Iteration

C++ provides three looping statements: `while`, `do while`, and `for`. Which you use depends on the needs of your program: whether the loop will be executed a fixed or variable number of times and whether the loop must always be executed at least once.

Using the while Statement

The `while` is the most common C++ looping structure. It has the following general syntax:

```
while (logical_expression)
{
    body of loop
}
```

If the body of the loop is only one statement, the surrounding braces aren't needed.

The important thing to remember about a `while` is that the logical expression in parentheses is evaluated at the top of the loop. This means that it is possible that a loop might never be executed. As an example, consider the following:

```
int Option;

Option = 9;
while (Option != 9)
{
    body of loop
}
```

Because the logical expression is false the first time the program encounters the `while`, control passes to the statement below the body of the loop, without ever executing the statements in the loop. This is not necessarily a bad thing. Consider, for example, the code in Listing 5.5. The purpose of the code is to move the decimal point in a positive floating point number so that the number is in the format .XXXX. It also needs to keep track of how many times the decimal point is moved. If the original number is greater than or equal to 1, it should be multiplied by 0.1; if the number is less than 0.1, it should be multiplied by 10. Listing 5.5 contains two `while` loops, one for condition. Rather than using an `if` to decide which loop to execute, the code takes advantage of the fact that the original value in `Number` will pass the test of no more than one `while`, ensuring that only the correct transformation is performed. (If the number is already in the correct format, neither loop will execute.)

Listing 5.5   Loops that intentionally may never be executed

```
float Number;
int timesMoved = 0;
:
:
while (Number >= 1)
{
    Number *= 0.1;
    timesMoved++;
}
while (Number < .1)
{
    Number *= 10;
    timesMoved++;
}
```

Using the do while Statement

The C++ `do while` is a variation on the `while`. It has the following general syntax:

```
do
{
    body of loop
}
while (logical_expression);
```

Notice that the logical expression that controls the loop appears at the bottom of the loop. A `do while` will therefore always execute at least once, until it reaches the `while` at the bottom where the control expression is actually evaluated.

Given that the body of a a `do while` is executed at least once, you might be tempted to use it frequently. You might, for example, want to use it to control a main program loop that terminates when the user chooses a Quit option from a main menu. The loop would then have the structure:

```
const QUIT = 9;
int Option;

do
{
    display menu
    cin >> Option;
    take action based on value of Option
}
while (Option != QUIT);
```

The advantage of this structure is that you don't have to give Option a value before the loop begins. If you use a while, the code must be written:

```
const QUIT = 9;
int Option = 0;

while (Option != QUIT)
{
    display menu
    cin >> Option;
    take action based on value of Option
}
```

In this example, Option must be initialized to something other than the value of QUIT so that the loop will execute the first time.

Nonetheless, using do while can make a program harder to understand and debug because the while (logical_expression); at the end of the loop looks an awful lot like a while without a body. Many programmers therefore prefer to avoid using do while as much as possible, even if it means remembering to initialize while control values.

Using the for Statement

The for structure is useful when you need a loop that increments a numeric control variable and stops when that variable reaches some predetermined value. In particular, it is convenient for processing an entire array, in order. The for structure has the following general syntax:

```
for (initial_control_value; terminating_condition; increment)
{
    body of loop
}
```

For example, assume that you have numbItems elements in an array. You want to process each element, beginning with the first. A for structure to control the loop would be written:

```
for (i = 0; i < numbItems; i++)
{
    body of loop
}
```

The first statement within the parentheses initializes the control variable. In this case, it is i, a variable that has been declared earlier in the program. The second statement within the parentheses is a logical expression. The loop continues as long as the condition is true. The final statement is an arithmetic expression that increments the control variable. In this particular example, the loop continues as long as the control variable is less than the number of items in the array. Each time the loop increments, the control variable is incremented by one. You will see how for is used in array processing in Chapter 6.

The break and continue Statements

As you saw earlier, the break statement is used within a switch to branch out of the switch after the program has matched a case value and executed the associated statements. The break statement, however, can be used in other ways, including branching out of a loop at any time. In particular, break can be very useful when there are many conditions that can terminate a loop, too many to put into a single logical expression.

Note

If you are familiar with assembly language, then it might help you to understand the operation of the break if you know that its action is to pop the address of the statement below the bottom of the loop off the stack and place that address in the CPU's program counter.

The continue statement causes a loop to iterate. Its use can speed up program execution by preventing a program from evaluating if statements whose logical expressions can't be true because a preceding if's logical expression is true.

As an example of both break and continue, consider the following while:

```
while (1 < 2)
{
    cin >> SomeValue;
    if (SomeValue > 100)
    {
        NewValue += SomeValue * 10;
        continue;
    }
    if (SomeValue > 50 && SomeValue <= 100)
    {
        NewValue += SomeValue / 10;
        break;
    }
    if (SomeValue > 25 NewValue <= 50)
    {
        NewValue += SomeValue - 10;
        break;
    }
    if (NewValue < 1)
        break;
}
```

Notice that the logical expression for this while generates an infinite loop. A loop of this type relies on if statements that contain breaks to terminate the loop.

The first if in the body of the loop traps values greater than 100. In this example, the loop should iterate after performing the multiplication. Although it wouldn't hurt to leave out the continue—the value won't meet either of the following if's logical expressions—the program will execute faster if C++ doesn't have to evaluate the remaining ifs.

The remaining three if structures in the loop contain logical expressions that terminate the loop. Although the logical expressions in the ifs could have been combined into a single while logical expression, doing so would have created a complicated logical expression that would be hard to understand. The structure in the example is easier to understand.

There is one drawback to placing logical expressions that terminate a loop inside the loop (rather than in the while): The program can be harder to debug and modify because it isn't immediately obvious which conditions in the body of the loop actually stop the loop. Most programmers therefore try to limit the use of break in a while to situations where a while's logical expression would be impractically complicated.

```
--- Welcome to the Hi/Lo Guessing Game ---

Enter your guess: 50
Your guess was too high.
Enter your guess: 25
Your guess was too high.
Enter your guess: 15
Your guess was too low.
Enter your guess: 20
Your guess was too low.
Enter your guess: 21
Your guess was too low.
Enter your guess: 22
You win!
Another game? (y or n): n

You played 1 and won 1
for a winning percentage of 100%.
```

Figure 5.2 Sample output from the Hi/Low Game program

The Hi/Low Game

The hi/lo game is a number guessing game. The computer chooses a random number between 0 and 100. The player's job is to discover the number in seven or less guesses. The implementation of the game that appears here also keeps statistics on how well the player is doing. As you can see in Figure 5.2, the program counts the number of games played, how many have been won, and at the end of play, reports the winning percentage.

The Header File

Like the currency converter program, the source code for the hi/lo game is stored in three files. The first—game.h—contains the definition for the program's single class, which represents a game being played. As you can see in Listing 5.6, a game has two variables: the correct answer, which the player is trying to guess, and the current guess made by the player. There are also prototypes for four functions: a constructor (Game), a function to initialize a new game by generating a new answer (InitGame), a function to determine whether a guess is above, below, or equal to the answer (evaluate Guess), and a function to return the correct answer for display by the main program (getAnswer).

Listing 5.6   game.h: Header file for the hi/low game

```
// class for hi/lo game
// game.h

const HI = 1;
const LO = -1;
const EQ = 0;
const MAX_GUESSES = 7;
const RAND_FACTOR = 325;

class Game
{
    private:
        int answer, guess;
    public:
        Game();      // constructor
        void InitGame();
        int evaluateGuess (int);
        int getAnswer ();
};
```

The Member Functions

The source code for the member functions is stored in `game.cpp`
(Listing 5.7). As you would expect, the constructor simply initializes the class
variables. The `InitGame` function uses the `rand` function from the standard
C library to generate a random number and then scales that number so that it
is in the range 0 to 100. The `rand` function, whose prototype appears in
`stdlib.h`, generates a number in the range 0 to 2^{15}. Because this program
requires a number between 0 and 100, the random number is divided by the
constant `RAND_FACTOR` (defined as 325 in `game.h`).

Listing 5.7   game.cpp: Member functions for the hi/lo game

// member functions for game program //

```
#include <stdlib.h>
#include "game.h"

Game::Game()
{
    answer = 0;
    guess = 0;
}
```

Continued next page

Listing 5.7 (Continued) game.cpp: Member functions for the hi/lo game

```
void Game::InitGame()
{
// generates the answer as random # between 0 and 100
    answer = rand() / RAND_FACTOR;
}

int Game::evaluateGuess (int guess)
{
    if (guess == answer)
        return EQ;
    else
        if (guess < answer)
            return LO;
        else
            return HI;
}

int Game::getAnswer()
{
    return answer;
}
```

Note

There is no secret to figuring out the scale factor for a random number. You just need to do a bit of algebra to find it:

```
scale factor = 2^15 / maximum number wanted
```

Each successive call to `rand` produces a different number, based on a starting number. To avoid getting the same sequence of numbers each time you run the program, you need to initialize the random number generator when the program run begins. Do this with a call to `srand`, another function from the standard C library whose prototype appears in `stdlib.h`. Call `srand` only once, as occurs in the main program for the game (`main.h` in Listing 5.8).

The `srand` function requires a seed value as a parameter. Although there is no way to generate a truly random seed value, you an approximate it by grabbing the current time from the system clock and then performing a modulo division to scale it back to an integer. To read the current time, use the `time` function. (Its prototype appears in `time.h`.) The function's single parameter is a pointer to a variable that will hold the time. However, in this

Listing 5.8   main.cpp: Main program for the Hi/Lo Game program

```cpp
#include <iostream.h>
#include <stdlib.h>
#include <time.h>
#include <ctype.h>
#include "game.h"

void main()
{
    int choice, count, result, guesses_made, games_played = 0, games_won = 0;
    char keep_going = 'Y';
    Game gamePlayed;

    srand (time(NULL) % 37); // initialize random number generator
    cout << "--- Welcome to the Hi/Lo Guessing Game ---" << endl << endl;

// This outer loop iterates once for each game played.
    while (toupper(keep_going) == 'Y')
    {
        count = 0;
        guesses_made = 0;
        result = LO;
        gamePlayed.InitGame(); // Initialize a game with a new answer
        games_played++;
// This inner loop iterates until the user has made the maximum number of guesses
// or until a guess equals the answer
        while (guesses_made++ < MAX_GUESSES && result != EQ)
        {
            cout << "Enter your guess: ";
            cin >> choice;
            result = gamePlayed.evaluateGuess (choice);
            switch (result)
            {
                case EQ:
                    cout << "You win!" << endl;
                    break;
                case LO:
                    cout << "Your guess was too low." << endl;
                    break;
                case HI:
                    cout << "Your guess was too high." << endl;
                    break;
            }
        }
```

Continued next page

Listing 5.8 (Continued) main.cpp: Main program for the Hi/Lo Game program

```cpp
// Although the inner loop has stopped, at this point there's no way to know precisely
// what caused it to stop. The purpose of this if structure is therefore to determine
// why the loop stopped and then to take the appropriate action.
        if (guesses_made > MAX_GUESSES)
        {
            cout << "You've exceeded your allotted " << MAX_GUESSES << "
                guesses." << endl;
            cout << "The correct answer was " << gamePlayed.getAnswer() << "."
                << endl;
        }
        else
            if (result == EQ) games_won++;
        cout << "Another game? (y or n): ";
        cin >> keep_going;
        cout << endl;
    }
    cout << "You played " << games_played << " and won " << games_won << endl;

// Notice that the computation of the percentage of the games won is typecast to a
// floating point value. If this didn't occur, the result would almost always be 0 because
// the variables used in the division are integer variables.
    cout << "for a winning percentage of " <<
        (float) games_won/games_played * 100 << "%.";
}
```

case the time isn't stored anywhere, but instead is divided by 37. The remainder of the division is then used directly by the `srand` function. There is no need to keep the time; a NULL can therefore be used instead of a pointer to a variable.

The `evaluateGuess` member function contains the nested `if` structure you saw earlier in this chapter to examine one guess made by the user. The constants `HI`, `LO`, and `EQ` that the function returns are defined in the header file. The remaining member function—`getAnswer`—simply returns the correct answer to the main program for display.

The Main Program

The program that uses objects created from the `Game` class uses two `while` loops, one nested within the other. The outer loop iterates once for each game played. The inner loop manages game play. It iterates until the user either makes the maximum number of guesses or guesses the correct answer.

As you study the main program, notice that there is no way to determine exactly which of the two conditions causes the inner loop to stop. The program must therefore use an if structure to explicitly test the two conditions and take action based on whichever it finds.

At the end of a game, the user is given the option of continuing to play another game or ending the program. The outer loop uses the value in the keep_going variable to decide whether to begin another game. Because a user might enter either an upper- or lowercase letter, the while in the outer loop uses the toupper function to convert the contents of keep_going to uppercase. (The prototype for this C library function can be found in ctype.h.) If keep_going already contains an uppercase character, toupper has no effect.

After the outer loop terminates, the main program has one more task: it computes the percentage of games won. The algorithm for the calculation involves dividing the number of games won by the number of games played and then multiplying by 100. Unfortunately, the games_played and games_won variables are integer. Unless the player wins every game, the result of the integer division will always be zero. The program therefore typecasts the result into a floating point value.

Functions Revisited

Now that you have seen two complete C++ programs, this is a good time to stop and generalize what you know about functions. To this point, you have seen four types of functions:

- Programmer-written member functions: Functions that are defined as members of classes.
- Programmer-written functions: Functions that aren't part of a class.
- Library member functions: Functions that are members of classes that are part of a class library. In most cases, this will be the ANSI C++ library and C++ libraries written to support a particular programming platform's user interface.
- Library functions: Functions that aren't members of classes that are part of a class library. In most cases, this will be the ANSI C library.

The difference between programmer-written functions and library functions lies primarily in where prototypes can be found. In the case of programmer-written functions, prototypes are found in class header files (for member functions) and main program header files (for functions that aren't member functions). In the case of very short programs, function prototypes may be included in the same file as the main program.

Calling Functions

Member functions—regardless of whether they are programmer-written or part of a class library—are called using slightly different syntax than functions that aren't part of a class. As you know, the way in which you call a member function depends on the type of binding you're using. To this point, you have seen static binding. (Dynamic binding, which requires the use of pointers, is discussed in Chapter 7.)

To call a member function for an object that has been created for use with static binding, you use the object's name, followed by a period, the name of the function, and any parameters needed by the function.

The period is known as either the *structure member operator* or the *dot operator*. It has two purposes. First, it lets the compiler know the object to which a variable or member function belongs. Second, it tells the compiler that you want the variable or member function statically bound to the object. In other words, you want the compiler to make the link between the variable or member function and the object when the program is compiled.

A function call using the dot operator has the following general syntax:

```
object_name.function_name (parameters);
```

For example, the function that initializes a new hi/lo game is called with the following syntax:

```
gamePlayed.InitGame();
```

By the same token, the ios member function that grabs a character from the keyboard is called with the name of the input stream, followed by the name of the function:

```
cin.get();
```

If the function returns a value with the `return` statement, then that return value can be assigned to a variable with the assignment operator, as in:

```
variable = object_name.function_name (parameters);
```

For example, the hi/lo game's main program calls the member function that evaluates a guess with the following:

```
result = gamePlayed.evaluateGuess (choice);
```

Because functions that aren't member functions aren't involved with objects, they can be called without specifying an object. The general syntax for calling a function that isn't a member function is:

```
function_name (parameters);
```

If the function returns a value, that value can be assigned to a variable:

```
variable = function_name (parameters);
```

The most important thing to notice from this discussion is that the only difference between calling member functions and calling functions that aren't part of a class is the presence or absence of an object name in the call.

Passing Parameters

As you know, parameters are data that are transferred into a function when a function is called. The act of actually transferring the data is known as *parameter passing*. To this point, you have seen parameters that are passed *by value*.

Parameters that are passed by value are sent into variables that can be used by the function receiving them. However, if the values in those parameters are changed by the function, the modified values are *not* sent back to the calling function. Parameters that are passed by value are therefore most useful as input data to a function.

So far, the only way you have seen to send a value back to the calling function is with the `return` statement. The drawback to using `return` is that it transmits only a single value. Although a function can contain many `return` statements, the first `return` the computer encounters not only sends back a value to the calling function, but terminates the function as well.

There are two alternatives to passing by value, both of which make it possible to return multiple values from a function. The first, *pass by reference*, places the address of variables in a function's formal parameter list. The second uses *pointer variables* (variables that contain the addresses of where data are stored). In both cases, modifying values in the function returns the modified data to the calling function. You will learn how to pass by reference and to use pointer variables in Chapter 7.

Summary

This chapter introduced the structured elements of the C++ language, including details on variables, selection, and iteration. It also generalized some of the procedures you have seen previously for working with functions.

C++ variables can be declared just about anywhere in a program. However, a variable is recognized by and can be used only by the portion of the program (function or compound statement) in which it is defined (the scope of the variable). Although C++ does support global variables, they should not be used because they can make a program harder to debug and modify.

C++ variables are assigned one of three storage classes. The default—`auto`—produces variables whose storage is released whenever the function in which the variable was declared terminates. To retain variables in memory until the program ends, change the variable's storage class to `static`. The final storage class—`register`—attempts to keep a variables contents in a CPU register whenever possible, decreasing the time needed to access the variable.

C++ supports the typical set of arithmetic operators found in a high-level programming language. However, there is no exponentiation operator; exponentiation is typically performed by using a library function. C++ also provides special operators for quickly incrementing and decrementing a value by one. C++ supports the typical logical operators of AND, OR, and NOT, along with bit-wise logical operators that perform logical operations on the individual bits in two storage locations.

During arithmetic operations, C++ automatically converts data types so that all values in the expression are the same data type. By default, conversion is to the data type with the greatest range and precision. A programmer can override automatic data conversion with typecasting, which forces a conversion to a specific type of data. Typecasting is the only way to force C++ to perform a floating point division with two integers.

C++ supports two selection structures: if and switch. The if structure is like that found in other high-level languages. It supports an else clause; if structures can be nested as needed. The switch structure is similar to the case statement found in Pascal and Modula-2. Its use it appropriate when a program needs to evaluate and take action on more than two values of the same variable.

C++ supports three iteration structures: while, do while, and for. The while structure places the test for stopping the loop at the top of the loop. It can therefore be used for all loops, even those that should not be executed under certain circumstances. The do while structure places the test for stopping the loop at the bottom of the loop. It is therefore always executed at least once. The for loop is a shorthand version of a while that bases the condition for stopping the loop on some value that it iterated each time the loop is executed.

Functions are called by using the name of the function and its formal parameters. Calls to member functions for objects created with static binding must be preceded by the name of the object on which the function is to operate and a period.

Simple variables (variables that aren't arrays) used as parameters that are passed through a function's formal parameter list are passed by value. Even if the values are changed inside the function, the changed values aren't returned to the calling program.

Exercises

1. Write and test a program that uses the class for a picture frame that you wrote for Exercise 1 at the end of Chapter 3. Create one object from the class. (The program handles one order for framing at a time.) The program should provide a menu from which the user can choose the following options:

   - Enter data to describe a picture framing order.
   - Compute and display the cost of the framing order. (*Hint*: Keep in mind that the total inches of framing used in the frame is twice the width plus twice the length.)
   - Display all the data for the picture framing order.
   - Quit the program.

2. Write and test a program that uses the class for an oil storage tank that you wrote for Exercise 2 at the end of Chapter 3. Create one object from the class. (The program handles one oil storage tank at a time.) The program should provide a menu from which the user can choose the following options:

    - Enter data to describe an oil tank.
    - Display the amount of oil in the tank expressed as a percentage of the tank's capacity.
    - Display the amount of available space in the tank expressed as a percentage of the tank's capacity.
    - Display all data for the storage tank.
    - Quit the program.

3. Write and test a program that uses a decision tree to identify a living creature that the user describes to the program. The way in which the program should make its decisions is diagrammed in Figure 5.3. The program collects information by asking the user questions such as "How many legs does the creature have?" and "Does the creature live in water?" Design your own class for this program. Define one object from that class. (The program should handle one creature at a time.)

4. Write and test a program that computes the pay for three categories of sales associates (junior sales associates, sales associates, and senior sales associates). Create a single class for a sales associate with variables for a sales associate's monthly sales goal, the commission rate paid if the goal is met, the commission rate paid if the goal isn't met, and base salary (may be zero). Create one object for each type of sales associate.

    Store the data for each object in a file. Read the data in at the beginning of each program run; write the data out at the end of each program run.

    Give the user a menu from which he or she can choose the following options:

    - Enter data for each type of sales associate. (This function is used to both initialize and modify the data stored in the objects.)
    - View the current data for each type of sales associate.

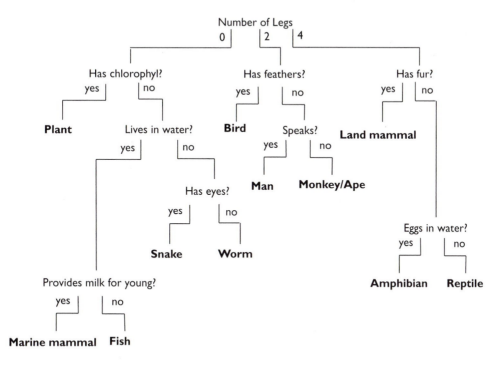

Figure 5.3 A decision tree for identifying a living creature

- Compute a sales associate's gross pay, based on monthly sales and the type of sales associate. (The monthly sales and type of associate are entered by the user.) Once the program has decided which commission rate to use, the gross pay is equal to:

```
commission rate * monthly sales + the base pay
```

- Quit the program

5. Write and test a program that computes the amount of principal in a certificate of deposit, where the interest paid is added to the principal each month. The formula for the principal after interest is paid for a given month is:

```
Principal = Amount of initial deposit *
      (1 + Monthly interest rate)Number of months on deposit
```

Decide what the class should be for this program. Create any necessary object(s).

Give the user the opportunity to enter the *annual* interest rate. (The program should compute the monthly interest rate.) Also give the user the choice of term for the CD (12, 24, or 26 months). Display the amount of principal on deposit for each month during the term of the CD.

6. Create a class that stores information about costs to produce a product, including the number of units produced in the past month, the direct materials cost per unit, the direct labor cost per unit, and the overhead per unit. Include a member function that computes the total cost for all units produced in the past month. Write a program that lets the user enter data for a product and then displays the total cost for that product.

7. Create a class to handle the conversion between 12-hour and 24-hour time. The class should include variables for the time (a four-digit integer) and whether it represents 12- or 24-hour time. Include a member function that performs the conversion based on the value in the "12 or 24" variable. Then display the result in an appropriate format. For example, 12-hour time should be displayed as HH:MM PM or HH:MM AM, where HH is the hour and MM is the minutes; 24-hour time should be displayed simply as HH:MM.

8. Create a class that handles the pricing of purchases of athletic uniforms for a uniform supply company. The class should include an ID number for the uniform, a price for the top, a price for the bottom, a price for purchasing the combination of top and bottom, and the percentage discount if 50 or more complete uniforms are purchased. Include a member function that computes the price of an order for uniforms. Write a program that demonstrates that the class and the member function work, where the user enters the prices and the number of uniforms being purchased.

9. Create a class for a local water and electric utility that handles a customer's monthly bill. The class should include the customer account number, the gallons of water used, and the number of kilowatt-hours (kwh) of electricity used. Include a member function that computes the amount of the bill based on the following rules:

- The first 1500 gallons of water cost $0.011 per gallon.
- Each gallon over 1500 costs $0.015 per gallon.
- The first 500 kwh of electricity cost $0.044 per kwh.
- 501 to 1000 kwh of electricity cost $0.065 per kwh.
- More than 1000 kwh of electricity cost $0.097 per kwh.

Write a program that demonstrates that your bill computation function works. The user should enter the gallons of water and the number of kwh of electricity used along with the customer number. The program should print out the customer number and the total bill.

10. Add a member function to the program you wrote for Exercise 4 at the end of Chapter 4. This function should compute the following:

- The percentage of people who inquired about information that actually applied to the college.
- The percentage of people who inquired that were accepted.
- The percentage of people who were accepted that actually attended the college. (Colleges call this the "conversion" rate.)

Prepare a nicely formatted report that displays these values for each of the four objects handled by the program.

6

Arrays

OBJECTIVES

In this chapter you will learn about:
- Creating one- and two-dimensional C++ arrays.
- Using arrays that are class variables.
- Manipulating arrays of objects.
- Reading arrays of objects from and writing arrays of objects to a text file.
- Sorting an array of objects.

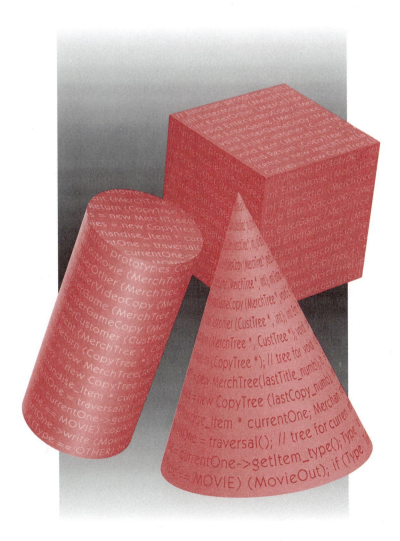

Arrays provide a way to organize and access values through a data structure that is often viewed as a list or table. Although most programming languages, including C++, support arrays with many dimensions, programmers commonly use only one- and two-dimensional arrays.

An object-oriented program uses arrays in three different ways. The first is as a local variable in functions that manipulate objects created from a class. This is the way in which you have used arrays in whichever high-level programming languages you know. Local variable arrays are accessible to the function in which they are defined and any functions into which they are passed.

The second way in which an array can be used in an object-oriented program is as a class variable. In other words, an array is defined as a variable for a class. In that case, each object created from the class has its own copy of the array and can manipulate that array with its member functions.

The third way in which object-oriented programs use arrays is with arrays of objects. The array is maintained by the program that manipulates the objects. Because the array isn't part of any single object—but instead is a collection of many objects—the array isn't accessible to the objects; it is accessible to the program that manipulates the objects.

The syntax for defining and accessing all three types of arrays is the same. However, because you are familiar with local variable arrays, this chapter looks specifically at the second and third type of arrays. It begins by looking at one- and two-dimensional arrays used as class variables. It then discusses arrays of objects, including loading arrays of objects from a data file, an introduction to passing arrays into functions, and sorting arrays of objects. As you will see, sorting arrays of objects can be somewhat cumbersome because the contents one object can't simply be assigned to another across the assignment operator.

Defining and Using One-Dimensional Arrays

The simplest type of array is a one-dimensional array, which can most easily be thought of as a single-column list where every row has the same data type. To declare a one-dimensional C++ array, use the following general syntax:

```
data_type variable_name [# of elements];
```

Like any other variable declaration, the data type is followed by the name of the variable. In this case, however, the variable name is followed by a pair of square brackets ([and]) within which are placed the number of elements in the array. For example, in the yearly sales average program that you will see shortly, the variable to hold 12 months' worth of sales is declared with:

```
long Sales [NUM_MON];
```

where NUM_MON is a constant defined in the program's header file.

Note

It is a good programming practice to define constants to use for the total number of elements when declaring arrays. It makes the program easier to read because the name of the constant tells you something about the meaning of the array. It also makes the program easier to modify because you don't have to go hunting through the program to find the array definition; you only need to change the constant, which is typically located at the beginning of a header file.

Warning

To this point, C++ should look very familiar to Pascal and Modula-2 programmers. However, there is one major, very important difference that you must remember when dealing with C++ arrays: When you reference the array, the elements are numbered beginning with 0, not 1! In other words, although you declare the array using the total number of elements in the array, the index (or subscript, as COBOL programmers may call it) of the last value in the array is one less than the total number of elements. For example, if NUM_MON is equal to 12, then the array indexes range from 0 to 11.

When an array is defined as a class variable, the entire array is accessible to an object created from that class. The program that manipulates the object can retrieve one element at a time or can access the entire array. (Retrieving an entire array from a function requires the use of pointers; it will therefore be discussed in Chapter 8.)

To explore how an array defined as a class variable can be used, we'll be looking at a program that computes average monthly sales over a one-year period when given total sales in even dollars for 12 individual months. The program lets the user enter the 12 sales values and then computes the average. It also displays the entire contents of the array (see Figure 6.1).

The header file for the Sales Average program can be found in Listing 6.1. It has one variable, the Sales array that holds 12 long integer values. The four member functions include the constructor, a function to place a

```
Pick a menu option:
1. Enter sales data
2. Compute average yearly sales
3. See monthly sales
9. Quit

Which one? 1

Enter sales for month #  1: 1200
Enter sales for month #  2: 1500
Enter sales for month #  3: 750
Enter sales for month #  4: 895
Enter sales for month #  5: 400
Enter sales for month #  6: 1000
Enter sales for month #  7: 850
Enter sales for month #  8: 2400
Enter sales for month #  9: 8500
Enter sales for month #10: 1750
Enter sales for month #11: 500
Enter sales for month #12: 750

Pick a menu option:
1. Enter sales data
2. Compute average yearly sales
3. See monthly sales
9. Quit

Which one? 2

Average sales for the year were $1707.92

Pick a menu option:
1. Enter sales data
2. Compute average yearly sales
3. See monthly sales
9. Quit

Which one? 3

The sales for this year are:
   Month #  1:    1200
   Month #  2:    1500
   Month #  3:     750
   Month #  4:     895
   Month #  5:     400
   Month #  6:    1000
   Month #  7:     850
   Month #  8:    2400
   Month #  9:    8500
   Month #10:    1750
   Month #11:     500
   Month #12:     750
```

Figure 6.1 Output from the Sales Average program

value into one element in the array (`InitSales`), a function to compute the average of values stored in the array (`AvgSales`), and a function to return one value from the array to the program manipulating an object (`getSales`).

Listing 6.1   sales.h: Header file for the sales average program

```
const NUM_MON=12;

class YearlySales
{
    private:
        long Sales [NUM_MON];
    public:
        YearlySales(); // constructor
        void InitSales(int, long); // Pass in array index and value
        float AvgSales(); // Compute the average of values stored in the array
        long getSales(int); // Pass in index value
};
```

The member functions are stored in the file sales.cpp (Listing 6.2). The constructor sets each element in the array to zero. The only way to do this is to use a loop that operates on one array element at a time, such as:

```
for (i = 0; i < NUM_MON; i++)
    Sales[i] = 0;
```

Ironically, C++ will allow an operation such as

```
Sales = 0;
```

Warning

However, this statement doesn't do what you might expect (assign 0 to every element in the array). The name of an array, without an index to indicate the element of the array that is being referenced, is the main memory address of the beginning of the array. When you assign a value to an array name, you change the location in memory referenced when you use the array name with an index. If you perform such as assignment by accident, at the very least you'll lose access to the memory assigned to the array. At the worst, you can crash your computer if you attempt to put values into the array after moving its location to an area occupied either by the operating system or another program.

The InitSales member function requires two parameters: the value to be inserted into the Sales array and the index of the element into which the value should be placed. The function uses these parameters to simply assign the value to the correct element in the array. Values are therefore inserted into the array one at a time.

Listing 6.2   sales.cpp: Member functions for the sales average program

```cpp
#include "sales.h"

YearlySales::YearlySales() // constructor
{
    int i;

    for (i = 0; i < NUM_MON; i++) // must use a loop to initialize the entire array
        Sales[i] = 0;
}

void YearlySales::InitSales (int i, long Amount)
{
    Sales[i] = Amount;
}

float YearlySales::AvgSales()
{
    long sum, i;

    sum = 0;
    for (i = 0; i < NUM_MON; i++)
        sum += Sales[i];
    return (float) sum/NUM_MON;
}

int YearlySales::getSales(int i)
{
    return Sales[i];
}
```

There is one alternative to the procedure used by `InitSales`. The program manipulating the object could accept all 12 values into an array of its own and then pass the array into the member function. Even in this case, however, the values would have to be transferred from the array used as an input parameter to the object's array one element at a time.

The `AvgSales` member function sums the contents of the array and divides by the total number of elements in the array. Although the values stored in the array are integers, it's unreasonable to assume that the average will also be an integer. The statement that computes the average therefore typecasts the result to a floating point value.

The final member function, `getSales`, accepts an index value as its single parameter. Its function is to return the contents of one element in the array to the calling program.

The program that manipulates a `Sales` object can be found in Listing 6.3. This program has one function of its own: `Menu`, which displays the menu from which a user chooses program functions. It creates one object from the `YearlySales` class (`SalesOjbect`).

The rest of the program is primarily made up of a `switch` statement that processes a menu choice. As you study the program, notice that the program can access the `Sales` array that is part of the object one element at a time by passing the index of the desired element to a member function. This is the method used to insert data into the array (the `InitSales` member function, used to process menu option #1) and to display the contents of the array (the `getSales` member function, used to process menu option #3).

The program can also receive a value from the object after the object has processed the entire array. For example, the `AvgSales` member function (used to process menu option #2) returns the average of the contents of the array. In this case, the program manipulating the object doesn't interact directly with the array.

Listing 6.3   main.cpp: Main program for the sales average program

```cpp
#include <iostream.h>
#include <iomanip.h>
#include "sales.h"

void main()
{
    int Menu(void);   // menu function prototype

    int menuChoice = 0, idx;
    long oneMonth;
    YearlySales SalesObject;

    while (menuChoice != 9)
    {
        menuChoice = Menu();
        switch (menuChoice)
        {
```

Continued next page

Listing 6.3 (Continued) main.cpp: Main program for the sales average program

```cpp
            case 1: // Accept input one month at a time
                for (idx = 0; idx < NUM_MON; idx++)
                {
                    setiosflags (ios::right);
                    cout << "Enter sales for month #" << setw(2) << idx+1
                        << ": ";
                    cin >> oneMonth;
                    SalesObject.InitSales(idx, oneMonth);
                }
                break;
            case 2: // Compute the average and display
                cout << setiosflags (ios::showpoint | ios::fixed)
                    << setprecision(2);
                cout << "Average sales for the year were $" <<
                    SalesObject.AvgSales() << endl;
                break;
            case 3: // Retrieve data from the array one month at a time and display
                cout << "The sales for this year are: " << endl;
                cout << setiosflags (ios::right);
                for (idx = 0; idx < NUM_MON; idx++)
                    cout << "  Month #" << setw(2) << idx+1 << ": " << setw(6)
                        << SalesObject.getSales(idx) << endl;
                break;
            case 9:
                break;
            default: // Always let the user know when input is incorrect
                cout << "You've entered an unavailable option." << endl;
        }
    }
}

int Menu()
{
    int choice;

    cout << "\nPick a menu option: " << endl;
    cout << "1. Enter sales data" << endl;
    cout << "2. Compute average yearly sales" << endl;
    cout << "3. See monthly sales" << endl;
    cout << "9. Quit" << endl;
    cout << "\nWhich one? ";
    cin >> choice;
    cout << endl;
    return choice;
}
```

Defining and Using Two-Dimensional Arrays

A two-dimensional array can be visualized as a table with columns and rows. Each element in the array is referenced by the combination of its row number and column number. For example, assume that you have an array that is three rows down by three columns across. The top left element has the coordinates 0,0; the bottom right element has the elements 2,2. (Don't forget that C++ arrays start array index numbers with 0 rather than 1.)

To declare this array, a C++ program contains a statement with the following general syntax:

```
data_type array_name [# rows] [# columns];
```

Assuming that each element in the three row by three column array stores a single character, you can see that the array could be declared as:

```
char grid [3][3];
```

Note

Two-dimensional arrays aren't stored in main memory as two-dimensional grids; they're stored linearly. For example, in the three by three array, element 0,0 is followed by 0,1; 0,2; 1, 0; 1,1; 1,2; 2,0; and so on. Notice that the second index varies more quickly. The first index changes only after all of the second index values have been used. This means that it actually makes no difference which index you use for columns and which for rows. You and your program simply have to be consistent in how you access and assign elements to the array. By convention, however, the first index represents rows and the second, column.

To make a program easier to understand and modify, a programmer wants to avoid using meaningful numeric constants wherever possible. A C++ program is therefore likely to contain the following three statements to define the array:

```
const ROWS = 3;
const COLS = 3;
char grid [ROWS][COLS];
```

The array named `grid` can be used as a playing field for a tic-tac-toe game in which a human plays against the computer. Play begins with the user choosing to play X or O and making the first move. (The first move alternates

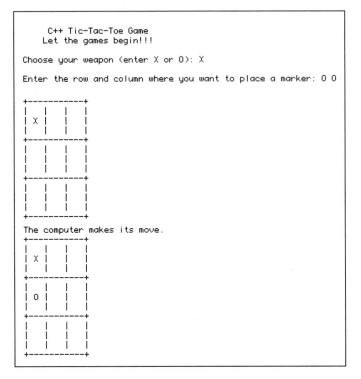

```
        C++ Tic-Tac-Toe Game
        Let the games begin!!!

Choose your weapon (enter X or 0): X

Enter the row and column where you want to place a marker: 0 0

+-----------+
|   |   |   |
| X |   |   |
|   |   |   |
+-----------+
|   |   |   |
|   |   |   |
|   |   |   |
+-----------+
|   |   |   |
|   |   |   |
|   |   |   |
+-----------+
The computer makes its move.
+-----------+
|   |   |   |
| X |   |   |
|   |   |   |
+-----------+
|   |   |   |
| 0 |   |   |
|   |   |   |
+-----------+
|   |   |   |
|   |   |   |
|   |   |   |
+-----------+
```

Figure 6.2   Opening play for the C++ tic-tac-toe game

between the player and the computer for each successive game.) The computer then makes its move. After the computer moves, the program displays the game grid (see Figure 6.2). Play continues to alternate between the user and the computer until either a winner is detected or the grid is filled, signifying a draw. At that point the user can play again or exit the program (see Figure 6.3).

The class used by the tic-tac-toe game program (tttGame) represents one entire game of tic-tac-toe. As you can see in the header file (Listing 6.4), the class contains an array for the playing gird along with variables to hold index values, the number of moves made by the player and the computer (used to detect a draw), and the marker (X or O) used by the player and computer.

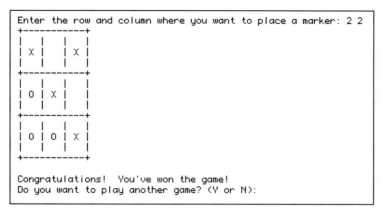

```
Enter the row and column where you want to place a marker: 2 2
+-----------+
|   |   |   |
| X |   | X |
|   |   |   |
+-----------+
|   |   |   |
| O | X |   |
|   |   |   |
+-----------+
|   |   |   |
| O | O | X |
|   |   |   |
+-----------+

Congratulations!  You've won the game!
Do you want to play another game? (Y or N):
```

Figure 6.3   End of game play for the tic-tac-toe program

Listing 6.4   ttt.h: Header file for the tic-tac-toe game

```
// Number of elements in the array
const ROWS = 3;
const COLS = 3;

// Flags to indicate result of making one move
const WIN = 1;
const TIE = 0;
const PLAY_ON = -1;  // neither win nor lose so "play on"

// Flags to indicate whether player or computer goes first
const PLAYER = 1;
const COMPUTER = 0;

const RAND_FACTOR = 10923;  // used to scale random number between 1 and 3

// Flags to indicate whether a player's move attempts to place a maker in an element
// that is already occupied
const GOOD = 1;
const BAD = 0;

class tttGame
{
    private:
        char grid [ROWS][COLS]; // game board
```

Continued next page

Listing 6.4 (Continued) ttt.h: Header file for the tic-tac-toe game

```
    int row, column; // indexes used in member functions
    int player_moves; // number of moves made by player; used to detect draw
    int computer_moves; // number of moves made by computer
    char player, computer; // X or O

public:
    tttGame();    // constructor; doesn't need to do anything
    void InitGame(); // initializes a new game
    void chooseMarker(char); // let player choose X or O
    void displayGrid(); // display the grid
    int playerMove(int, int); // send in row and column of space
    void computerMove(); // generate a move for the computer;
    int checkGrid(); // check for draw or winner
    int whoWon(); // find out who won
};
```

The Member Functions

There are eight member functions in the tic-tac-toe program (see Listing 6.5). These functions fall into three categories: setting up the game, making moves, and determining the status of the game at the end of a move. As you study these functions, notice how they illustrate the way in which an object and a program can interact with a two-dimensional array that is part of an object.

Listing 6.5   ttt.cpp: Member functions for the tic-tac-toe game

```
#include <iostream.h>
#include <stdlib.h>
#include <time.h>
#include "ttt.h"

tttGame::tttGame()  // constructor initializes random number generator
{
    srand(time(NULL) % 37); // initialize random number generator
}

void tttGame::InitGame()
{
    int x,y;
```

Continued next page

Listing 6.5 (Continued) ttt.cpp: Member functions for the tic-tac-toe game

```cpp
    for (x = 0; x < ROWS; x++) // must initialize each element individually
        for (y = 0; y < COLS; y++)
            grid [x][y] = ' ';
    row = 0;
    column = 0;
    player_moves = 0, computer_moves = 0;
}

void tttGame::chooseMarker (char marker)
{
    player = marker;
    if (player == 'X')
        computer = 'O';
    else
        computer = 'X';
}

void tttGame::displayGrid() // uses nested for loops to display each element in grid
{
    int x, y;

    for (x = 0; x < ROWS; x++)
    {
        cout << "+-----------+" << endl;
        cout << "|    |    |    |" << endl;
        cout << "|";
        for (y = 0; y < COLS; y++)
        {
            cout << " " << grid[x][y] << "  |";

        }
        cout << "\n|    |    |    |" << endl;
    }
    cout << "+-----------+" << endl;
}

int tttGame::playerMove (int prow, int pcol)
{
    if (grid[prow][pcol] != ' ')
        return BAD;
    grid[prow][pcol] = player;   // insert the player's marker
    player_moves++;
    return GOOD;
}
```

Continued next page

Listing 6.5 (Continued) ttt.cpp: Member functions for the tic-tac-toe game

```
// Computer's strategy is random. Pick random number between 1 and 3 for column and
// row. Subtract 1 to get the right index range. If cell is filled, try the next one.
void tttGame::computerMove()
{
    int row, column;

    row = (rand() / RAND_FACTOR) - 1;
    column = (rand() / RAND_FACTOR) - 1;
    while (grid[row][column] != ' ')
    {
        row ++;
        if (row == ROWS) row = 0;
        if (grid[row][column] != ' ')
        {
            column++;
            if (column == COLS) column = 0;
        }
    }
    grid[row][column] = computer;
    computer_moves++;
}

int tttGame::checkGrid()
{
    int x, y;

    for (x = 0; x < ROWS; x++)   // look for winner across rows
        if (grid[x][0] != ' ' && grid[x][0] == grid[x][1] &&
            grid[x][1] == grid[x][2])
            return WIN;
    for (y = 0; y < COLS; y++)   // look for winner down columns
        if (grid[0][y] !=+ ' ' && grid[0][y] == grid[1][y] &&
            grid[1][y] == grid[2][y])
            return WIN;
    // check for diagonal win
    if ((grid[0][0] == grid[1][1] && grid[1][1] == grid[2][2] &&
        grid[0][0] != ' ') || (grid[0][2] == grid [1][1] &&
        grid[1][1] == grid[2][0] && grid[0][2] != ' '))
        return WIN;
    // 9 moves mean grid is full
    if (player_moves + computer_moves == 9) return TIE;
    // if no win or tie, keep playing
    return PLAY_ON;
}
```

Continued next page

Listing 6.5 (Continued) ttt.cpp: Member functions for the tic-tac-toe game

```
int tttGame::whoWon() // find out who won
{
    if (player_moves > computer_moves)
        return PLAYER;
    else
        return COMPUTER;
}
```

Setting Up the Game

The first member function encountered by the program is the constructor (tttGame). Because the grid and variables such as the number of player and computer moves have to be reinitialized for each new game, there's no point in using the constructor to perform initialization. Instead, it initializes the random number generator.

The InitGame function is called every time a new game begins. It assigns a blank to each element in the grid. (A blank is used rather than a NULL to ensure that the grid displays correctly on the screen even if an element isn't occupied by an X or O. Keep in mind that a blank is a character, just like X or O.) Notice that just as with one-dimensional arrays, the only way to insert values is to access each element individually. In the case of a two-dimensional array, we frequently use nested for loops, as was done in this function.

The third setup function, chooseMarker, accepts the character chosen by the user as its single input parameter. It then assigns that character to the player and assigns the unused marker to the computer. Like InitGame, it is executed once for each new game.

Displaying the Grid

The function that displays the contents of the two-dimensional array (displayGrid) intentionally violates the principle that input from the user and output to the user should not be part of a class's member functions (unless that class is intended to support the user interface). In cases where games use a specialized display for portions of game play, it is up to the programmer to decide whether it is more important to hide the details of the display from the program manipulating the tttGame object or to keep the class system-independent by relieving it of any I/O responsibilities. This particular program chooses to hide the details of the display of the grid from the main program. However, if the game were to be ported to several operating systems, a programmer might choose to remove this I/O from the member function.

Another reason for keeping the display code entirely within the class is that it simplifies coding. The grid array is a private variable; a program using an object created from the class can't access the contents of the array directly. If a program were to perform the display, a member function would have to be written that returns one element of the array. The function would need to have the row and column indexes passed in as parameters. To use such a function, the calling program would then use nested `for` loops to access each element in the array, one at a time. By hiding this logic in a member function, the program using an object created from the class is simpler.

To display the grid, the `displayGrid` function uses nested `for` loops. The outer loop controls displaying one row at a time, including the bar at the top of a row and the blank line below the bar. The inner loop then displays all columns for the row, followed by another blank line. After all three rows have been displayed, the function finishes by displaying the bar at the bottom of the grid. Notice that just like initializing the array, the only way to access the contents of the array is one element at a time, using both a row and column index to identify each element.

Making Moves

There are two types of moves, one made by the player and the other made by the computer. The player move (handled by `playerMove`) function accepts the row and column indexes from the program manipulating the object. If the array element indicated by the indexes contains a blank, the player's marker is inserted into the element using an assignment operator and the total number of moves made by the player is incremented. Otherwise, the element is occupied, and a flag indicating that the move isn't valid is returned to the calling program.

The computer's move (handled by `computerMove`) is a bit more complex because the computer must generate the move itself. For this program, the computer generates two random numbers between 1 and 3 and then subtracts 1 from each to bring the values into the correct range for the array's indexes. If the array element indicated by the random values is unoccupied (in other words, it contains a blank), then the computer inserts its marker and increments the number of moves it has made.

If the randomly selected element is occupied, the computer looks in the next row. If the next row is occupied, it looks in the next column. The process repeats until the computer finds an open element. Notice that the function detects when the "next" index is 3 and resets it to 0 so the index values don't exceed those available in the array.

Note

There are certainly better strategies for picking moves in a tic-tac-toe game. (This one might be described as somewhat brain dead.) However, strategies that analyze the current position of markers on the board require much more code than the random strategy. Since the purpose of this program is to demonstrate how to use two-dimensional arrays rather than to make the computer a good game player, the random strategy has been used.

Finding Winners and Ties

The status of the game at the end of each move is detected with the `check-Winners` function. The function's first job is to look for a winner, a process for which there is no simple algorithm. The function therefore first checks each row to see if the elements aren't blank and that they contain the same marker. If there is no winner across the rows, the function checks down the columns. If there is no winner down the columns, then the function looks diagonally. When the computer finds a winner, it returns a flag indicating that either the computer or the player has won.

Assuming there is no winner, the function then checks for a tie. If the sum of the number of moves made by the computer and the player is 9, then the grid is full and the game is a draw. Otherwise, play continues.

The `checkWinner`'s function doesn't detect whether the computer or the player has won. That is performed by the `whoWon` function, which looks to see which of the two has made more moves. Whoever has made more moves is the winner.

The Main Program

The program that manipulates the `tttGame` class can be found in Listing 6.6. It begins by creating one object (`inPlay`) and then enters a loop that plays games until the user indicates that he or she wants to quit. At the start of each new game, the program lets the user choose a marker, decides whether the computer or the player goes first, initializes the grid with a call to `InitGrid`, and then transfers the user's chosen marker to the object.

Listing 6.6   main.cpp: Main program for the tic-tac-toe game

```cpp
#include <iostream.h>
#include <stdlib.h>
#include <ctype.h>
#include "ttt.h"
void main(void)
{
    tttGame inPlay;
    char X_or_O, another = 'y';
    int move_OK, keepPlaying = PLAY_ON;
    int prow, pcol, goes_first = COMPUTER;

    cout << "     C++ Tic Tac Toe Game" << endl;
    cout << "     Let the games begin!!!" << endl << endl;
```

// This loop plays repeated games until the user enters something other than 'y' for the
// variable named "another."

```cpp
    while (toupper(another) == 'Y')
    {
```

// Let the user choose a marker.

```cpp
        cout << "Choose your weapon (enter X or O): ";
        cin >> X_or_O;
        if (goes_first == COMPUTER)
            goes_first = PLAYER;      // alternate who goes first
        else
            goes_first = COMPUTER;
        inPlay.InitGame(); // initialize the grid for each new game
        inPlay.chooseMarker (toupper(X_or_O)); // set the marker
```

// This loop iterates as long as a single game is in play.

```cpp
        while (keepPlaying == PLAY_ON)
        {
            if (goes_first == PLAYER)
            {

                // used to check if player tried to put marker in element that is
                // already occupied
                move_OK = BAD;
                while (move_OK == BAD)
                {
                cout <<
                "\nEnter the row and column where you want to place a marker: ";
                    cin >> prow >> pcol;
                    move_OK = inPlay.playerMove (prow, pcol);
                    if (move_OK == BAD)
                        cout << "\nThat square is already occupied";
                }
            }
```

Continued next page

Listing 6.6 (Continued) main.cpp: Main program for the tic-tac-toe game

```cpp
        else
        {
            cout << "\nThe computer makes its move." << endl;
            inPlay.computerMove();
        }
        inPlay.displayGrid();  // display the grid
        keepPlaying = inPlay.checkGrid();   // check to see if game is over
        if (keepPlaying != PLAY_ON)
            break;      // break out of loop if game is over
        if (goes_first == PLAYER)
        {
            cout << "\nThe computer makes its move." << endl;
            inPlay.computerMove();
        }
        else
        {
            move_OK = BAD;
            while (move_OK == BAD)
                {
        cout <<
        "\nEnter the row and column where you want to place a marker: ";
                cin >> prow >> pcol;
                move_OK = inPlay.playerMove (prow, pcol);
                if (move_OK == BAD)
                    cout << "\nThat square is already occupied";
            }
        }
        inPlay.displayGrid();
        keepPlaying = inPlay.checkGrid();
    }
    if (keepPlaying == WIN)  // find out who won the game
    {
        if (inPlay.whoWon() == PLAYER)
            cout << "\nCongratulations!  You've won the game!";
        else
            cout << "\nThe computer won this one. So it goes...";
    }
    else
        if (keepPlaying == TIE)
            cout << "\nThis won ended in a draw.";
    cout << "\nDo you want to play another game? (Y or N): ";
    cin >> another;
    if (toupper(another) == 'Y')
        keepPlaying = PLAY_ON;
    }
}
```

The program then begins a second loop that iterates as long as a single game is in play. Based on whether the user or computer goes first, the program accepts a move from the user or generates a move for the computer by calling either playerMove or computerMove, as appropriate. After two moves have been made, the program displays the grid using the displayGrid function and calls checkGrid to determine if the game has ended. If the game has ended, the program issues a break statement to exit the inner loop.

To finish the game, the program either determines and displays who won (using whoWon) or displays a message indicating that the game has ended in a draw. Finally, the user is given the choice whether to play another game. The user's response determines whether the outer loop continues.

When studying this program, the most important point to remember is that because the grid array is a private variable belonging to the inPlay object, the only way the program can gain access to the contents of the array, without using pointers, is to pass a member function the row and column indexes of one element at a time. For example, this is the way in which the playerMove function is written. As you will see in Chapter 8, a program can gain access to an array defined as a class variable if an object created from the class passes a pointer to the array to the program.

Handling Multiple Objects of the Same Class

Business information systems usually deal with data that describe many objects of a single class rather than just a single object. For example, the program to manage a pharmacy's prescriptions, to which you were introduced in Chapter 3, must handle many customers, many types of drugs, and many prescriptions. There are four ways in which a program can manage multiple objects of the same class:

- Create a separately named variable for each object created from a class. Unless the number of objects is very small, this solution isn't very practical. As you can see in Figure 6.4, the objects aren't necessarily stored next to one another in main memory. To access an object, you must use the object's individual name. If you want to call the same member function for each object, you must write one statement for each object.

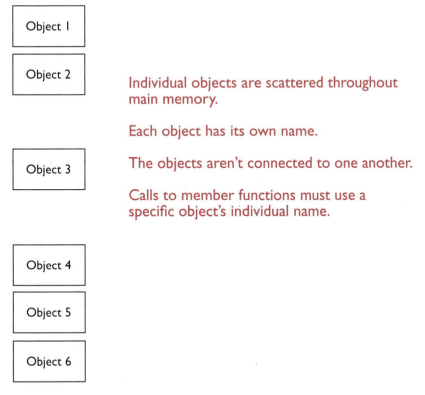

Individual objects are scattered throughout main memory.

Each object has its own name.

The objects aren't connected to one another.

Calls to member functions must use a specific object's individual name.

Figure 6.4   Storing individual objects from the same class

- Create an array of objects for static binding, such as that in Figure 6.5. Such an array is declared in the program manipulating the objects. Arrays of objects are easy to use, but have three drawbacks. First, they can waste storage space because space for an entire array is allocated when the array is declared, regardless of whether the array is completely filled with data. Second, the number of objects is limited to the number of elements declared in the array. Finally, the program in which the array is declared must be concerned with the details of manipulating the array. You will see how to create and use arrays of objects in this section.

objectArray

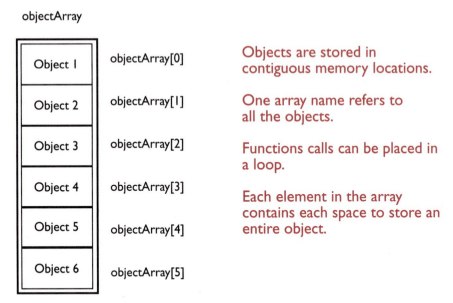

Objects are stored in
contiguous memory locations.

One array name refers to
all the objects.

Functions calls can be placed in
a loop.

Each element in the array
contains each space to store an
entire object.

Figure 6.5   An array of objects

- Create an array of pointers to objects (see Figure 6.6). Used with dynamic binding, this technique provides good memory management for objects, but limits the number of objects to the number of elements in the pointer array. In addition, the number of elements you can allocate to any array of objects or pointers to objects is ultimately limited to the amount of main memory available to the program. Arrays of pointers to objects can be managed by special classes designed for that purpose, hiding the details of array manipulation from the program using the array. You will learn about this strategy for handling arrays of pointers to objects in Chapter 9.

- Create a linked list of objects. A linked list is a data structure in which objects are chained together by including a pointer to the next object in the list as part of an object's data (see Figure 6.7). Linked lists are used with dynamic binding and provide good memory management. They may include a special object that manages the list, hiding the details of the list from the class that owns it. Because objects are chained together, the number of objects that can

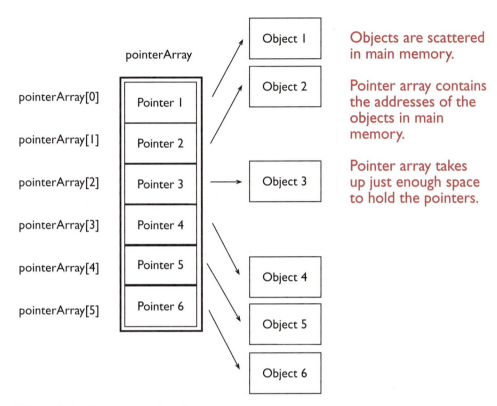

pointerArray

pointerArray[0]   Pointer 1

pointerArray[1]   Pointer 2

pointerArray[2]   Pointer 3

pointerArray[3]   Pointer 4

pointerArray[4]   Pointer 5

pointerArray[5]   Pointer 6

Object 1

Object 2

Object 3

Object 4

Object 5

Object 6

Objects are scattered in main memory.

Pointer array contains the addresses of the objects in main memory.

Pointer array takes up just enough space to hold the pointers.

Figure 6.6   An array of pointers

be created is limited only by available main memory space. However, linked lists are more difficult to manipulate than arrays of pointers. You will be introduced to linked lists of objects in Chapter 9.

As an example of a program that handles an array of objects, we will be looking at the survey analysis program, for which the class was introduced in Chapter 3. The complete header file can be found again in Listing 6.7. Remember that the class is made up of variables for the survey number, the gender and age of the respondent, and eight values for the number of pairs of shoes that the respondent owns and has purchased in the past year.

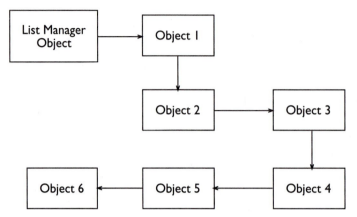

Figure 6.7   A linked list of objects

Listing 6.7   survey.h: Header file for the marketing survey program

```
const SWAP_MADE = 1;
const NO_SWAP = 0;
class OneSurvey
{
    private:
        int Survey_numb;
        char Gender;
        int Age, AthleticOwned, AthleticBought, DressOwned, DressBought,
            BootsOwned,BootsBought, SandalsOwned, SandalsBought;
    public:
        OneSurvey(); // constructor
        void InitSurvey (int, char, int, int, int, int, int, int, int, int,
            int);
        char getGender();
        int getAge();
        int getAthleticOwned();
        int getAthleticBought();
        int getDressOwned();
        int getDressBought();
        int getBootsOwned();
        int. getBootsBought();
        int getSandalsOwned();
        int getSandalsBought();
        // copy data from another object of the same type
        void copy (OneSurvey);
};
```

With one exception, the member functions for the OneSurvey class perform actions you have seen before (see Listing 6.8). The constructor, for example, initializes the integer variables to 0 and sets the single-character variable to NULL. The InitSurvey member function accepts data from the program manipulating an object and inserts those data into the object's variables. Other than the copy function, the remaining member functions simply return the contents of one of the object's variables to a calling function. As you will see shortly, the purpose of the copy function is to copy data from one OneSurvey object to another. It is used when sorting an array of objects.

Listing 6.8   survey.cpp: Member functions for the marketing survey program

```
#include "survey.h"
OneSurvey::OneSurvey()    // constructor
{
    Survey_numb = 0;
    Gender = '';
    Age = 0;
    AthleticOwned = 0;
    AthleticBought = 0;
    DressOwned = 0;
    DressBought = 0;
    BootsOwned = 0;
    BootsBought = 0;
    SandalsOwned = 0;
    SandalsBought = 0;
}

void OneSurvey::InitSurvey (int iSurvey_numb, char iGender, int iAge,
    int iAOwned, int iABought, int iDOwned, int iDBought, int iBOwned,
    int iBBought, int iSOwned, int iSBought)
{
    Survey_numb = iSurvey_numb;
    Gender = iGender;
    Age = iAge;
    AthleticOwned = iAOwned;
    AthleticBought = iABought;
    DressOwned = iDOwned;
    DressBought = iDBought;
    BootsOwned = iBOwned;
    BootsBought = iBBought;
    SandalsOwned = iSOwned;
    SandalsBought = iSBought;
}
```

Continued next page

Listing 6.8 (Continued) survey.cpp: Member functions for the marketing survey program

```
char OneSurvey::getGender()
    { return Gender; }

int OneSurvey::getAge()
    { return Age; }

int OneSurvey::getAthleticOwned()
    { return AthleticOwned; }

int OneSurvey::getAthleticBought()
    { return AthleticBought;}

int OneSurvey::getDressOwned()
    { return DressOwned; }

int OneSurvey::getDressBought()
    { return DressBought; }

int OneSurvey::getBootsOwned()
    { return BootsOwned; }

int OneSurvey::getBootsBought()
    { return BootsBought; }

int OneSurvey::getSandalsOwned()
    { return SandalsOwned; }

int OneSurvey::getSandalsBought()
    { return SandalsBought; }

void OneSurvey::copy (OneSurvey inputObject)   // copy one object into another
{
    Survey_numb = inputObject.Survey_numb;
    Gender = inputObject.Gender;
    Age = inputObject.Age;
    AthleticOwned = inputObject.AthleticOwned;
    AthleticBought = inputObject.AthleticBought;
    DressOwned = inputObject.DressOwned;
    DressBought = inputObject.DressBought;
    BootsOwned = inputObject.BootsOwned;
    BootsBought = inputObject.BootsBought;
    SandalsOwned = inputObject.SandalsOwned;
    SandalsBought = inputObject.SandalsBought;
}
```

The program that manipulates objects created from the OneSurvey class can be found in Listing 6.9. As you can see from the sample run in Figure 6.8, the program computes averages for each type of shoe ownership and purchase. It also computes those averages, separating the data by the gender of the recipient, as well as presenting a frequency distribution for the entire group of surveys.

As written, this program illustrates most of the concepts that will be covered in the rest of this chapter. Nonetheless, it is far from complete. There are many more things that it should do, including computing standard deviations, medians, modes, and statistics based on groupings of respondents by age. In addition, the program needs better error checking and more I/O capabilities. (You will get a chance to add some of the missing pieces for the exercises at the end of this chapter.)

Declaring and Referencing Arrays of Objects

In principle, an array of objects isn't much different from any other array. To declare an array of objects using static binding, you add the number of objects in the array to the declaration:

```
type_of_object array_name [#_of_objects];
```

The array that holds objects for the survey analysis program is defined with:

```
OneSurvey surveyData[50];
```

This allocates space for 50 objects of the class OneSurvey. Each individual object can then be referenced by the name of the array and the index of the object's position in the array. The third object, for example, is specified with surveyData[3].

In other words, the name of an object that is part of an array of objects includes the object's array index. This means that when a program calls a member function, it must use the object's entire name, including the array index. For example, to retrieve the value in the Gender variable, the program uses:

```
Lgender = inputData[i].getGender();
```

where Lgender is a local character variable and i contains the index of the desired array element.

```
Choose an option:

1. Compute averages
2. Compute averages by gender
3. Frequencies
9. Quit

Which one? 1

This function computes the average for the entire sample.

Choose the field to analyze:

1. Number of pairs of athletic shoes owned
2. Number of pairs of athleitic shoes purchased
3. Number of pairs of dress shoes owned
4. Number of pairs of dress shoes purchased
5. Number of pairs of boots owned
6. Number of pairs of boots purchased
7. Number of pairs of sandals owned
8. Number of pairs of sandals purchased
9. Exit without making a choice

Which one? 4

The average is 5.333333

Choose an option:

1. Compute averages
2. Compute averages by gender
3. Frequencies
9. Quit

Which one? 4

Choose the field to analyze:

1. Number of pairs of athletic shoes owned
2. Number of pairs of athleitic shoes purchased
3. Number of pairs of dress shoes owned
4. Number of pairs of dress shoes purchased
5. Number of pairs of boots owned
6. Number of pairs of boots purchased
7. Number of pairs of sandals owned
8. Number of pairs of sandals purchased
9. Exit without making a choice

Which one? 4

The average for men is 6.400000
The average for women is 4.363636

Choose an option:

1. Compute averages
2. Compute averages by gender
3. Frequencies
9. Quit

Which one? 3

Choose the field to analyze:

1. Number of pairs of athletic shoes owned
2. Number of pairs of athleitic shoes purchased
3. Number of pairs of dress shoes owned
4. Number of pairs of dress shoes purchased
5. Number of pairs of boots owned
6. Number of pairs of boots purchased
7. Number of pairs of sandals owned
8. Number of pairs of sandals purchased
9. Exit without making a choice

Which one? 4

VALUE COUNT
   0     2
   1     1
   2     1
   3     3
   5     1
   6     5
   7     3
   8     4
```

Figure 6.8 Sample output from the marketing survey program

Listing 6.9   main.cpp: Main program for the marketing survey program

```cpp
#include <iostream.h>
#include <fstream.h>
#include <iomanip.h>
#include "survey.h"

void main()
{
    int Menu(void); // function to handle program menu
    int FieldMenu(void); // function to handle menu of data fields
    int grabOne (int, OneSurvey);
    void Averages(OneSurvey[], int);
    void GAverages(OneSurvey[], int);
    void Frequencies (OneSurvey[], int);

    int choice = 0, count = 0;
    OneSurvey surveyData[50];   // Array to hold data from file
    int LSurvey_numb,LAge,LAthleticOwned,LAthleticBought,LDressOwned,
        LDressBought,LBootsOwned,LBootsBought,LSandalsOwned,LSandalsBought;
    char LGender;

// attempt to open the text file containing the data
    ifstream readFile ("Survey");
    if (!readFile) // if data file can't be found, exit the program
    {
        cout << "\nThe survey data file wasn't found.";
        return;
    }

    while (readFile)   // keep going until an error occurs
    {
        readFile >> LSurvey_numb >> LGender >> LAge >> LAthleticOwned >>
            LAthleticBought >> LDressOwned >> LDressBought >> LBootsOwned >>
            LBootsBought >> LSandalsOwned >> LSandalsBought;
// Send data to the next object in the array. Increment the number of objects when done.
        surveyData[count++].InitSurvey
            (LSurvey_numb,LGender,LAge,LAthleticOwned,LAthleticBought,
            LDressOwned,LDressBought,LBootsOwned,LBootsBought,
            LSandalsOwned,LSandalsBought);
    }
```

Continued next page

Listing 6.9 (Continued) main.cpp: Main program for the marketing survey program

```cpp
// something other than end-of-file encountered. Quit program
    if (!readFile.eof)
    {
        cout <<
            "\nError occurred while reading input file. Unable to continue.";
        return;
    }
    count--; // count is one too many at this point because of postincrement

    while (choice != 9)
    {
        choice = Menu();
        switch(choice)
        {
            case 1:
                Averages(surveyData, count);
                break;
            case 2:
                GAverages(surveyData, count);
                break;
            case 3:
                Frequencies(surveyData, count);
                break;
            case 9:
                break;
            default:
                cout << "\nYou've entered an unavailable option.";
        }
    }
}

int Menu()
{
    int option;

    cout << "\nChoose an option:" << endl << endl;
    cout << "1. Compute averages" << endl;
    cout << "2. Compute averages by gender" << endl;
    cout << "3. Frequencies" << endl;
    cout << "9. Quit" << endl << endl;
    cout << "Which one? ";
    cin >> option;
    return option;
}
```

Continued next page

Listing 6.9 (Continued) main.cpp: Main program for the marketing survey program

```
int FieldMenu( ) // This function lets the user choose one field to analyze
{
    int option;

    cout << "\nChoose the field to analyze:" << endl << endl;
    cout << "1. Number of pairs of athletic shoes owned" << endl;
    cout << "2. Number of pairs of athletic shoes purchased" << endl;
    cout << "3. Number of pairs of dress shoes owned" << endl;
    cout << "4. Number of pairs of dress shoes purchased" << endl;
    cout << "5. Number of pairs of boots owned" << endl;
    cout << "6. Number of pairs of boots purchased" << endl;
    cout << "7. Number of pairs of sandals owned" << endl;
    cout << "8. Number of pairs of sandals purchased" << endl;
    cout << "9. Exit without making a choice" << endl << endl;
    cout << "Which one? ";
    cin >> option;
    return option;
}


void Averages (OneSurvey inputData[], int count)
{
    int choice, i, sum;
    cout << setiosflags (ios::showpoint) << setprecision(6);
    cout << "\nThis function computes the average for the entire sample."
        << endl;
    choice = FieldMenu();
// This gets the user out without doing any computations
    if (choice == 9) return;
    sum = 0;
    for (i = 0; i <= count; i++)
        sum += grabOne (choice, inputData[i]);
    cout << "\nThe average is " << (float) sum / (count + 1) << endl;

}


void GAverages (OneSurvey inputData[], int count)
{
    cout << setiosflags (ios::showpoint) << setprecision(6);
    int choice, i, sumM, sumF, countM, countF;
    char Lgender;

    sumM = 0; sumF = 0; countM = 0; countF = 0;
    choice = FieldMenu();
    if (choice == 9) return; // get the user out without doing computations
```

Continued next page

Listing 6.9 (Continued) main.cpp: Main program for the marketing survey program

```cpp
for (i = 0; i <= count; i++)
{
    Lgender = inputData[i].getGender();
    if (Lgender == 'M')
    {
        countM++;
        sumM += grabOne (choice, inputData[i]);
    }
    else
    {
        countF++;
        sumF += grabOne (choice, inputData[i]);
    }
}
cout << "\nThe average for men is " << (float) sumM / countM << endl;
cout << "The average for women is " << (float) sumF / countF << endl;
}

void Frequencies (OneSurvey inputData[], int count)
{
    int choice, i, result, Value, ValueBelow, howMany;
    OneSurvey tempSurvey; // temporary object for use by bubble sort
    choice = FieldMenu();
    if (choice == 9) return; // get user out without doing anything
    resetiosflags (0);
    // This code is a bubble sort that sorts the array of objects on the chosen field
    result = SWAP_MADE;
    while (result == SWAP_MADE)
    {
        result = NO_SWAP;
        for (i = 0; i < count; i++)
        {
            Value = grabOne (choice, inputData[i]);
            ValueBelow = grabOne (choice, inputData[i+1]);
            if (Value > ValueBelow)
            {
                tempSurvey.copy(inputData[i]); // put current data into temp. object
                inputData[i].copy(inputData[i+1]); // copy in object below
                // copy original from temporary object
                inputData[i+1].copy(tempSurvey);
                result = SWAP_MADE;
            }
        }
    }
```

Continued next page

**Listing 6.9 (Continued) main.cpp: Main program for the marketing
                survey program**

// end of bubble sort; now scan the sorted table to generate the frequency distribution

```cpp
    Value = grabOne (choice, inputData[0]);    // get first value
    howMany = 1;
    cout << "\nVALUE COUNT" << endl;
    for (i = 1; i <= count; i++)
    {
        ValueBelow = grabOne (choice, inputData[i]);
        if (ValueBelow == Value)
            howMany++;
        else
        {
            cout << "  " << setw(2) << Value << "     " << setw(2) << howMany <<
    endl;
            Value = ValueBelow;
            howMany = 1;
        }
    }
}
```

```cpp
// This function retrieves data from one field in one object, based on the field the user
// chose earlier. It avoids using tons of repeated code.
int grabOne (int choice, OneSurvey chosenSurvey)
{
    int Value;

    switch(choice)
    {
        case 1: Value = chosenSurvey.getAthleticOwned(); break;
        case 2: Value = chosenSurvey.getAthleticBought(); break;
        case 3: Value = chosenSurvey.getDressOwned(); break;
        case 4: Value = chosenSurvey.getDressBought(); break;
        case 5: Value = chosenSurvey.getBootsOwned(); break;
        case 6: Value = chosenSurvey.getBootsBought(); break;
        case 7: Value = chosenSurvey.getSandalsOwned(); break;
        case 8: Value = chosenSurvey.getSandalsBought(); break;
    }
    return Value;
}
```

Passing Arrays into Functions

The structure of the program that manipulates the array of OneSurvey
objects is organized around a group of functions, each of which either displays
a menu (Menu and FieldMenu), retrieves one value from one object

(grabOne), or performs statistical analysis (Averages, GAverages, and Frequencies). The three functions that perform the statistical analysis need access to the entire array of objects. The array must therefore be sent from the main function, where it is declared, into any function that will be using it.

Passing One-Dimensional Arrays

Handling arrays as formal parameters is somewhat different from handling simple variables. First, the prototype of the function that will be accepting the array must indicate that the parameter is an array. For a one-dimensional array, the prototype doesn't need to specify the number of elements in the array; just include the brackets that normally surround the index. The prototype for the Averages function, for example, is written:

```
void Averages(OneSurvey[], int);
```

The function takes two format parameters: an array of objects of the type One-Survey and an integer (the index of the highest numbered element of the array that contains data).

The function declaration also doesn't need to indicate the number of elements in the array. The declaration of Averages is therefore written as:

```
void Averages (OneSurvey inputData[], int count)
```

When the array arrives in the function, it will be called inputData. Notice that the parameter list contains the data type—in this case a class—along with the name to be given the parameter in the function. The brackets next to the parameter's name indicate that it's an array.

The function that receives the array really doesn't need to know how many elements are in the array. It only needs to know the data type of the array's value. This is because C++ accesses elements in a one-dimensional array by multiplying the array index by the number of bytes in each element and then adding that offset to the starting address of the array.

Warning

The major implication of the way in which C++ accesses an array is that it really doesn't keep track of the size of an array. Once space is allocated when an array is declared, all C++ does is perform its multiplication and addition to generate an address for data access. This means you can read data beyond the end of an array or write data beyond the end of an array. Doing the former gives you a wrong value; doing the latter may well destroy the contents of a memory location actually allocated to another variable. It is therefore up to the programmer to ensure that a program doesn't overflow the bounds of an array; C++ won't do it for you!

When you call a function that has an entire array as a formal parameter, use the array's name, without any brackets. For example, the Averages function is called with:

```
Averages(surveyData, count);
```

Passing an array as a formal parameter may look very similar to passing a simple variable, but what gets passed is very different. When you pass a simple variable, such as count, the program copies the variable's value into the function's parameter, leaving the contents of the original value alone. However, *the name of an array is the address of the beginning of the array.* When you pass an entire array, you are actually sending the array's starting address into the function; no copy of the array is made and transferred into the function's parameter. In other words, *arrays are always passed by reference.* (It's impossible to pass an array by value.) This means that when a function modifies the contents of an array, the modifications are made to the original array in main memory.

Passing Two-Dimensional Arrays

A two-dimensional array presents a bit of a challenge to a function: It must be able to figure out where one row begins and another ends. If you don't give a function some idea about how many columns there are in each row, then the function won't know how to interpret array indexes. This means that when you pass a two-dimensional array into a function, you can leave the number of rows empty, but you must indicate how many columns there are. A prototype therefore includes the number of columns, as in:

```
void someFunction (int [][NUM_COLUMNS);
```

By the same token, the function header must also include the number of columns:

```
void someFunction (int myArray[][NUM_COLUMNS)
```

When you call the function, it is called using just the name of the array as an input parameter:

```
anObject.someFunction (myArray);
```

The function can then use the starting address of the array, the size of the elements in the array, and the number of columns to calculate the starting address of any element in the array.

Loading Objects from a Text File

The survey analysis program reads its data from a text file (`Sample`). Unfortunately, the program has no way of knowing how many objects are represented by the text file. It therefore can't use a `for` loop to read one set of data after another. The solution is to read data until there aren't any more data in the file, until an *end-of-file* condition arises. An end-of-file condition indicates that a program has attempted to read beyond the last valid data in a file.

The `ifstream` class contains a flag (`eof`) that indicates the end-of-file condition. You can test to determine that the flag has been set (an end-of-file has occurred) with the syntax

```
if (stream_name.eof)
```

By the same token, you might decide to read repeated groups of data from a file with a `while` loop such as

```
while (!stream_name.eof)
{
    read from the file
}
```

However, there is a major risk in doing so: If an error other than an end-of-file arises when reading from the file, the program will be stuck in an infinite loop. Therefore, programs typically loop until *any* error arises and then determine exactly what error occurred. The survey analysis program, for example, contains the loop

```
while (readFile)
{
    read one object's data
    copy data to object with InitSurvey function
}
```

Each iteration of the loop reads one survey's worth of data from the file. It then calls the `InitSurvey` member function to insert the data into an object in the array of objects. Counting the number of objects as they are read is handled by the postincrement of the array's index variable.

The preceding loop stops whenever any file error occurs. At that point, it is up to the program to check the exact type of error. In this case, the program looks for any error that isn't an end-of-file:

```
if (!readFile.eof)
{
    display error message
    return; // exit program
}
```

If an unexpected error condition has arisen, the program displays an error message to the user and then quits. There isn't any requirement that a program stop execution if an unexpected file error occurs, but the way the survey analysis program is written, it will have no data to analyze if a problem with the file occurs.

Note

Systems vary in the way in which they mark the end of a file. For example, UNIX systems tend to use a CTRL-D as an end-of-file character; MS-DOS and OS/2 use CTRL-Z. Fortunately, C++, like most programming languages, make it easy to test for the end of a file without knowing exactly how the end is indicated in the file itself.

Sorting an Array of Objects

The easiest way to produce a frequency distribution like that generated by the survey analysis program is to sort the values and then scan them from low to high, counting how many times each value occurs. The `Frequencies` function of the survey analysis program must therefore be able to sort the `survey-Data` array by any of the eight variables dealing with pairs of shoes.

There are many ways to sort an array. One of the simplest to understand and program is a *bubble sort*. It is also relatively efficient when the values originally are more in order than out of order (only a few values need to be rearranged) and when the number of values to be sorted are relatively few.

A bubble sort looks at successive pairs of values and swaps their positions in the array if they are in the wrong order. For example, if the value in array element 2 is greater than the value in array element 3, the bubble sort swaps the values in those two elements, placing them in the correct low-to-high order. The sort then proceeds to examine elements 3 and 4, 4 and 5, and so on to the end of the array. Reaching the bottom of the array, the sort returns to the top to begin examining pairs of values again. Once the program makes a scan through the entire array without swapping any values, the array is in the correct low-to-high order.

To manage the sort, the `Frequencies` function uses two loops. The outer—a `while`—keeps going until the `result` variable indicates that no swaps have been made. (This is where the `SWAP_MADE` and `NO_SWAP` constants come in.) The inner loop—a `for`—makes one pass through the array.

Whenever the need for a swap is detected, the bubble sort copies the array element with the lower index into a temporary storage location. It can then copy the object below into the location of the object being held in temporary storage. Finally, the object in temporary storage can be copied into its new location in the array (one array element below where it was originally located).

To perform the swap, the `Frequencies` function defines an object from the `OneSurvey` class named `tempSurvey`. (This is not an array; it is a single object.) Then, the program calls the `copy` function to transfer data from the array to the temporary object with the syntax:

```
tempSurvey.copy(inputData[i]);
```

This takes one object from the array of objects and uses it as an input parameter to the `copy` function, which acts on the `tempSurvey` object. The `copy` function (look back at Listing 6.8) transfers the data one variable at a time.

Note

There is an easier way to copy one object into another, using a special pointer variable called `this`. You will be introduced to it in Chapter 8.

The next step is to copy up the value below:

```
inputData[i].copy(inputData[i+1]);
```

In this case, the object below the one that was just placed in temporary storage is copied into the preceding element in the array. Finally, the object in temporary storage is copied into its new location in the array:

```
inputData[i+1].copy(tempSurvey);
```

Summary

Like high-level languages, C++ supports arrays. Arrays can be used as class variables or as local variables in functions that manipulate objects. In addition, a program that manipulates objects may use arrays to hold groups of objects.

To declare a one-dimensional C++ array, place the number of elements in the array within brackets following the name of the array. A two-dimensional array requires two sets of brackets, one for each dimension.

The elements in a C++ array are numbered beginning with zero. Although an array declaration requires the total number of elements in the array, the index of the highest element in the array is therefore one less than the total number of elements.

To assign a value to an array, a program uses the name of the array followed by brackets containing the index of the element to which the value is to be assigned. However, when the array is an array of objects, each element must be assigned a value or copied one class variable at a time.

The name of an array is the address of the beginning of the array in main memory. When an array is passed into a function, the address of the array is passed rather than a copy of the contents of the array. Because arrays are always passed by reference in this way, modifying the contents of an array in a function changes the array in main memory.

Arrays of objects can be loaded from a text file. In most cases, data are read from the file until an error condition occurs. The program then checks to see if an end-of-file condition has arisen. Any other type of error indicates an unexpected problem with file input.

Exercises

1. Write a class that contains an array of the closing Dow Jones Averages for the past two weeks. The program that manipulates an object of this class should allow the user to enter the averages and then initialize the object with those numbers. The program should finish by calling a member func-

tion that computes the average of the values in the array and returns that average to the calling function, which should then display the average for the user.

2. Write a class that contains a two-dimensional array for the credit card purchases made by one employee during a seven-day period. Allow the employee to make up to 10 purchases each day. The program that manipulates an object of this class should prompt the user to enter data for the array and then initialize the object's array. Write member functions to calculate the total purchases made on one day and the total purchases made for the entire seven-day period. Then, prepare a nicely formatted report that shows the purchases made on each day, the total for each day, and—at the end of the report—the grand total of the purchases made.

3. Write a class that contains summary information for a bank. The class should include the customer's number. It should also include a two-dimensional array that holds an account number and a deposit account balance (checking account, CD, NOW account, passbook savings account). Write a program to test the class that includes an array of customer objects. The program should do the following:

   • Permit interactive entry of data.
   • Compute the total worth of each customer. Display each customer's number followed by the sum of all of his or her account balances. At the end of the report, compute the total amount on deposit at the bank.

4. Create a class that stores information about the salespeople for a cosmetics company. The class should include the salesperson's ID number and the dollar value of sales made during each of the past five weeks (one month).Write a program to test the class that computes the amount paid each salesperson for the month, based on the following rules:

   • Base pay is $250 a week plus 10% of sales.
   • If a salesperson sells over $10,000 in the month, he or she receives a bonus of $500.

The program should include an array of objects that store data entered interactively. Once the data are in the array, compute and display the number of salespeople receiving pay in the following ranges:

- Less than $1,000
- $1,000–$2,499.99
- $2,500–$4,999.99
- $5,000 or more

Store the counts in an array in your program and display the result once all computations are completed.

5. Modify Exercise 6 from Chapter 5 so that it handles an array of product objects. Add a function to the program so that it displays the costs for all products, one at a time, followed by the total cost for all products.

6. Create a class that stores and evaluates a poker hand. The class should contain a two-dimensional array to store the five-card hand. In one column, store the suit (1 = Diamonds, 2 = Hearts, 3 = Clubs, 4 = Spades); in the other column, store the card value (11 = Jack, 12 = Queen, 13 = King). Include a member function that evaluates a hand and reports back to the program calling the function whether the hand contains a flush (all the same suit), a straight (all five cards in numeric order), a straight flush (all five cards in the same suit in numeric order), four of a kind, a full house (three of a kind plus two of a kind), three of a kind, two pair, one pair, or nothing. Write a program that demonstrates that the hand evaluation function works.

7. Write a program that tracks which rooms in a hotel are currently occupied. Base the program on a class that describes a room (room number, maximum number of occupants, and an integer flag indicating whether the room is occupied). Include member functions to indicate when a room becomes occupied and when a room becomes unoccupied. Demonstrate that the class and its member functions work by writing a program to manipulate an array of room objects. The program should do the following:

- Allow interactive entry of data to initialize room objects. (File storage is also useful.)
- Display the total number of unoccupied rooms.
- Display the number of unoccupied rooms of each size (size = maximum number of occupants).
- Find an unoccupied room of a given size and set that room as occupied.
- Set a room as unoccupied.

8. As you know, the survey data analysis program that was used as an example isn't complete. Along with additional functionality, it also needs more error trapping and I/O. Add the following to the program:

- Error trapping when reading the data file: Add code that stops reading the data file when the array is full. Display an appropriate error message. Then give the user the choice of proceeding with data currently in the array or exiting the program.
- Interactive I/O: Add code that accepts data for new objects from the keyboard and inserts them into the array of objects. Be sure to check to make sure that the array isn't full.
- File save: Once interactive I/O has been added to the program, the contents of the array of objects must be written back to the text file when the program ends. Add code to write to the file.
- Standard deviation: The standard deviation is a measure of the degree of spread of data values around the average. It has the formula:

$$s = \sqrt{\frac{\Sigma (X_i - \bar{X})^2}{N}}$$

In this formula, X is a data value, $\bar{X}$ is the average (mean) of all data values, and N is the total number of data values. The symbol Σ means to sum all the values. The formula therefore tells you first to compute the mean. Then subtract the mean from each data value and square that difference. Add up all the differences and divide them by the total number of values. Finally, take the square root. (*Hint*: Use the `sqrt` function that is prototyped in `math.h`.)

Add computations for the standard deviation to the `Averages` and `GAverages` functions.

- Median and Mode: The median is a data value chosen so that half the values are above it and half below it. The mode is that data value (or values) that have the highest frequency. Add code that produces median and mode to the frequency distribution functions.
- Statistics grouped by age range: Add a function that creates groups of objects based on the age of the respondent. For example, age ranges might be defined as all people under 16, 17–21, 22–30, 31–40, and so on. Then, compute means, medians, and modes for each age group.

7

Strings

OBJECTIVES

In this chapter you will learn about:
- Defining and initializing strings.
- Performing string I/O.
- Reading strings from and writing strings to files.
- Using functions that manipulate strings.
- Strings as function parameters.
- Searching and sorting arrays of strings.
- Using strings to create a generic menu class.

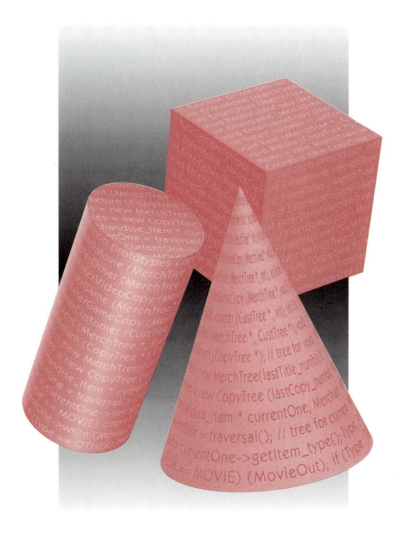

By its very nature, business data contain a lot of text: names, phone numbers, addresses, product descriptions, and so on. It is therefore extremely important that business application programmers who are working in C++ be proficient in handling strings.

In this chapter you will learn how C++ represents strings. You will also be introduced to performing string I/O, manipulating arrays of strings, and passing arrays to and from functions. In addition, you will see a generic menu class that you can use in your programs to simplify support for a text-based menu-driven interface.

The Sample Programs

The major examples in this chapter are taken from two programs. (You will also see some shorter sample programs.) As the first major example of a program that handles strings, we'll be looking at a program to manage the office supplies inventory. (You were introduced to this program in Chapter 3.) The program lets the user enter new items into the inventory, update the quantities on hand each month, and print a reorder list (see Figure 7.1). The program also saves the inventory to disk each time the program ends and reads it back into memory whenever the program is run.

The second program is an implementation of the program for the pharmacy that also first appeared in Chapter 2. A complete prescription-management program for a pharmacy is a very lengthy program; it usually requires years to develop. Even the limited version written for this book is too long to publish in the body of the text. However, you will find the complete source code in Appendix B. Significant portions of the code are also included in the text in this and the following two chapters, where the language features the program was written to demonstrate are discussed.

Note

The original design of the pharmacy program that appeared in Chapter 2 used inheritance to represent prescriptions. However, because you won't be learning about inheritance until Chapter 10, the implementation written for this book uses only one class for prescriptions.

```
Please choose a menu option:

1. Enter a new item
2. Update inventory
3. View the reorder list
9. Quit

Which one? 1
Description: Pencils, #2
Item number: 9
Amount currently in inventory: 20
Reorder point: 3

Description:

Please choose a menu option:

1. Enter a new item
2. Update inventory
3. View the reorder list
9. Quit

Which one? 2
Enter current inventory amount for each item (-1 = no change)
Pens, red (15): -1
Pens, blue (10): 15
Pens, black (15): -1
Tablets, yellow lined (25): 50
Envelopes, #10 (500): 10
Tape, masking (5): 1
Staples (3): 1
Tape, cellphane (1): -1
Pencils, #2 (20): -1

Please choose a menu option:

1. Enter a new item
2. Update inventory
3. View the reorder list
9. Quit

Which one? 3

ITEMS TO REORDER
----------------

Envelopes, #10: On hand (10)  Reorder point (25)
Tape, masking: On hand (1)  Reorder point (2)
Staples: On hand (1)  Reorder point (5)
Tape, cellphane: On hand (1)  Reorder point (5)
```

Figure 7.1   Output from the supply inventory program

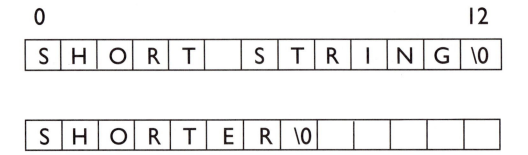

Figure 7.2   String storage in main memory

Declaring Strings

C++ has no "string" data type. Instead, strings are stored as arrays of type char. The end of the string is marked with a null, the character '\0'. Although this character might look like two characters, it is actually stored as one—the ASCII code for null. The \ preceding the 0 is the escape character, telling the compiler that what follows isn't a zero, but should instead be interpreted as a special character.

When defining an array to hold a string, you must allocate one extra element beyond the maximum number of characters in the string to hold the terminating null. For example, if you want to define a 12-character string, you will use the following declaration:

```
char oneLine [13];
```

Although the storage space is 13 characters long, a string needn't use all of it. As you can see in Figure 7.2, a string occupies only as much of the allocated storage space as needed to hold its characters. The null in the last position simply marks the ending position, wherever it may fall.

Note

The special way in which strings are stored means that you can't use the normal operators for operations such as assignment and logical comparisons. Because a string is an array and its name is a main memory address, if you attempt to assign a value using the assignment operator you'll be assigning an address to the variable, rather than changing its contents. If you use the comparison operators with a string name, you'll be comparing the address of the string, not its contents. You'll therefore be using functions from the C libraries to perform string operations.

If a program contains many strings that need the same amount of storage space, you can simplify string declaration by defining a new data type with typedef. (As you will see later in this chapter, this is particularly useful for working with arrays of strings.) To define a "string" data type, use something like

```
typedef char string[81];
```

The result is a data type named string that can be used to define other variables, just like any of the simple variable types.

The class for the supply inventory program (Listing 7.1) uses an 80-character string to store the supply item's description. As you can see from the header file, the remainder of the variables are integers.

Listing 7.1   supplies.h: Header file for the supply inventory program

```
class Item
{
    private:
        int Item_numb, On_hand, Reorder_pt;
        char Desc[81]; // string to hold the supply item description

    public:
        Item(); // constructor
        void InitItem (int, int, int, char[]);
        int getItem_numb ();
        int getOn_hand ();
        int getReorder_pt ();
// returns a pointer to a string array; details will appear later in this chapter.
        char * getDesc ();
        void ModOn_hand(int);
};
```

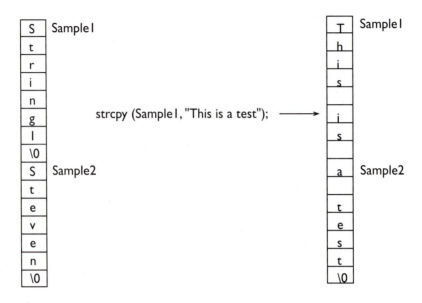

Figure 7.3   The effect of string overflow

Warning

C++ compilers don't detect operations that attempt to assign or retrieve values beyond the end of a string. References to arrays are handled as pointers. As you know, the name of an array (or the first element in an array) is a pointer to the array's starting location in main memory. Access to other elements in the array are computed by multiplying the number of bytes occupied by an element by the element number and then adding that to the array's starting address.

If a program does store data beyond the end of an array, it will overwrite storage for another variable. To make this a bit clearer, take a look at Figure 7.3. At the left you will see some consecutive memory locations that have been used to store two strings, Sample1 and Sample2. Both have been declared to hold a maximum of seven characters (eight memory locations including the terminating null). The program manipulating these strings performs a strcpy operation, placing "This is a test" into Sample1. Although the string constant is longer than the amount of space declared for Sample1, the computer executes the function. As a result, the string overlays the original values for Sample2. The effect is to place "This is a test" in Sample1 and "a test" in Sample2.

The most common indication that a program has overflowed a string storage location is when the values of variables change without direct modification by a program. To identify where the problem is occurring, use a debugger and view the contents of variables whose contents are mysteriously changing. Step through the program line by line, checking to see which action causes the value of the variables to change. In many cases, it will be a statement that assigns a value to a string. Once you know which string is at fault, you can check the length of the string's array against the length of values being assigned to that array.

Accessing Strings

As arrays of characters, string variables behave much like other arrays. The name of the string variable represents the starting address of the string in main memory. Each individual character in the string can also be accessed like a single element in any other type of array. For example, `arrayName[0]` is a single-character variable that also happens to be the first element in a string. You can assign a value to it just as you would any other simple variable or array element:

```
arrayName[0] = 'J';
```

In contrast, `arrayName` represents the starting address of the array. You can also obtain the starting address of the array by using the notation `&arrayName[0]`. The ampersand operator tells the computer that you want the address of a variable rather than its contents. That being the case, the notation `&arrayName[5]` gives you the starting address of a substring of the original that begins at the sixth position in the string and continues until the terminating null. (You will learn more about using this operator in Chapter 8.)

Initializing and Assigning Values to Strings

Strings can be initialized when they are declared, just like any other variable. However, you can't assign a value to a string using an assignment operator; you must use a library function for that purpose.

Initializing Strings

To initialize a string at the time it is declared, surround the string with double quotes and assign it to the string variable, as in

```
char menuTitle[] = "MAIN MENU";
```

Notice that when you initialize a string in this way, you don't need to tell C++ how much space to allocate for the string array. The compiler will allocate exactly enough space to hold the string.

There is a very important difference in surrounding a single character with single quotes and with double quotes. If you initialize a variable with

```
char yes_no = 'y';
```

you are requesting a single-byte storage location. The single quotes generates a simple character variable, without the trailing null. However, if you initialize a variable with

```
char yes_no[] = "y";
```

you are requesting two bytes of storage, one for the character and the other for the terminating null.

Assigning Values to Strings

To assign a value to a string, you must use the `strcpy` function. Like most other string functions, its prototype is in the header file `string.h`. The function has the general syntax

```
strcpy (destination_string, source_string);
```

The destination string is a string variable. The source string can be another string variable or a string constant (characters surrounded by double quotes).

The supply inventory program uses the `strcpy` function in its constructor and in the member function that initializes an object. (You can find those functions, along with the rest of the program's member functions, in Listing 7.2.) Notice that in the constructor, the `strcpy` function places a null (two single or double quotes right next to one another) in the `Desc` variable. In the `InitItem` function, however, the `strcpy` function assigns the value in the input parameter (`iDesc`) to the object's variable.

If you don't want to copy an entire string, but just part of a string, use `strncpy`, a variant of `strcpy` that lets you specify exactly how many characters you want to copy:

```
strncpy(destination_string,source_string,#characters);
```

Listing 7.2   supplies.cpp: Member functions for the supply inventory program

```cpp
#include "supplies.h"
#include <string.h>

Item::Item()
{
    Item_numb = 0;
    On_hand = 0;
    Reorder_pt = 0;
    strcpy (Desc, '');
}

void Item::InitItem (int iItem_numb, int iOn_hand, int iReorder_pt, char
    iDesc[])
{
    Item_numb = iItem_numb;
    On_hand = iOn_hand;
    Reorder_pt = iReorder_pt;
    strcpy (Desc, iDesc); // assign value in input parameter to object's variable
}

int Item::getItem_numb ()
{
    return Item_numb;
}

int Item::getOn_hand ()
{
    return On_hand;
}

int Item::getReorder_pt ()
{
    return Reorder_pt;
}

char * Item::getDesc ()
{
// returning the name of an array returns a pointer to its first element.
    return Desc;
}

void Item::ModOn_hand (int newAmount)
{
    On_hand = newAmount;
}
```

For example, if `string1` contains "This is a test," then the following expression copies "This is ":

```
strncpy (string2, string1, 7)
```

To change the starting position in the source string, use the ampersand notation to specify a specific character with which to begin:

```
strncpy (string2, &string1[7], 7)
```

After the above function call is completed, `string2` contains " a test" (including the blank preceding *a*). The `strncpy` function copies as many characters as specified in the function call or until the computer encounters a terminating null in the source string.

Concatenating Strings

A common operation performed with strings is to create a long string by combining two strings, one after the other. Known as *concatenation*, this operation copies the source string onto the end of the destination string. The destination string's storage allocation must therefore be long enough to hold the combined string.

The `strcat` function as the general syntax

```
strcat (destination_string, source_string);
```

As an example, consider the following:

```
char One[30] = "First string";
char Two[30] = "Second string";
strcat (One, Two);
```

The contents of `Two` will be unaltered; the contents of `Two` will be "First stringSecond string." To get a space between the words, it needs to be inserted explicitly. If a program executes

```
strcat (One, " ");
strcat (One, Two);
```

the result will be "First string Second string."

```
First name: John
Last name: Dough
Street: 195 805th Ave.
City: Anytown
State: NY
Zip: 12345


John Dough
195 805th Ave.
Anytown, NY 12345
```

Figure 7.4 Output of the address label program

To explore how string concatenation can be used, let's look at a program that takes data about a customer stored in individual variables and formats output strings that have correct spacing for a mailing label. This is a common task that many business programs perform. In general, data are stored in the smallest units possible and combined for output. For example, rather than storing city, state, and zipcode in one variable, they are stored in three. This makes it easier to sort and search the data on any one of the variables.

Note

Later in this chapter you will see another way of producing a mailing label that involves formatting an output stream in main memory.

As you can see in Figure 7.4, this program asks the user for the individual elements of the customer information and then displays a properly formatting mailing label. The program is based on the Customer class (Listing 7.3), which has individual variables for the pieces of the customer's information and three member functions (a constructor, a function to initialize an object, and a function to format and display the label).

The member functions for this program can be found in Listing 7.4. The constructor copies a null (two double quotes directly next to one another) into each variable; the init function copies data from input strings into each variable. Formatting and display of the mailing label occurs in displayFormatted. (The cout statements appear inside the function because we haven't yet discussed returning strings from functions.)

As you study displayString, notice that when the function formats a line for the address label, it begins by *copying* the first piece of data into the output string. This is essential because you want to erase any previous contents

Listing 7.3   label.h: Header file for the mailing label program

```
typedef char string80[81];
typedef char string50[51];
typedef char string25[26];

class Customer
{
    private:
        string25 first, last, city;
        string50 street;
        char state[3], zip[6];
    public:
        Customer ();
        void init (string25, string25, string50, string25, char [], char[]);
        void displayFormatted ();
};
```

Listing 7.4   label.cpp: Member functions for the mailing label
             program

```
#include <iostream.h>
#include <string.h>
#include "label.h"

Customer::Customer()
{
    strcpy (first,"");
    strcpy (last,"");
    strcpy (street,"");
    strcpy (city,"");
    strcpy (state,"");
    strcpy (zip,"");
}

void Customer::init (string25 ifirst, string25 ilast, string50 istreet,
    string25 icity, char istate[], char izip[])
{
    strcpy (first,ifirst);
    strcpy (last,ilast);
    strcpy (street,istreet);
    strcpy (city,icity);
    strcpy (state,istate);
    strcpy (zip,izip);
}
```

Continued next page

Listing 7.4 (Continued) label.cpp: Member functions for the mailing label program

```
void Customer::displayFormatted ()
{
    string50 wholeName;
    string80 CSZ;

    cout << endl << endl;
    strcpy (wholeName, first);
    strcat (wholeName, " ");
    strcat (wholeName, last);
    cout << wholeName << endl;
    cout << street << endl;

    strcpy (CSZ, city);
    strcat (CSZ, ", ");
    strcat (CSZ, state);
    strcat (CSZ, " ");
    strcat (CSZ, zip);
    cout << CSZ;
}
```

in the output string. Then, the remainder of the data are *concatenated* onto the string. Formatting, such as blanks and commas, are added as literal strings; other values are taken from class variables.

The main function that drives the address label program can be found in Listing 7.5. It collects the data used to initialize the object onePerson and then calls the init function to send the input data to the object. In this case, the strings are passed by name, just like any other array. The function finishes by calling the displayFormatted function to perform this program's actual work.

Finding the Length of a String

Because the end of a string is marked with a null, a string doesn't have to fill every position in its array. After you have been playing with strings using the strcpy and strcat functions, you may not know exactly how many characters are in a string. Nonetheless, you may need to access each character in the string individually. The easiest way to do this is to set up a for loop that begins at array element 0 and continues until it reaches the length of the string.

Listing 7.5　main.cpp: Main program for the address label program

```
#include <iostream.h>
#include <string.h>
#include <stdio.h>
#include "label.h"

void main()
{
    Customer onePerson;  // delcare an object

    string25 ifirst, ilast, icity;
    string50 istreet;
    char istate[3], izip[6];

    cout << "First name: ";
    gets (ifirst);
    cout << "Last name: ";
    gets (ilast);
    cout << "Street: ";
    gets (istreet);
    cout << "City: ";
    gets (icity);
    cout << "State: ";
    gets (istate);
    cout << "Zip: ";
    gets (izip);

    onePerson.init (ifirst, ilast, istreet, icity, istate, izip);
    onePerson.displayFormatted();
}
```

The key to finding the length of a string is the `strlen` function. Its only input parameter is the name of a string variable:

```
strlen (string_variable_name)
```

It returns an integer that represents the number of characters in the string, excluding the trailing null. In other words, if a string variable contains `abc-defghij\0`, the string length is 10, not 11.

To use the function, you can assign its result to an integer variable or place it in any expression that expects an integer. For example, the following code displays each character of a string on a separate line:

```
char aString[50] = "This is a test";
for (int i = 0; i <= strlen(aString); i++)
    cout << "Character #: " << aString[i] << endl;
```

```
Enter a date in the format YY/MM/DD: 96/10/05
Enter a date to compare: 95/09/12
The date in the class is later.
```

Figure 7.5   Output of the date comparison program

Comparing Strings

Because strings are arrays, they can't be compared like simple data types. If you attempt something like if (Array1 > Array 2), C++ will assume that you are asking for an analysis of the starting addresses of the arrays, not their contents.

The solution is a function called strcmp, which has the following general syntax:

```
result = strcmp(first_string, second_string);
```

If the two strings are identical, result is 0. However, if first_string follows second_string in alphabetical order, the result is greater than 1; if first_string precedes second_string, the result is less than 1.

As an example of comparing strings, we'll be looking at a program that compares dates stored as strings in the format YY/MM/DD. (Because string comparisons are made in alphabetical rather than numeric order, this is the only string date format that will also be evaluated in correct chronological order.)

The program (Figure 7.5) collects a date from the user that it stores in an object created from a class named Date (Listing 7.6). It then stores that date in a class object. The program collects a second date from the user, compares it to the date stored in the object, and then reports back to the user which date comes first.

The function that initializes an object created from the Date class (init) performs some basic validation on the input date. It returns an integer that indicates whether the month or day is out of range. (The logic is incomplete, however, because it doesn't match the number of days in a month to the specific month.) As you can see in Listing 7.7, the program displays an error message and terminates if the date intended for storage in the class isn't valid.

Listing 7.6   date.h: Header file for the date comparison program

```
const BAD_MON = 1;
const BAD_DAY = 2;
const OK = 0;

class Date
{
    private:
        char stringDate[9];
    public:
        Date ();
        int init (char []);
        int compareDates (char []);
};
```

Listing 7.7   main.cpp: Main program for the date comparison
program

```
#include <string.h>
#include <stdio.h>
#include <iostream.h>
#include "dates.h"

void main ()
{
    char iDate[9];
    int result;
    Date oneDay; // declare an object

    cout << "Enter a date in the format YY/MM/DD: ";
    gets (iDate);
    result = oneDay.init (iDate);
    if (result == BAD_MON)
    {
        cout << iDate << " contains an invalid month";
        return;
    }
    else if (result == BAD_DAY)
    {
        cout << iDate << "contains an invalid day.";
        return;
    }

    cout << "Enter a date to compare: ";
    gets (iDate);
    result = oneDay.compareDates (iDate);
```

Continued next page

**Listing 7.7 (Continued) main.cpp: Main program for the date comparison
program**

```
    if (result == 0)
        cout << "The dates are the same.";
    else if (result < 0)
        cout << "The date in the class is earlier.";
    else
        cout << "The date in the class is later.";
}
```

After initializing the object, the main function collects a date for comparison from the user and then calls the compareDates member function to actually perform the comparison. It finishes by evaluating the result returned by compareDates and displays an appropriate message to the user.

The member functions that perform the actual work for this program can be found in Listing 7.8. First take a look at the init function. It uses strncpy to isolate the characters for the month into a separate variable. It then compares those two characters to string constants that represent valid months. Assuming the check for the month is passed, the function then isolates the characters that represent the day and compares them to string constants that represent valid months. If the check for the day is passed, the function finishes by copying the input date into the object and returns a value that signals the calling function that the date is valid.

The compareDates function is quite simple. It performs a strcmp and returns the result. Why then use this function rather than just performing the comparison in the main function? Because the stringDate variable is a private variable and therefore not directly accessible to a function outside the class. It would need to be sent to the calling function by a member function. It is therefore simpler to perform the comparison in a member function.

String I/O

Strings present special challenges for stream I/O because streams use spaces or commas to separate values. Therefore, although you can use cin with the stream extraction operator to read in one word, you can't use it to read in an entire sentence. The same problem arises when you are attempting to read data from a text file. In this section you will be introduced to the special techniques used to manage stream I/O when strings are involved.

Listing 7.8   date.cpp: Member functions for the date comparison program

```
#include <string.h>
#include "dates.h"

Date::Date()
    { strcpy (stringDate,""); }

int Date::init (char iDate[])
{
    char MM[3], DD[3];

    strncpy (MM,&iDate[3],2);
    if (strcmp(MM,"01") < 0 || strcmp (MM,"12") > 0)
        return BAD_MON;
    strncpy (DD,&iDate[6],2); // isolate the day
    if (strcmp(DD,"01") < 0 || strcmp (DD,"31") > 0)
        return BAD_DAY;
    strcpy (stringDate,iDate);
    return OK;
}

int Date::compareDates (char iDate[])
    { return strcmp (stringDate,iDate); }
```

The example code to which this discussion will refer can be found in the supply inventory program (Listing 7.9). Before reading any further, spend some time looking at the program so you have a feeling for its overall structure and operation.

Listing 7.9   main.cpp: Main program for the supply inventory program

```
#include <iostream.h>
#include <string.h>
#include <fstream.h>
#include <ctype.h>
#include <stdio.h>
#include <iomanip.h>
#include "supplies.h"

void main()
{
    int NewItem (int, Item[]); // interactive I/O for new items
    // update each item after inventory has been taken
    void MonthlyUpdate (int, Item[]);
```

Continued next page

Listing 7.9 (Continued) main.cpp: Main program for the supply inventory program

```cpp
void ReorderList (int, Item[]); // display the reorder list
int Menu (); // main menu

Item ourSupplies[50]; // array to hold supply objects
int iItem_numb, iOn_hand, iReorder_pt;
char iDesc[81], yes_no, white_space;
// set count to -1 to handle situation where no file exists
int choice = 0, count = -1;

ifstream readFile ("Items");

if (!readFile)   // handle situation where data file can't be found
{
    cout << "No data file could be found. Do you want to continue? ";
    cin >> yes_no;
    if (toupper(yes_no) == 'N')
        return;
}
else
{
// The following strategy simplifies working with text files that contain strings

    readFile >> count; // get number of objects from first part of file
    for (int i = 0; i <= count ; i++) // load data in from the file
    {
        readFile.getline (iDesc, 80, '\0');
        readFile >> iItem_numb >> iOn_hand >> iReorder_pt;
        readFile.get (white_space);
        ourSupplies[i].InitItem (iItem_numb, iOn_hand, iReorder_pt, iDesc);
    }

    if (!readFile)   // file error occurred
    {
    cout <<"Unexpected file input error occurred.Do you want to continue?";
        cin >> yes_no;
        if (toupper(yes_no) == 'N')
        return;
    }
    readFile.close();
}
```

Continued next page

Listing 7.9 (Continued) main.cpp: Main program for the supply inventory program

```cpp
    while (choice != 9)
    {
        choice = Menu();
        switch (choice)
        {
            case 1:
                count = NewItem(count, ourSupplies);   // enter new items
                break;
            case 2:
                MonthlyUpdate(count, ourSupplies); // update all items each month
                break;
            case 3:
                ReorderList(count, ourSupplies); // display reorder list
                break;
            case 9:
                break;
            default:
                cout << "\nYou've entered an unavailable option.";
        }
    }

    ofstream writeFile ("Items");
    if (!writeFile)
        cout << "Unexpected file error occurred when opening output file.";
    else
    {
        writeFile << count; // write the number of items in the array
        for (int i = 0; i <= count; i++)
        {
            writeFile << ourSupplies[i].getDesc() << '\0';
            writeFile << ourSupplies[i].getItem_numb() << ' ';
            writeFile << ourSupplies[i].getOn_hand() << ' ';
            writeFile << ourSupplies[i].getReorder_pt() << ' ';

        }
    }
}

int NewItem(int howMany, Item itemArray[])
{
    int iItem_numb, iOn_hand, iReorder_pt;
    char iDesc[81];

    cout << "Description: ";
```

Continued next page

Listing 7.9 (Continued) main.cpp: Main program for the supply inventory program

```cpp
    gets (iDesc);
    while (strlen(iDesc) != 0)   // keep going until "Enter" signals end of input
    {
    // Notice preincrement of howMany. This is necessary because the value of "count"
    // passed in to this function is the highest array index used.

        iItem_numb = ++howMany + 1; // automatically generate the new item number
        cout << "Item number: " << iItem_numb << endl;
        cout << "Amount currently in inventory: ";
        cin >> iOn_hand;
        cout << "Reorder point: ";
        cin >> iReorder_pt;
        itemArray[howMany].InitItem (iItem_numb, iOn_hand, iReorder_pt, iDesc);
        cout << "\nDescription: ";
        gets (iDesc);
    }
    return howMany;
}

void MonthlyUpdate(int howMany, Item itemArray[])
{
    int newAmount;

    cout << "Enter current inventory amount for each item (-1 = no change)"
        << endl;
    for (int i = 0; i <= howMany; i++)
    {
        cout << itemArray[i].getDesc() << " (" << itemArray[i].getOn_hand()
            << "): ";
        cin >> newAmount;
        if (newAmount != -1)
            itemArray[i].ModOn_hand (newAmount);
    }
}

void ReorderList(int howMany,Item itemArray[])
{
    int inStock, Minimum;

    cout << "\nITEMS TO REORDER" << endl;
    cout << "----------------" << endl << endl;
    for (int i = 0; i <= howMany; i++)
    {
        inStock = itemArray[i].getOn_hand();
```

Continued next page

Listing 7.9 (Continued) main.cpp: Main program for the supply inventory program

```
            Minimum = itemArray[i].getReorder_pt();
            if (inStock <= Minimum)
                cout << itemArray[i].getDesc() << ": On hand (" << inStock <<
                    ")  Reorder point (" << Minimum << ")" << endl;
        }
    }

int Menu()
{
    int option;

    cout << "\nPlease choose a menu option:" << endl << endl;
    cout << "1. Enter a new item" << endl;
    cout << "2. Update inventory" << endl;
    cout << "3. View the reorder list" << endl;
    cout << "9. Quit" << endl << endl;
    cout << "Which one? ";
    cin >> option;
    return option;
}
```

Interactive Output

To display the contents of a string variable on the screen, simply insert the variable's name into the cout stream. For example, assuming that iDesc has been declared as an 80-character string,

```
        cout << iDesc;
```

writes the contents of the variable on the screen. The cout stream displays characters until it reaches the terminating null. It does not pad the output field to the width of the array.

Interactive Input

Although there are several ways to perform interactive string input, probably the easiest is to use the gets function, which takes all the characters the user types before pressing the Enter key and inserts them into a string variable. To use gets, include stdio.h in your source file and then simply place the name of the string variable that is to receive the input in the function's parameter list. For example, the supply inventory program accepts a value into the iDesc variable with the following:

```
cout << "Description: ";
gets (iDesc);
```

You can combine gets with the function that checks the length of a string (strlen) to let a user indicate the end of input with a press of the Enter key. The strlen function returns an integer value, the number of characters in a string, not including the terminating null. Therefore, if a program checks the length of a string and finds that the length is zero, the user has pressed Enter without entering any characters. The supply inventory program uses this technique for interactive input of new supply items:

```
cout << "\nDescription: ";
gets (iDesc);

while (strlen(iDesc) != 0)
{
    iItem_numb = ++howMany + 1;
    cout << "Item number: " << iItem_numb << endl;
    cout << "Amount currently in inventory: ";
    cin >> iOn_hand;
    cout << "Reorder point: ";
    cin >> iReorder_pt;
    itemArray[howMany].InitItem (iItem_numb,
        iOn_hand, iReorder_pt, iDesc);
    cout << "\nDescription: ";
    gets (iDesc);
}
```

Notice that this block of code collects a value for iDesc before entering the while loop. This gives the user a chance to prevent any input: If the user presses Enter in response to the first gets. the while loop never executes.

The strlen function takes the name of a string variable or a string constant as its single parameter. The integer result can be assigned to an integer variable, or as in this case, placed in another statement that uses an integer.

Text File Output

When you insert a string into an output stream, the terminating null isn't included. That means that when you write a string to a text file, you must explicitly write the null. In addition, you need to explicitly write a blank after each value that comes from a simple variable. For example, the supply inventory program uses the following statements to write the contents of one Item object to a text file:

```
writeFile << ourSupplies[i].getDesc() << '\0';
writeFile << ourSupplies[i].getItem_numb() << ' ';
writeFile << ourSupplies[i].getOn_hand() << ' ';
writeFile << ourSupplies[i].getReorder_pt() << ' ';
```

File Input

Input from text files that contain strings is subject to the same problems as keyboard input: stream extraction assumes that a space marks the end of a value. The solution is to use an ifstream member function, getline, to read a block of data. The getline function has the following general syntax:

```
stream_name.getline (buffer, size, terminator);
```

The buffer is a string variable that will hold the result of the input. The size parameter is the number of characters that are to be read. The third parameter is optional. If included, it contains the character that marks the end of the string. In that case, the size parameter indicates the maximum number of characters to be read; getline reads characters until it either encounters the terminator or the maximum number of characters have been read. The supply inventory program therefore uses the following statements to read one Item object from a file:

```
readFile.getline (iDesc, 80, '\0');
readFile >> iItem_numb >> iOn_hand >> iReorder_pt;
readFile.get (white_space);
```

The first statement, a call of the getline member function, reads either 80 characters or until a null is encountered. The second statement uses the stream extraction operator to retrieve the three integer values. At this point, the space marking the end of the iReorder_pt value is still in the file. If the program issues another `getline` call immediately, the string read in will have a leading blank that really isn't a part of the string. (No, you can't leave out the final blank; it is needed to mark the end of the third integer value.)

The trick is therefore to read the blank, placing it in a variable whose value is probably never used. The easiest way to read the character is to use the `ifstream` member function `get`, which reads just one character.

Note

To be completely accurate, in some circumstances you can get away without a blank between the end of a number and the beginning of a string. The program stops reading the number when it encounters a character that isn't part of a legal number (for example, a letter). However, this isn't a good programming practice because there is always the chance that a string will begin with a number or a period. It also introduces ambiguity into the file. If you look at it with a text editor, for example, it will be difficult to determine where one data value ends and another begins. Therefore, always put a blank after a number and before a string. Use the `get` function to gobble up the extra blank during input as demonstrated above.

Strings and Functions

Passing a string into a function as a formal parameter is straightforward. However, returning a string from a function with the `return` statement can't be performed without using a pointer. You will see how to perform both of these actions in this section.

Passing Strings into Functions

Because strings are arrays, they are passed into functions just like other arrays. Therefore, using the name of an array as a formal parameter passes the starting address of the array in main memory. Given that this is a pass by reference, any modification you make to the string in the receiving function is made in main memory to the string's original storage location. The change is therefore available to the calling function.

Returning Strings Via the return Statement

When you return an array from a function using the `return` statement, you actually return the array's address, not the data themselves. This value is a pointer to the array's location. You must therefore use pointer notation when declaring a function that returns an array. As a first example, consider the `getDesc` member function used by the `Item` class. Its prototype is as follows:

```
char * getDesc ();
```

The `*` in the return data type means that you will be returning a pointer. In this case, it's a pointer to character data.

Note

There is a bit of a "which came first? the chicken or the egg?" problem when it comes to teaching C++ arrays and pointers. It's tough to explain pointers without first knowing about arrays, but it's also virtually impossible to deal with arrays without dealing with pointers. This book has chosen to look at arrays first. You will therefore find much more about pointers in Chapters 8 and 9.

The function declaration also uses the pointer notation for its return data type.

```
char * Item::getDesc ()
{
    return Desc;
}
```

To return the `Desc` variable, which holds the description of an office supply item, the name of the variable is placed after the `return` statement. As you would expect, this returns the address of the starting point of the array.

Manipulating Arrays of Strings

An array of strings is a two-dimensional array in which each row is one string. Although you can access such an array using two index values, it is generally easier to eliminate the column subscript by using a `typedef` statement to create a string data type. As an example, consider the following statements:

```
typedef char string[81];
string children[10];
```

The children array holds 10 strings, each of which can be up to 80 characters long plus a terminating null. To reference the third string in the array, you would then use children[2]. This produces the starting address of the array's third element, which in turn is an array 81 elements long.

Arrays of strings are used extensively by the program written for the corner pharmacy. For example, in Listing 7.10 you can see the declaration of the Drug class. This class includes three integers (the drug number, a count of the number of generic equivalents, and a count of the number of conflicting drugs). The strings all hold drug names. Their storage allocations are based on the typedef of the string data type that you saw in the preceding paragraph.

The drug name is therefore an 81-character array (an 80-character string with an extra space for the terminating null). The names of generic equivalents for and the names of drugs that conflict with the drug are contained in arrays of strings. Using the string data type means that arrays of strings can be handled as one-dimensional strings, without worrying about specifying the second dimension. The generics array has room for five generic equivalents; the conflicts array can hold 20 interacting drugs.

Listing 7.10   The Drug class from the pharmacy program

```
class Drug
{
    private:
        int drug_numb;
        string drug_name;
        string generics[GENERICS]; // an array for generic equivalents
        string conflicts[CONFLICTS]; // array for conflicting drugs
        int numb_generics, numb_conflicts;

    public:
        // constructor that loads data from disk--stream is passed in
        Drug(ifstream &);
        // constructor that handles interactive I/O
        Drug(int, int, int, string, string[], string[]);
        void writeDrug(ofstream&); // function that writes to disk
        int checkInteraction (string); // check for drug interaction
        int getDrug_numb();
        char * getDrug_name();
        string * getGenerics(int *);
        string * getConflicts(int *);
};
```

Note

The class in Listing 7.10 contains some concepts to which you have not been introduced. For example, there are two constructors, each with different parameter lists. C++ uses a combination of a function's name and its parameter list to distinguish one function from another. Therefore, the two constructors are actually different functions, despite having the same name. You will read and learn about this technique (known as *overloading*) and other techniques employed by the pharmacy program throughout the rest of this book.

Sorting Arrays of Strings

To sort an array of strings, placing its contents in alphabetical order, you need to compare two strings and decide which precedes the other. Regardless of the method of sorting you use, the process is based on the strcmp function to which you were introduced earlier in this chapter.

The pharmacy program uses strcmp in a bubble sort to order the contents of the generics and conflicts arrays. Both arrays are sorted by the same function (sortArray in Listing 7.11). This function takes two parameters: the array and a count of the number of items in the array. When looking at this code, remember that an array used as a formal parameter is always passed by reference. Therefore, any changes made to the array in the function are made to the original array rather than a copy that is local to the function.

As you will remember from your first look at the bubble sort in Chapter 6, the algorithm swaps two elements in the array when the value in an element is greater than the value in the following element. To make this evaluation, sortArray uses the strcmp function. If the result is greater than 1 (the string in element i alphabetically follows the string in element i+1), the strings are swapped. The swap involves copying the string in element i to a temporary storage location, copying string i+1 to element i, and then restoring the value currently in the temporary location to array element i+1. Notice that the only real difference between this sort and the sort in Chapter 6 is that the copying takes place using the strcpy function rather than the assignment operator.

Listing 7.11   The sortArray function

```
void sortArray (string source[], int count)
{
    int result, i;
    string temp;

    result = SWAP_MADE;
    while (result == SWAP_MADE)
    {
        result = NO_SWAP;
        for (i = 0; i < count; i++)
        {
            if (strcmp(source[i],source[i+1]) > 0)
            {
                strcpy(temp,source[i]);
                strcpy(source[i],source[i+1]);
                strcpy(source[i+1],temp);
                result = SWAP_MADE;
            }
        }
    }
}
```

Searching Arrays of Strings

There are many ways to search arrays. If the array contains only a few elements, then a sequential search, a search in which a program examines every element in the array, beginning at element 0, is relatively efficient. Because the `conflicts` array holds no more than 20 strings, the pharmacy program uses a sequential search to determine whether a particular drug conflicts with the drug described by a given object. This search is handled by the `checkInteraction` member function (Listing 7.12).

Listing 7.12   The checkInteraction function

```
int Drug::checkInteraction (string drug2check)
{
    for (int i = 0; i <= numb_conflicts; i++)
    {
        if (strcmp (drug2check, conflicts[i]) == 0 )
            return TRUE;
    }
    return FALSE;
}
```

The function accepts a string as an input parameter. This is a drug name supplied by the calling program. The function then looks at each element in the `conflicts` array. If the `strcmp` function finds a match, the function returns a 1 (the constant `TRUE`); if no match can be found after all elements in the `conflicts` array have been checked, the function returns a 0 (the constant `FALSE`).

Note

As the number of elements in an array gets larger, a sequential search becomes less and less efficient. Probably the most efficient search technique is a binary search, which you will see in Chapter 9. The drawback to a binary search is that it must be performed on an ordered list. In other words, if you are going to use it on an array of strings, they must first be sorted in alphabetical order.

Using Strings to Implement a Generic Menu Class

Throughout this book you have been encouraged to separate system-dependent I/O from the implementation of classes. That does not mean that objects are never used to handle I/O. In fact, most graphic user interfaces are supported in an object-oriented environment through a hierarchy of classes that provide windows, menus, dialog boxes, and so on. Because user interface class libraries are highly system-dependent, the details of any specific user interface are beyond the scope of this book. However, to give you a feeling for how such classes work, this section contains a text-based menu class that you can use to implement menus for any C++ program with a text-based interface.

The declaration for the `menu` class can be found in Listing 7.13. This class provides for menus of up to 20 items, each of which can be up to 40 characters long. (The 41st element in the `menuoption` array is to hold the terminating null.) A menu also has a title of up to 25 characters.

A `menu` object knows how to do three things: initialize itself, display its title and options, and accept a choice of a menu option from a user. As you can see in Listing 7.14, the constructor requires a string for the menu's title, the array containing the menu options (an array of strings), and a count of the number of menu options.

From where do these values come? Typically, specifications of elements of the user interface are placed in a *resource file*. (A *resource* is a program element, such as a menu or window, used by a program.) Although resource definitions could be placed in the main program file, the main program will be

Listing 7.13   menu.h: Header file for a generic menu class

```
const ITEM_LEN = 41;
const MAX_ITEMS = 20;
typedef char menuoption [ITEM_LEN];

class menu        // class for a menu of up to MAX_ITEMS
{
    private:
        char menutitle[26];
        menuoption menuitems [MAX_ITEMS];   // array to hold the items
        int count;  // # of options in the menu

    public:
        menu (char [], menuoption [], int); // constructor
        void displaymenu (void);
        int chooseoption (void);
};
```

cleaner and shorter if resources are defined in their own file. In addition, keeping resources separate form the code that uses them hides the details of the interface from the rest of the program, making it easier to change resources without modifying other parts of the program. Resource files also make it much easier to port a program from one graphic user interface to another and provide a way to incorporate resources developed by other programmers into a program.

The resource file for the pharmacy program appears in Listing 7.15. This file creates one string for each menu title and one array of menu options for each menu. Notice that to initialize the arrays of strings, the values are placed inside braces and that the individual strings are separated by commas. The resource file also takes care of initializing variables for the number of options in each menu. In addition, it sets up constants that can be used in switch statements to make identifying selected menu options easier.

How a resource file is used is highly dependent on the environment in which you are working. In this particular case, the resource file is actually nothing more than a special-purpose header file. It is therefore included in the main program's file with a #include directive. The variables defined in the resource file are then available to the main program, which can use them when it defines menu objects. The main program therefore includes the object definitions in Listing 7.16.

Listing 7.14   menu.cpp: Member functions for a generic menu class

```
#include <iostream.h>
#include <string.h>
#include "menu.h"

menu::menu (char title[], menuoption menutext[], int numbitems)
{
    strcpy (menutitle, title);
    count = numbitems;
    for (int i = 0; i <= count; i++)
        strcpy (menuitems[i], menutext[i]);
}

void menu::displaymenu ()
{
    cout << endl;
    cout << "---------- " << menutitle << " ----------" << endl << endl;
    for (int i = 0; i <= count; i++)
        cout << menuitems[i] << endl;
    cout << endl;
}

int menu::chooseoption ()
{
    int choice;

    cout << "Enter an option: ";
    cin >> choice;
    return choice;
}
```

Listing 7.15   menu.rsc: Resource file to be used by a generic
                   menu class

```
#include "menu.h"

menuoption maintitle = "MAIN MENU";
menuoption mainmenu [] = {"1. Manage drug information",
                          "2. Manage customer information",
                          "3. Manage prescriptions",
                          "9. Quit"};

int mainmenucount = 4;

const DRUGS = 1;
const CUSTOMERS = 2;
const PRESCRIPTS = 3;
```

Continued next page

Listing 7.15 (Continued) menu.rsc: Resource file to be used by a generic menu class

```
const MAIN_QUIT = 9;

menuoption drugtitle = "DRUG MENU";
menuoption drugmenu [] = {"1. Enter a new drug",
                          "2. View all drugs",
                          "9. Return to main menu"};

int drugmenucount = 3;

const NEW_DRUG = 1;
const SEE_DRUGS = 2;
const DRUG_QUIT = 9;

menuoption custtitle = "CUSTOMER MENU";
menuoption custmenu [] = {"1. Enter a new customer",
                          "2. View all customers",
                          "3. Print mailing labels",
                          "9. Return to main menu"};

int custmenucount = 4;

const NEW_CUST = 1;
const SEE_CUST = 2;
const LABELS = 3;
const CUST_QUIT = 9;

menuoption prescripttitle = "PRESCRIPTION MENU";
menuoption prescriptmenu [] = {"1. Enter a new prescription",
                               "2. Print a prescription label",
                               "3. Refill a prescription",
                               "9. Return to main menu"};

int prescriptmenucount = 4;

const NEW_PRESCRIPT = 1;
const BOTTLE = 2;
const REFILL = 3;
const PRESCRIPT_QUIT = 9;
```

Listing 7.16   Menu object declarations

```
menu MainMenu (maintitle, mainmenu, mainmenucount),
    DrugMenu (drugtitle, drugmenu, drugmenucount),
    CustMenu (custtitle, custmenu, custmenucount),
    PrescriptMenu (prescripttitle, prescriptmenu,prescriptmenucount);
```

The result is four menu objects, each of which uses one set of data from the resource file.

To display a menu, the program uses the `displaymenu` function for the appropriate menu object. To let the user make a choice from the menu, the program can call the `chooseoption` function. For example, managing the main menu is handled with:

```
MainMenu.displaymenu();
chosenOption = MainMenu.chooseoption();
```

Why should you bother to implement menus in this way? First, once you have the menu class and its member functions declared, you can use them in any text-based program, without having to rewrite menu code each time you create a new program. All you have to do is create a resource file that is tailored to a given program's specific needs. Second, it further separates platform-dependent I/O code from other parts of the program. Should you choose to port your program to another environment, you can use other menu objects and resource files, reducing (but not eliminating) the amount of modification you need to make to other parts of the program.

Summary

C++ implements strings as arrays of characters. Each string is terminated by a null, which is represented as the character '\0'. An array declared to contain a string should therefore be one character longer than needed so there is room for the terminating null.

The fact that strings are arrays has numerous implications for how they are stored and manipulated. In particular, most string operations are performed using C library functions rather than the standard operators. The most commonly used functions include:

- `strcpy` (copy a string from one storage location to another)
- `strcat` (concatenate one string on the end of another)
- `strlen` (determine the number of characters in a string)
- `strcmp` (compare to strings to determine their relative position in an alphabetical ordering sequence)

String I/O is complicated by the presence of blanks, which the default I/O streams view as the end of a value. To input an entire string from the keyboard, use the `gets` function, which takes everything up to the press of the Enter key as part of one string. To output a string to the screen, simply include the string variable's name in the `cout` stream.

When working with text files, strings must be explicitly followed by nulls; the values of simple variables written to the same file must be explicitly followed by blanks. When reading such files, the blank preceding a string must be read and discarded. The strings themselves are read with the `ifstream` member function `getline`.

Like other arrays, the name of a string variable is the address of the beginning of the array in main memory. All strings are passed to functions by reference. When a string is a return value from a function, its address is passed to the calling function.

Arrays of strings are two-dimensional arrays. Working with them can be simplified by using `typedef` to define a data type for a string, which can then be used when declaring the array. This makes it possible to reference entire strings within the array using only a single index.

Exercises

1. Create a class that holds a string of up to 80 characters. Include a member function that reverses the order of the characters in the string. Write a program that demonstrates that the reversal function works.

2. Write a program that manipulates a class that stores a person's name. The name is entered in the format "Last, First." The class should include a member program that reformats the name so it is displayed in the format "First Last." Create the program so that it demonstrates that the name reversal function works.

3. Assume that you are an industrial spy trying to break the data encryption scheme used by one of your employer's competitors. One of your basic techniques is to examine the frequency of characters in a block of text. Create a class that holds a string of up to 256 characters. Include a member function that scans the string and counts the frequency with which each letter in the string appears. (Ignore spaces and punctuation marks; treat

uppercase and lowercase letters the same.) When the scan is finished, display the frequency counts. Write a program that demonstrates that the frequency count member function works.

4. Create a class that manages a game of Hangman (the word guessing game). The class should store the solution word (the word the player is trying to guess), the correct guesses so far, the number of guesses made, and the maximum guesses allowed. (Maximum guesses are equal to the length of the solution word plus seven.) Write a program that plays the game. Create a text file for the program that contains a list of words to be used as solutions. When the program begins, read those words into an array of strings. At the beginning of each game, randomly select a word from the solutions array and store it in the game object. Member functions of the class should include evaluating a guess against the solution, storing a correct guess in its proper position in the word (use this string for output after each guess), and storing the number of guesses made. After each guess, the game object should determine the game status (won, in progress, or maximum number of guesses exceeded). After each guess that doesn't result in a win or a loss, print out the letters guessed correctly in their correct position in the word, using underscores (_) as placeholders for letters not yet guessed. Be sure to allow the player to play many games without exiting the program.

5. Write a program that performs simple arithmetic (add, subtract, multiply, divide) using Roman numerals. The class on which this program is based should include a string for a Roman numeral and an integer for its integer equivalent. The class will need functions to convert from a Roman numeral to an integer and from an integer to a Roman numeral.

    The program that manipulates objects created from the class should let users enter expressions in typical arithmetic format, such as:

    XXX- XV

    The program should then scan the string to find the Roman numerals and the operator. You should consider writing functions that scan a string for a specific character and, once the character has been found, extracting parts of a string based on the position of that character in the string. (Note: There are C library functions that do these things, but you will learn much more about manipulating strings if you write them yourself.)

Once the program has performed the arithmetic, it should convert the result back to a Roman numeral for display.

6. Write a program that grades true/false exams of up to 30 questions. The key to the exam should be stored in a single string, such as "TFT-FFFFFFF." Student data should be stored in objects created from a class that contains the student ID, a string for the student's responses on the exam, and the number of correct responses. The class should include a member function that scores the exam. The program that manipulates objects should include an array for student objects. After scoring all the exams, the program should prepare and display a frequency distribution of correct responses along with a display of the ID number and score for each student, sorted in descending order by score.

7. The HHH Hardware House employs a number of salespeople, each of whom works within one of the company's five sales territories. At the end of each year, the company prepares an annual sales summary. Write a program that produces this summary. The program should be based on a class that stores a salesperson's name, territory, and total sales for the year. Use an array to store objects created from the class.

The summary report should be organized by sales territory. Within each territory, display the salespeople and their total sales, sorted in descending order by sales. Compute the total sales for each territory (displayed immediately after all the salespeople from that territory). At the end of the program, display the total sales for the entire company.

8. (General Ledger) Create a class that represents one account from a chart of accounts. Include the account number, the name of the account, the type of account, and the account's current balance. Write a program to test the class that does the following:

Long

- Reads accounts in from a text file.
- Creates new accounts interactively.

- Writes accounts back to a text file.
- Sorts the accounts by account number and displays a chart of accounts.

Include member functions as needed to support the functionality of the program.

Long

9. (Purchasing) Create the four classes that will form the basis of a purchasing program: Vendor, Item, Purchase Order, and Line Item. Write a program to test the classes that does the following:

- Reads each class in from a text file.
- Creates new objects interactively.
- Writes each class back to a text file.
- Displays the contents of the objects on the screen.

Include member functions as needed to support the functionality of the program.

Long

10. (Temporary Employment Agency) Create the three classes that will form the basis of a program to handle the assignments of workers for a temporary employment agency: Employee, Employer, and Work Assignment. Write a program to test the classes that does the following:

- Reads each class in from a text file.
- Creates new objects interactively.
- Writes each class back to a text file.
- Displays the contents of objects on the screen.

Include member functions as needed to support the functionality of the program.

8

Introducing Pointers

OBJECTIVES

In this chapter you will learn about:
- Declaring and initializing pointer variables.
- Accessing data in pointer variables.
- Using the "this" pointer.
- Using dynamic binding to create objects and access member functions.
- Returning multiple values from functions.
- Using the addresses of I/O streams as function parameters.

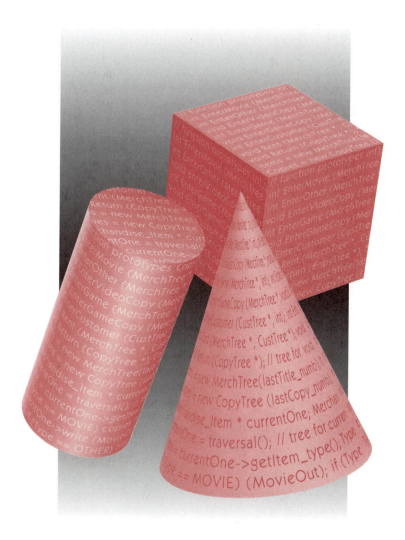

As you know, a pointer is the starting address of a value in main memory. A pointer can point to a simple variable type (for example, an integer or a character), to an array, or to an object. Pointers make it possible to return more than one value from a function. They can also be used to ease and speed access to objects and arrays.

In this chapter you will be introduced to using pointers and pointer variables, manipulating pointers to access memory, using dynamic binding to create objects, and using pointers to pass values to and from functions. Chapter 9 looks at ways in which you can use pointers to speed up sorting and searching as well as the use of pointers to create some common data structures.

To show you how pointers work, we will be looking at the pharmacy program to which you were introduced in Chapter 7 along with some small programs that demonstrate the uses of pointers. These samples include two versions of a program that counts the number of values in a string. The vowel statistics program produces output like that in Figure 8.1. (The difference between the two versions of the program lies in how values are passed into and returned from a function; the output is the same.)

Working with Pointer Variables

A *pointer variable* is a variable that is declared to hold a pointer to some type of data storage. The contents of a pointer variable are therefore interpreted as a main memory address rather than a data value. To make this a bit clearer,

```
Enter a string of up to 80 characters:
Then, several people ran up to him and sang a joyous song

The vowels in the string are:
   A: 5
   E: 5
   I: 1
   O: 5
   U: 2

There are 18 vowels.
```

Figure 8.1 Output from the vowel statistics program

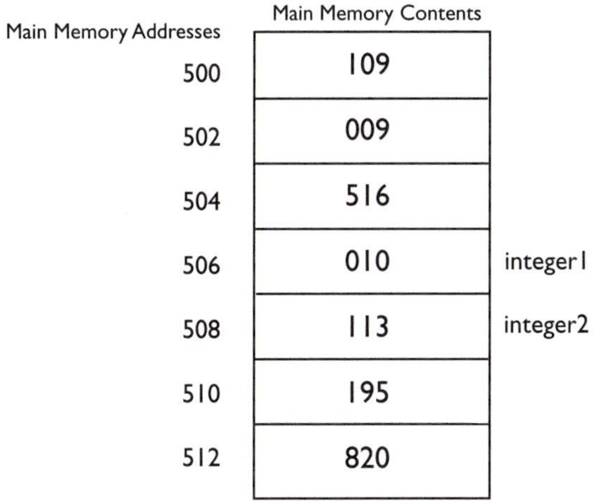

Figure 8.2   Sample contents of memory locations

consider Figure 8.2, which contains a portion of a computer's memory. This memory segment contains a group of 16-bit integers. Therefore, the addresses on the left increase by two. (Remember that main memory addresses are assigned to individual bytes. A 16-bit integer therefore occupies two bytes, and a block of integers in main memory will have starting addresses two bytes from each other.)

Two of the memory locations are referenced by the variables `integer1` and `integer2`. When a program uses `integer1`, the computer accesses memory location 506 and uses the 010 that it finds in that location. By the same token, when a program uses `integer2`, the computer accesses memory location 508 and uses the 113 it finds in that location. In the next section, you will see exactly how pointer variables can provide access to the same locations but in a different way.

Declaring Pointer Variables

To declare a pointer variable, use the following general syntax:

```
data_type * variable_name;
```

The asterisk tells the compiler that the following variable will hold a pointer to the specified type of storage. For example, you could declare pointer variables that would ultimately hold the addresses of `integer1` and `integer2` with:

```
int * integer1Ptr, * integer2Ptr;
```

Although there is no formal naming convention for pointer variables, we often append the characters *Ptr* to the name of the variable to which the pointer variable will point.

One version of the vowel statistics includes the following declarations in its main program:

```
int A, * APtr, E, * EPtr, I, * IPtr, O, * OPtr,
    U, * UPtr, theTotal, * TotalPtr;
```

This statement sets aside six integer variables (A. E, I, O, U, theTotal) that will hold the counts of the vowels in a string. It also sets aside a pointer variable for each integer variable (APtr, EPtr, IPtr, OPtr, Uptr, TotalPtr). Notice that an asterisk precedes each pointer variable.

Pointers to Objects

One of the most common uses of pointer variables in an object-oriented program is to hold pointers to objects. For example, the pharmacy program uses an array of pointers to hold references to Drug objects:

```
Drug * drugs[DRUG_MAX];
```

The preceding declaration sets up an array named drugs. Each element in the array contains a pointer to an object of class Drug. Each of those pointers indicates the starting location in memory for an object created from the Drug class. (The objects are created with dynamic binding, and their addresses are assigned to elements in this array. You will see how to do this later in this chapter.)

A class may also contain pointer variables. As an example, take a look at the Prescription class in Listing 8.1. Objects created from this class participate in two data structures. The first—a linked list—joins the prescription to other prescriptions for the same customer. The "next" prescription in the list is indicated by a pointer variable called nextPrescript. The second data structure is a binary tree, which maintains the prescriptions in prescription number order so that a single prescription can be found quickly. To maintain the binary tree, a prescription needs two additional pointers, one to its right child in the tree (`right`) and one to its left child in the tree (`left`). Notice that the data type of these variables is `Prescription`, the same as the class.

Listing 8.1   The Prescription class

```
class Prescription
{
    private:
        int drug_numb;
        int prescription_numb, numb_refills, refills_left, FDA_numb,
            controlled;
        char doctor[31], doctor_phone[13];
        date_string prescription_date, refill_dates[10];
        Prescription * nextPrescript; // pointer to next in list
        Prescription * right; // pointer to right child in tree
        Prescription * left; // pointer to left child in tree

    public:
        Prescription(ifstream &);
        Prescription(int, int, int, int, char [], char[], date_string);
        void writePrescription(ofstream &);
        void setPrescriptPtr (Prescription *);
        int refill();
        void bottleLabel(Customer *, strstream &, drugArray *);
        Prescription * getNextPrescript(); // get next prescription in list
        void setRight (Prescription *); // set right child pointer in tree
        Prescription * getRight (); // return right child pointer in tree
        void setLeft (Prescription *); // set left child pointer in tree
        Prescription * getLeft (); // return left child pointer in tree
        char * getDoc();
        char * getDocPhone();
        int getPrescript_numb ();
        int getDrug_numb ();
};
```

Note   The `Prescription` class, and the `Customer` class that you will see shortly, have more than one constructor. This isn't an error; it's an object-oriented technique known as *overloading*. You will learn about overloading in Chapter 11.

Note

Linked lists and binary trees are *data structures*, ways in which you can organize groups of objects. You will learn much more about them in Chapter 9.

A class might also contain a pointer to an object of a different type. For example, the pharmacy program's Customer class includes a pointer to the next customer in a list of customers, but also includes a pointer to a special object (PrescriptList) that manages the customer's list of prescriptions.

Listing 8.2   The Customer class

```
class Customer
{
    private:
        char fname[16], lname[16], street[31], city [21], state[3], zip[6],
            phone [13];
        PrescriptList * PrescriptHeader; // pointer to prescription list object
        Customer * nextCust; // pointer to next customer

    public:
        Customer(ifstream &);
        Customer(char [], char [], char [], char [], char [], char [], char []);
        void setPrescriptPtr (PrescriptList *); // pointer to prescription object
        void setNextPtr (Customer *); // pointer to next customer
        void writeCustomer(ofstream &);
        Customer * getNext (); // pointer to next customer
        void mailingLabel (strstream &);
        char * getZip ();
        char * getLName ();
        char * getFName ();
        char * getStreet ();
        char * getCSZ();
        char * getPhone ();
        PrescriptList * getPrescriptHeader(); // pointer to prescription header
        int checkNewDrug (string, drugArray *);
};
```

Forward References

When you start including pointers to objects of a different class within a class definition, you can run into a problem. The compiler won't accept a pointer to a class until the class has been defined. This presents a bit of a dilemma for the pharmacy program. The objects that manipulate data structures have to be declared before they can be used in other classes, but the other classes need to include pointers to the objects that manipulate data structures. There is a simple way around this circular problem: include a *forward reference* to a class in a header file, before the class is defined.

A forward reference includes the keyword `class` and the name of the class. It tells the compiler that a class by that name will be defined later. For example, the header file for the pharmacy program includes the statement:

```
class PrescriptList;
```

By placing this statement before the definition of the `Customer` class, the compiler won't flag an error when it encounters a reference to the `PrescriptList` class prior to the class's declaration.

Initializing Pointer Variables

To initialize a pointer variable, a program uses the assignment operator to copy the address of a storage location. Placing an ampersand (&) in front of a variable name indicates that you want the address of a variable rather than its contents. For example, you could initialize the integer pointer variables that we've been considering with:

```
integer1Ptr = &integer1;
integer2Ptr = &integer2;
```

After the initialization, `integer1Ptr` contains 506; `integer2Ptr` contains 508.

The following statements from one version of the vowel statistics program place the address of an integer variable into a variable that holds an integer pointer:

```
APtr = &A;
EPtr = &E;
IPtr = &I;
OPtr = &O;
UPtr = &U;
TotalPtr = &theTotal;
```

A pointer variable can also be initialized by assigning it the result of a function that returns a pointer. As you will see shortly, this is exactly what happens when you create an object using dynamic binding.

Because the name of an array is a pointer to the start of the array in main memory, you can use the name of an array, without any array indexes, as if it were a pointer variable. However, as you will see shortly, some uses of pointers include modifying the value of the pointer itself. If the pointer variable happens to be the name of an array, changing it in any way will cause the program to lose track of where the array's contents are actually stored. To avoid that problem, declare a separate pointer variable to hold the array's address and initialize it to the address of the array:

```
char stringArray[81];
char * stringArrayPtr;
stringArrayPtr = stringArray;
```

Once `stringArrayPtr` has been initialized, it points to the same location as `stringArray`. However, because `stringArrayPtr` is a separate variable from `stringArray`, you can modify the contents of `stringArrayPtr` without losing track of the original beginning of the array.

Accessing Values Using the Contents of Pointer Variables

To access a value in a location pointed to by a pointer variable, you must tell the C++ compiler that you want the contents of the storage location rather than the address of the location. This is known as *dereferencing* the pointer. Dereferencing is performed by placing an asterisk in front of the pointer variable's name. For example, you can gain contents to `integer1Ptr` and `integer2Ptr` with:

```
*integer1Ptr
*integer2Ptr
```

Using the first expression in a program provides 010 (the contents of location 506); using the second expression provides 113 (the contents of location 508).

Dereferencing can occur on the right or left side of an assignment operator. For example, the member function that computes vowel statistics initializes the variables that count the number of vowels with the following statements:

Why bother to use a pointer variable? Wouldn't it be easier to simply use the original variable? If a variable is going to be used locally within only one function, then it is certainly easier to use the variable without working with a pointer. However, if the variable needs to be passed into a function where it will be modified and returned, you may want to use pointer notation to return multiple values from the function. (You will be introduced to this technique at the end of this chapter.)

Pointer Arithmetic

One of the most common uses of dereferencing pointers is to simplify stepping through blocks of storage in main memory. You do this by performing *pointer arithmetic* (any arithmetic operation performed on a main memory address). As an example, let's look at a program that performs two operations on a string. The first is to determine where one string begins within another; the second generates a substring. The program collects a string that is stored in an object. It then asks the user for a shorter string for which it is to search and reports where the shorter string begins in the object's string. Finally, the program asks for the starting position and length of a substring and finishes by displaying a substring. A sample run of this program can be found in Figure 8.3.

```
Enter a string to store: This is the string being tested
Enter a string to match: the string being
The first string begins at position 8 in the second.

Enter starting position for substring: 8
Enter length of substring: 5

The substring is "the s"
```

Figure 8.3   Output of the String Stuff program

The class on which the String Stuff program is based appears in Listing 8.3. It has just one class variable—a string. The four member functions are the constructor, an initialization function that assigns data to the string, the function that searches for one string within the other (searchString), and the function that produces the substring (subString).

The class on which the String Stuff program is based appears in Listing 8.3. It has just one class variable—a string. The four member functions are the constructor, an initialization function that assigns data to the string, the function that searches for one string within the other (`searchString`), and the function that produces the substring (`subString`).

Listing 8.3 match.h: Header file for the String Stuff program

```
class stringStuff
{
    private:
        char theString[81];
    public:
        stringStuff();
        void init (char []);
        int searchString (char []);
        char * subString (int, int);
};
```

The `main` function that controls the String Stuff program is relatively simple. (Most of the work in this program occurs in the member functions.) As you can see in Listing 8.4, it gathers the string that is stored in the `string-Stuff` object and initializes the object. Then, it gathers the string for the matching function, calls the function, and displays the result. The `main` function then immediately gathers the data for the substring function. It calls the function and shows the substring (if it was possible to extract a substring).

Listing 8.4 Main.cpp for the String Stuff program

```
#include <iostream.h>
#include <stdio.h>
#include "match.h"

void main ()
{
    stringStuff oneString; // delcare an object
    char ustring[81]; // utility string
    char * stringPtr;
    int matchPos, istart, ilength;

    cout << "Enter a string to store: ";
    gets (ustring);
    oneString.init (ustring); // initialize the object
```

Listing 8.4 (Continued) Main.cpp for the String Stuff program

```
cout << "Enter a string to match: ";
gets (ustring);
matchPos = oneString.searchString(ustring);
cout << "The second string begins at position " << matchPos << " in the
second.";

cout << "\n\nEnter starting position for substring: " ;
```
Continued next page
```
cin >> istart;
cout << "Enter length of substring: ";
cin >> ilength;
stringPtr = oneString.subString (istart, ilength);
if (ustring == 0)
    cout << "\nCouldn't take the substring.";
else
    cout << "\nThe substring is \"" << stringPtr << "\"";
}
```

Taking a Substring

As just mentioned, the real work of the String Stuff program occurs in the member functions. To begin examining how pointer arithmetic is used to access the contents of arrays, let's look first at the subString function, which extracts a portion of a string, given a starting position in the original string and the number of characters to extract (Listing 8.5).

Listing 8.5   The subString member function from the String Stuff Program

```
char * stringStuff::subString (int start, int length)
{
    static char SubString[81]; // storage for substring; must be static
    char * SubStringPtr; // need to be able to step through string
    char * theStringPtr; // don't want to modify value stored in class

    theStringPtr = theString;
    SubStringPtr = SubString;
    if (start < strlen(theString))
    {
        theStringPtr = theStringPtr + start;
        while ((length--) && (*theStringPtr != '\0'))
            *SubStringPtr++ = *theStringPtr++;
        *SubStringPtr = '\0'; // add terminating null
        return SubString;
    }
```

Listing 8.5 The subString member function from the String Stuff Program

```
return 0; // couldn't take substring
}
```

The function begins by declaring a variable in which the substring will be stored (SubString). Notice that this variable's storage class has been changed from the default auto to static. This has been done to make sure that the variable isn't destroyed when the function terminates. The function returns a pointer to the substring. The string itself therefore must be left in main memory so that there are meaningful data in the pointer's location when the calling function attempts to access it.

The subString function also uses two pointer variables. The first, SubStringPtr, is initialized to the address of the SubString variable. Although the name of an array can be used as a pointer variable, the function is going to be doing arithmetic with the pointer. Using this pointer variable means that the address of SubString remains unchanged and can therefore be used as the function's return value.

The second pointer variable (theStringPtr) is initialized to the address of the class variable theString. The function uses this variable, rather than the class variable, because pointer arithmetic would change the location of an object's data, making the entire string inaccessible.

To begin, the subString function performs a simple error check: If the starting position of the substring is greater than or equal to the length of theString, then it isn't possible to create a substring. In that case, the program returns 0.

However, if the substring can be taken, then the program enters a while loop that copies characters from theString into SubString. It does so by using the pointer variables. A single character in theString is referenced by writing *theStringPtr; a single character in SubString is referenced by *SubStringPtr. The increment operator (++) following each pointer variable name increases the values in the pointer variables by one byte after copying a character.

The important thing to keep in mind about pointer arithmetic is that the amount that is added to or subtracted from a pointer depends on the type of data to which the pointer points. For example, if you have set up a pointer to an array of long integers and your computer uses 32-bit long integers, then incrementing the pointer adds four bytes to the pointer; adding 2 to the pointer adds eight bytes. If your pointer variable points to an array of floating point values, then each increment of 1 adds the number of bytes in your computer's floating point format. In the String Stuff program, each array element is a character. The increment therefore adds one byte to the address stored in each pointer variable.

Once all the characters have been copied, the subString function appends a null to the end of the substring. It can then return the address of the SubString variable. If you look back at Listing 8.4, you'll notice that the main function has declared a pointer to a string variable into which the return value is placed.

Looking for One String Within Another

The searchString function, which looks for one string within another, can be found in Listing 8.6. To determine whether the input string (stored in iString) is completely contained within theString, the function compares every character in iString to every character in theString. However, it's not enough to begin the comparison with the first character of theString. Because iString could begin anywhere within theString, the function must perform repeated comparisons, beginning with each character in theString.

The searchString function uses three pointer variables:

- theStringPtr: a pointer to theString that can be used in pointer arithmetic so that the address of theString doesn't need to be changed.
- moveablePtr: another pointer to theString that can be used in pointer arithmetic.
- iStringPtr: a pointer to iString that can be used in pointer arithmetic, leaving the address of iString intact.

The function also uses two variables (theStringCount and iStringCount) that hold the length of the two strings.

Before checking to see if the input string is contained within the class's string, the searchString function needs to figure out at what point it should stop checking. When there are fewer characters left in theString than there are in the input string, there's no reason to continue; it would be impossible for the input string to be contained within theString. The computation of the stopping point is stored in the variable charCount, which is decre-

Listing 8.6   The searchString member function from the String Stuff program

```
// locate where input string begins inside theString
// return index of where first matching character occurs (-1 if not found)
int stringStuff::searchString (char iString[])
{
    // create pointer variables for the strings so we don't modify the
    // original strings in main memory
    char * theStringPtr, * moveablePtr, * iStringPtr;
    int theStringCount, iStringCount; // variables to hold lengths of strings
    int theStringPos = 0, charCount, iStringPos;

    theStringCount = strlen(theString);
    iStringCount = strlen(iString);

    charCount = theStringCount - iStringCount + 1;
    moveablePtr = theString;

    while (charCount--)
    {
        theStringPtr = moveablePtr++; // moves beginning of theStringPtr
        iStringPtr = iString; // start over each time @ beginning of iString
        iStringPos = iStringCount;

    // compare against current state of theString (pointed to by theStringPtr)
    // this loops through every character in iString
        while ((*(iStringPtr++)) == *(theStringPtr++)) && (iStringPos--))
            ; // this is an empty while loop

        if (iStringPos == 0) // match was found
            return theStringPos;
        else
            theStringPos++;
    }
    return -1;
}
```

mented as the outer `while` loop iterates. If `charCount` drops to zero without finding a match, then the function returns a -1 to indicate that no match was found.

Inside the outer while, `searchString` uses an empty `while` loop (a loop with nothing in its body) to step through the characters being compared. The loop's control condition dereferences each of the string pointers to compare the contents of individual storage locations. The control condition also keeps track of how many characters in the input string have been checked.

After evaluating the control condition, the computer increments each pointer variable and decrements the counter. If the counter drops to zero and the characters in the two strings have been identical, a match has been found. The function can then return an integer that represents the position in theString where the match begins.

The this Pointer

A C++ programs maintains a special pointer that contains the address of the object with which the program is currently working: this. The this pointer can be used in several ways. For example, it can greatly simplify copying one object to another. Remember the laborious variable-by-variable copy function used in the bubble sort of an array of objects in Chapter 6? That entire function can be replaced with the following:

```
void OneSurvey::copy (OneSurvey inputObject)
{
    *this = inputObject;
}
```

The assignment statement that now forms the body of the function takes each variable in the object that is being passed in as a formal parameter and assigns those values to the current object. Notice that the this pointer is dereferenced, indicating the assignment is not to assign the address of inputObject to the current object, but instead to modify the contents of the current object.

The assignment you have just seen is actually provided by the compiler. In other words, the compiler includes code in the object file that copies the contents of each variable from the source object to the destination object, just as the copy function from Chapter 6 acted. If this happens to be what you want, then use this type of assignment. However, if you aren't doing a direct copy, but instead are manipulating the data in some other way as you perform the copy, then you'll need to handle the copying of each variable individually.

Dynamic Binding

Dynamic binding is a technique for creating objects while a program is running. It has two major advantages over static binding. First, a programmer doesn't need to be able to predict how many objects will be needed; they can be created on the fly. Second, dynamic binding provides better memory management. No storage is set aside for objects that might not be used; memory can be released when objects are no longer needed. In this section you will learn how to create objects using dynamic binding and how to access member functions for objects that are created in this way.

Creating Objects for Use with Dynamic Binding

To create an object using dynamic binding, use the keyword new, followed by the name of the class from which the object is to be created and a parameter list that matches the class's constructor. The new operation returns a pointer to the object just created. For example, the pharmacy program uses the code in Listing 8.7 to create a new Customer object. This code, which forms a part of a function in the main program, collects the data needed to initialize the new object and then passes that data into the constructor, which is executed automatically when the object is created.

Listing 8.7   Creating a new customer using dynamic binding

```
char ifname[16], ilname[16], istreet[31], icity [21], istate[3], izip[6],
    iphone [13];
Customer * newCust; // need a place to put the pointer to the newly created object

cout << "\nFirst name: ";
gets (ifname);
cout << "\nLast name: ";
gets (ilname);
cout << "\nStreet: ";
gets (istreet);
cout << "\nCity: ";
gets (icity);
cout << "\nState: ";
gets (istate);
cout << "\nZip: ";
gets (izip);
cout << "\nPhone: ";
gets (iphone);
newCust = new Customer (ifname, ilname, istreet, icity, istate, izip, iphone);
```

The vowel statistics program also uses dynamic binding. The program is based on one class: string (Listing 8.8), which is the same for both versions of the program. The main program for either version can therefore create an object from the class with the following:

```
cout << "Enter a string of up to 80 characters:"
    << endl;
gets (itext);
theString = new string (itext);
```

Note that the theString variable must be declared as a pointer to the string class with string * theString;.

Listing 8.8   stats.h: Header file for the vowel statistics program

```
class string
{
    private:
        char text[81];
        int length;

    public:
        string (char *);
        void stats (int *, int *, int *, int *, int *, int *);
};
```

Removing Objects Created for Use with Dynamic Binding

When a program no longer needs an object created with dynamic binding, it can be removed from memory, freeing up the space to be used by other objects. To remove an object from memory, use the following general syntax:

```
delete object_name;
```

The vowel statistics program, for example, removes an object from memory with:

```
delete theString;
```

Accessing Objects and Member Functions Created for Use with Dynamic Binding

As well as changing the way objects are created, using dynamic binding changes the way in which a program calls a member function. Instead of using a period between the object name and the name of the member function, dynamic binding uses an arrow made up of a hyphen and a greater than symbol (->, the *arrow operator*). For example, one version of the vowel statistics program uses the following statement to call the member function that counts vowels:

```
theString->stats (APtr, EPtr, IPtr, OPtr, UPtr, TotalPtr);
```

The arrow operator tells the computer to dereference the pointer to the object. In other words, the following two expressions are equivalent:

```
pointer2object->functioName();
(*pointer2object).functionName();
```

This means that you actually can use the arrow operator with objects that are declared as variables. All you need to do is create a pointer variable for the object. For example, the following statements let you use the arrow operator with an object that was allocated space in main memory when the program was run:

```
className someObject;
className * someObjectPtr;
someObjectPtr = &someObject;
someObjectPtr->functionName();
```

Pointers and Function Parameters

One of the most important things you can do with pointers is return more than one value from a function. To be completely accurate, a function can only return one value. However, a function *can* make modifications directly to a variable's original storage location in main memory.

There are actually two ways to pass parameters so that modifications to variables are made to the original storage locations. The first method, a pass by reference, involves sending the *address of a regular variable* into a function. The second involves sending the *contents of a pointer variable* into a function. In most cases, you'll use the address of a regular variable when there is no reason to create a pointer variable. You'll use a pointer variable when you've created the pointer variable for other purposes.

To illustrate the subtle difference between these methods, we will be looking at the two versions of the vowel statistics program. Both programs use the same member functions for the string class. As you can see in Listing 8.9, the stats function, which counts the vowels in a string, expects six addresses as input parameters. Each of these parameters identifies the location of a variable declared in the main program. Whether the main program variable is a regular variable or a pointer variable depends on the way in which you decide to send the address to the member function.

Listing 8.9   stats.cpp: Member functions for the vowel statistics program

```
#include <string.h>
#include <iostream.h>
#include "stats.h"
string::string (char * itext)
{
    strcpy (text, itext);
    length = strlen (text);
}

void string::stats (int * A, int * E, int * I, int * O, int * U, int * total)
{
    *A = 0;
    *E = 0;
    *I = 0;
    *O = 0;
    *U = 0;
    *total = 0;
    for (int i = 0; i < length; i++)
    {
        *total += 1;
        switch (text[i])
        {
            case 'A':
            case 'a':
                *A += 1;
                break;
            case 'E':
            case 'e':
                *E += 1;
                break;
            case 'I':
            case 'i':
                *I += 1;
                break;
            case 'O':
            case 'o':
                *O +=+ 1;
                break;
```

Continued next page

Listing 8.9 (Continued) stats.cpp: Member functions for the vowel statistics program

```
        case 'U':
        case 'u':
            *U += 1;
            break;
        default:
            *total -= 1;  // not a vowel
    }
  }
}
```

Notice that because the member function expects addresses as parameters, all modification to those parameters in the member function are made using pointer notation. In other words, whenever the member function modifies a value, it uses an asterisk to dereference the pointer.

Passing by Reference

Passing by reference is the simplest way to return multiple values from a function. As you can see in Listing 8.10, the main program defines an integer variable for each of the six counts the `stats` member function will produce. Then, to pass the address of those variables into the member function, the program prefaces each variable with an ampersand.

Listing 8.10 main.cpp for the vowel statistics program, demonstrating pass by reference

```
#include <iostream.h>
#include <string.h>
#include <stdio.h>
#include "stats.h"

void main()
{
    string * theString;  // pointer variable for new string object
    char itext[81];
    int A, E, I, O, U, theTotal;

    cout << "Enter a string of up to 80 characters:" << endl;
    gets (itext);
    theString = new string (itext);
```

Continued next page

Listing 8.10 (Continued) main.cpp for the vowel statistics program,
            demonstrating pass by reference

```
// Send addresses to the member function by prefacing variable names with an &
theString->stats(&A,&E,&I,&O,&U,&theTotal);
cout << "\nThe vowels in the string are:" << endl;
cout << "   A: " << A << endl;
cout << "   E: " << E << endl;
cout << "   I: " << I << endl;
cout << "   O: " << O << endl;
cout << "   U: " << U << endl;
cout << "\nThere are " << theTotal << " vowels." << endl;
delete theString;
}
```

When you pass by reference, the program doesn't send a copy of the contents of a variable into the called function. Instead, it sends just the main memory address of the variable. Modifications of those variables are made directly to the variable in main memory, thus making the changes available to the calling function, in which the variables were declared.

Passing Pointer Variables

The second way to pass the address of a variable into a function is to use a pointer variable as a parameter. To see how this differs from passing by reference, take a look at Listing 8.11. This program includes both a regular variable and a pointer variable for each vowel count. The program initializes the pointer variables and then passes them to the function. Notice that because the pointer variables contain addresses, there is no need to use an ampersand in front of them. In fact, if you did use the ampersand, you would be sending the address of the pointer variables, not the address of the regular variables.

Using I/O Streams as Function Parameters

The addresses of data are not the only types of addresses that a C++ program can handle. An I/O stream, such as a file stream, also has an address that can be passed into a function as a parameter, allowing the function to interact with an I/O stream that was created elsewhere. There are two useful things you can do with this capability. The first is to allow objects to save themselves to a file and to read themselves back from that file, using an I/O stream created by a main program. The second is to allow objects to format out in main memory and

Listing 8.11   main.cpp for the vowels statistics program, demonstrating passing an address using a pointer variable

```
#include <iostream.h>
#include <string.h>
#include <stdio.h>
#include "stats.h"

void main()
{
    string * theString; // pointer variable for new string object
    char itext[81];
    int A, * APtr, E, * EPtr, I, * IPtr, O, * OPtr, U, * UPtr, theTotal, *
    TotalPtr;

    // initialize the pointer variables
    APtr = &A;
    EPtr = &E;
    IPtr = &I;
    OPtr = &O;
    UPtr = &U;
    TotalPtr = &theTotal;
    cout << "Enter a string of up to 80 characters:" << endl;
    gets (itext);
    theString = new string (itext);
    // pass addresses to the member function by sending the contents of pointer variables
    theString->stats(APtr,EPtr,IPtr,OPtr,UPtr,TotalPtr);
    cout << "\nThe vowels in the string are:" << endl;
    cout << "   A: " << A << endl;
    cout << "   E: " << E << endl;
    cout << "   I: " << I << endl;
    cout << "   O: " << O << endl;
    cout << "   U: " << U << endl;
    cout << "\nThere are " << theTotal << " vowels." << endl;
    delete theString;
}
```

then return the formatting output to the calling function, where it can be displayed as needed. Both of these operations are discussed in the following section.

I/O Streams and Persistent Objects

One of the biggest problems with most of the short programs you have seen thus far in this book is that the objects created by those programs disappear when the program stops running. However, most business applications operate on stored data, data that must exist from one program run to another. The obvious way to handle the problem is to store objects in a file before a program ends and read them in again the next time a program is run. You have already seen one way to do this in Chapter 4.

The drawback to the methods presented in Chapter 4 is that the main program needs to know about the structure of the file containing the objects. A more "object-oriented" way to deal with saving and restoring objects is to write *persistent objects*. A persistent object is an object that reads itself in from a file when it is created and writes itself to a file when it is destroyed. (As you will see in Appendix A, persistent objects underlie object-oriented databases.)

To support persistent objects, a program opens an I/O stream and then passes the address of that stream into a class's constructor when an object is created. The constructor can then use that stream to read in and initialize the newly created object.

To see how this works, consider a constructor for the pharmacy program's `Drug` class. The constructor has the following prototype:

```
Drug(ifstream &);
```

This prototype defines its single input parameter as an object of class `ifstream` (an input file stream). The ampersand indicates that the function expects a reference to that stream to be passed in.

The function that corresponds to the preceding prototype can be found in Listing 8.12. Notice that the declaration's format parameter list includes the class (`ifstream`), the ampersand indicating that a reference to the stream is coming, and a name for the stream to be used within the function (`fin`). Notice also that the local name of the stream is used within the function without pointer notation. This is therefore different than the way addresses of data are handled.

To initiate the constructor in Listing 8.12, the pharmacy program creates a new `Drug` object with the following statement:

```
newDrug = new Drug (drugIn);
```

In this example, `newDrug` is a pointer to an object of class `Drug`; `drugIn` is a file input stream defined for the file storing drug data. Notice that the stream is passed simply by including its name in the parameter list. Like an array, the name of a stream is an address rather than the contents of the stream.

Listing 8.12   A member function to read in one Drug object from a data file

```
Drug::Drug(ifstream & fin)     // constructor that loads one from disk
{
    char dummy;
    fin >> drug_numb;
    fin.get (dummy); // skip over blank
    fin.getline (drug_name,80,'\0');
    fin >> numb_generics;
    fin.get (dummy); // skip over blank
    for (int i = 0; i <= numb_generics; i++)
        fin.getline (generics[i],80,'\0');
    fin >> numb_conflicts;
    fin.get (dummy); // skip over blank
    for (i = 0; i <= numb_conflicts; i++)
        fin.getline (conflicts[i],80,'\0');
}
```

Note

Because the pharmacy program deals with a data file with a specific data format, the constructor that reads from the file must know the way in which the file was written. That means that even though the layout of the file is hidden from the main program, that layout isn't isolated from the class using the file. Therefore, even though the pharmacy program has persistent objects, it isn't a database management system, which requires isolating application programs from physical data storage layouts.

Formatting I/O Streams in Main Memory

A C++ output stream can be formatted in main memory, without immediately displaying the contents of the stream. The formatted stream can then be sent from one function to another to be displayed or printed whenever needed. This is particularly useful when you want to output data contained in an object's private variables and want to avoid having to retrieve and format those values directly.

For example, the pharmacy program prints a label for a prescription bottle or box each time a new prescription is created or an existing prescription refilled. The label uses data from several objects, including the customer, the drug, and the prescription. Rather than interact directly with all those objects and with the objects' private variables, the main program creates an in-memory stream that is passed into a member function of the prescription object. The member function formats the stream and then returns control to the calling program. Because the stream is passed by reference, just like the file stream you saw in the preceding section, the main program has access to the formatted stream and can display or print it as needed.

Streams for in-memory use are created as objects of the strstream class. Because strstream is longer than the eight characters allowed for MS-DOS/Windows files names, many compilers have shortened the name of the header file to strstrea.h. Even if this is this case for your compiler, you must use the entire class name when creating an object from it.

To prepare for formatting the label, the pharmacy program's main function contains a statement to create an object from the strstream class:

```
strstream label;
```

This in-memory stream object can then be passed into a function as a formal parameter.

The function, which is a member function of the Prescription class, has the following prototype:

```
void bottleLabel(Customer *, strstream &, drugArray *);
```

The first parameter is a pointer to a Customer object; the third parameter is a pointer to an object that manages the array of drug objects. (You will learn more about this array manager in Chapter 9.) The middle parameter is a reference to the strstream object. Notice that this reference uses the ampersand notation, just as the function you saw previously did for its ifstream object reference.

To call the function, the main program places the names of the objects to be passed into the function's parameter list:

```
newPrescript->bottleLabel (whichCust,label,drugs);
```

In this example, newPrescript is a pointer variable holding the address of a prescription object that has been created using dynamic binding.; label is the strstream object created earlier.

The function that accepts the `label` stream as an input parameter formats the stream using the stream insertion operator, just as a program would format a `cout` or `ofstream` object. As you can see in Listing 8.13, the statements look very much like `cout` statements. The major difference is that nothing appears on the screen; the stream is assembled in main memory.

Listing 8.13   Formatting a stream in memory

```
void Prescription::bottleLabel(Customer * whichCustomer, strstream & label,
    drugArray * drugs)
{
    Drug * whichDrug;

    label << "*****************************************" << endl;
    label << " Prescription #" << prescription_numb << "        "
        << prescription_date << endl;
    label << " " << endl;
    label << " " << whichCustomer->getFName() << " "
        << whichCustomer->getLName() << endl;
    label << " Dr. " << doctor << endl;
    label << " " << endl;
    whichDrug = drugs->findDrug(drug_numb);
    label << " " << whichDrug->getDrug_name() << "   Refills: " << numb_refills
        << endl;
    label << "*****************************************";
}
```

To display the contents of an in-memory stream, a program uses the stream's `str` member function, inserting it into a `cout` stream, as in:

```
cout << label.str();
```

A sample label produced by the code in Listing 8.13 can be found in Figure 8.4.

Warning

The `str` function initializes a pointer to the head of the in-memory stream and also freezes the stream so it can't be modified. This latter characteristic of in-memory streams can be a bit of a "gotcha" if you want to repeatedly modify and display an in-memory stream. Unless the stream is destroyed or unfrozen, you won't be able to modify it. Like other local variables, a stream is destroyed when the function in which it was created exits. As far as the prescription bottle/box labels are concerned, this presents no problem. The

```
**************************************************
  Prescription #5      10-31-94

  John Doe
  Dr. Hyde


  Hemlock    Refills: 12
**************************************************
```

Figure 8.4   A sample prescription bottle/box label

program exits the functions that create new or refilled prescriptions immediately after displaying the label. The stream is therefore deleted and created anew for each new prescription or refill.

However, if the pharmacy wants to print mailing labels for all its customers, the situation is a bit different. In this case, a single function loops through all the customers, without exiting the function. Nonetheless, the stream must be unfrozen after display or it can't be used for more than one mailing label.

There are two possible solutions. The first is to put the code that deals with the in-memory stream in a small function all its own, as in Listing 8.14. The DisplayLabel function is called once each time the loop in the see-Cust function iterates. Because the stream is created inside the DisplayLabel function, it is destroyed each time that function exits.

Alternatively, a program can unfreeze a stream with the freeze member function. If you pass the function a parameter of 0, it will unfreeze the stream:

```
label.freeze(0);
```

Binary Files

To this point, all the files used by the programs you have seen are text files. Text files are relatively easy to program, but they have one major drawback: They can be opened and read by a word processor or text editor. If you are storing data that should be protected from unauthorized viewing, then you should

Listing 8.14   Destroying an in-memory stream after displaying

```
void seeCust (CustList * LinkedCusts)
{
    Customer * currentCust;
    int i;
    char dummy[2];

    int Count = LinkedCusts->getCount();
    currentCust = LinkedCusts->getFirst();

    for (i = 1; i <= Count; i++) // loop through all customers
    {
        DisplayLabel (currentCust);
        cout << " " << endl; // blank line between
        currentCust = currentCust->getNext(); // get next customer in linked list
    }
}

void DisplayLabel (Customer * currentCust)
{
    strstream label; // need to kill object and recreate each time because of freeze
    currentCust->mailingLabel (label);
    cout << label.str();
}
```

consider a type of file storage that is unintelligible to the casual viewer. Although not as secure as using data encryption, using binary files is an effective way to protect your data against many attempts at unauthorized access.

A *binary file* stores data as a stream of bits that don't translate into readable ASCII characters. The file is therefore unintelligible to a word processor or text editor. By the same token, a program can't use the standard stream insertion and extraction operators to write and read data.

Creating and Opening Binary Files

Creating and opening a binary file is very similar to creating and opening a text file. Because a text file is the default, a program must specifically indicate that it wants a binary file. To do so, add the flag ios::binary to the statement that opens the file, as in:

```
ifstream drugIn (drugFile, ios::binary);
ofstream drugOut (drugFile, ios::binary);
```

Writing to Binary Files

In Listing 8.15 you will find a function that writes a `Customer` object to a binary file. It uses the member function `write` to output a stream of unformatted bytes of characters (arrays of characters). The `write` function has the following general syntax:

```
stream.write (address_of_data, #_characters);
```

The `write` function requires the starting address of the characters to be written to the file. If a program is writing from an array of characters (a string), then the name of the variable is sufficient. However, if the data are stored in a simple variable (for example, an integer or floating point variable), then the variable's name must be preceded by the ampersand to indicate the address of the variable.

The `write` function doesn't recognize the null that terminates a string. A program must therefore tell `write` how many characters are to be output. For example, to write a customer's first name to the file, the program uses:

```
fout.write (fname, sizeof(fname));
```

The `sizeof` function returns the number of bytes in a C++ data structure (even an object). Although you could certainly use the length of the `fname` string as a constant, the use of the `sizeof` function means that the `write` will not need to be modified if the length of `fname` variable ever changes.

Listing 8.15   Writing to a binary file

```
void Customer::writeCustomer(ofstream & fout)
{
    fout.write ((unsigned char *) &numb_prescripts, sizeof(numb_prescripts));
    fout.write (fname, sizeof(fname));
    fout.write (lname, sizeof(lname));
    fout.write (street, sizeof(street));
    fout.write (city, sizeof(city));
    fout.write (state,sizeof(state));
    fout.write (zip, sizeof(zip));
    fout.write (phone, sizeof(phone));
}
```

Because `write` only outputs characters, the address of numeric data must be typecast into a character pointer as the data are written. For example, the following syntax typecasts the address of an integer variable:

```
(unsigned char *) &numb_prescripts
```

Reading from Binary Files

Reading from a binary file is precisely the opposite of writing to the file. It uses the function `read`, which has the following general syntax:

```
stream.read (address_of_storage, #_characters);
```

The function expects two parameters: the address of the storage location where the data should be stored as they are input and the number of characters to input. Notice in Listing 8.16, a function to read a customer from a binary file, that the addresses of variables that aren't character arrays must once more be typecast into character pointers. Because the first element of a character array is a pointer, the name of a character array can be used without typecasting.

Listing 8.16   Reading from a binary file

```
Customer::Customer(ifstream & fin)
{
    fin.read ((unsigned char *) &numb_prescripts, sizeof(numb_prescripts));
    fin.read (fname,sizeof(fname));
    fin.read (lname,sizeof(lname));
    fin.read (street,sizeof(street));
    fin.read (city,sizeof(city));
    fin.read (state,sizeof(state));
    fin.read (zip,sizeof(zip));
    fin.read (phone,sizeof(phone));
    // create header for prescription list
    PrescriptHeader = new PrescriptList (this, PrescriptCount);
    nextCust = 0; // defaults to zero but will be replaced for all but last customer
}
```

Summary

In this chapter you have learned about using pointers to access data and objects. C++ provides two mechanisms for handling addresses. The first uses ampersand notation: placing an ampersand in front of a variable name or the name of an object created with static binding generates the address at which that variable or object's storage begins in main memory. The exception to this is arrays, whose names are addresses without being preceded by an ampersand.

The second mechanism stores an address in a variable declared to hold a pointer. Pointer variables are used to return multiple values from a function and to hold pointers to objects created with dynamic binding.

To access the data pointed to by a pointer variable, a program must dereference the pointer by placing an asterisk in front of the variable's name. For example, *Data refers to the contents of the main memory location stored in the Data variable.

C++ maintains a special pointer called this, which holds a pointer to the current object. The this pointer can be used, for example, to simplify copying one object into another.

Dynamic binding lets a program create and destroy objects as needed, rather than having to declare all objects when the program is written. The new keyword creates a new object using dynamic binding and returns a pointer to that object. To access member functions of objects created with dynamic binding, use arrow notation (->).

To return multiple values from a function, the function must expect pointer to variables as input parameters. It must then use pointer notation to modify values. The calling function can either pass in the address of a variable (using ampersand notation) or the contents of a pointer variable.

The addresses of I/O streams can be passed into functions as parameters. The streams can be modified by the functions. Because the name of a stream is the main memory address of its starting location, a stream is passed simply by using its name. The function to which the stream is a parameter uses ampersand notation in its parameter list because the function is expecting a reference to the stream. The stream name is then used dereferencing in the function.

Binary files store bytes of unformatted character data. To write to a binary file, a program uses the write function, which uses the address of the data to be written along with the number of bytes to write. The read function works in exactly the opposite manner to input data from a binary file. In either case, addresses of noncharacter array variables must be typecast into character pointers before writing data to or reading data from a binary file.

Exercises

1. Create a class that manages payroll information about employees who are paid hourly. The class should store the employee's ID number, his or her hourly pay rate, and the hours worked during a given week. Include a member function that computes an employee's weekly pay. Each employee is paid according to the following schedule:

   - For the first 40 hours worked, pay is equal to the hourly rate times the number of hours worked.
   - For hours over 40, pay is equal to 1.5 times the hourly rate times the number of overtime hours worked.

   The pay computation function should return the pay for the first 40 hours of work, the overtime pay amount, and the total gross pay. Write a program that demonstrates that the class and its payroll computation function work.

2. Create a class that includes an array variable that stores up to 25 floating point values. Include a member function that uses pointer arithmetic to sum the values in the array and returns the sum to the calling function. Write a program that demonstrates that the sum function works correctly.

3. Add a member function to the String Stuff program you read about in this chapter that converts a number stored as a string to an integer. The function should accept a string array as an input parameter and return the equivalent integer value. Be sure to check the input string to determine if it contains only characters that constitute a valid integer. Use pointer arithmetic to examine the characters in the string one by one, checking and converting them as you go. Add code to the program's main function that demonstrates that your conversion function works.

4. To help the local tax assessor, create a class that describes properties in a town. The class should include the ID number of the property and the market value of the property. Include a function that computes and returns the assessed value of the property and the tax owed. The computations use the following rules:

- A property's assessed value is 33% of its market value.
- The tax rate is 130 mils for each dollar of assessed value. (One mil = 0.1 cent.)

Write a program that demonstrates that your class and the tax computation function work.

5. Create a class that can be used to help surgical patients manage their medication schedule after they are released from the hospital. The class should store the name of the medication, the dosage of the medication, and the times at which the medication must be taken (e.g., 2:00 PM, 6:00 PM). Write a program that uses an array of objects to store data about all of a patient's medication. Include a function in the program that prints a daily medication schedule for the patient, showing which medication(s) should be taken each hour during the day and the dosage for each of the medications. The program's output should be organized by hour rather than by type of medication. (*Hint*: This is a bit trickier than it looks, because most medications are taken more than once a day. Consider carefully how you're going to store the times within the class.)

6. (Purchasing) Modify the purchasing system program you began developing in Chapter 7. Add a variable to the Purchase Order class that is a pointer to the vendor to whom the purchase order was sent. Consider carefully how the program will obtain and maintain this pointer, since the pointer can't be stored when the purchase order is written to a file.

Long

Add a variable to the Line Item class that is a pointer to the item being ordered. As the pointer from the purchase order to the vendor, consider carefully how this pointer can be recreated when a Line Item object is read in from a file.

7. (Temporary Employment Agency) Modify the temporary employment agency program you began developing in Chapter 7. Add a class to the program that stores data about the hours an employee worked during a given week. The class should identify the employee, the employer, the number of hours worked, the base pay (if any), and the hourly rate. Include a member function that computes weekly pay according to the following rules:

Long

- For 40 or fewer hours a week, gross pay is equal to the hourly rate times the number of hours worked, plus the base pay (if any).
- For hours over 40, overtime pay is calculated as 1.5 times the hourly rate for those hours over 40.

The pay computation function should report number of hours worked, the pay for the first 40 hours plus base pay, any overtime pay, and the total net pay.

Demonstrate that the pay computation works by computing and displaying pay information for all employees for one week.

9

Using Pointers

OBJECTIVES

In this chapter you will learn about:

- Managing arrays of pointers to objects.
- Creating and using linked lists of objects.
- Creating a binary search tree of objects.
- Using special objects to manage data structures of other objects.

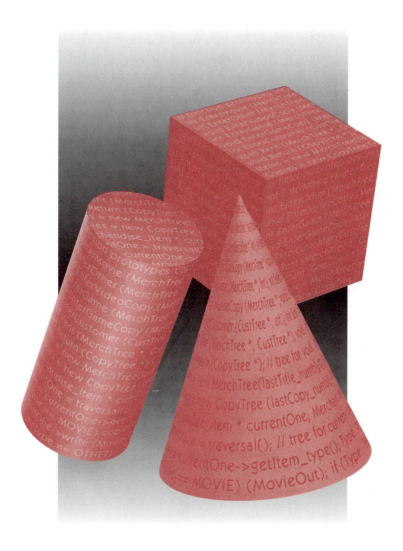

As you know, using dynamic binding to create an object gives a program better control over main memory and relieves the programmer from having to know the number of objects needed during a program run. This alone is sufficient reason to work with pointers to objects instead of the object variables created with static binding. However, there is an even more compelling reason to use dynamic binding: The pointers to objects created with dynamic binding form the basis of a variety of data structures that organize and provide access to a collection of objects.

In this chapter you will read about three types of data structures that can be created using pointers to objects (arrays, linked lists, and binary search trees). You will also see how special objects are created and used to manage those data structures, isolating the program using the data structures from the details of their operation. All of these data structures have been implemented in the pharmacy program, which uses them to handle the drugs (an array of pointers in alphabetical order by drug name), the customers (a linked list of customers in alphabetical order by name), and the prescriptions (a linked list to relate customers to their prescriptions and a binary search tree in prescription number order).

Pointers and Arrays

In Chapter 6 you learned how to use arrays of objects that were created using static binding. Each element in such an array is an object. When the array is sorted, entire objects are moved in main memory. There are two drawbacks to this approach.

First, moving objects around in memory can, over the length of a program run, lead to memory fragmentation and ultimately to program crashes. Moving entire objects in memory also takes more time than simply moving a pointer. Therefore, if an array consists of pointers to objects, rather than the objects themselves, a program can avoid ever moving an object; only pointers are moved.

Second, the array has to be managed by the program that created the objects. Any other program that wants to use the same array of objects must also include its own code to handle the array. Optimally, the declaration and manipulation of the array should be transparent to program using the array. This can only be achieved by creating an object to manage the array.

Keep in mind, however, that no matter how you write it, an array isn't a dynamic data structure. In other words, a program is limited to the maximum number of elements indicated when the array is declared. If you find that an array doesn't have enough elements, the only solution is to make the change to the source code and recompile the program.

An Object to Manage an Array of Objects

The first step in programming an array of object pointers is to declare the object that will manage the array. As you can see in Listing 9.1, the class drugArray has two variables, an array that holds pointers to objects created from the class Drug and the number of drugs in the array at any given time. The member functions include the following:

- Two constructors, one for when there is no file from which drug data can be loaded and another for when drug data are loaded from a file.
- Two insert functions, the first for inserting new pointers into the array when a drug is created interactively and the second for inserting new pointers when data are read from a file. In the first case, the array has to be sorted. In the second, it does not because the drugs are written to the file in sorted order.
- Two find functions, one to search by drug name, the other by drug number.
- A function to return the number of drugs in the array.
- A function to return a pointer to a drug identified by a drug number.

There are two additional things to keep in mind about the drugArray class. First, the number of elements available for an array when an object is created from this class is limited by the constant DRUG_MAX. As noted earlier, if you want more space in the array, the constant needs to be changed in this header file and the program recompiled.

Second, the function using a drugArray object must create an object from that class. For example, the main pharmacy program first sets aside a pointer variable to hold a pointer to the object:

```
drugArray * drugs;
```

Listing 9.1   array.h: Header file for an object that manages an array of prescription and over-the-counter pharmaceuticals

```
const DRUG_MAX = 25;

class drugArray
{
    private:
        Drug * drugs[DRUG_MAX]; // array to hold drugs
        int drugCount; // number of drugs currently in array

    public:
        drugArray ();
        drugArray (int);
        void iInsert (Drug *); // interactive insert
        void fInsert (Drug *, int); // file insert
        Drug * findDrug (string); // search by drug name
        Drug * findDrug (int); // search by drug number
        int getDrugCount();
        Drug * getDrug (int);
};
```

Then, it can create the object using dynamic binding. If there is no file containing drug data, the object is created with:

```
drugs = new DrugArray();
```

However, if a file is present, the program first reads the number of drugs from the file and then passes that count to a constructor:

```
drugIn >> drugCount;
drugs = new drugArray (drugCount);
```

In both cases, the constructors are very similar. As you can see in Listing 9.2, each initializes both the drugCount variable and the array of pointers. The only difference is that the constructor that is invoked when a data file is present uses the drug count that was read from the file.

Listing 9.2 Constructors for the drugArray class

```
drugArray::drugArray() // constructor for when there's no file
{
    drugCount = 0;
    for (int i = 0; i < DRUG_MAX; i++)
        drugs[i] = 0;
}

drugArray::drugArray (int iCount) // constructor for file input
{
    drugCount = iCount;
    for (int i = 0; i < DRUG_MAX; i++)
        drugs[i] = 0; // will be replaced as drugs are loaded from file
}
```

Sorting Arrays of Pointers

The array of drug pointers is kept in alphabetical order by drug name. This means that every time a new drug object is created, its pointer must be inserted in the correct place so that if the program were to look at the drug names, the new drug would be in the correct order.

When drugs are loaded from the file, no sorting is needed because the drugs were written to the file in sorted order. The fInsert function in Listing 9.3 therefore uses a pointer to a new drug and the drug's index in the array to simply insert the drug. The loop that loads from the file is managed by the main program. As you can see in Listing 9.4, the program first reads the number of drugs from the file and then uses that value to create the drugArray object that will manage the drug array. At that point, it begins a for loop that creates Drug objects.

As you will remember from Chapter 8, one of the constructors for a Drug object reads the object from the file and initializes the object's variables. This constructor is invoked by including the name of the file input stream (drugIn) as a parameter when the object is created. A pointer to the new object is stored in the pointer variable newDrug. Once the Drug object is created, the program calls the drugArray object's fInsert function to place the Drug object's pointer into the array.

When a user enters a new drug interactively, however, the drug array must be sorted during the array insertion process. Therefore, the iInsert function (seen in Listing 9.3) contains a version of the bubble sort that makes

Listing 9.3 Inserting drugs into the array of drug pointers

```
void drugArray::iInsert (Drug * newDrug) // interactive insert
{
    Drug * Tdrug;
    int result;

    drugs[++drugCount] = newDrug;

    // sort moves pointers to objects rather than the objects themselves
    result = SWAP_MADE;
    while (result == SWAP_MADE)
    {
        result = NO_SWAP;
        for (int i = 0; i < drugCount; i++)
        // compare the drug names, but...
        if (strcmp(drugs[i]->getDrug_name(),drugs[i+1]->getDrug_name()) > 0)
            { // ... move the pointers!
                Tdrug = drugs[i];
                drugs[i] = drugs[i+1];
                drugs [i+1] = Tdrug;
                result = SWAP_MADE;
            }
        }
    }
}

void drugArray::fInsert (Drug * newDrug, int index)
    { drugs[index] = newDrug; }
```

Listing 9.4 Reading objects from the drug file and inserting them into the drug array

```
drugIn >> drugCount;
drugs = new drugArray (drugCount); // create object to manage drug array
for (int ind = 0; ind <= drugCount; ind++)
{
    newDrug = new Drug(drugIn);   // constructor reads the object
    drugs->fInsert (newDrug, ind); // insert drug into array by drug name
}
drugIn.close();
```

its decision whether to swap two array elements based on a comparison of the drug names. However, when the time comes to make a swap, the objects aren't moved; just the pointers to the objects in the array are moved.

Note

There are certainly other sort algorithms besides the bubble sort. Some are more efficient. However, the drug array sorting routine was written using the bubble sort so that you could compare it to the sort you saw in Chapter 6, where entire objects were moved.

Searching Arrays of Pointers

The main reason for keeping the array of drugs in alphabetical order by name is to provide for efficient searching. Consider, for example, the two findDrug functions in Listing 9.5. The second, which uses the drug number as its input parameter, is a *sequential search*. Because the drugs aren't ordered on the drug number, the only way to search the array is to start at the first drug and look at each drug in order, checking to see if the drug is the target of the search.

A sequential search is a very easy search to write; it requires only a for loop. However, it isn't very efficient. If, for example, an array has 1,000 elements, then on average a program will have to look at 500 elements to find the desired element. A program will have to look at all 1,000 elements to determine that the desired element isn't in the array.

A much more efficient alternative is a *binary search*. A binary search is based on the premise that if you look at the middle element in an ordered list, you can eliminate half the elements in the list by determining in which half of the elements the desired element lies. Using a binary search, a program only needs to look at 10 to 12 elements in a list of 1,000 elements to determine that the value for which the program is searching isn't present. A successful search needs to consult even fewer elements. Even in the worst case, where the search value isn't present in the list, a binary search is 10 times better than a sequential search. As the number of elements in the list goes up, the difference between a sequential search and a binary search becomes even more pronounced.

To use a binary search, a data structure must be ordered on the data that form the basis of the search. The data structure must also provide direct access to its elements. An array provides direct access because you can access any element by simply specifying its index.

Listing 9.5   Searching the array of drug pointers

```
Drug * drugArray::findDrug (string idrug_name) // use a binary search
{
    int top, bottom, mid, test;

    top = -1; // top is one less than minimum array index
    bottom = drugCount + 1; // bottom is one more than maximum array index
    mid = (top + bottom) / 2; // compute the middle of the range

    while (top < mid)
    {
        // check drug pointed to by pointer in the middle of the range
        test = strcmp (idrug_name, drugs[mid]->getDrug_name());
        // if correct drug found, return the pointer to the Drug object
        if (test == 0)
            return drugs[mid];
        if (test < 0) // if search value is above the middle, move up the bottom
            bottom = mid;
        else // otherwise, move down the top
            top = mid;
        mid = (top + bottom) / 2; // compute a middle of the new range
    }
    return 0; // drug wasn't found
}

Drug * drugArray::findDrug (int idrug_numb) // use a sequential search
{
    for (int i = 0; i <= drugCount; i++)
        if (drugs[i]->getDrug_numb() == idrug_numb)
            return drugs[i];
    return 0; // drug not found
}
```

Looking at the first findDrug function in Listing 9.5, you can see that the binary search begins by initializing variables to hold the edges of the range of indexes being considered. The top of the range is initialized to one less than the minimum index in the array (in this case, -1). The bottom of the range is initialized to one more than the maximum index used in the array (in this case, drugCount + 1). Then, the function computes the middle of the range and stores the index of the middle value in the variable mid.

The binary search checks the Drug object pointed to by array element mid. If it matches the drug for which the program is searching, the function returns the Drug pointer. If the value for which the program is searching is less than (or alphabetically precedes) the value pointed to by mid, the search can eliminate all values greater than the value pointed to by mid; the function therefore moves the bottom index up to mid. By the same token, if the value for which the program is searching is greater than (or alphabetically follows) the value pointed to by mid, the search can eliminate a values less than mid. It therefore moves the top index down to mid.

Using the adjusted range of indexes, the binary search recomputes a new middle point and repeats the entire process. If the top index becomes greater than or equal to the current midpoint of the range, then search has failed. In that case, the function returns a zero.

Note

An array of pointers can be thought of as an index to a group of objects. In this situation, the term *index* is being used to refer to something that is similar to the index in a book. You can maintain as many indexes as you need to a group of objects. The pharmacy program could, for example, maintain a second array of pointers to the Drug objects, sorted by any other variable in the object.

Using Pointers to Create Linked Lists of Objects

A linked list is a dynamic data structure that chains together objects by having one object point to the "next" object in the list. Because you can lengthen the list by simply adding another object to the chain, the number of objects in a linked list is theoretically limited only by the amount of main memory available for the program's data storage.

The pharmacy program uses two types of linked lists. The first links the customers together in alphabetical order by customer name. The second links prescriptions to customers. The way in which these lists order the objects can be seen in Figure 9.1. Each rectangle represents an object; the word in the rectangle is the class from which the object was created.

The CustList class (Listing 9.6) manages the linked list of customer objects (see the class declaration in Listing 9.7). The pharmacy program creates just one object from the CustList class. (There is only one linked list of customers.) It stores the number of customers in the linked list and a pointer to the first customer in the list. This object also provides a convenient place to store the highest prescription number used so that each new prescription can automatically be assigned the next unused number.

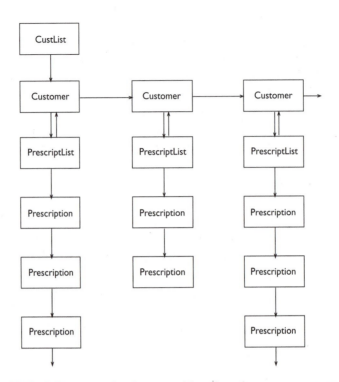

Figure 9.1   Linked list organization used by the pharmacy program

Listing 9.6   The CustList class from the pharmacy program

```
class CustList
{
    private:
        Customer * firstCust;
        int custCount, lastPrescript_numb;

    public:
        CustList (Customer *, int, int); // constructor when coming from file
        CustList (); // constructor when no file and therefore no customers
        void Insert (Customer *, int); // insert new customer into list
        Customer * findCust (char [], char []); // traverse list to find customer
        int getCount (); // return customer count
        Customer * getFirst(); // return pointer to first in list
        void incLastPrescript_numb (); // increment last prescription number
        int getLastPrescript_numb();
};
```

Listing 9.7 The Customer class from the pharmacy program

```
class Customer
{
    private:
        char fname[16], lname[16], street[31], city [21], state[3],
            zip[6], phone [13];
        PrescriptList * PrescriptHeader; // pointer to prescription list object
        Customer * nextCust; // pointer to next customer

    public:
        Customer(ifstream &);
        Customer(char [], char [], char [], char [], char [], char [], char []);
        void setPrescriptPtr (PrescriptList *); // pointer to prescription object
        void setNextPtr (Customer *); // pointer to next customer
        void writeCustomer(ofstream &);
        Customer * getNext (); // pointer to next customer
        void mailingLabel (strstream &);
        char * getZip ();
        char * getLName ();
        char * getFName ();
        char * getStreet ();
        char * getCSZ();
        char * getPhone ();
        PrescriptList * getPrescriptHeader(); // pointer to prescription header
        int checkNewDrug (string, drugArray *);
};
```

Each Customer object contains a pointer to the next Customer object in the list. The pointer in the last Customer object points to nothing, indicated by placing a zero in the pointer variable.

A linked list is a sequential access data structure. In this case, because the only pointers are to the next Customer object, access is from first, to next, to next, and so on, until the last object in the list is reached. If the Customer class also included a pointer to the prior object in the list, then access to the preceding object would also be possible. To enable prior access, the CustList object would also need to contain a pointer to the last Customer object in the list.

Note

How do you decide what pointers to include in a linked list? The decision is usually based on the type of access you think a program will need. Having both next and prior pointers provides more flexible access. However, using both pointers takes a bit more space to store each object and also increases the work that needs to be done to insert and remove objects from the list.

In addition to a pointer to the next customer, each `Customer` object also contains a pointer to a `PrescriptList` object. The `PrescriptList` object (Listing 9.8) manages the linked list of prescriptions for a single customer. There is therefore one `PrescriptList` object for each customer, each of which manages its own list of prescriptions.

Listing 9.8   The PrescriptList class from the pharmacy program

```
class PrescriptList
{
    private:
        Customer * owner; // pointer to customer that owns it
        Prescription * firstPrescript;
        int PrescriptCount;
        int IFLAG; // detects interactive insert

    public:
        PrescriptList (Customer *); // interactive constructor
        PrescriptList (Customer *, int); // file constructor
        void Insert (Prescription *, int); // IFLAG = TRUE for interactive
        Prescription * findPrescript (int iprescript_numb);
        void incCount (); // increment prescription count
        int getPrescriptCount ();
        Prescription * getFirst();
};
```

The `PrescriptList` class contains a pointer to the `Customer` object that owns the linked list of prescriptions. It also contains a pointer to the first `Prescription` object and the total number of prescriptions in the list. The `IFLAG` variable is used to indicate whether a prescription being inserted into a list is coming from a data file or is being entered interactively by a user.

Searching a Linked List

As mentioned earlier, the only way to search a linked list is sequentially, beginning at the first or last object in the list and moving through the objects in order. Although the Customer objects are maintained in alphabetical order, a program can't use a binary search because the linked list structure doesn't provide the direct access required for the faster search technique.

The basic strategy for searching a linked list is to initialize a pointer to first object in the list. In Listing 9.9, for example, the findCust function initializes the currentCust pointer to the value in the CustList object's firstCust variable. Once the pointer to the first object is available, the sequential search enters a while loop. The body of the loop determines if the current object is the desired object. If it is, the function returns a pointer to the object. If the current object isn't the desired object, the function retrieves the pointer to the next object. (The Customer class's GetNext function returns the pointer to the next object.) The process repeats until the function either finds the desired object or it encounters the end of the list.

Listing 9.9   Searching the linked list for a customer in the pharmacy program

```
Customer * CustList::findCust (char iLname[], char iFname[])
{
    Customer * nextCust, * currentCust;
    char longName[31], searchName[31];

    strcpy (searchName,iLname);
    strcat (searchName,iFname);
    currentCust = firstCust;
    while (currentCust != 0)
    {
        strcpy (longName,currentCust->getLName());
        strcat (longName,currentCust->getFName());
        if (strcmp (searchName,longName) == 0)
            return currentCust;
        currentCust = currentCust->getNext(); // follow link to next
    }
    return 0; // customer not found
}
```

Inserting Objects into a Linked List

Objects are inserted into a linked list under two circumstances: either data are being read in from a file or an object is being created interactively. Why does a program need to recreate a list if the objects in the list are stored in a file before the program ends? Because the pointers that create a linked list won't be the same each time the program is run. There is no way to guarantee that a program always loads in memory at the same place. (A program's location in memory depends on what other programs are running when the program is launched.) Each time an object is created, it will almost certainly be located at a main memory address different from where it was the last time the program was run. In fact, using pointers from a previous program run will corrupt any other program running concurrently that happens to be occupying the memory locations pointed to by the stored pointers. A program must therefore recreate the pointers that define linked lists as data are read in from a file. By the same token, a program shouldn't bother to store the pointers that define a linked list in a data file.

There are several strategies for inserting a new object into a linked list. In the case of the `Customer` objects, new objects are inserted in sorted order. `Prescription` objects, however, are always inserted at the head of the list. This maintains them in relatively descending chronological order. The rationale behind this strategy is that more recent prescriptions are more likely to be accessed than older prescriptions. Alternatively, a program might decide to insert new objects at the end of a list, prior to the current object, or after the current object.

Regardless of where a new object is inserted into a linked list, at least two pointers have to modified to make the insertion:

- The "next" pointer in the preceding object must be modified to point to the new object. If the object is being inserted at the beginning of the list, the "first" pointer in the list management object (for example, a `PrescriptList` object) must be modified.
- The "next" pointer in the new object must be modified to point to the next object in the list.

If there are prior pointers in the list, they will need to be modified as well. As you will see in the following two sections, the procedure for inserting an object into a linked list is relatively straightforward, regardless of where the object is inserted.

Inserting First

To insert a new prescription at the head of the linked list of prescriptions, the pharmacy program must modify the PrescriptList object so that it points to the new prescription. The program must then modify the new prescription so that it points to the previous first prescription, which then becomes second in the list. As you can see in Listing 9.10, the Insert function uses the Prescription object's setPrescriptPtr function to modify the value of the new prescription's nextPrescript variable.

Listing 9.10   Inserting a new object as the first object in a linked list in the pharmacy program

```
void PrescriptList::Insert (Prescription * newPrescript, int IFLAG)
{
    Prescription * oldFirst;

    // new prescription always goes first
    oldFirst = firstPrescript; // save current value of firstPrescript
    firstPrescript = newPrescript; // set new object as first prescription in list
    // set new prescription to point to previous first prescription, which is now second.
    // don't bother if first prescription.
    if (oldFirst) newPrescript->setPrescriptPtr(oldFirst);
    if (IFLAG) PrescriptCount++; // if interactive, increment the number of prescriptions
}
```

Inserting Sorted

Inserting an object into a sorted list requires finding the correct place for the new object before moving any pointers. The function to insert a customer into the linked list of customers (Listing 9.11) therefore includes code that looks similar to the sequential search of the list. The search begins at the first object in the list and continues until either the end of the list is reached or the name of the new customer is alphabetically greater than the name of the customer just checked. When the latter condition arises, the new customer is inserted between the customer just checked and the object that follows it.

Listing 9.11   Inserting a new object into a sorted list of objects in the pharmacy program

```
void CustList::Insert (Customer * newCust, int IFLAG)
{
    string newLongname, oldLongname;
    Customer * currentCust, * previousCust;

    if (custCount == 0) // handle first customer separately
    {
        firstCust = newCust;
        custCount = 1;
    }
    else
    {
        int i = 1;
        int first = TRUE;
        currentCust = firstCust; // start at head of list
        // must do the concatenations and copying outside while to avoid modifying
        // good data
        strcpy (newLongname,newCust->getLName());
        strcat (newLongname,newCust->getFName());
        strcpy (oldLongname,currentCust->getLName());
        strcat (oldLongname,currentCust->getFName());
        while (strcmp(newLongname, oldLongname) > 0 && i++ <= custCount)
        {
            first = FALSE;
            // save preceding because there aren't backward pointers
            previousCust = currentCust;
            currentCust = currentCust->getNext();
            strcpy (oldLongname,currentCust->getLName());
            strcat (oldLongname,currentCust->getFName());
        }

        // set previous customer to point to new customer except when new one is
        // first in list
        if (!first)
            previousCust->setNextPtr (newCust);
        else
            firstCust = newCust; // have new first in list

        // set new customer to point to following customer
        newCust->setNextPtr (currentCust);
        if (IFLAG) custCount++; // increment number of customers only if interactive
    }
}
```

To make the insertion, the function sets the previous customer to point to the new customer using the previous customer's `setNextPtr` function. It then uses the same member function for the new customer to set it to point to the following customer.

There are two special cases that need to be handled by this insert function. The first is when the program is inserting the first customer into the list. If that is the case, there is no need to perform a search. The function can simply set the `CustList` object to point to the first customer.

The second special case arises when a new customer must be inserted at the head of the list. (In other words, it alphabetically precedes all other customers in the list.) In that situation, the function modifies the `CustList` object to point to the new customer and the new customer object to point to the `Customer` object that was previously first in the list.

Note

Removing an object from a linked list is just the opposite of inserting it. A program simply changes the pointer in the object prior to the object being removed to point to the object following the object being removed. You will get a chance to write a removal function in the exercises at the end of this chapter.

Using Pointers to Create a Binary Search Tree

The biggest drawback to a linked list is that it is a sequential data structure. Even if it is ordered like the linked list of customers, it still can only be searched using a sequential search. Many programs therefore use other data structures that are specially designed to support fast searches. One of the most efficient is a *binary search tree*.

A binary tree is a hierarchical data structure in which each object has no more than two objects below it. Figure 9.2, for example, shows a sample tree based on prescription number. Notice first that the prescription numbers aren't necessarily continuous; in other words, the numbers don't run without gaps from 1 on. The tree is effective whether or not the numbers are continuous. Notice also that at first glance the numbers don't appear to be in numerical order. Nonetheless, this structure does order the numbers and provides a very fast way to search for any specific number.

Each object in a tree is called a *node*; the node at the top of the tree (node 1 in Figure 9.2) is called the *root*. Each of the objects pointed to by a node is a *child*. The right child represents a value less than a node's value; the

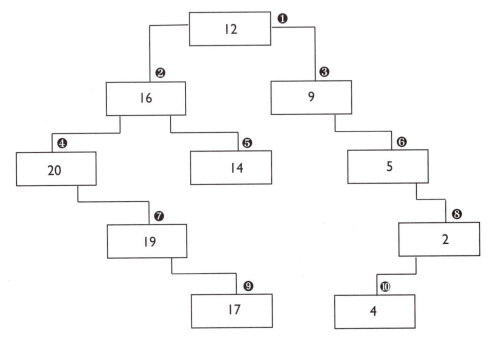

Figure 9.2   A binary search tree

left child represents a value greater than a node's value. As you will see in the next section, this organization is created as nodes are added to the tree and is used to search the tree quickly.

The pharmacy program's binary search tree is managed by an object of the PrescriptTree class (Listing 9.12). The class contains a pointer to the root of the tree. Like the linked lists used to manage customers and their pre- scriptions, the tree is reinitialized and rebuilt each time data are loaded from a data file at the beginning of a program run.

To support membership in the binary tree, the Prescription class includes two pointer variables (right and left) that point to other prescrip- tion objects. The class also includes functions to return the values in each pointer (getLeft and getRight) and functions to set the values in each pointer (setLeft and setRight), the source code for which can be found in Listing 9.13.

Listing 9.12   The PrescriptTree class for the pharmacy program

```
class PrescriptTree
{
    private:
        Prescription * root;

    public:
        PrescriptTree (); // constructor
        void Insert (Prescription *, int); // insert into tree
        Prescription * findPrescript (int); // find a prescription by number
};
```

Listing 9.13   Functions to retrieve and set pointer variables used to support
              membership in a binary tree for the pharmacy program

```
Prescription * Prescription::getLeft()
    { return left; }

Prescription * Prescription::getRight()
    { return right; }

void Prescription::setLeft (Prescription * newPrescript)
    { left = newPrescript; }

void Prescription::setRight (Prescription * newPrescript)
    { right = newPrescript; }
```

Searching the Tree

To search the tree, a program begins at the root node. If the value sought by the search is less than the value in the root node, the program moves to the right child; if the value sought by the search is greater than the value in the root node, the program moves to the left node. The process continues, choosing the right node for a smaller value or the left node for a larger value, until either the correct node is found or a node without a needed child is found. In the latter case, the search is unsuccessful. The maximum number of nodes that will have to be checked to determine that a search value isn't present is therefore equal to the number of levels in the tree.

As an example of the process, assume that a program wants to find prescription #19 (node #7 in Figure 9.2). The search enters the tree at the root (node #1, prescription #12). Because the search value is greater than the current node's value, the search goes to the left child, which becomes the current node.

The process now repeats with the new current node. The search value is greater than the value in the current node (node #2, prescription #16). The path is therefore again to the left child (node #4, prescription #20). Because the search value is less than the value in the current, the search moves to the right child. At this point, the search has found the correct object.

The way in which the pharmacy program implements this type of search can be found in Listing 9.14. Notice that an unsuccessful search is detected when an attempt to access a child is unsuccessful. In other words, the current node has a zero for a child pointer in the direction the search was attempting to take.

Listing 9.14   Searching a binary tree in the pharmacy program

```
Prescription * PrescriptTree::findPrescript (int iPrescript_numb)
{
    Prescription * current;

    if (root) // make sure there is at least one node
    {
        current = root;
        while (current) // as long as there's a pointer
        {
            if (current->getPrescript_numb() == iPrescript_numb)
                return current; // send back pointer to drug object
            // if less, go down right side
            if (current->getPrescript_numb() < iPrescript_numb)
                current = current->getRight();
            // if greater, go down left side
            else
                current = current->getLeft();
        }
    }
    return 0; // prescription not found
}
```

Inserting Values into a Binary Search Tree

To insert a value into a binary search tree, a program searches the tree until it finds a node without a child on the correct side. As an example, assume that the pharmacy program wants to insert prescription #10 into the tree in Figure 9.2. As with a search for a specific node, the process begins with the root node. Because the value of the new prescription is less than the value in the root node (node #1, prescription #20), the program moves to the right child.

The value of the new prescription is greater than the value in the root's right child (node #3, prescription #9). The program therefore looks for a left child. In this instance, however, there is no left child. The program has found the correct place to insert the new node; it becomes node #3's left child.

The pharmacy program's implementation of the tree insertion process can be found in Listing 9.15. Notice the similarity of this function to the search function in Listing 9.14. The major difference is that when an unsuccessful search is detected, the search function returns a value to that effect. In contrast, the insert function inserts the new node.

Summary

Pointers are commonly used in a C++ program to set up and manipulate data structures that organize and provide access to collections of objects. In this chapter you have learned about three types of data structures: arrays of pointers to objects, linked lists, and binary trees.

In each case, the data structure is managed by a special object created for that purpose. The data structure management object isolates the program using the data structure from needing to know about details such as inserting and searching for objects.

An array of pointers makes manipulating an array of objects more efficient. Rather than moving entire objects in memory when objects are inserted or removed or when the array is sorted, only pointers are moved. This can speed up program execution and prevent memory from being fragmented. There is one drawback to an array of pointers: the number of objects the array can handle are limited by the size declared for the array. However, an array provides direct access to the pointers, which supports fast search techniques such as the binary search.

Listing 9.15   Inserting a node into a binary search tree in the pharmacy program

```
void PrescriptTree::Insert (Prescription * newPrescript, int prescript_numb)
{
    Prescription * current, * child;

    if (root) // if root node exists
    {
        current = root;
        while (current) // keep going while there's a pointer
        {
            if (current->getPrescript_numb() < prescript_numb)
            {
                // go down right side
                child = current->getRight();
                if (!child) // if no right child, insert
                {
                    current->setRight (newPrescript);
                    return;
                }
            }
            else
            {
                // go down left side
                child = current->getLeft();
                if (!child) // if no left child, insert
                {
                    current->setLeft (newPrescript);
                    return;
                }
            }
            current = child;
        }
    }
    else
        root = newPrescript;
}
```

A linked list is a sequential data structure that links objects together by having each object point to the next (and perhaps also the prior) object in the list. A linked list has no preset limit on the number of objects that can be added to the list. (The limit is usually the amount of memory available to the program.) However, because it is a sequential data structure, it can only be searched sequentially (from first, to next, to next, and so on).

A binary search tree is a hierarchical data structure in which each node has at most two child nodes. The right child is an object with a data value less than the node's value; the left child is an object with a data value greater than the node's value. The number of objects that can be added to a binary search tree is usually limited only by the amount of memory available to a program. It can also be searched very rapidly.

Exercises

1. Create two classes, one to store data about a college student and another to store the courses taken by a student. The course class should include the name and number of the course, the semester/quarter in which the course was taken, the number of course credits, and the grade earned. Create a class that manipulates a linked list that connects course objects to a student object. Also create a class that manipulates an array of student objects. Write a program that tests the classes. The program should do the following:

   - Permit interactive entry of student and course data. The constructor for the student class should insert the student into the array of student objects; the constructor for the course class should insert the course into the correct student's linked list of courses. Optionally, write member functions that store the classes in a data file when the program ends and read the objects into main memory when the program begins.
   - Compute a student's grade point average (GPA) and store the value in the student object. The program should recalculate the GPA each time a new course is added.
   - Display a student's transcript.
   - Determine if or when a specific student has taken a specific course. The user enters the student number and the course number; the program does the rest.

2. Modify Exercise 3 from Chapter 6, creating a class that manipulates the array of product objects. Make the function that computes and displays product costs a member function of the array manipulation class, rather than a function of the main program.

3. Modify Exercise 3 from Chapter 8, creating a class that manipulates the array of medication objects. Make the function that assembles and displays the medication schedule a member function of the array manipulation class, rather than a function of the main program.

4. Write a program that provides lists of the passengers scheduled to fly on an airline's flights. This program needs three classes: a flight (flight number, date, time, and maximum number of passengers), a passenger (name, address, and phone number), and a list manager to handle a linked list of passengers for each flight. Allow users to create new flights, add passengers to a flight, remove passengers from a flight, and display a list of a flight's passengers. Be sure to avoid overbooking!

5. Modify the program you wrote for Exercise 5 above so that it uses binary search trees of passengers rather than linked lists.

6. Write a program that produces an alphabetical list and frequency count of all the words in a text document. The document should be stored in a text file. Maintain the word list in a binary search tree, where each node is an object that stores a word and its frequency. Once the entire file has been processed, the program should print out the contents of the tree, in order. (Note: This is tougher than it appears at first glance. Consider carefully how you will read text in from the file. If you read it in a line at a time, what should the program do if there isn't a blank or a punctuation mark at the end of the line, indicating that the end of the line is in the middle of a word? How should the program detect the situation where there are two or more blanks in a row?)

7. Modify the program you wrote for Exercise 7 at the end of Chapter 7 so that it includes a class for the territories that manipulates an array of salesperson objects and a class for the company that manipulates an array of territory objects. The company class should include a member function that totals sales for the company; the territory class should include a function that sorts its array and totals sales for the territory.

8. The Suddenly Summer Bathing Suit Company needs a program to manage telephone messages that come into the home office for its salespeople. The telephone is answered by a secretary, who types the message into a

computer. Write a program that can be used to store and retrieve messages. The program is based on three classes: a salesperson class (name and password), a message class (the text of the message—up to 256 characters, the date and time of the message, whether the message has been read), and a class to manipulate a linked list of the messages waiting for a given salesperson. The program should allow a secretary to enter messages. A salesperson should be able to retrieve his or her unread messages, all messages (read and unread), and delete messages. Note that a secretary can enter messages for any salesperson. However, a salesperson must supply a recognized name and password to retrieve or delete messages. To make this practical, of course, salesperson data and messages must be maintained in data files that are read when the program is run and written when the program stops.

9. The pharmacy program needs some work to make it more functional and less error-prone. Add and test the following capabilities:

   - Add array-bounds checking to the `drugArray` class's `Insert` checking. If the user attempts to insert a new drug when the drug array is full, display an appropriate message to the user.
   - Write a function for the `drugArray` class to delete a drug.
   - Write a function for the `CustList` class to delete a customer. (Don't forget to remove the customer object from memory after it's been removed from the linked list.)
   - Write a function for the `CustList` class that modifies a customer's name. Keep in mind that changing a customer's name means that the customer object may need also to change its position in the linked list.
   - When a customer is deleted, the pharmacy program should also delete all the customer's prescriptions. Therefore, write a function that deletes a prescription. This function should remove the prescription from the linked list of prescriptions. Once you've tested the prescription deletion function, modify the function that deletes a customer so that it traverses the customer's linked list of prescriptions, deleting all prescriptions in the list. Then, remove the `PrescriptList` object that manages the prescription list from memory.
   - When a prescription is deleted, it should also be removed from the binary tree of prescriptions. Write a function to remove a prescrip-

tion from that tree. (Note: This isn't as easy as it seems at first glance. Think about which object remaining in the tree should be moved into the position of the object being deleted and develop your logic based on that principle.) Once the function is working, add it to the function that deletes a customer and the customer's prescriptions.

10. (General Ledger) Add a class to the general ledger program that you began developing in Chapter 7 to handle a general ledger journal entry. Consider what data structure(s) will be needed to handle multiple journal entries. Each time a journal entry is created, update the appropriate account in the chart of accounts. (Note: You may also want to replace the program array used to manage the chart of accounts with an array-management object.) Add functions to the program so that it can display journal entries in order by number or by date. Also add code to display a current balance sheet.

Long

11. (Purchasing) Add data structures to the purchasing program that you began developing in Chapter 7. The data structures should link vendors to their purchase orders and purchase orders to the line items that appear on them. Also add data structures to manage multiple Vendor objects and multiple Item objects. Demonstrate that the data structures work by adding functions to the program to display a complete purchase order.

Long

12. (Manufacturing) Create the three classes that will form the basis of a manufacturing management system: Raw Material, Assembly, Product. In this program, an assembly is made up of raw materials and possibly, other assemblies. A product is made up of assemblies and raw materials that aren't part of an assembly. The classes should track quantities of raw materials used to make assemblies and products as well as inventory levels of all raw materials, assemblies, and products. Include appropriate data structures to link raw materials, assemblies, and products.

Long

Write a program that demonstrates that the classes work. In particular, the program should allow a user to retrieve the instructions for creating any specific product, including all assemblies and raw materials used in any way to create that product. Keep in mind that this program is useful only if it can store its data in files.

10

Overloading

OBJECTIVES

In this chapter you will learn about:
- Using overloading to give functions more than one implementation within the same class.
- Using overloading to give operators more than one meaning.
- Defining overloaded operators for a class that traverses a binary tree.

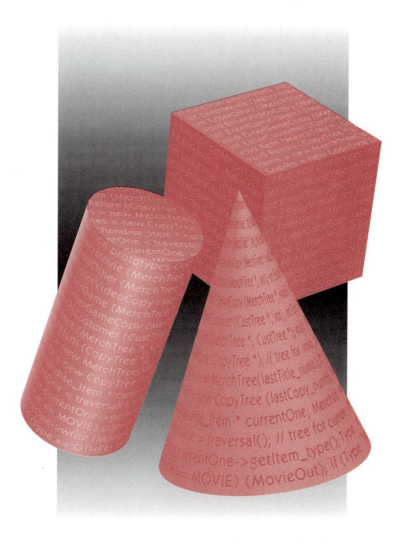

Overloading is a technique for giving operators and functions multiple definitions so that using the same operator or calling the same function results in different actions, depending on the way in which the operator or function is used. The major benefit of overloading is that it simplifies the use of classes by helping to present a consistent interface to the programmer.

Although you may not be aware of it, you have already used overloaded operators. For example, the stream insertion and extraction operators are redefinitions of the C++ operators that shift the bits in a storage location to the right (>>) or left (<<). The instances in the pharmacy program in which classes have more than one constructor is also an example of overloading.

In this chapter you will learn how to overload functions so that the same action can easily be performed in the same way under slightly different circumstances. You will also learn how to create your own overloaded operators to simplify the way in which a program can manipulate an object and see how overloaded operators can be used to implement the traversal of a binary tree.

Overloading Member Functions

When a C++ compiler compiles member functions, it identifies a function by more than just its name. A function's *signature* is made up of its name along with the number, type, and order of its parameters. It is therefore acceptable to define more than one function by the same name in the same class, as long as the functions have different signatures. For example, the following functions are recognized by a C++ compiler as different:

```
Object * find (char *, int);
Object * find (int, char *);
```

Although the two functions return the same type of value and have the same name, number of parameters, and parameter types, the order of their parameters is distinct. When you define two or more member functions in the same class with the same name, distinguishing them by their parameters, you are using function overloading.

Note

Using the same function name in different classes isn't precisely the same as overloading within a single class. A C++ compiler identifies member functions in terms of the classes in which they are defined. You can therefore define two functions with exactly the same name and parameter list for two distinct classes without a problem. The program knows which class's member function to use based on the type of object issuing the function call.

Overloading Constructors

One of the most common uses of overloading is to provide multiple constructors for the same class. The pharmacy program, for example, has two constructors for each of the Drug, Customer, and Prescription classes, one for data that are entered from the keyboard and the other for data that are read from a file. In each case, the function signatures are significantly different:

```
Drug(ifstream &);
Drug(int, int, int, string, string[], string[]);
```

The first constructor above has only one parameter—an input stream reference. The second constructor's parameters are three integers, a string (a type defined by the program to hold an 80-character string), and two arrays of strings.

As you can see in Listing 10.1, the implementations of the two functions are also considerably different. Keep in mind, however, that the C++ compiler knows which function to bind to an object based on the entire function signature, not just the function name.

Note

Because C++ compilers identify functions by the entire function signature and not just the name of the function, compilers can identify many errors that involve the wrong types and/or numbers of parameters passed to functions by comparing the parameter list in a function call to the parameter list in a prototype. In most cases, the compiler's error message will tell you that the compiler can't find a function that matches the signature in a function call. It's then up to you to figure out where the function call's parameter list differs from that of the function's prototype.

Listing 10.1   Overloaded constructors for the Drug class from the pharmacy program

```
Drug::Drug(ifstream & fin)     // constructor that loads one from disk
{
    char dummy;
    fin >> drug_numb;
    fin.get (dummy); // skip over blank
    fin.getline (drug_name,80,'\0');
    fin >> numb_generics;
    fin.get (dummy); // skip over blank
    for (int i = 0; i <= numb_generics; i++)
        fin.getline (generics[i],80,'\0');
    fin >> numb_conflicts;
    fin.get (dummy); // skip over blank
    for (i = 0; i <= numb_conflicts; i++)
        fin.getline (conflicts[i],80,'\0');
}

// constructor for interactive drug entry
Drug::Drug(int idrug_numb, int inumb_generics, int inumb_conflicts, string
    idrug_name, string igenerics[], string iconflicts[])
{
    drug_numb = idrug_numb;
    strcpy (drug_name, idrug_name);
    numb_generics = inumb_generics;
    for (int i = 0; i <= numb_generics; i++)
        strcpy (generics[i], igenerics[i]);
    numb_conflicts = inumb_conflicts;
    for (i = 0; i <= numb_conflicts; i++)
        strcpy (conflicts[i], iconflicts[i]);
}
```

Copy Constructors

Many classes contain a third type of constructor known as a *copy constructor.* It is an overloaded member function, just like the constructors you have seen for interactive and file input. The purpose of a copy constructor is to initialize a new object with data copied from another object of the same class. For example, the Drug class might declare a copy constructor as:

```
Drug (Drug);
```

The function then can be implemented simply with:

```
Drug::Drug (Drug copyDrug)
    { *this = copyDrug; }
```

Using the default assignment in the preceding example will work only if the class contains no pointers. If the class contains pointers, then you will end up having two objects pointing to the same place in main memory because the contents of pointer variables will be copied along with the contents of regular variables. Therefore, if a class contains pointers, a copy constructor must initialize each variable individually.

For example, assume that a class named sampleClass contains the following variables:

```
someClass * anObject;
int ID_numb;
char name[31], address[81];
```

If you attempt to use the default *this assignment for these variables, you will end up with two classes pointing to the same object created from someClass because the assignment will copy the address of the object rather than creating a new one. This means that you can't use *this to copy from one object to another but must write a copy constructor that creates an object from the someClass. A sample copy constructor might appear like the one in Listing 10.2. Notice that the regular variables are copied using an assignment statement but that the anObject pointer is filled by using the new statement to actually create the object.

Listing 10.2   A copy constructor

```
sampleClass::sampleClass (sampleClass & original)
{
    ID_numb = original.ID_numb;
    strcpy (name, original.name);
    strcpy (addres, original.address);
    anObject = new someClass ();
}
```

You can invoke a copy constructor when you declare an object as a variable. For example, assume that a program contains the following:

```
sampleClass firstObject (0,"", "");
sampleClass secondObject = firstObject;
```

The first declaration creates an object from `sampleClass` and passes the data for the class into a constructor designed for interactive input. (The `ID_numb` variable receives the zero; the two string variables receive nulls). Although the second declaration looks like an assignment statement, it actually creates `secondObject` and invokes the copy constructor, passing `firstObject` into the constructor.

Overloading Operators

Overloading functions is easy; all you need to do is make sure that the overloaded functions have different signatures. There are no other restrictions on the overloaded functions. Overloading operators is very different. Although overloaded operators are implemented as functions, there are significant restrictions on where they are defined and the number and type of parameters they can accept.

If operator overloading is surrounded by more restrictions than function overloading, why bother to do it at all? Because overloaded operators can greatly simplify the interface between a programmer and the classes he or she is using. For example, suppose you decided on a single output format that you always wanted to use for the data in a given class. One way to handle that output would be to provide the output formatting in a member function. A program using that format could then include the statement:

```
cout << Object_name;
```

to display the object's data. In this case, the `<<` operator has been overloaded to invoke the function that performs the actual output. The overloading provides a logically consistent way to access the output function.

Note

The idea behind overloaded operators is to define new behaviors for operators that are consistent with the operators' default behaviors. It is confusing to the programmer if operator overloading drastically changes an operator's behavior. For example, overloading a multiplication operator to perform an addition is confusing. However, overloading a multiplication operator so that it multiplies the values contained in two objects makes sense.

Introducing the Direct Mail Program

As a first look at overloading operators, we'll be examining a program that selects people from a mailing list based on a computed demographic index. The purpose of the program is to allow a company marketing by direct mail to select advertising targets that are likely to purchase its products.

Each factor the program stores about a person (age, income, educational level, marital status, and occupation) is given a numeric value. The index is generated by adding together the values assigned each characteristic. Higher index values represent wealthier, older, and more highly educated individuals.

The header file for the direct mail program can be found in Listing 10.3. You can recognize functions that implement overloaded operators by the presence of the keyword `operator`. Notice that the overloaded operators appear in two different places. The first three—those at the top of the class definition—are preceded by the keyword `friend`. Friend functions (and classes) are defined outside the class but have access to all the class's private members. The remaining overloaded functions are declared just like other public member functions.

There are actually three functions in Listing 10.3 that have the name `operator==`. Each, however, has a different signature. In this case, the overloaded operators are also overloaded functions! You will see shortly why the functions have been declared in this way.

Operators Available for Overloading

Most of C++'s operators are available for overloading, including those in Table 10.1. Notice that the operators are divided into two types, unary and binary. Unary operators are those that work on a single value. For example, the

Listing 10.3   mail.h: Header file for the direct mail program

```
typedef char string[81];
const ARRAY_MAX = 25;

class Direct_mail
{
    friend ostream & operator<< (ostream &, Direct_mail *);
    friend int operator== (Direct_mail, int);
    friend int operator== (int, Direct_mail);

    private:
        int age_group, income;
        int married, occupation, ed_level;
        string fname, lname, street, city;
        char state[3], zip[6];
        // compute weighted index of demographic factors
        int computeIndex ();
    public:
        Direct_mail (int, int, int, int, int, string, string, string, string,
            char [], char []);
        // compare two marketing targets
        int operator== (Direct_mail);
        int operator> (Direct_mail);
        int operator>= (Direct_mail);
        int operator< (Direct_mail);
        int operator<= (Direct_mail);
        // compare current marketing target against constants
        int operator> (int);
        int operator>= (int);
        int operator< (int);
        int operator<= (int);
};

class Mail_array
{
    private:
        // array of 25 pointers
        Direct_mail * people[ARRAY_MAX];
        // last index used in array
        int Count;
    public:
        Mail_array();
        void Insert (Direct_mail *);
        int getCount();
        Direct_mail * getOne (int);
        void sortArray ();
};
```

+ operator can be used to change the sign of a single value, as in +sales. However, when the same operator is used between two other values, as in sales + tax, it is a binary operator that adds the two values together.

Table 10.1   Some of the C++ operators available for overloading

Operator	Type	Operator	Type	Operator	Type
+	Unary	++	Unary	!	Unary
-	Unary	--	Unary	( )	Unary
+	Binary	*	Binary	[ ]	Unary
-	Binary	/	Binary	%	Binary
==	Binary	=	Binary	&	Binary
!=	Binary	+=	Binary	&&	Binary
<	Binary	-=	Binary	|	Binary
<=	Binary	*=	Binary	||	Binary
>=	Binary	/=	Binary	<<	Binary
>	Binary	%=	Binary	>>	Binary

The distinction between unary and binary operators may seem trivial. However, as you will see shortly, the rules for where you define overloaded operator functions and the number of parameters they can take depend in some part on whether an operator is unary or binary.

The Rules for Operator Overloading

As mentioned earlier, the implementation of operator overloading is rather restrictive. The rules that you will be encountering as we go through examples of operator overloading include the following:

• Operator overloading can be used only to redefine the behavior of existing operators. It cannot be used to define new ones.

- Overloading for a unary operator can be declared as a member function with no parameters. The operator then always acts on the current object.
- Overloading for a unary operator can be declared as a friend function with one parameter, which must be an object of the class or a pointer to an object of the class.
- Overloading for a binary operator can be declared as a member function with one parameter. In this case, the current object must always be used on the left of the operator. The object or value on the right of the operator is taken from the parameter passed into the function.
- Overloading for a binary operator can be declared as a friend function with two parameters, one of which must be an object of the class or a pointer to an object of the class. The first parameter is the value or object that is used on the left of the operator; the second parameter is the value or object that is used on the right.

How do you choose whether to implement an overloaded operator as a member function or a friend function? The answer is tied to the nature of friend functions and the flexibility you need for the overloaded operator. A friend function has access to all the private variables and functions in the class for which it is declared as a friend. Using friend functions therefore violates the object-oriented principle of information hiding. Many programmers therefore prefer not to use friend functions if they can be avoided.

However, when you overload a binary operator as a member function, it can only take one parameter. For example, if the demographic index for an object is to be compared to a constant, an overloaded operator can be declared as

```
int operator== (int);
```

The problem with this declaration is that when the overloaded operator is used, the object must always be on the left side of the operator, as in

```
Object_name == 7
```

In other words, the operation isn't commutative. If you want it to be commutative, so that the object and the constant can be on either side of the operator, then you must implement the overloading using two friend functions, each of which can take two parameters:

```
friend int operator== (Direct_mail, int);
friend int operator== (int, Direct_mail);
```

Because the overloaded operator sends the object or value on the left side of the operator into the first parameter and the object or value on the right side of the operator into the second parameter, the compiler chooses whichever of the two functions above matches the use of the operator in a program. When you want an overloaded operator to be commutative, you have no alternative but to use friend functions in the above fashion.

Overloading Operators Using Member Functions

To overload an operator as a member function, first declare a function prototype in which the name of the function is the keyword operator followed by the operator being overloaded. Then, define a function that performs the actions you want to occur when the overloaded operator is used with an object.

Overloading to Compare an Object with a Constant

The direct mail program overloads the relationship operators as member functions to compare the current object with a constant using the following declarations:

```
int operator> (int);
int operator>= (int);
int operator< (int);
int operator<= (int);
```

Notice that each function has a return type. In the case of a relationship operator, the return value should be either true or false (1 or 0). The first four operators above compare the demographic index of the current object with the index of a second object. The second four operators compare the demographic index of the current object with a constant.

The implementation of the functions is the same as any other member function. As you can see in Listing 10.4 (the implementation of the Direct_mail class), each function performs a comparison between the index value computed for the current object (returned by the computeIndex function) and the input parameter (either a constant or the result of the computeIndex function performed on another object). The result of the comparison (either 1 or 0) is sent back to the program using the overloaded operator.

Listing 10.4 The Direct_mail class from the direct mail program

```
#include <string.h>
#include <iostream.h>
#include "mail.h"

Direct_mail::Direct_mail (int iage, int isalary, int imarried, int ijob, int
    ied_level, string ifname, string ilname, string istreet, string icity, char
    istate[], char izip[])
{
    age_group = iage;
    income = isalary;
    married = imarried;
    occupation = ijob;
    ed_level = ied_level;
    strcpy (fname, ifname);
    strcpy (lname, ilname);
    strcpy (street, istreet);
    strcpy (city, icity);
    strcpy (state, istate);
    strcpy (zip, izip);
}

int Direct_mail::computeIndex ()
{
    return (age_group + income + married + occupation + ed_level);
}

int Direct_mail::operator== (Direct_mail person2)
{
    return (computeIndex() == person2.computeIndex());
}

int Direct_mail::operator> (Direct_mail person2)
{
    return (computeIndex() > person2.computeIndex());
}
```

Continued next page

Listing 10.4 (Continued) The Direct_mail class from the direct mail program

```
int Direct_mail::operator>= (Direct_mail person2)
{
    return (computeIndex() >= person2.computeIndex());
}

int Direct_mail::operator< (Direct_mail person2)
{
    return (computeIndex() < person2.computeIndex());
}

int Direct_mail::operator<= (Direct_mail person2)
{
    return (computeIndex() < person2.computeIndex());
}

int Direct_mail::operator> (int compare_value)
{
    return (computeIndex() > compare_value);
}

int Direct_mail::operator>= (int compare_value)
{
    return (computeIndex() >= compare_value);
}

int Direct_mail::operator< (int compare_value)
{
    return (computeIndex() < compare_value);
}

int Direct_mail::operator<= (int compare_value)
{
    return (computeIndex() <= compare_value);
}
```

An overloaded operator works on an entire object, using the same syntax employed when the operator is used without being overloaded. For example, to determine if the demographic index of the current object is less than a value entered by the user (stored in the variable index_value), the direct mail program uses:

```
if (*currentOne <= index_value)
    cout << currentOne << endl;
```

The variable `currentOne` contains a pointer to the current object. Therefore, to use the overloaded operator, a program must dereference the pointer to gain access to the contents of the object. However, if the object was declared for static binding and the variable contained the object rather than a pointer to it, dereferencing would be unnecessary.

The complete program that uses the overloaded operators can be found in Listing 10.5. As you study the code, notice that because the overloaded operators were declared as member functions, an object or a pointer to an object *must* appear on the left side of the operator. The single parameter accepted by the overloaded operator's function *must* appear on the right side.

Note

The user interface in the direct mail program isn't particularly good. To keep the code short enough to include in this chapter, the user is asked to enter integers that correspond to the coded values for demographic characteristics. A better interface would allow the user to enter data as characters. The program would then convert the characters to the coded values, out of sight of the user. This program is also written only for interactive input. In the real world, a program of this type would generally read its input from a file. If the mailing list were too large to keep in memory, the file I/O would process objects as they were read from a file, rather than processing them from an array.

Listing 10.5   main.cpp: Main program for the direct mail program

```
#include <iostream.h>
#include <stdio.h>
#include "mail.h"

void main()
{
    void Enter (Mail_array *); // enter a new person
    void choosePeople (Mail_array *); // choose people
    void sortAndDisplay (Mail_array *); // sort by demographic index
    int quickMenu ();

    Mail_array * Data_source;
    Data_source = new Mail_array();

    int choice = 0;
```

Continued next page

Listing 10.5 (Continued) main.cpp: Main program for the direct mail program

```cpp
    while (choice != 9)
    {
        choice = quickMenu ();
        switch (choice)
        {
            case 1:
                Enter (Data_source);
                break;
            case 2:
                choosePeople (Data_source);
                break;
            case 3:
                sortAndDisplay (Data_source);
                break;
            case 9:
                break;
            default:
                cout << "You've entered an unavailable option." << endl;
        }
    }
}

void Enter (Mail_array * Data_source)
{
    int imarried, ijob, ied_level, isalary, ihow_old;
    string ifname, ilname, istreet, icity;
    char istate[3], izip[6];

    Direct_mail * newPerson;

    cout << "First name: ";
    gets (ifname);
    cout << "Last name: ";
    gets (ilname);
    cout << "Street: ";
    gets (istreet);
    cout << "City: ";
    gets (icity);
    cout << "State: ";
    gets (istate);
    cout << "Zip code: ";
    gets (izip);
    cout << "Age group (0:under20, 1:under30, 2:under45, 3:under60, 4:under75,
        5:over75): ";
    cin >> ihow_old;
```

Continued next page

Listing 10.5 (Continued) main.cpp: Main program for the direct mail program

```cpp
        cout <<"Income group (0:LT10, 1:LT20, 2:LT40, 3:LT60, 4:LT100, 5:GT100): ";
        cin >> isalary;
        cout << "Married? (1:TRUE, 0:FALSE): ";
        cin >> imarried;
        cout << "Occupation group (0:unskilled, 1:blueCollar, 2:whiteCollar,
        3:professional): ";
        cin >> ijob;
        cout << "Education level" << endl;
        cout << "  (0:no_grade, 1:grade, 2:some_hi, 3:hi, 4:some_college,
            5:college, 6:some_grad, 7:grad): ";
        cin >> ied_level;
        newPerson = new Direct_mail (ihow_old, isalary, imarried, ijob, ied_level,
            ifname, ilname, istreet, icity, istate, izip);
        Data_source->Insert (newPerson);
}

void choosePeople (Mail_array * Data_source)
{
    int index_value, comparison, i, currentIndex;
    Direct_mail * currentOne;

    cout << "Enter the index value for matching: ";
    cin >> index_value;
    cout << "Choose the operator (0:EQ, 1:LT, 2:LE, 3:GT, 4:GE): ";
    cin >> comparison;
    for (i = 0; i <= Data_source->getCount(); i++)
    {
        currentOne = Data_source->getOne(i);
        switch (comparison)
        {
            case 0:
                if (*currentOne == index_value)
                    cout << currentOne << endl;
                break;
            case 1:
                if (*currentOne < index_value)
                    cout << currentOne << endl;
                break;
            case 2:
                if (*currentOne <= index_value)
                    cout << currentOne << endl;
                break;
            case 3:
                if (*currentOne > index_value)
                    cout << currentOne << endl;
```

Continued next page

Listing 10.5 (Continued) main.cpp: Main program for the direct mail program

```
                break;
            case 4:
                if (*currentOne >= index_value)
                    cout << currentOne << endl;
        }
    }

}

void sortAndDisplay (Mail_array * Data_source)
{
    Direct_mail * onePerson;

    Data_source->sortArray();
    for (int i = 0; i <= Data_source->getCount(); i++)
    {
        onePerson = Data_source->getOne(i);
        cout << onePerson << endl << endl;
    }
}

int quickMenu()
{
    int choice;
    cout << "\n\nYou can do any of the following:" << endl;
    cout << " 1. Enter a new person into the mailing list" << endl;
    cout << " 2. Select people by weighted demographic index" << endl;
    cout << " 3. Sort by weighted demographic index and display" << endl;
    cout << " 9. Quit" << endl << endl;
    cout << "Pick one: ";
    cin >> choice;
    return choice;
}
```

Overloading to Compare Two Objects

Overloaded operators can compare the current object to another object. The direct mail program declares the following member functions for that purpose:

```
int operator== (Direct_mail);
int operator> (Direct_mail);
int operator>= (Direct_mail);
int operator< (Direct_mail);
int operator<= (Direct_mail);
```

These operators are to simplify the coding of a function that sorts the entire array of Direct_mail objects in ascending order by demographic index.

The code for this sort can be found in Listing 10.6, which contains the implementation of the Mail_array class. The sort used in this case is a *Shell sort*, a sorting method that is more efficient than a bubble sort because it limits the number of comparisons that are made.

Listing 10.6   Implementation of the Mail_array class for the direct mail program

```
Mail_array::Mail_array()
{
    Count = -1;
    for (int i = 0; i < ARRAY_MAX; i++)
        people[i] = 0;
}

void Mail_array::Insert (Direct_mail * newPerson)
{
    people[++Count] = newPerson;
}

int Mail_array::getCount()
{
    return Count;
}

Direct_mail * Mail_array::getOne(int index)
{
    return people[index];
}

void Mail_array::sortArray ()   // shell sort
{
    int distance, limit, current, working, Xflag;
    Direct_mail * Tmail;

    distance = Count/2;
    while (distance > 0)
    {
        // set limit so sort doesn't go beyond bottom of array
        limit = Count - distance;
        current = 0;
```

Continued next page

Listing 10.6 (Continued) Implementation of the Mail_array class for the direct mail program

```
    // stop when a comparison would go beyond bottom of array
    while (current <= limit)
    {
        // use an overloaded operator to make a comparison between the
        // demographic indexes of two Direct_mail objects
        if (*people[current] > *people[current+distance])
        {
            // save current so you can back up without disturbing it
            working = current;
            Xflag = TRUE;
            while (Xflag)
            {
                // start swap
                Tmail = people[working];
                people[working] = people[working+distance];
                people[working+distance] = Tmail;
                // end swap
                // back up if possible
                working = working - distance;
                // check to see if backup went beyond beginning of array
                if (working >= 0)
                {
                    if (*people[working] <= *people[working+distance])
                        Xflag = FALSE;
                }
                else
                    Xflag = FALSE;
            }
        }
        current++;
    }
    distance /= 2;
    }
}
Mail_array::Mail_array()
{
    Count = -1;
    for (int i = 0; i < ARRAY_MAX; i++)
        people[i] = 0;
}
```

Rather than comparing adjacent values during every pass like the bubble sort, the shell sort compares values that are some distance apart and swaps those values if they are in the wrong order. The distance is initially set to half the size of the array (distance = Count /2;). Comparisons are then made between the current object and the object that is distance places away from it. The comparisons are stopped by a limit that prevents the sort from attempting to access an element beyond the end of the array. Therefore, in the first pass, the sort only looks at half the possible pairs of values; a bubble sort would look at every possible pair.

When the shell sort finds two values that are out of order, it swaps those values. If possible (if doing so doesn't go beyond the bounds of the array), the sort then backs up to compare pairs of values above the current value, swapping any values that aren't in order. At the end of a pass through the array, the array will be in better order than it was, although individual elements will not necessarily be in their final position.

Each pass through the array, the shell sort shortens the distance between the items being compared. On the last pass, the distance will be one. During that last pass, the shell short does compare all possible pairs, functioning much like a bubble sort. However, because the other passes examine fewer pairs, this sorting technique usually runs faster than a bubble sort.

Overloading Operators Using Friend Functions

When you want to use two arguments with an overloaded operator, you need to declare the function for the overloading as a friend function. In this section you will be introduced to friend functions and classes and learn how friends can be used to implement operator overloading, including overloading stream operators.

Declaring Friend Classes and Functions

As you have read, a friend is something that has access to all of a class's private data and functions. A program can declare either a class or a function as a friend. To declare a friend class, include the keyword friend followed by the name of the class in the declaration of the class to which the first class should be a friend. For example, in the following declaration, the Employee class is a friend to the Project class:

```
class Project
{
    friend Employee;
    private:
        ...
    public:
        ...
};
```

This means that all parts of the Employee class have access to all parts of the Project class, including private variables and private functions.

To declare a friend function, include the keyword friend followed by the function's prototype in the declaration of the class to which the function will be a friend. The Direct_mail class includes the following friend function declarations:

```
friend ostream & operator<< (ostream &, Direct_mail *);
friend int operator== (Direct_mail, int);
friend int operator== (int, Direct_mail);
```

Because the use of friend classes and functions violates the object-oriented principles of information hiding, many programmers prefer to avoid using friends except when absolutely necessary. Declaring overloaded operators using two parameters is one of those situations.

Overloading Stream Operators

You can overload the stream insertion and extraction operators to make it easier to perform input and output with an object. To do so using a friend function, the function prototype must include a reference to the stream as the first parameter and the object or a pointer to the object as the second parameter. This operation will never be commutative; when stream insertion or extraction is performed, the name of the stream always precedes operator, which precedes the object.

In the case of a generic output stream, the stream reference parameter is to an object of class ostream; in the case of an input stream, the stream reference is to an object of class istream. A function that overloads the stream insertion operator must also return a reference to the stream, as in:

```
friend ostream & operator<< (ostream &, Direct_mail *);
```

The implementation of the friend function that overloads the stream insertion operator for the direct mail program can be found in Listing 10.7. Notice that the body of the operator<< function inserts values into the stream just as a program would if it were using the cout stream. The function's final action is to return the stream to the calling function.

Listing 10.7   friends.cpp: Member functions implementing overloaded operators as friend functions for the direct mail program

```
#include <iostream.h>
#include "mail.h"

// overloading stream insertion operator so cout will output entire object
ostream & operator << (ostream & out_stream, Direct_mail * Mptr)
{
    out_stream << Mptr->fname << " " << Mptr->lname << endl;
    out_stream << Mptr->street << endl;
    out_stream << Mptr->city << ", " << Mptr->state << " " << Mptr->zip << endl;
    out_stream << "  Weighted demographic index: " << Mptr->computeIndex();
    return out_stream;
}

int operator== (Direct_mail person, int compare_value)
{
    return (person.computeIndex() == compare_value)
}

int operator== (int compare_value, Direct_mail person)
{
    return (person.computeIndex() == compare_value)
}
```

To use an overloaded stream operator, follow the name of the stream with the operator and an object from a class for which the overloaded operator has been defined. For example, the direct mail program displays the contents of a Direct_mail object using the following:

```
cout << onePerson << endl << endl;
```

Note

The drawback of overloading the stream insertion and extraction operators is that member functions have to perform I/O. To facilitate cross-platform code, however, a programmer often wants to avoid making I/O part of member functions. There is therefore a tradeoff with using overloaded operators for I/O. Although the overloading operators make coding easier, they can be a problem when you want to reuse the class using a different user interface.

Overloading Operators to Make Them Commutative

As mentioned earlier, when you overload a binary operator as a member function, the operator must be used so that the current object is always to the left and value for the input parameter is always to the right. If you want to make the use of the operator commutative, you must declare two overloaded operator functions as friends, as in:

```
friend int operator== (Direct_mail, int);
friend int operator== (int, Direct_mail);
```

The definitions of these two functions appear in Listing 10.7. Notice that the only difference between them is the order of their input parameters. That means that either of the following expressions is acceptable:

```
(*Direct_mail_object_pointer == integer_value)
(integer_value == *Direct_mail_object_pointer)
```

Overloading Unary Operators to Traverse a Binary Tree

When studying the pharmacy program, you learned how to insert objects into a binary tree and use that tree to perform fast searches. As well as searching a binary tree, you may need to access all the objects in the tree, in order. This is known as *traversing* the tree. Although there are several ways to access the nodes in a tree, one of the most common is an *in-order traversal*, in which a program processes the nodes in the order imposed by the tree (for example, alphabetical, numeric, or chronological order). The object-oriented implementation of an in-order traversal makes extensive use of overloaded unary operators.

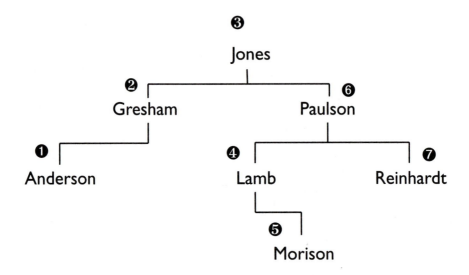

Figure 10.1   in-order traversal of a binary tree

The Algorithm Behind an In-Order Traversal

To help understand the algorithm used to perform an in-order traversal, take a look at the sample tree in Figure 10.1. The numbers by the nodes indicate the order in which the nodes should be processed. The first problem that faces a program trying to perform such a traversal is that entry to the tree is through the root node, which, in this example, is actually the third node in alphabetical order. Once the first three nodes have been processed, the program must then deal with the right side of the tree, where the next nodes are two and three layers down. To make the situation even more complicated, there's no way a program can predict in which order the nodes will need to be accessed before actually entering the tree; the access order is determined to some extent by the order in which the nodes were entered into the tree. For example, in Figure 10.1, Morison entered the tree *after* Lamb. However, if Morison entered the tree first, it would be a left child of Paulson. When Lamb entered, it would end up a left child of Morison. A program must therefore have a generalized algorithm for locating the nodes in the correct order.

An in-order tree traversal uses the following procedure:

1. Enter the tree at the root.
2. If there is a left child, save the previous node and move to the left child.
3. Repeat step 2 until there are no more left children.
4. Process the current node.
5. If there is a right child, save the right child and go to step 2. Otherwise, move back to the most recently saved node. Repeat step 4.
6. Continue the procedure until all nodes have been processed.

The trick to this process is coming up with a way to save nodes as the program moves down through a chain of left child nodes. The answer is a data structure called a *stack*.

Operation of the Stack

A stack is a linear data structure in which data are entered and removed from only one end. The last piece of data entered is therefore the first piece of data removed. It often helps to think of a stack as a spring-loaded tube (something akin to a Pez candy dispenser) like that in Figure 10.2. Data are *pushed* onto the top of the stack one at a time. Because the bottom of the stack is closed, the only way to remove data is to *pop* a value off the top.

Because a stack is a linear data structure that doesn't need direct access to its elements, it can be implemented using either a linked list or an array. In either case, the program using the stack needs to keep track of the top of the stack (a *stack pointer*). A push function increments the stack pointer and stores a new item on the stack. By the same token, a pop function removes an item from the stack and then decrements the stack pointer.

The in-order tree traversal algorithm you saw earlier uses a stack to traverse the tree in Figure 10.1 in the following way:

1. Enter the tree through the root.
2. Push Jones onto the stack.
3. Push Gresham onto the stack.
4. Push Anderson onto the stack.
5. Because Anderson has no left child, pop Anderson off the stack and process it.
6. Check to see if Anderson has a right child. Because Anderson has no

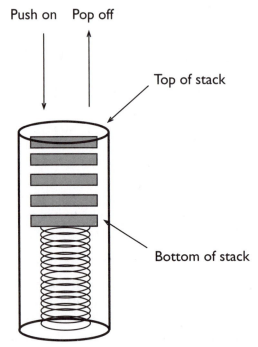

Push on   Pop off

Top of stack

Bottom of stack

Figure 10.2   The operation of a stack

right child, pop Gresham off the stack and process it.

7. Check to see if Gresham has a right child. Because Gresham has no right child, pop Jones off the stack and process it.

8. Check to see if Jones has a right child. Because Jones has a right child, push Paulson onto the stack.

9. Push Lamb onto the stack.

10. Because Lamb has no left child, pop Lamb off the stack and process it.

11. Check to see if Lamb has a right child. Because Lamb has a right child, push Morison onto the stack.

12. Because Morison has no left child, pop Morison off the stack and process it.

13. Because Morison has no right child, pop Paulson off the stack and process it.

14. Check to see if Paulson has a right child. Because Paulson has a right

child, push Reinhardt onto the stack.

15. Because Reinhardt has no left child, pop it off the stack and process it.

16. Because Reinhardt has no right child and there are no nodes waiting on the stack to be processed, stop.

Implementing the In-Order Traversal

There are many ways to actually write code to perform an in-order tree traversal. The object-oriented method uses a special class known as an *iterator*. Iterators can be defined for any type of data structure (an array, a list, or tree). Their purpose is to process the nodes in the data structure, one node at a time.

A tree iterator manages its stack, keeping track of the stack pointer and pushing and popping items from that stack. It also returns a node to the program for processing and detects the end of the traversal when the stack is empty. Overloaded operators are used to move from one node to another, to check for the end of the process, and to return the current node for processing.

As an example of an in-order tree traversal, we will be taking a first look at a program that manages a video store. (You will see much more of this program in Chapter 11; the complete source code is in Appendix B.) The merchandise items stocked by the store (movies, other videos, and games) are organized in a single binary search tree by title. The nodes in the tree are pointers to a class named Merchandise_Item; the class that manages the tree is named MerchTree. The functions for inserting items into the tree and finding items by title work exactly the same way as the binary search tree implemented for the pharmacy program.

The iterator for a MerchTree, the class MerchItr, can be found in Listing 10.8. Its variables include the stack, a pointer to the root of the tree, and a stack pointer. For demonstration purposes, the stack has been implemented as an array. The stack pointer is therefore an integer that represents the element that is currently the top of the stack.

Note

When implemented as an array, a stack can grow from low addresses up or from high addresses down. A stack array can be filled beginning with element 0 or beginning with the highest element.

Listing 10.8   The MerchItr class from the video store program

```
class MerchItr
{
    private:
        Merchandise_Item * stack[25], * root;
        int stackPtr;
        void push (Merchandise_Item *); // push onto stack
        Merchandise_Item * pop (); // pop from stack
        void goLeft (Merchandise_Item *); // push left children onto stack
    public:
        MerchItr ();
        int Init (MerchTree *);
        int operator++ (); // find next node to process
        int operator! (); // check for end of traversal
        Merchandise_Item * operator() (); // return pointer to current object
};
```

To traverse the tree, the video store program uses a `MerchItr` object as in Listing 10.9. First, the program opens the files to which data will be written. It then declares an object of the `MerchItr` class. The iteration itself is controlled by a `for` loop.

Listing 10.9   Using a tree iterator in the video store program

```
// open data files for writing
ofstream MovieOut ("Movies");
ofstream OtherOut ("Others");
ofstream GameOut ("Games");
// declare an iterator object
MerchItr traversal;
// control the iteration with a for loop
for (traversal.Init (Items); !traversal; ++traversal)
{
    int Type;
    Merchandise_Item * currentOne;
    // retrieve a pointer to the current node
    currentOne = traversal();
    Type = currentOne->getItem_type();
    if (Type == MOVIE)
        currentOne->write (MovieOut);
    else if (Type == OTHER)
        currentOne->write (OtherOut);
    else
        currentOne->write (GameOut);
}
```

The loop is initialized by the MerchItr class's Init function, which is passed a pointer to the tree of Merchandise_Item objects. As you can see in Listing 10.10, the Init function initializes the stack pointer to one less than the minimum array index. (This value will be used to determine whether the stack is empty.) The Init function also retrieves the root of the tree and then executes the goLeft function to push left children onto the stack until a node without a left child is reached. It returns TRUE (1) because the stack is not empty; even if there is only one node in the tree, the track will contain the root node.

Listing 10.10   The implementation of the MerchItr class for the video store program

```
MerchItr::MerchItr()
{
    stackPtr = 0;
    root = 0;
}

int MerchItr::Init (MerchTree * tree)
{
    stackPtr = -1; // set stack as empty
    root = tree->getRoot(); // initialize current node to root
    goLeft (root); // go down left side of tree
    return stackPtr >= 0; // is stack empty?
}

int MerchItr::operator++ ()
{
    Merchandise_Item * parent, * child;

    if (stackPtr >= 0)
    {
        parent = pop();
        child = parent->getRight();
        if (child)
            goLeft (child);
    }
    return stackPtr >= 0;
}

Merchandise_Item * MerchItr::operator() ()
    { return stack[stackPtr]; }   // current node is top of stack
```

Continued next page

Listing 10.10 (Continued) The implementation of the Merchltr class for the video store program

```
void MerchItr::goLeft (Merchandise_Item * Item)
{
    while (Item)
    {
        push (Item);
        Item = Item->getLeft();
    }
}

int MerchItr::operator! ()
    { return stackPtr >= 0; }  // check for end of traversal

void MerchItr::push (Merchandise_Item * Item)
    { stack[++stackPtr] = Item; }

Merchandise_Item * MerchItr::pop ()
    { return stack[stackPtr--]; }
```

The second part of the `for` loop uses the overloaded ! operator to determine whether the stack is empty. This condition stops the loop. As you can see in Listing 10.10, the `operator!` function simply returns TRUE if the stack pointer is greater than or equal to zero (there is at least one item on the stack) and FALSE if the stack is empty.

The final part of the `for` loop uses the overloaded ++ operator to manipulate the stack so that each time the loop iterates the next node in tree traversal order is at the top of the stack. The code for this operator, which appears in Listing 10.10, first pops the top node off the stack. It then looks for a right child. If there is a right child, the function pushes all left children onto the stack until it runs into a node without a left child.

Note

Notice that there is no way for a compiler to tell whether `operator++ ()` represents the postincrement or preincrement use of the ++ operator. If you are overloading only one of the two, you can use the operator as either postincrement or preincrement, but not both. If you need to overload both, the second function must include a parameter, as in `operator++ (int)`. This gives the second function a different signature. When using the operator, the parameter is simply inserted as a zero (for example, `object++(0)`). The value of the parameter doesn't necessarily have to be used in the function.

The body of the `for` loop uses the overloaded `( )` operator to return the node that is on the top of the stack. Once the body of the loop has the pointer to the current object, it can retrieve the object type and write the data to the correct file.

Why bother to go through the trouble of creating the iterator class and defining the overloaded operators? Because it makes writing the main program easier. The `for` loop that performs the iteration is easy to write and easy to understand. For example, using the `++` operator to move to the next node in tree traversal order is consistent with the operator's default behavior. In addition, using the iterator class and the overloaded operators hides the details of tree manipulation from the main program. Assuming that iterators for all data structures overload the `!`, `++`, and `( )` operators to perform the functions you have just seen, the programmer is also presented with a consistent interface for data structure iteration.

Note

If you want to learn more about implementing object-oriented data structures using C++, see *Classic Data Structures in C++* by Timothy A. Budd (Addison-Wesley, 1994).

Summary

In this chapter you have learned how overloading of functions and operators is used to provide a simpler, more consistent interface to a programmer. Function overloading occurs when two member functions of the same class have the same name but different parameter lists. The C++ compiler identifies a function based on its signature, which is made up of the function's name along with the number, type, and order of its parameters. As long as the parameters differ in number, type, and/or order, a compiler will see two functions with the same name as distinct. When a function is called, the compiler uses the function whose signature matches the syntax of the function call.

Function overloading is commonly used to give classes more than one constructor. Typically, one constructor is used for interactive data input, another for input from a file, and a third to copy data into a new object from another object of the same class.

Operator overloading gives alternative meanings to C++ operators. Most C++ operators can be overloaded to make it easier for a programmer to work with objects. Overloaded operators are implemented as functions whose names are made up of the keyword `operator` followed by the operator being overloaded.

When functions that define binary overloaded operators are declared as member functions, they can take only one input parameter. That parameter must be placed on the right side of the operator when the operator is used; an object of the class in which the overloading is defined must appear on the left side of the operator. The operations of overloaded operators defined as member functions are therefore not commutative.

Functions that define overloaded operators can also be declared as friend functions. A friend function or class has access to the private variables and functions of the class to which it is declared a friend. The drawback to using friends is that they violate the object-oriented principle of information hiding. However, overloaded binary operators defined as friends can take two parameters. By defining two overloaded operator functions with parameters in opposite order, an overloaded operator can be made commutative.

Overloaded operators can also make working with data structures easier. A special type of class—an iterator—can be defined to traverse through a data structure in order. An iterator uses overloaded operators to present a consistent method for stepping through a data structure, regardless of whether the data structure is an array, list, or tree.

Exercises

1. Create a class that lets you store a date in three integer variables (month, day, and year). Overload the arithmetic operators so that you can perform date arithmetic to determine the number of days between two dates (for example, `Date2 - Date1`) or add one date to another (for example, `Date2 + 30`). Overload the relationship operators so that you can evaluate expressions like `Date1 < (Date2 + 60)`. Write a program that demonstrates that the overloaded operators work correctly.

2. Modify the program you wrote for Exercise 4 from Chapter 7 to use operator overloading for the arithmetic operators, allowing you to include code in the form Object1 + Object2, Object1 - Object2, and so on.

3. (Manufacturing) Modify the manufacturing program so that it can compute the typical cost of making a product. First, add a variable to the Raw Material class that stores the current average cost of a material. Then, add a variable to the Assembly class that stores the cost of the assembly (computed by adding together the cost of the raw materials and other assemblies used). Finally, add a variable to the Product that stores the cost of the product (computed by adding the cost of the raw materials and assemblies used). Overload the addition operator for the Raw Material and Assembly classes so that the arithmetic can be performed in the following manner:

```
cost += raw_material; or
cost += assembly;
```

where `raw_material` and `assembly` are objects of the named type.

4. (Purchasing) Add the date class you developed for Exercise 1 in this chapter to the Purchasing program. Then, add the following functions to the program:

   • Receipts of objects: write a function that can be used to indicate which items on which purchase orders have been received. Indicate the date on which the items were received and the number received. (The number received may not be the same as the number ordered.) Modify classes and data structures as needed to support this function.
   • Analyze a purchase order to determine whether it has been completely filled.
   • List purchase orders that have not been filled within 30, 60, and 90 days of the order date.

5. (Temporary Employment Agency) Add a class to the Employment Agency program that stores the hours an employee worked on a single day. Also add a time class that stores the time as two integers (hour and minutes). Include two Time objects in the Hours Worked object (one for start time and one for the end time). Overload the arithmetic operators for the Time class so that the Hours Worked class can calculate the time worked with syntax like `EndTime - StartTime`, where `EndTime` and `StartTime` are objects of the Time class.

Implement the data structures needed to link Hours Worked objects to employees. Then, add a function to the Employee object that computes the time worked for a week by adding the time worked for each day in the week.

If necessary, modify the salary computing function so that it can accommodate the changes you have made to the Employee object.

Suggestion: Add the date class from Exercise 1 to this program. Use it to store the date to which a Hours Worked object applies. Then, modify the salary computation function to compute salary for any date interval (any week, month, or year, specified by a starting date and an ending date).

Inheritance and Polymorphism

OBJECTIVES

In this chapter you will learn about:

- Using inheritance to allow similar classes to share data and functions.
- Where inheritance is appropriate and where it isn't.
- How polymorphism, implemented through virtual functions, allows objects from related classes to react differently to the same message.

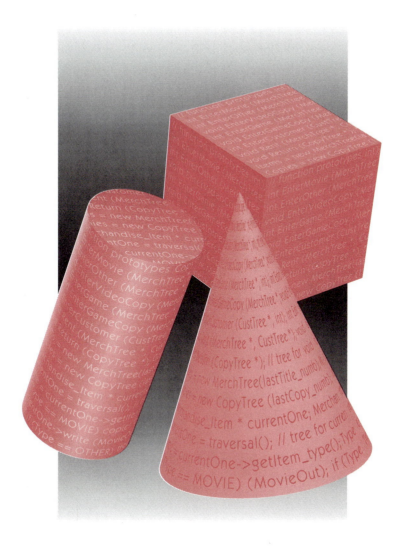

This chapter introduces one of the most important features of the object-oriented paradigm: inheritance. Inheritance makes it possible for similar objects to share variable and function definitions. Inheritance also supports *polymorphism*, through which different objects can respond to the same message in different ways.

The example used throughout this chapter is a program to manage rentals at a video store. Like the pharmacy program, the entire program listing is too long to print in the body of the book. Although you will see significant parts of the code in this chapter, the complete listing can be found in the second half of Appendix A.

Where Inheritance Makes Sense

As you read in Chapter 2, using inheritance creates a hierarchy of classes through which the variables and functions for classes higher in the hierarchy are passed down to classes below. This means that when similar classes share variables and functions, you only need to declare them once, rather than repeating them for each class in which they appear.

The idea of inheritance can be a bit confusing, especially if you've studied data management. Although inheritance initially looks a lot like the relationships between entities in a database system, it is a different concept. To see where inheritance is appropriate and where inheritance hurts rather than helps, let's take a look at the design of the merchandise classes for the video store program.

The first thing to understand about a video store is that the store needs to store data about the type of merchandise it carries. However, the store doesn't rent a type of merchandise; it rents *copies* of those types. There are therefore two major groups of classes that a video store program must handle: classes about the types of merchandise and classes about merchandise copies.

In Figure 11.1, each box represents a class. (There is also a customer class that doesn't appear in the diagram.) The hierarchy at the top of the diagram, connected by solid lines, describes types of merchandise carried by the store. The hierarchy at the bottom of the diagram, also connected by solid lines, describes the copies of the types of merchandise that are actually rented to customers. The dashed lines in the middle of the diagram indicate where inheritance isn't appropriate. You'll read more about this shortly.

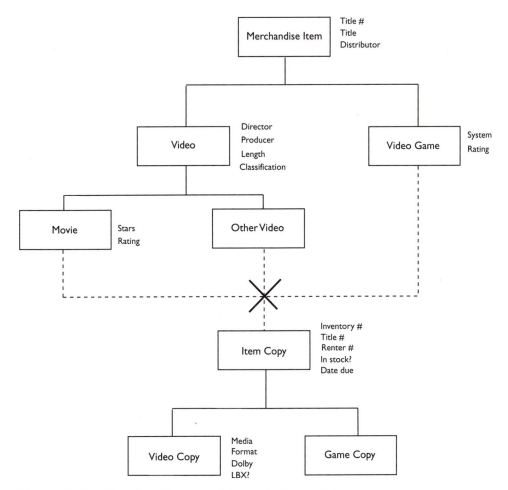

Figure 11.1   Merchandise class hierarchy for a video store

The base class of the type of merchandise hierarchy is a generic Merchandise Item. As you can see in Figure 11.1, it contains data that are applicable to movies, other videos, *and* video games (the three types of merchandise rented by the store). Two classes are derived from the Merchandise Item class, one for videos and another for video games. The Video Game class inherits all the variables from the Merchandise Item class and adds two variables that are specifically applicable to games. The Video class also inherits the Merchandise

Item class's variables and adds variables of its own. However, the Video class has two classes derived from it (Movie and Other Video). Video is therefore both a base class and a derived class.

Objects are created from only three of the classes in the merchandise item hierarchy: Movie, Other Video, and Game. Notice that these are classes at the bottom of the hierarchy, classes from which no other classes are derived. Although this is not always the case, it is not uncommon for objects to be created only from classes at the bottom of a hierarchy.

The copy hierarchy begins with the base class Item Copy. It contains variables that apply to all copies of merchandise items, regardless of the type of item. The Video Copy derived class adds variables that apply only to videos. The Game Copy class doesn't need any additional data. As with the merchandise item hierarchy, objects are created only from the two classes at the bottom of the hierarchy and never from the Item Copy class.

One question arises at this point. If the Other Video and Game Copy classes don't add any variables to those they inherit from their respective base classes, why include these classes in the design at all? Because the classes behave differently even when they receive the same message. For example, the Other Video class behaves differently from the Movie class when it receives the message as "write yourself to a file."

If you have taken a database course, then you are probably also wondering why the Item Copy class and its derived classes aren't part of the merchandise item hierarchy. It is very true that the store stocks many copies of each merchandise item. In fact, a database system would represent this as a one-to-many relationship. Keep in mind, however, that inheritance *copies* all the variables from a base class into a derived class.

If Video Copy, for example, was derived from Movie, each copy of a given movie would repeat all the data about the movie, including its title, distributor, producer, director, stars, and rating. The result would be a great deal of unnecessary duplicated data. The fact that the extra data waste disk space is the least of the problems. As you may know from your database course, the presence of unnecessary duplicated data sooner or later leads to data inconsistency, a situation in which data that should be the same are not. A search for a movie by title would never find any copy that had even one incorrect letter in its title, perhaps causing someone at the store to believe that no copies of a given title were in stock.

In this situation, inheritance isn't appropriate. Use inheritance where the derived classes actually need every variable from their base classes. (A copy of a merchandise item doesn't need all the data describing the item; it only needs an identifier, such as an inventory number, that can be used to locate the object that contains the descriptive data.) Use inheritance where the inherited variables don't represent unnecessary duplicated data.

Another way to help determine when inheritance is appropriate is to recognize that in most cases, inheritance represents the special relationship "is a," in which a derived class is a more specific example of its base class. In other words, a Video "is a" Merchandise Item; a Movie "is a" Video. If you can express the relationship between two classes using the "is a" relationship, then inheritance is probably appropriate.

Declaring Derived Classes

The declaration of a derived class is very similar to the declaration of a base class. The major difference is that the declaration must include the name of the class from which the new class is derived and the type of inheritance that is in effect. As an example, consider the merchandise item hierarchy in Listing 11.1. Notice that the first line of the declaration of the derived classes has the following format:

```
class class_name : inheritance_type base_class_name
```

The same pattern can be found in the hierarchy for copies of merchandise items (Listing 11.2).

Listing 11.1   Declarations of the classes in the merchandise item hierarchy for the video store program

```
class Item_copy;
class MerchTree;
class CopyTree;

class Merchandise_Item
{
    protected:
        int Title_numb, Copy_count, Item_type;
        string Title;
        string Distributor;
        Merchandise_Item * Left, * Right; // binary search tree of titles
```
Continued next page

Listing 11.1 (Continued) Declarations of the classes in the merchandise item hierarchy for the video store program

```
        Item_copy * First, * Last; // linked list of items
    public:
        Merchandise_Item (int, string, string);
        Merchandise_Item (ifstream &);
        char * getTitle();
        int getCopy_count(); // return number of copies
        Merchandise_Item * getLeft();
        Merchandise_Item * getRight();
        void setLeft (Merchandise_Item *);
        void setRight (Merchandise_Item *);
        void Insert (Item_copy *);
        Item_copy * getLast ();
        int getItem_type ();
        int getTitle_numb();
        Item_copy * available (); // check to see if any copies are available
        virtual void write (ofstream &) = 0;

};

class Video : public Merchandise_Item
{
    protected:
        string Director;
        string Producer;
        string Classification;
        int Length;
    public:
        Video (int, string, string, string, string, string, int);
        Video (ifstream &);
        virtual void write (ofstream &) = 0;
};

class Movie : public Video
{
    private:
        string Stars[MAX_STARS]; // array of strings for stars
        int numbStars;
        rate_string Rating;
    public:
        Movie (int, string, string, string, string, string, int, int, string
    [], rate_string, MerchTree *);
        Movie (ifstream &, MerchTree *);
        void write (ofstream &);
};
```

Listing 11.1 (Continued) Declarations of the classes in the merchandise item hierarchy for the video store program

```
class Other : public Video
{
    public:
        Other (int, string, string, string, string, string, int, MerchTree *);
        Other (ifstream &, MerchTree *);
        void write (ofstream &);
};

class Game : public Merchandise_Item
{
    private:
        string System;
        rate_string Rating;
    public:
        Game (int, string, string, string, rate_string, MerchTree *);
        Game (ifstream &, MerchTree *);
        void write (ofstream &);
};
```

Listing 11.2 Declarations of the classes in the copies of merchandise items hierarchy for the video store program

```
class Customer;

class Item_copy
{
    protected:
        int Inventory_numb, Title_numb, Renter_numb;
        int In_stock; // boolean
        date_string Date_due;
        Item_copy * Next, * Right, * Left;
    public:
        Item_copy (int, int);
        Item_copy (ifstream &);
        void Rent (Customer *, date_string);
        void Return ();
        int getStatus();
        int getInventory_numb();
        Item_copy * getNext();
        void setNext (Item_copy *);
        void setRight (Item_copy *);
        void setLeft (Item_copy *);
        Item_copy * getRight ();
```

Continued next page

```
        Item_copy * getLeft ();
        virtual void write (ofstream &) = 0;
};

class Video_copy : public Item_copy
{
    private:
        string Media, Format;
        int Dolby, LBX; // these are all booleans
    public:
        Video_copy (int, int, string, string, int, int, Merchandise_Item *,
    CopyTree *);
        Video_copy (ifstream &, Merchandise_Item *, CopyTree *);
        void write (ofstream &);
};

class Game_copy : public Item_copy
{
    public:
        Game_copy (int, int, Merchandise_Item *, CopyTree *);
        Game_copy (ifstream &, Merchandise_Item *, CopyTree *);
        void write (ofstream &);
};
```

Types of Inheritance

To this point, you have worked with public and private variables and functions. Public items are accessible to all functions; private items are accessible only to members of the class in which they are defined. Inheritance can also be public and private, although private is used very rarely. In addition, inheritance can take advantage of a third type of variables and functions (protected).

Regardless of the type of inheritance, a derived class cannot access private variables and functions of its base class. To get around this problem and still hide the internals of the base class from classes and functions outside the class hierarchy, a base class usually uses protected items rather than private items. Assuming public inheritance, protected items are accessible to member functions in all derived classes. Notice in Listing 11.1, for example, that the Merchandise_Item and Video classes have protected rather than private variables. The classes at the bottom of the hierarchy, however, have private variables to hide them from the outside world.

In general, public inheritance means that a derived class has access to the public and protected items of its base class. Public items are inherited as public items; protected items remain protected. Private inheritance, however, means that a derived class has no access to any of its base class's items. Types of inheritance and derived class accessibility are summarized in Table 11.1.

Warning

By default, inheritance is private. If you accidentally leave out the keyword `public`, base class items will be inaccessible. The type of inheritance is therefore one of the first things you should check if a compiler returns an error message that says variables and/or functions are inaccessible.

Table 11.1   Variable and function access based on type of inheritance

Type of Inheritance	Type of Item	Accessible to Derived Class?
public	public	yes
	protected	yes
	private	no
private	public	no
	protected	no
	private	no

We rarely use private inheritance. Even if you currently don't see a need for a derived class to access variables or member functions from its base class, you can't be certain that you won't need to modify the program in the future in such a way so that you *do* need to access base class contents.

Limitations to Inheritance

A derived class inherits all of its base class's public and protected variables, but it doesn't inherit all of its functions. The following functions aren't inherited:

- constructors
- destructors
- overloaded operators
- friends

Inheritance and Constructors

Although constructors aren't inherited, the situation isn't as limiting as it might appear. When an object is created from a derived class, the program automatically calls the base class's constructor. When the hierarchy is more than two levels deep, the program calls constructors all the way up the hierarchy.

When constructors take input parameters, the compiler has no way of knowing which parameters should be passed to a base class constructor and which are intended only for local use. In such a case, a program needs to indicate explicitly how parameters should be transferred.

You can find the interactive constructors for the `Video` and `Movie` classes in Listing 11.3. Notice that the input parameter list for each constructor is followed by a colon and a call to the base class constructor. This is the *only* circumstance under which a derived function can explicitly call its base class's constructor. Once the constructors have been run, the base class constructor becomes inaccessible.

Using Base Class Pointers

One of the most useful aspects of inheritance is the ability to reference an object created from a derived class with a base class pointer. For example, although the video store creates objects only from the `Movie`, `Other`, and `Game` classes, all three are ultimately derived from `Merchandise_Item`. It is therefore possible to create an object to manage a binary search tree that uses pointers to `Merchandise_Item` as nodes (see Listing 11.4). When you copy a derived class pointer into a base class pointer, there is an implicit typecasting of the derived class pointer into a base class pointer.

Listing 11.3   Derived class constructors that pass parameters to a base class constructor, used by the video store program

```
Video::Video (int iTnumb, string iTitle, string iDistributor, string iDirector,
    string iProducer, string iClass, int iLength)
    : Merchandise_Item (iTnumb, iTitle, iDistributor) // call base class constructor
{   strcpy (Director, iDirector);
    strcpy (Producer, iProducer);
    strcpy (Classification, iClass);
    Length = iLength;
    First = 0;
    Last = 0; }

Movie::Movie (int iTnumb, string iTitle, string iDistributor, string iDirector,
    string iProducer, string iClass, int iLength, int inumbStars, string
    iStars[], rate_string iRating, MerchTree * Items)
    : Video (iTnumb, iTitle, iDistributor, iDirector, iProducer, iClass,
    iLength)
{   numbStars = inumbStars;
    for (int i = 0; i <= numbStars; i++)
        strcpy (Stars[i], iStars[i]);
    strcpy (Rating, iRating);
    Left = 0;
    Right = 0;
    Item_type = MOVIE;
    Items->Insert (this, Title); }
```

As a result, the same tree can organize movies, other videos, and games—even though the structures of the objects aren't precisely the same—making it possible to search through all the items carried by the video store at one time.

Note

As you look at Listing 11.4 and compare it to the binary tree used by the pharmacy program, you'll see that the two classes are very much alike. The video store program also uses similar tree classes for customers and copies of merchandise items. For the most part, these trees differ only in the data type of the pointer used as a node. The result is a great deal of similar, but not quite identical, code. Ideally, there should be some way to avoid this repetition. The answer is something called a *template*, which lets a programmer use a placeholder for the type of data used by a class. When you create an object from a template, you specify the type of data to be substituted for the placeholder. Unfortunately, not all C++ compilers support templates, and those that do, do not do so in a the same way.

Listing 11.4 Defining a tree that uses base class pointers for the video store program

```
// Can use a single tree to hold all merchandise items
// Alternatively, could define one tree from for each type of merchandise
// Base class pointer can hold pointers to any of the derived classes
class MerchTree
{
    private:
        Merchandise_Item * root;
        int Item_count, lastTitle_numb;
    public:
        MerchTree (int);
        void Insert (Merchandise_Item *, string);
        Merchandise_Item * find (string);
        int getItem_count();
        void setItem_count (int);
        int getlastTitle_numb ();
        int inclastTitle_numb ();
        Merchandise_Item * getRoot();
};
```

By the same token, the video game program can use a base class pointer whenever it needs to handle copies of items in a generic manner. For example, the functions to rent and return items are declared as part of the `Item_Copy` class (see Listing 11.5). The function to determine whether any copies of a merchandise item are available for rental is declared as part of the `Merchandise_Item` class; the function returns a pointer to an `Item_Copy` object (see Listing 11.6).

Listing 11.5 Member functions to rent and return copies of merchandise items for the video store program

```
void Item_copy::Rent (Customer * Renter, date_string Due)
{
    Renter_numb = Renter->getRenter_numb();
    strcpy (Date_due, Due);
    In_stock = FALSE;
}

void Item_copy::Return()
{
    Renter_numb = 0;
    strcpy (Date_due, "");
    In_stock = TRUE;
}
```

Listing 11.6   The member function to determine whether any copies of a merchandise item are available for the video store program

```
Item_copy * Merchandise_Item::available()
{
    Item_copy * current;

    current = First;
    while (current)
    {
        if (current->getStatus() == TRUE)
            return current;
        current = current->getNext();
    }
    return 0; // no copies available
}
```

The main program also uses base class pointers to refer to merchandise items and copies of merchandise items. As you can see in Listing 11.7, the `Rent` and `Return` main program functions use a `Merchandise_Item` pointer to refer to either a movie, other video, or game; an `Item_copy` pointer refers to a copy of either a video or a game. The beauty of this capability is that the program can handle all three types of merchandise items in exactly the same way, without being concerned about the specific structure of an object and without needing to contain duplicated code for each type of merchandise item.

Listing 11.7   Main program functions to rent and return copies of merchandise items for the video store program

```
void Rent (MerchTree * Items, CustTree * Customers)
{
    string iTitle, ifname, ilname;
    Customer * renter;
    int cust_numb;
    Merchandise_Item * item;
    Item_copy * whichItem;
    date_string due;

    cout << "Customer's first name: ";
    gets (ifname);
    cout << "Customer's last name: ";
    gets (ilname);
    renter = Customers->find (ifname, ilname);
```

Continued next page

Listing 11.7 (Continued) Main program functions to rent and return copies of merchandise items for the video store program

```
    if (renter == 0)
    {
        cout << "That customer isn't on file.";
        return;
    }
    cout << "Title: ";
    gets (iTitle);
    item = Items->find (iTitle);
    if (item == 0)
    {
        cout << "We don't stock that title.";
        return;
    }
    whichItem = item->available();
    if (whichItem == 0)
    {
        cout << "No copies of " << iTitle << " are available.";
        return;
    }
    cout << "Date due: ";
    gets (due);
    whichItem->Rent (renter, due);
}

void Return (CopyTree * Copies)
{
    Item_copy * item;
    int copy_numb;

    cout << "Inventory #: ";
    cin >> copy_numb;
    item = Copies->find (copy_numb);
    if (item == 0)
    {
        cout << "That inventory number isn't in use.";
        return;
    }
    item->Return();
}
```

Polymorphism

One of the most powerful capabilities of inheritance is its support for *polymorphism*, the ability to have classes in the same inheritance hierarchy respond differently to the same message. A program is using polymorphism when member functions in different classes have the same signature but differ in the content of the function body. As an example, consider the three `write` functions in Listing 11.8. Each is defined in a different class and had exactly the same signature. However, the body of each function is different. In other words, the functions receive the same message and yet behave in a different way.

Listing 11.8 Polymorphic functions used by the video store program

```
void Movie::write (ofstream & fout)
{
    fout << Title_numb << ' ';
    fout << Copy_count << ' ';
    fout << Title << '\0';
    fout << Distributor << '\0';
    fout << Director << '\0';
    fout << Producer << '\0';
    fout << Classification << '\0';
    fout << Length << ' ' << numbStars << ' ';
    for (int i = 0; i <= numbStars; i++)
        fout << Stars[i] << '\0';
    fout << Rating << '\0';
}

void Other::write (ofstream & fout)
{
    fout << Title_numb << ' ';
    fout << Copy_count << ' ';
    fout << Title << '\0';
    fout << Distributor << '\0';
    fout << Director << '\0';
    fout << Producer << '\0';
    fout << Classification << '\0';
    fout << Length << ' ';
}

void Game::write (ofstream & fout)
{
    fout << Title_numb << ' ';
    fout << Copy_count << ' ';
    fout << Title << '\0';
    fout << Distributor << '\0';
    fout << System << '\0';
    fout << Rating << '\0';
}
```

Note

It's important to keep in mind the difference between function overloading and polymorphism. Function overloading occurs when more than one function in the same class has the same name but a different signature. Polymorphism occurs when functions in different classes in the same inheritance hierarchy have the same signature but different bodies.

Virtual Functions

A program uses *virtual functions* to implement polymorphism. A virtual function is a function that needs to be called with a pointer (dynamic binding) so that the program will know exactly which function to use: The pointer to an object that precedes the -> and the name of the function identifies the class from which the correct function should be taken.

To declare a function virtual, precede its prototype with the keyword `virtual`, just as was done with the `write` functions in Listing 11.1 and Listing 11.2. Once declared, a function is virtual all the way down the inheritance hierarchy. A derived class can redefine a virtual function, giving that function behavior appropriate to the derived class, or it can simply inherit the function from its base class. In the video store program, the `write` function is redefined by the `Movie`, `Other`, and `Game` classes.

Note

Once a function has been declared virtual in a base class, it isn't necessary to include the keyword `virtual` in any derived classes. However, many programmers choose to do so because it makes class definitions easier to understand.

Pure Functions and Abstract Classes

In some circumstances, you may want to use a base class only as a source for derived classes; you never intend to create objects from that class. (`Merchandise_Item` and `Item_copy` are such classes.) To prevent any program from ever creating objects from a class, make it an *abstract class*. (A program can only create objects from *concrete classes*, classes that aren't abstract.)

An abstract class is a class that contains at least one *pure function*, a virtual function that is declared in a class but not defined. In other words, the function has only a prototype. Pure functions are identified by following their prototypes with = 0. The Merchandise_Item class declaration, for example, includes the following declaration for the write function:

```
virtual void write (ofstream & fout) = 0;
```

This declaration is repeated in the Video class, which is also an abstract base class.

Pure functions are ultimately redefined in concrete classes. For example, the write function is redefined by Movie, Other, and Game, the three concrete classes in the merchandise item hierarchy.

Why bother to use polymorphism, virtual functions, and abstract base classes? Because they simplify a program, providing a consistent interface to the programmer. They also generalize object behavior. With a polymorphic write function such as that used by the video store program, the programmer knows that whenever object data should be written to a file, he or she can simply use a function named write, regardless of the details needed to actually perform the output. This not only makes a program easier to write, debug, and understand, but also makes it easier to reuse classes in multiple programs.

Summary

Inheritance provides a mechanism for allowing similar classes to share variables and functions in a hierarchical manner. Inheritance is appropriate when the classes are related by the "is a" relationship: A derived class "is a" more specific instance of a base class.

By default, inheritance is private. Private inheritance means that no variables or functions of a base class are accessible to its derived classes. However, in most cases inheritance is public. With public inheritance, public items in the base class are inherited as public items and protected items are inherited as protected. However, even with public inheritance private items are inaccessible to a derived class.

Not everything can be inherited. Constructors, destructors, overloaded operators, and friends can't be inherited. However, when an object is created from a derived class, the base class constructor is called automatically, along with the derived class constructor.

Pointers to base classes can be used to provide a generic way to access objects created from classes derived from the same base class.

Polymorphism provides a way to allow objects created from different classes to respond to the same message in different ways. Polymorphism is implemented using virtual functions, functions that must be referenced with a pointer (using dynamic binding). Polymorphic functions must have the same signature. This is in direct contrast to function overloading, in which functions that are part of the same class have different signatures.

Base classes from which no objects can be created are known as abstract base classes; classes from which objects can be created are called concrete classes. An abstract base class contains at least one pure virtual function (a function whose prototype ends with the initialization = 0). Pure functions are declared but not defined; they have a prototype but no body. Pure functions are redefined by concrete classes in the hierarchy.

Exercises

1. Create a class hierarchy to manage the live animal inventory for a pet shop that handles cats, dogs, aquarium fish, reptiles, and small mammals (for example, rabbits, gerbils, and hamsters). Include data such as the type of animal, its living conditions, its feeding and care requirements, and the number of individuals currently in stock. Write member functions that display data about a given type of animal, enter new individuals into inventory, and remove individuals from inventory when sold. Create a single data structure (array or binary tree) to manage the entire inventory. Write a program that demonstrates that the classes and their member functions work.

2. Create at least one class hierarchy to manage a corporation's office furniture and equipment, which includes items such as desks, chairs, file cabinets, computers, copiers, and fax machines. (Consider carefully whether there should be one or two class hierarchies.) Classes should include variables for the name of an item, its manufacturer, a description of the item (using as many variables as necessary), an internal corporate identification number, the date of purchase, purchase price, and current value. Develop necessary data structures to manage objects. Include member functions to enter new items and to display data describing items of a given type (e.g., desks). In

addition, include member functions to compute the total current value of all assets of a given type, of all assets, and of all assets organized by type (a control break report).

3. Create classes to manage the "cars wanted" list of an exotic car dealership. The classes should handle data about the customers along with descriptions of the vehicles for which customers are searching. Decide which classes can be part of a class hierarchy and which need to be related to others using data structures. Include member functions to enter customers and customer requests, display the requests of a specific customer, and find out whether a specific car matches any request currently stored. Write a program that demonstrates that the classes and their member functions work.

4. Create a class hierarchy to manage an investment portfolio, including stocks, bonds, CDs, and mutual funds. Include data about the name of the investment, the amount held, and the current unit value. Include member functions to enter new investments, modify the current value of all investments held, and the total value of the portfolio. Use any data structures needed to manage the objects. Write a program that demonstrates that the classes and their member functions work.

5. Modify the program you wrote for Exercise 4 so that it handles multiple investment profiles. Also add a class to manage the investors. Allow a single investor to own multiple portfolios; allow a single portfolio to be owned by multiple investors. Consider carefully how this "many-to-many" relationship can be implemented, either through a class hierarchy or through data structures.

Beyond Programming

OBJECTIVES

In this chapter you will learn about:

- The state-of-the-art of object-oriented database management systems.
- How object-oriented database management systems represent data relationships.
- What it means for an operating system to be object-oriented.
- What the user of an object-oriented sees.
- The programming environment for an application developer writing programs for an object-oriented operating system.

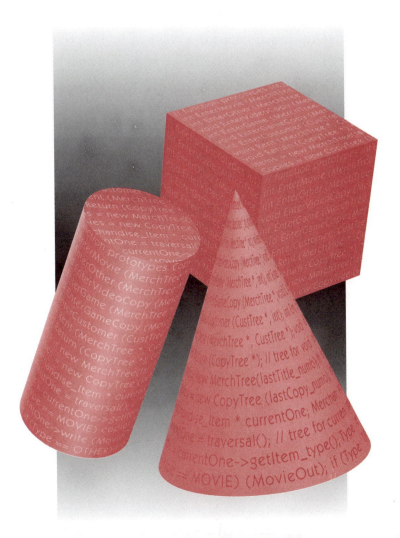

The object-oriented paradigm isn't limited to programming. It has permeated many aspects of information systems, including database management and operating systems. In this appendix you will be introduced to the basic concepts and state-of-the-art in both of these areas.

Object-Oriented Databases

Although throughout this book you have learned to use files to store data, a large proportion of today's business data processing is centered around a database. Application programs are written to interact with a database management system, which then acts as an interface to the physical files.

The object-oriented paradigm can easily be extended to support the definition of data relationships for a database system. As you will see in this chapter, object-oriented databases are a natural extension of the concepts with which you have been working. Nonetheless, object-oriented database management systems (ODBMSs) are just beginning to appear on the market. It is too early to predict what impact they will have on business database processing, whether they will supplant or merely supplement relational databases.

The Status of Object-Oriented Database Management

Depending on who you talk to and whose articles you read, ODBMSs are either too immature to be used for mission-critical applications or a viable alternative to relational databases. The relatively few that were available when this book was written are based on persistent objects.

As you know, a persistent object is an object that reads itself in from disk when it is created and writes itself to disk when it is destroyed. At a minimum, an ODBMS that is based on persistent objects must provide functions to support that persistence. Those functions must include storing the object in a database and loading it into memory when the object is requested by an application program or an end-user. In addition, the ODBMS must provide functions that retrieve objects based on logical search criteria.

Navigational Versus Nonnavigational Databases

It is important to realize that, in contrast to relational databases, object-oriented databases are *navigational*. This means that access to data is performed by using relationships explicitly defined in the database's schema. Such relationships are typically defined by including pointers to related objects as variables that are part of a class.

Relational databases, on the other hand, don't store relationships; relationships are created "on the fly" by joining tables, usually between primary and foreign keys. This has been one of the biggest attractions of the relational database model because it provides significant support for ad hoc querying capabilities. It also makes it very easy to modify the logical structure of the database. In contrast, navigational databases are less flexible than relational databases because data retrieval is restricted to preplanned relationships; changing relationships means changing the database schema.

On the other hand, navigational databases generally perform better than relational databases. Performing a join requires significant processing overhead. Many SQL-based relational DBMSs perform a join by taking the relational product of the two tables being joined, forming all possible combinations of rows, and then choosing only those rows that meet the join condition. For example, if the two tables being joined have 100 and 1,000 rows, the intermediate product table will have 100,000 rows. Manipulating that much data heavily loads memory and the CPU, slowing DBMS performance. Navigational databases, however, retrieve exactly the data needed and therefore avoid the overhead of large joins.

Note

The older data models—hierarchical, simple network, complex network—are also navigational. In large measure, this characteristic led to their being replaced with relational databases.

SQL Versus the ODBMS

The developers of ODBMs recognize that people who work with databases today are comfortable with using SQL for queries. Some have therefore provided SQL interfaces for their products. SQL for ODBMs isn't standardized in the same way as SQL is for relational DBMSs. You will therefore discover that some implementations are intended only for embedding in C++ or SmallTalk programs; other implementations provide interactive access so that end-users can formulate their own queries.

The nature of ODBMs presents some challenges for SQL. SQL is designed for a database that adheres to the design constraints of the relational data model. In particular, SQL expects to find only one value at the intersection of a column and a row (no multivalued attributes). An ODBMS doesn't impose that restriction on its variables; a variable can be an array or a set (a collection of objects or pointers to objects, about which you will learn more shortly). This means that SQL designed for an ODBMS must have extensions to the language that handle the data structures specific to an ODBMS. However, in most cases the translation between standard SQL syntax and an ODBMS is performed without user or application programmer intervention.

Representing Data Relationships

Like the relational data model, an object-oriented database is able to handle one-to-one and many-to-many relationships. However, unlike the relational data model, an object-oriented database is able to implement a many-to-many relationship directly. (The relational data model requires an extra entity whose sole purpose it to represent the many-to-many relationship between two other entities.)

In Figure 12.1 you will find an entity-relationship (ER) diagram for an object-oriented database for a video store. Notice that the entities in this diagram are the same as the classes used in the video store program that was discussed in Chapter 11. However, the relationships aren't quite the same as the inheritance hierarchies used by the C++ program. The entities are also different from those that would be used in a relational implementation of a video store database; the relationships are also different.

Each entity that was part of an inheritance hierarchy in the C++ program is related to the other entities in the hierarchy with the "is a" relationship. The types of merchandise items (Movies, Other Videos, and Games) are also related to their copies in a one-to-many relationship. (This is the relationship for which inheritance was inappropriate in the C++ program.)

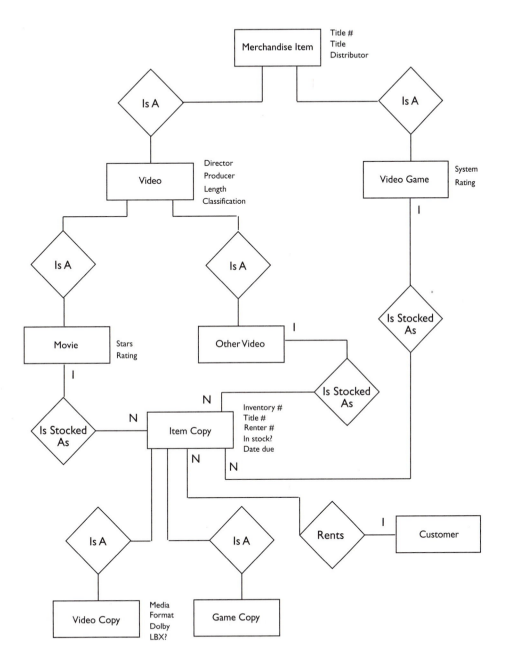

Figure 12.1   An ER diagram for an object-oriented database for a video store

Defining a Class for an ODBMS

Unlike SQL for relational databases, there is no standard language for defining the structure of an object-oriented database. The way in which you express entities and data relationships varies from one product to another. In this section, we'll take a look at some sample database declarations, just to give you a feeling for how persistent database objects might be defined.

Note

The syntax in this section is actually used by an ODBMS named POET.

Each entity in an ODMBS that is based on persistent objects is implemented as a persistent class. For example, Listing A.1 shows a persistent object for the `Merchandise_Item` entity. Notice that the keyword `persistent` precedes the class name, identifying it as a database entity rather than a class for a program. The class also contains a set (pointers to the copies of this merchandise item).

Listing A.1   Declaring a persistent class

```
persistent class Merchandise_Item
{
    protected:
        int Title_numb, Item_type;
        string, Title, Distributor;
    public:
        cset<ondemand<Item_copy *>> copies; // set of copies
        int getTitle_numb ();
        int getItem_type ();
        char * getTitle ();
        virtual ostream & displayData (ostream &);
};
```

This class is certainly similar to the class used in Chapter 11's video store program. However, it is missing some of its variables and all of its member functions. First, it doesn't need the pointers for the data structures that the C++ program uses to organize its objects. For example, the linked list that connected merchandise items to copies isn't required because the persistent class contains the set of pointers to all copy objects.

The persistent class also doesn't have many member functions. This is because functions to read objects from disk, write objects to disk, and search for objects are provided as a part of the ODBMS. (These are the functions that an ODBMS typically provides.) Assuming that interactive I/O is performed by the C++ program manipulating the database, most persistent classes don't need any member functions.

Defining "Is A" Relationships

Persistent classes implement the "is a" relationship through inheritance. As you can see in Listing A.2, each of the derived classes in the merchandise item hierarchy uses the same syntax to specify the class from which a class is derived as was used in the C++ program. The major differences between the declarations in Listing A.2 and those for the C++ program are the presence of the `persistent` keyword and the absence of many member functions.

Sets and Data Relationships

An object-oriented database organizes objects from the same class into units called *sets*. Sets can be used to access all objects of the same class or to implement both one-to-many and many-to-many relationships. A set is implemented as a class that has pointers to the members of the class as data values.

One-to-many and many-to-many relationships are implemented using sets as persistent class variables. In the examples we have been considering, the class for a set used as a variable is `cset`, which can be thought of as a "container" for any type of data. To establish a relationship with objects created from another class, a `cset` contains pointers to the related objects.

As you know, when member variables are declared for a class, the declaration must include the type of data. This presents a problem to the `cset` class because there is no way to know in advance what type of data it must handle. The solution is to use a template, which provides a placeholder for the data type.

To establish a one-to-many relationship between classes, an ODBMS can declare a `cset` in the class at the "one" end of the relationship to contain pointers to the class at the "many" end. For example, to establish the relationship between a merchandise item and its copies, the class declaration could contain:

```
cset<Item_copy *> copies;
```

Listing A.2   Declaring derived persistent classes

```
persistent class Video : public Merchandise_item
{
    protected:
        string Director, Producer, Classification;
        int Length;
    public:
        virtual ostream & displayData (ostream &);
};

persistent class Movie : public Video
{
    protected:
        string Stars[MAX_STARS];
        int numbStars;
        rate_string Rating;
    public:
        ostream & displayData (ostream &); // display all data
};

persistent class Other : public Video
{
    protected:

    public:
        ostream & displayData (ostream &); // display all data
};

persistent class Game : public Merchandise_Item
{
    protected:
        string System;
        rate_string Rating;
    public:
        ostream & displayData (ostream &); // display all data
};
```

There are two possible problems with the preceding declaration. First, if you think back to the data structures that have been used throughout this book, you'll remember that the pointers that maintained the data structures weren't stored in the files along with the objects they related; the data structures were reconstructed each time data were read from a file into main memory. This is because the pointers change each time data are loaded in memory. A database system is faced with the same issue. To get around this problem, an object-oriented database stores object references (internal unique identifiers) rather than actual memory addresses. This means that the objects referenced by the `Item_copy` pointers will always be locatable, regardless of where they are placed in main memory.

The second problem also concerns memory: As a database grows large, it won't be possible to store all objects in memory at the same time. Some choice has to be made as to which objects will be memory resident and which will be loaded only when needed. An object that is loaded when needed is known as an "on demand" object. It might be maintained by an object of the class `onde-mand`, which in turn is implemented using template syntax. To make the copies of a merchandise item on demand objects, the declaration of the on demand object can be embedded in the set declaration:

```
cset<ondemand<Item_copy *>>
```

An application program can explicitly load the on demand object whenever it is needed for processing.

The `Customer` class (Listing A.3) also participates in a one-to-many relationship with the `Item_copy` class. This relationship is used to indicate which customer is currently renting which copy.

Listing A.3   The persistent Customer class

```
persistent class Customer
{
    protected:
        int Renter_numb;
        string fname, lname, street, CSZ, phone, credit_card_numb;
    public:
        cset <ondemand<Item_copy *>; // items currently rented
};
```

To complete a one-to-many relationship, an ODBMS includes a pointer to the class at the "one" end of the relationship as a variable in the class at the "many" end of the relationship. For example, in Listing A.4 the `Item_copy` class contains two pointers, one to a merchandise item and another to a customer. In both cases, the copy is at the "many" end of a relationship with the other class.

Listing A.4   A persistent class that is at the "many" end of one-to-many relationships

```
persistent class Item_copy
{
    protected:
        int Inventory_numb, In_stock;
        Merchandise_Item * Item;  // identifies which merchandise item
        Customer * Renter;  // identifies who has rented the item
        date_string Date_due;
    public:
        void Rent (Customer *, date_string);
        void Return ();
        int getStatus ();
        Merchandise_Item * getItem ();
        Customer * getRenter ();
};
```

The `Video_Copy` and `Game_copy` persistent classes (Listing A.5) inherit the relationship pointers from their base class. As you can see, the `Video_copy` class adds only the variables that are specific to a video; the `Game_copy` class adds nothing at all to the base class.

Listing A.5   Derived persistent classes at the "many" end of one-to-many relationships

```
persistent class Video_copy : public Item_copy
{
    private:
        string Media, Format;
        int Dolby, LBX;
    public:
};

persistent class Game_copy : public Item_copy
{
    private:
    public:
};
```

Note

To establish a many-to-many relationship, an object-oriented database declares a set in each of the two classes participating in the relationship, rather than using a pointer to a single object to define the object at the "one" end of the relationship.

Programming for an ODBMS

The way in which you access data stored in an object-oriented database varies significantly from one ODBMS to another. In some cases, access is provided as a group of library functions that can be called from a C++ program. In others, you may be able to use a variant of SQL that can be embedded in C++. Regardless of which you do, the statements that you place in a program that access a DBMS won't be acceptable to a C++ compiler because they aren't part of C++.

The solution is a *precompiler*, a stand-alone program that processes a source code file containing database manipulation statements. (This technique is used whenever database access statements are used in a general-purpose high-level language.) Whenever the precompiler encounters a database manipulation statement, it either removes the statement or turns it into a comment and inserts a class to an external library function that provides the functionality of the database manipulation statement. The result is a source file that can be compiled by a standard language compiler. The external function libraries, of course, must be linked to the compiled program before the program will run.

This means that the process of preparing applications to access an object-oriented database is somewhat more involved than simply preparing a C++ program. After creating your source code, you must then run the program through the compiler and correct any errors in database access syntax that the precompiler detects. Only then will you be able to successfully compile the program with a C++ compiler.

Object-Oriented Operating Systems

As well as changing the way we look at database management, objects have also had an impact on the design and implementation of operating systems. At least two vendors have been working on object-oriented operating systems. In this section of this appendix, we'll first look at some of the characteristics an object-oriented operating system should exhibit and then turn to whether current software actually has those characteristics.

Inside an Object-Oriented Operating System

Assuming that an operating system were to be created based on object-oriented principles, how should that operating system be structured? How should the parts of the OS interact? If we can answer these questions, we can provide a framework for looking at current efforts to create an object-oriented operating system.

Characteristics of an Object-Oriented OS

A multitasking, multiuser operating system performs the following general functions:

- Process (task) management
- Memory management (real and virtual)
- File system management
- I/O management
- User interface management

Most of today's operating systems are based on a *kernel*, which includes the fundamental functions of the OS. In particular, the kernel contains the portions of the OS that are hardware dependent and those portions that are executed frequently. In many cases, the kernel is written in assembly language for performance reasons.

The rest of the OS is implemented as a collection of add-on programs, which can be written in a portable, high-level language such as C++. The kernel-based design brings two major advantages. First, the OS is easy to extend; a systems programmer simply writes another program that interacts with the kernel and other OS programs. Second, the OS becomes easier to port to other hardware platforms. Only the kernel and user interface modules need to be rewritten; the remainder of the OS usually only needs to be recompiled.

Process Management

The process management portion of an operating system is responsible for scheduling process access to the CPU. It must handle swapping processes into and out of the CPU, keep track of which processes are executing, where processes are located in main memory, and handle interrupts such as the completion of I/O operations.

In most multiuser operating systems, a process is created for a user when the user logs in. Every process the user creates by running programs is then connected to the login process in some way. The OS can therefore keep track of which process belongs to which user. The logout process usually involves stopping (killing) the user's login process.

Note

What happens when a user logs out with processes other than the login process still running varies from one OS to another. In some cases, the logout automatically kills all the user's processes. In others, the user can indicate which processes should continue to run after logout. This latter capability makes it possible for a user to start a long program run and then log out while the program is still running.

An object-oriented operating system would need to use a process management object that knew where all the user login process objects were located. Each user login process object would need to know where all its process objects could be found. However, the process management object also needs to know where all processes are located so that it can schedule processes for CPU time. To perform process scheduling, the process management object needs to order processes in some way and then manipulate that order as processes run, leave the CPU, wait for I/O to complete, and finish.

As you can see from the very simple example in Figure 13.2, the data structures that simply keep track of which processes are running and where they are located in memory become very complex. Adding to the problem is the possibility that a process might not be physically located in RAM, but might be residing in a virtual memory swap file on disk. This means that a process object needs to share a great deal of information with memory management objects.

Complicating the issue even further is support for *threads*, processes or parts of processes created from the same program that can run concurrently. When multiple threads are running at the same time, the operating system must keep track of the process to which each thread is related, where the thread is in memory, the state of each thread, what to do if a thread that has completed its task must wait for the completion of another, and so on. The same thread may also be shared by more than one process, in particular when more than one user is running the same program.

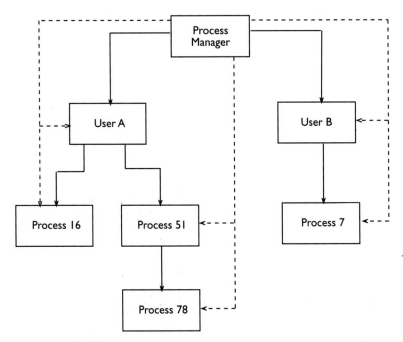

Figure 13.2 A small group of related operating system process objects

Memory Management

Memory management is concerned with keeping track of how memory is allocated. A multitasking operating system often has a total memory space larger than the amount of physical RAM installed in the computer. To manage the entire memory space, the OS uses a *virtual memory* scheme in which memory not physically present in the computer is simulated by a disk file. A virtual memory swap file on disk holds data and programs that won't fit into physical RAM at any given time. Blocks of data are swapped from disk to RAM and back again as needed. (Don't forget that a program must be in physical RAM to execute.)

The block of memory that is swapped between physical RAM and disk is known as a *page*, or in some cases, a *segment*. (For this discussion, we will simply refer to blocks of memory as pages.) Main memory is therefore broken into page-sized chunks (*page frames*). An object-oriented OS can therefore use a page object to represent each page and a page frame object to represent each slot in RAM into which a page can be placed.

A page object must contain information about where the page is located (in RAM or on disk), the process to which the page belongs, and the order of the page in the collection of pages used by the process. Because a process can occupy memory larger than a single page, the process object must also be linked in some way to its page objects.

When a page is swapped from disk to RAM, the page usually is placed in any available page frame. There is, however, nothing to guarantee that it is swapped into the location it occupied the last time it was in RAM. Therefore, page, page frame, and process objects must be modified every time a process is swapped between disk and RAM.

File System Management

In addition to handling processes and memory, an operating system must organize external storage. Most of today's OSs provide a hierarchical structure of directories (often represented graphically as folders) and files, which naturally lends itself to an object-oriented model.

Each individual directory hierarchy (a *file system*) might be represented by a file system object. This object also represents the top of the directory hierarchy (the *root directory*). Each file or directory within the hierarchy is also represented by an object. If these objects were the only consideration, a binary tree would be a sufficient data structure to handle a directory hierarchy. However, not all file systems are on direct access devices (disks). Tapes, such as those used for backup, also require file systems. Because tape is a sequential access medium, an operating system must have some way of providing a sequential data structure for a tape's file system.

A file object must include data that describe the file. In addition, it must keep track of whether the file is in use and if so, by which users. File use data must also be available to processes using the files. In particular, an OS must have some way of handling multiple users attempting to update the same file. Process objects must therefore be able to communicate with the file objects they are using and with other processes using the same file objects.

File Linking

A file system must do more than just manage directories and files. Most of today's operating systems support the ability to link one physical copy of a file or directory to many locations in one or more file systems. Both *soft links* (pointers to files or directories in the same file system) and *hard links* (path names of files and directories in the same or other file system) appear to the user as if they were physical copies of the linked item. Anything the user does to the link—opening a directory, running a program, modifying a file—affects the original rather than the link.

In the case of soft links, the operating system must keep track of how many links exist for an item and refrain from deleting the item from disk until the link count drops to zero, even if the command is given to delete the original, physical item. An object that manages a soft link must therefore be related to the file or directory object it represents; the destructor for a soft link object must modify the file or directory object by decrementing the link count.

Operating systems that support hard links (for example, some versions of UNIX and the Macintosh Operating System) typically don't keep track of how many hard links exist. It is therefore possible to delete (or move) the original and still leave the link in place. A hard link object must be able to gracefully handle the situation where the original item can't be located.

Multiple File Systems

Complicating a file system's task is the need to deal with multiple file systems. Most of today's desktop operating systems use one file system for each disk or disk partition. For example, each floppy disk and tape has its own file system; the same is true for each hard disk partition and each CD-ROM. The operating system must provide some way to integrate these individual file systems.

To make a new file system available to an OS, you *mount* the file system. Mounting attaches the new file system's root directory to some existing directory in the file system of the boot drive. For example, under UNIX, file systems often attach to the /mnt or /dsk directory; under the Macintosh Operating System, file systems are attached to the Desktop directory. (MS-DOS does not have a single attach point for multiple file systems; the file systems exist as separate entities.) Although there are typical attach points for a file system, an OS such as UNIX allows a user to mount a file system in any directory in any currently mounted file system.

To support the ability to mount a file system, an object representing a directory in a file system must be capable of handling mounting and unmounting of other file systems. In other words, every directory object must be capable of functioning as the parent of the root of another file system.

Note

Many operating systems do not mount tape file systems. Instead, a user must run software specifically designed to access files on tape. This method is used to make backups of disks under MS-DOS, Windows NT, and the Macintosh Operating System. UNIX, however, can mount some types of tape file systems.

I/O Management

Typically a file system doesn't include input and output capabilities; it simply organizes items on external storage. An operating system therefore must also provide a means for reading from and writing to disks and tapes. The I/O management portion of an OS accepts requests for I/O from processes, allocates I/O devices, and manages the transfer of data to and from the I/O device.

If the computer hardware supports *direct memory access* (DMA), the operating system must manage the direct transfer of data between the I/O device and RAM. Otherwise, the OS must pass all data transfers through the CPU. Nonetheless, each I/O data transfer involves at least one process, each of which can be represented as an object, just like any user process.

Each I/O device can also be represented as an object. The object's member functions implement data transfer, either through the CPU or directly to memory. When DMA is available, the I/O device object must interact with the memory manager and page objects to ensure that data are read from the correct locations and written to the correct locations. When DMA is not available, an I/O device object must interact closely with the process manager to gain access to the CPU for I/O processes.

Most of today's operating systems are *interrupt-driven*. This means that processes that handle I/O have precedence for access to the CPU over most other processes. Because I/O is generally the slowest part of a computer system, an operating system is written to minimize the amount of time a CPU must spend waiting for I/O. Therefore, most I/O transfers begin with a command from the CPU. The CPU then handles another process while the I/O is in progress. When the I/O operation is completed, the I/O devices signals (or *interrupts*) the CPU, requesting CPU time to complete the I/O transfer. Systems that support DMA can perform an entire I/O transfer once the CPU gives the command for the I/O operation to begin. However, systems that require I/O transfers through the CPU interrupt the CPU as soon as an I/O buffer is filled during a read or emptied during a write.

The thing to keep in mind is that I/O introduces another type of process object to the operating system along with additional data structures. I/O process objects have different behaviors and priorities than user process objects. The OS must know which I/O devices are available, the state of the devices, and which I/O process objects are linked to them. The process manager must also be able to incorporate member functions that handle interrupts as part of its process scheduling.

User Interface Management

As you have discovered throughout this book, a graphic user interface (GUI) is particularly amenable to object-oriented representation. Menus, menu options, windows, and the contents of windows can all easily be represented as objects. It is therefore not unusual today to find that support for an application's user interface is provided as a set of class libraries that implement the major functions of a GUI's components.

An object-oriented GUI isn't part of an operating system's kernel. Its classes are developed in a high-level language, which in turn are used by application programs written in a high-level language. This makes the GUI less dependent on the hardware on which it is running and more dependent on the operating system itself. The X Window GUI, for example, is specific to UNIX, but has been implemented on many types of hardware. It also means that a GUI might be object-oriented even though the rest of the operating system is not.

Object-Oriented OS Products

As this book was being written, the only "object-oriented" operating system on the market was NextStep, a product of Next Computer. Although NextStep uses a few object-oriented concepts internally and supports a totally object-oriented application development environment, it is really a UNIX variant. NextStep therefore isn't object-oriented from the ground up.

In addition, a major operating systems development project was underway at Taligent, a company set up and managed jointly by IBM and Apple. Taligent originally set out to build an object-oriented operating system from the ground up. However, as of this writing, the Taligent project has produced only a collection of object-oriented application program interfaces (APIs) and has announced plans for a user interface based on an underlying object-oriented structure. Plans for an underlying object-oriented OS seem to have been scaled down considerably.

Also in the works is Cairo, a Microsoft project that has been under development since the late 1980s. Although Cairo was designed initially to be completely object-oriented, it too seems to be metamorphosing into a set of object-oriented application development tools that will run on top of a nonobject-oriented OS.

Why is this the case? Why is it proving to be so difficult to write an operating system that is object-oriented internally? The answer lies in the complexity of the interactions between the various parts of an operating system. If you think back to the discussion earlier in this chapter about how a completely object-oriented operating system should work, you'll remember that the objects must interact in many ways. For example, process objects and memory page objects must share a great deal of information; both types of objects must be updated repeatedly as processes change states (running, ready to run, waiting for I/O, and so on) and are swapped from RAM to disk. Process objects must also interact with file objects to handle attempts by multiple processes to write to the same file. Today's object-oriented development tools simply aren't robust enough to handle the interwoven relationships and data structures required by an operating system.

Summary

Today's object-oriented databases are based on persistent objects. Most are closely tied to C++, using C++ syntax to declare persistent objects that are to be stored in a database.

Object-oriented databases provide four types of data relationships: one-to-one, one-to-many, many-to-many, and "is a." One-to-one relationships are established by including a pointer to the related object as a variable in another object. A one-to-many relationship is established by storing a set of pointers to related objects in the object at the "one" end of the relationship and a pointer to the single related object in an object at the "many" end of the relationship. Many-to-many relationships are implemented directly by including sets of pointers to related objects in objects on both sides of the relationship. The "is a" relationship is implemented through inheritance.

Because data relationships are represented using pointers, object-oriented databases are navigational. That means that they are limited to retrieving data based on the pointer structures that are defined in database objects. Although changes to data relationships require changes to class structures, data retrieval using the embedded pointers is quite fast.

Some object-oriented database management systems have a SQL-like query language. However, because object-oriented databases use sets, a concept not found in relational databases, SQL implementations for object-oriented databases must include extensions to the query language to handle multivalued variables.

An operating system might be viewed as object-oriented in three ways: from the user's point of view, from the application developer's point of view, and internally. Today's operating systems attempt to provide the user with a graphic user interface that uses a familiar desktop metaphor, isolating the user from object-oriented concepts. There are currently no attempts to develop an OS that impose object-oriented principles on the user.

Operating systems that are currently labeled as object-oriented provide object-oriented application development tools, including class libraries to support object-oriented graphic user interfaces. In addition, such operating systems often support only object-oriented programming languages.

Although many parts of the internals of an operating system lend themselves to representation as objects, developers of today's operating systems have discovered that the relationships between the objects are too complex for implementation using current tools. Therefore, at this time there are no operating systems that are completely based on an object-oriented internal model.

Exercises

1. In this exercise, you will be comparing the object-oriented and relational implementations of a database for the Corner Pharmacy (the pharmacy for which a C++ program was discussed earlier in this book).

    *   Draw an ER diagram for a relational database implementation of the pharmacy database.
    *   Draw an ER diagram for an object-oriented implementation of the pharmacy database.

- Describe the similarities and differences between the two designs. Would you choose a relational or object-oriented design for this environment? Justify your answer.

2. (General Ledger) Draw an ER diagram for an object-oriented database that handles general ledger functions. Compare this diagram to a C++ implementation of a general ledger program.

3. (Purchasing) Draw an ER diagram for an object-oriented database that handles a purchasing system. Compare this diagram to a C++ implementation of a purchasing system.

4. The development of object-oriented operating systems is going on while you are reading this exercise. Next, Taligent, and Microsoft are continuing to work on their products, which means that the current state of the products is almost certainly different from what you have just read. To find out the state-of-the-art in object-oriented operating systems, visit the library and research the most recent efforts in the development of NextStep, the Taligent Operating System, and Cairo. As you read the articles that you find, evaluate whether these products are moving closer to or farther away from an object-oriented structure.

5. Use the library to find out if there are any new object-oriented operating systems under development. If so, determine if the focus of these new products is similar to or different from the Next, Taligent, and Microsoft offerings.

Program Listings

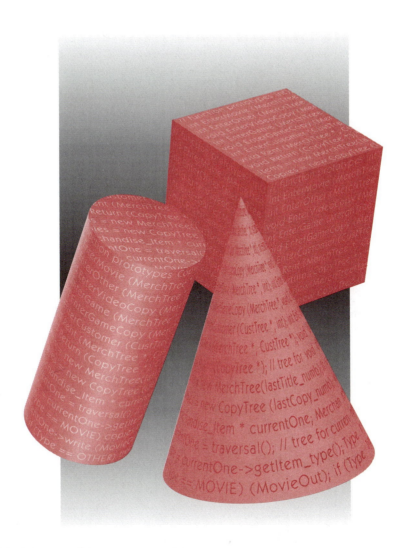

The Corner Pharmacy Program

Listing B.1   pharmacy.h

```cpp
const GENERICS = 5;   // maximum generic equivalents
const CONFLICTS = 20;   // maximum number of conflicting drugs
const SWAP_MADE = 1;
const NO_SWAP = 0;
#define TRUE 1
#define FALSE 0
typedef char string[81];   // define a new data type for an 80-character string
typedef char date_string[9]; // define a new data type for an 8-character date

class Drug
{
    private:
        int drug_numb;
        string drug_name;
        string generics[GENERICS]; // an array for generic equivalents
        string conflicts[CONFLICTS]; // array for conflicting drugs
        int numb_generics, numb_conflicts;

    public:
        Drug(ifstream &); // constructor that loads data from disk--stream is passed in
        // constructor that handles interactive I/O
        Drug(int, int, int, string, string[], string[]);
        void writeDrug(ofstream&); // function that writes to disk
        int checkInteraction (string);   // check for drug interaction
        int getDrug_numb();
        char * getDrug_name();
        string * getGenerics(int *);
        string * getConflicts(int *);
};


// These are forward declarations

class Customer;
class PrescriptList;
class PrescriptTree;
class drugArray;

class Prescription
{
    private:
        int drug_numb;
```

Listing B.1 (Continued)   pharmacy.h

```
      int prescription_numb, numb_refills, refills_left, FDA_numb,
  controlled;
      char doctor[31], doctor_phone[13];
      date_string prescription_date, refill_dates[10];
      Prescription * nextPrescript; // pointer to next in list
      Prescription * right; // pointer to right child in tree
      Prescription * left; // pointer to left child in tree

  public:
      Prescription(ifstream &);
      Prescription(int, int, int, int, char [], char[], date_string);
      void writePrescription(ofstream &);
      void setPrescriptPtr (Prescription *);
      int refill();
      void bottleLabel(Customer *, strstream &, drugArray *);
      Prescription * getNextPrescript(); // get next prescription in list
      void setRight (Prescription *); // set right child pointer in tree
      Prescription * getRight (); // return right child pointer in tree
      void setLeft (Prescription *); // set left child pointer in tree
      Prescription * getLeft (); // return left child pointer in tree
      char * getDoc();
      char * getDocPhone();
      int getPrescript_numb ();
      int getDrug_numb ();
};

class Customer
{
    private:
      char fname[16], lname[16], street[31], city [21], state[3], zip[6],
  phone [13];
      PrescriptList * PrescriptHeader; // pointer to prescription list object
      Customer * nextCust; // pointer to next customer

    public:
      Customer(ifstream &);
      Customer(char [], char [], char [], char [], char [], char [], char []);
      void setPrescriptPtr (PrescriptList *); // pointer to prescription object
      void setNextPtr (Customer *); // pointer to next customer
      void writeCustomer(ofstream &);
      Customer * getNext (); // pointer to next customer
      void mailingLabel (strstream &);
      char * getZip ();
      char * getLName ();
```

Listing B.1 (Continued)   pharmacy.h

```
        char * getFName ();
        char * getStreet ();
        char * getCSZ();
        char * getPhone ();
        PrescriptList * getPrescriptHeader(); // pointer to prescription header
        int checkNewDrug (string, drugArray *);
};
```

Listing B.2   customer.cpp

```
#include <fstream.h>
#include <string.h>
#include <strstrea.h>
#include "pharmacy.h"
#include "list.h"
#include "array.h"

Customer::Customer(ifstream & fin)
{
    int PrescriptCount;
    char dummy;

    fin.getline (fname, 80, '\0');
    fin.getline (lname, 80, '\0');
    fin.getline (street, 80, '\0');
    fin.getline (city, 80, '\0');
    fin.getline (state, 80, '\0');
    fin.getline (zip, 80, '\0');
    fin.getline (phone, 80, '\0');
    fin >> PrescriptCount;
    fin.get (dummy); // skip over trailing blank
    // create header for prescription list
    PrescriptHeader = new PrescriptList (this, PrescriptCount);
    // defaults to zero but will be replaced for all but last customer
    nextCust = 0;
}

// commented out; choose either this or the text file function for both
// the customer and prescription object. You can therefore use either text or
// binary files, but certainly not both!
// If you switch to binary, don't forget to add the ios::binary flag to the
// statement that opens the file.
/*Customer::Customer(ifstream & fin)
{
```

Listing B.2 (Continued)   customer.cpp

```
      fin.read ((unsigned char *) &numb_prescripts, sizeof(numb_prescripts));
      fin.read (fname,sizeof(fname));
      fin.read (lname,sizeof(lname));
      fin.read (street,sizeof(street));
      fin.read (city,sizeof(city));
      fin.read (state,sizeof(state));
      fin.read (zip,sizeof(zip));
      fin.read (phone,sizeof(phone));
      // create header for prescription list
      PrescriptHeader = new PrescriptList (this, PrescriptCount);
      // defaults to zero but will be replaced for all but last customer
      nextCust = 0;
}*/

Customer::Customer(char ifname[], char ilname[], char istreet[], char icity[],
      char istate[], char izip[], char iphone[])
{
      strcpy (fname, ifname);
      strcpy (lname, ilname);
      strcpy (street, istreet);
      strcpy (city, icity);
      strcpy (state, istate);
      strcpy (zip, izip);
      strcpy (phone, iphone);
      // create header for prescription list
      PrescriptHeader = new PrescriptList (this);
      // defaults to zero but will be replaced for all but last customer
      nextCust = 0;
}

void Customer::writeCustomer(ofstream & fout)
{
      fout << fname << '\0';
      fout << lname << '\0';
      fout << street << '\0';
      fout << city << '\0';
      fout << state << '\0';
      fout << zip  << '\0';
      fout << phone << '\0';
      fout << PrescriptHeader->getPrescriptCount() << ' ';
}

// commented out. See note above for binary input.
/*void Customer::writeCustomer(ofstream & fout)
{
```

Listing B.2 (Continued)   customer.cpp

```cpp
    fout.write ((unsigned char *) &numb_prescripts, sizeof(numb_prescripts));
    fout.write (fname, sizeof(fname));
    fout.write (lname, sizeof(lname));
    fout.write (street, sizeof(street));
    fout.write (city, sizeof(city));
    fout.write (state,sizeof(state));
    fout.write (zip, sizeof(zip));
    fout.write (phone, sizeof(phone));
}*/

void Customer::setPrescriptPtr (PrescriptList * iPrescriptHeader)
{
    // set link to head of prescription list
    PrescriptHeader = iPrescriptHeader;
}

int Customer::checkNewDrug (string idrug_name, drugArray * drugs)
    // look for drug interactions
{
    Prescription * currentPrescript;
    Drug * currentDrug;
    int OK;

    currentPrescript = PrescriptHeader->getFirst();
    while (currentPrescript)
    {
        currentDrug = drugs->findDrug (currentPrescript->getDrug_numb());
        OK = currentDrug->checkInteraction (idrug_name);
        if (!OK)
            return FALSE;  // interaction was found; prescription not OK
        currentPrescript = currentPrescript->getNextPrescript();
    }
    return TRUE; // all checked and no problem found
}

void Customer::setNextPtr (Customer * custPtr)
{
    nextCust = custPtr;
}

Customer * Customer::getNext()
    { return nextCust; }

PrescriptList * Customer::getPrescriptHeader()
    { return PrescriptHeader; }
```

Listing B.2 (Continued)   customer.cpp

```
void Customer::mailingLabel (strstream & label)
{
    label << fname << " " << lname << endl;
    label << street << endl;
    label << city << ", " << state << " " << zip << endl;
}

char * Customer::getZip ()
    { return zip; }

char * Customer::getLName ()
    { return lname; }

char * Customer::getFName ()
    { return fname; }

char * Customer::getStreet ()
    { return street; }

char * Customer::getCSZ ()
{
    static string CSZLine;

    strcpy (CSZLine, city);
    strcat (CSZLine, ", ");
    strcat (CSZLine, state);
    strcat (CSZLine, " ");
    strcat (CSZLine, zip);
    return CSZLine;
}

char * Customer::getPhone ()
    {return phone; }
```

Listing B.3   drug.cpp

```
#include <string.h>
#include <fstream.h>
#include <strstrea.h>
#include "pharmacy.h"

Drug::Drug(ifstream & fin)     // constructor that loads one from disk
{
    char dummy;
    fin >> drug_numb;
```

Listing B.3 (Continued)   drug.cpp

```cpp
    fin.get (dummy); // skip over blank
    fin.getline (drug_name,80,'\0');
    fin >> numb_generics;
    fin.get (dummy); // skip over blank
    for (int i = 0; i <= numb_generics; i++)
        fin.getline (generics[i],80,'\0');
    fin >> numb_conflicts;
    fin.get (dummy); // skip over blank
    for (i = 0; i <= numb_conflicts; i++)
        fin.getline (conflicts[i],80,'\0');
}

// constructor for interactive drug entry
Drug::Drug(int idrug_numb, int inumb_generics, int inumb_conflicts, string
    idrug_name, string igenerics[], string iconflicts[])
{
    drug_numb = idrug_numb;
    strcpy (drug_name, idrug_name);
    numb_generics = inumb_generics;
    for (int i = 0; i <= numb_generics; i++)
        strcpy (generics[i], igenerics[i]);
    numb_conflicts = inumb_conflicts;
    for (i = 0; i <= numb_conflicts; i++)
        strcpy (conflicts[i], iconflicts[i]);
}

void Drug::writeDrug(ofstream & fout)
{
    fout << drug_numb << ' ';
    fout << drug_name << '\0';
    fout << numb_generics << ' ';
    for (int i = 0; i <= numb_generics; i++)
        fout << generics[i] << '\0';
    fout << numb_conflicts << ' ';
    for (i = 0; i <= numb_conflicts; i++)
        fout << conflicts[i] << '\0';
}

int Drug::checkInteraction (string drug2check)
{
    for (int i = 0; i < numb_conflicts; i++)
    {
        if (strcmp (drug2check, conflicts[i]) == 0 )
            return FALSE;  // drug not OK
    }
    return TRUE;
```

Listing B.3 (Continued)   drug.cpp

```
}

int Drug::getDrug_numb()
    { return drug_numb; }

char * Drug::getDrug_name()
    { return drug_name; }

string * Drug::getGenerics (int * count)
{
    *count = numb_generics; // send back # generics
    return generics;
}

string * Drug::getConflicts(int * count)
{
    *count = numb_conflicts; // send back # conflicts
    return conflicts;
}
```

Listing B.4   prescription.cpp

```
#include <fstream.h>
#include <string.h>
#include <strstrea.h>
#include "pharmacy.h"
#include "tree.h"
#include "array.h"

Prescription::Prescription (ifstream & fin)
{
    nextPrescript = 0;
    right = 0;
    left = 0;
    char dummy;
    fin >> drug_numb;
    fin >> prescription_numb;
    fin >> numb_refills;
    fin >> refills_left;
    fin >> FDA_numb;
    fin >> controlled;
    fin.get (dummy); // grab the blank
    fin.getline (doctor, 80,'\0');
    fin.getline (doctor_phone, 80,'\0');
    fin.getline (prescription_date, 80,'\0');
```

Listing B.4 (Continued)   prescription.cpp

```
    for (int i = 0; i < (numb_refills - refills_left); i++)
        fin.getline (refill_dates[i], 80,'\0');
}
```

```
// commented out; choose either this or the text file function for both
// the customer and the prescription object. You can therefore use either
// text or binary files, but certainly not both!
// If you switch to binary, don't forget to add the ios::binary flag to the
// statement that opens the file.
/*Prescription::Prescription (ifstream & fin)
{
    fin.read ((unsigned char *) &drug_numb, sizeof(drug_numb));
    fin.read ((unsigned char *) &prescription_numb, sizeof(prescription_numb));
    fin.read ((unsigned char *) &numb_refills, sizeof(numb_refills));
    fin.read ((unsigned char *) &refills_left, sizeof(refills_left));
    fin.read ((unsigned char *) &FDA_numb, sizeof(FDA_numb));
    fin.read ((unsigned char *) &controlled, sizeof(controlled));
    fin.read (doctor, sizeof(doctor));
    fin.read (doctor_phone, sizeof(doctor_phone));
    fin.read (prescription_date, sizeof(prescription_date));
    for (int i = 0; i < (numb_refills - refills_left); i++)
        fin.read (refill_dates[i], sizeof(refill_dates[i]));
}*/


Prescription::Prescription (int idrug_numb, int iprescription_numb, int
    inumb_refills, int iFDA_numb, char idoctor[], char idoctor_phone[],
    date_string iprescription_date)
{
    nextPrescript = 0;
    right = 0;
    left = 0;
    drug_numb = idrug_numb;
    prescription_numb = iprescription_numb;
    numb_refills = inumb_refills;
    refills_left = numb_refills;
    FDA_numb = iFDA_numb;
    controlled = 0;
    strcpy (doctor, idoctor);
    strcpy (doctor_phone, idoctor_phone);
    strcpy (prescription_date, iprescription_date);
    for (int i = 0; i <= 9; i++)
        strcpy (refill_dates[i], "");

}
```

Listing B.4 (Continued)   prescription.cpp

```cpp
void Prescription::writePrescription(ofstream & fout)
{
    fout << drug_numb << ' ';
    fout << prescription_numb << ' ';
    fout << numb_refills << ' ';
    fout << refills_left << ' ';
    fout << FDA_numb << ' ';
    fout << controlled << ' ';
    fout << doctor << '\0';
    fout << doctor_phone << '\0';
    fout << prescription_date << '\0';
    for (int i = 0; i < (numb_refills - refills_left); i++)
        fout << refill_dates[i] << '\0';
}
```

// commented out. See note above for binary input.

```cpp
/*void Prescription::writePrescription(ofstream & fout)
{
    fout.write ((unsigned char *) &drug_numb, sizeof(drug_numb));
    fout.write ((unsigned char *) &prescription_numb,
    sizeof(prescription_numb));
    fout.write ((unsigned char *) &numb_refills, sizeof(numb_refills));
    fout.write ((unsigned char *) &refills_left, sizeof(refills_left));
    fout.write ((unsigned char *) &FDA_numb, sizeof(FDA_numb));
    fout.write ((unsigned char *) &controlled, sizeof(controlled));
    fout.write (doctor, sizeof(doctor));
    fout.write (doctor_phone, sizeof(doctor_phone));
    fout.write (prescription_date, sizeof(prescription_date));
    for (int i = 0; i < (numb_refills - refills_left); i++)
        fout.write (refill_dates[i], sizeof(refill_dates[i]));
}*/

int Prescription::refill()
{
    if (refills_left > 0)
    {
        refills_left--;
        return TRUE;
    }
    else
        return FALSE;
}

void Prescription::setPrescriptPtr (Prescription * prescriptPtr)
{
    nextPrescript = prescriptPtr;
}
```

Listing B.4 (Continued)   prescription.cpp

```cpp
void Prescription::bottleLabel(Customer * whichCustomer, strstream & label,
    drugArray * drugs)
{
    Drug * whichDrug;

    label << "*****************************************" << endl;
    label << " Prescription #" << prescription_numb << "      "
        << prescription_date << endl;
    label << " " << endl;
    label << " " << whichCustomer->getFName() << " "
        << whichCustomer->getLName() << endl;
    label << " Dr. " << doctor << endl;
    label << " " << endl;
    whichDrug = drugs->findDrug(drug_numb);
    label << " " << whichDrug->getDrug_name() << "    Refills: "
        << numb_refills << endl;
    label << "*****************************************";
}

Prescription * Prescription::getNextPrescript()
    { return nextPrescript; }

int Prescription::getPrescript_numb()
    { return prescription_numb; }

Prescription * Prescription::getLeft()
    { return left; }

Prescription * Prescription::getRight()
    { return right; }

void Prescription::setLeft (Prescription * newPrescript)
    { left = newPrescript; }

void Prescription::setRight (Prescription * newPrescript)
    { right = newPrescript; }

int Prescription::getDrug_numb()
    { return drug_numb; }
```

Listing B.5   array.h

```cpp
const DRUG_MAX = ¿
```

Listing B.5 (Continued)   array.h

```
class drugArray
{
    private:
        Drug * drugs[DRUG_MAX]; // array to hold drugs
        int drugCount; // number of drugs currently in array

    public:
        drugArray ();
        drugArray (int);
        void iInsert (Drug *); // interactive insert
        void fInsert (Drug *, int); // file insert
        Drug * findDrug (string);
        Drug * findDrug (int);
        int getDrugCount();
        Drug * getDrug (int);
};
```

Listing B.6   array.cpp

```
#include <string.h>
#include <iostream.h>
#include <fstream.h>
#include <strstream.h>
#include "pharmacy.h"
#include "array.h"

drugArray::drugArray() // constructor for when there's no file
{
    drugCount = 0;
    for (int i = 0; i < DRUG_MAX; i++)
        drugs[i] = 0;
}

drugArray::drugArray (int iCount) // constructor for file input
{
    drugCount = iCount;
    for (int i = 0; i < DRUG_MAX; i++)
        drugs[i] = 0; // will be replaced as drugs are loaded from file
}

void drugArray::iInsert (Drug * newDrug) // interactive insert
{
    Drug * Tdrug;
    int result;
```

Listing B.6 (Continued)   array.cpp

```cpp
    drugs[++drugCount] = newDrug;

    // sort moves pointers to objects rather than the objects themselves
    result = SWAP_MADE;
    while (result == SWAP_MADE)
    {
        result = NO_SWAP;
        for (int i = 0; i < drugCount; i++)
        { // compare the drugs names, but...
            if (strcmp(drugs[i]->getDrug_name(),
                drugs[i+1]->getDrug_name()) > 0)
            { // ... move the pointers!
                Tdrug = drugs[i];
                drugs[i] = drugs[i+1];
                drugs [i+1] = Tdrug;
                result = SWAP_MADE;
            }
        }
    }
}

void drugArray::fInsert (Drug * newDrug, int index)
    { drugs[index] = newDrug; }

Drug * drugArray::findDrug (string idrug_name)
{
    int top, bottom, mid, test;

    top = -1;
    bottom = drugCount + 1;
    mid = (top + bottom) / 2;

    while (top < mid)
    {
        test = strcmp (idrug_name, drugs[mid]->getDrug_name());
        if (test == 0)
            return drugs[mid]; // return pointer to drug object
        if (test < 0)
            bottom = mid;
        else
            top = mid;
        mid = (top + bottom) / 2;
    }
    return 0; // drug wasn't found
}
```

Listing B.6 (Continued)   array.cpp

```
Drug * drugArray::findDrug (int idrug_numb)
{
    for (int i = 0; i <= drugCount; i++)
        if (drugs[i]->getDrug_numb() == idrug_numb)
            return drugs[i];
    return 0; // drug not found
}

int drugArray::getDrugCount()
    { return drugCount; }

Drug * drugArray::getDrug (int index) // get drug based on array index
    { return drugs[index]; }
```

Listing B.7   list.h

```
class CustList
{
    private:
        Customer * firstCust;
        int custCount, lastPrescript_numb;

    public:
        CustList (Customer *, int, int); // constructor when coming from file
        CustList (); // constructor when no file and therefore no customers
        void Insert (Customer *, int); // insert new customer into list
        Customer * findCust (char [], char []); // traverse list to find customer
        int getCount (); // return customer count
        Customer * getFirst(); // return pointer to first in list
        void incLastPrescript_numb (); // increment last prescription number
        int getLastPrescript_numb();
};

class PrescriptList
{
    private:
        Customer * owner; // pointer to customer that owns it
        Prescription * firstPrescript;
        int PrescriptCount;
        int IFLAG; // detects interactive insert
```

Listing B.7 (Continued)   list.h

```cpp
public:
    PrescriptList (Customer *); // interactive constructor
    PrescriptList (Customer *, int); // file constructor
    void Insert (Prescription *, int); // IFLAG = 1 for interactive
    Prescription * findPrescript (int iprescript_numb);
    void incCount (); // increment prescription count
    int getPrescriptCount ();
    Prescription * getFirst();
};
```

Listing B.8   list.cpp

```cpp
#include <string.h>
#include <fstream.h>
#include <iostream.h>
#include <strstrea.h>
#include "pharmacy.h"
#include "list.h"

CustList::CustList (Customer * ifirstCust, int icustCount, int
    ilastPrescript_numb)
{
    firstCust = ifirstCust;
    custCount = icustCount;
    lastPrescript_numb = ilastPrescript_numb;
}

CustList::CustList()
{
    firstCust = 0;
    custCount = 0;
    lastPrescript_numb = 0;
}

void CustList::Insert (Customer * newCust, int IFLAG)
{
    string newLongname, oldLongname;
    Customer * currentCust, * previousCust;

    if (custCount == 0) // handle first customer separately
    {
        firstCust = newCust;
        custCount = 1;
    }
```

Listing B.8 (Continued)   list.cpp

```
    else
    {
        int i = 1;
        int first = TRUE;
        currentCust = firstCust; // start at head of list
        // must do outside while to avoid modifying good data
        strcpy (newLongname,newCust->getLName());
        strcat (newLongname,newCust->getFName());
        strcpy (oldLongname,currentCust->getLName());
        strcat (oldLongname,currentCust->getFName());
        while (strcmp(newLongname, oldLongname) > 0 && i++ <= custCount)
        {
            first = FALSE;
            // save preceding because there aren't backward pointers
            previousCust = currentCust;
            currentCust = currentCust->getNext();
            strcpy (oldLongname,currentCust->getLName());
            strcat (oldLongname,currentCust->getFName());
        }

        // set previous customer to point to new customer except when
        // new one is first in list
        if (!first)
            previousCust->setNextPtr (newCust);
        else
            firstCust = newCust; // have new first in list

        // set new customer to point to following custsomer
        newCust->setNextPtr (currentCust);
        // increment number of customers only if interactive
        if (IFLAG) custCount++;
    }
}

Customer * CustList::findCust (char iLname[], char iFname[])
{
    Customer * nextCust, * currentCust;
    char longName[31], searchName[31];

    strcpy (searchName,iLname);
    strcat (searchName,iFname);
    currentCust = firstCust;
    while (currentCust != 0)
    {
        strcpy (longName,currentCust->getLName());
```

Listing B.8 (Continued)   list.cpp

```cpp
        strcat (longName,currentCust->getFName());
        if (strcmp (searchName,longName) == 0)
            return currentCust;
        currentCust = currentCust->getNext();  // follow link to next
    }
    return 0;  // customer not found
}

int CustList::getCount()
    { return custCount; }

Customer * CustList::getFirst()
    { return firstCust; }

void CustList::incLastPrescript_numb ()
    { lastPrescript_numb++; }

int CustList::getLastPrescript_numb()
    { return lastPrescript_numb; }

PrescriptList::PrescriptList (Customer * iOwner)
{
    owner = iOwner;
    firstPrescript = 0;
    PrescriptCount = 0;
}

PrescriptList::PrescriptList (Customer * iOwner, int iPrescriptCount)
{
    owner = iOwner;
    firstPrescript = 0;
    PrescriptCount = iPrescriptCount;
}

void PrescriptList::Insert (Prescription * newPrescript, int IFLAG)
{
    Prescription * oldFirst;

    // new prescription always goes first
    oldFirst = firstPrescript;
    firstPrescript = newPrescript;
    newPrescript->setPrescriptPtr(oldFirst);
    if (IFLAG) PrescriptCount++;
}

int PrescriptList::getPrescriptCount ()
```

Listing B.8 (Continued)   list.cpp

```
    { return PrescriptCount; }

Prescription * PrescriptList::getFirst ()
    { return firstPrescript; }
```

Listing B.9   tree.h

```
class PrescriptTree
{
    private:
        Prescription * root;

    public:
        PrescriptTree (); // constructor
        void Insert (Prescription *, int); // insert into tree
        Prescription * findPrescript (int); // find a prescription by number
};
```

Listing B.10   tree.cpp

```
#include <iostream.h>
#include <fstream.h>
#include <strstrea.h>
#include <string.h>
#include "pharmacy.h"
#include "tree.h"

PrescriptTree::PrescriptTree ()
{
    root = 0;
}

void PrescriptTree::Insert (Prescription * newPrescript, int prescript_numb)
{
    Prescription * current, * child;

    if (root) // if root node exists
    {
        current = root;
        while (current) // keep going while there's a pointer
        {
            if (current->getPrescript_numb() < prescript_numb)
```

Listing B.10 (Continued)   tree.cpp

```cpp
        {
            // go down right side
            child = current->getRight();
            if (!child) // if no right child, insert
            {
                    current->setRight (newPrescript);
                return;
            }
        }
        else
        {
            // go down left side
            child = current->getLeft();
            if (!child) // if no left child, insert
            {
                current->setLeft (newPrescript);
                return;
            }
        }
        current = child;
    }
    }
    else
        root = newPrescript;
}

Prescription * PrescriptTree::findPrescript (int iPrescript_numb)
{
    Prescription * current;

    if (root) // make sure there is at least one node
    {
        current = root;
        while (current) // as long as there's a pointer
        {
            if (current->getPrescript_numb() == iPrescript_numb)
                return current; // send back pointer to drug object
            // if less, go down right side
            if (current->getPrescript_numb() < iPrescript_numb)
                current = current->getRight();
            // if greater, go down left side
            else
                current = current->getLeft();
        }
    }
```

Listing B.10 (Continued)   tree.cpp

```
    return 0;  // prescription not found
}
```

Listing B.11   menu.h

```
const ITEM_LEN = 41;
const MAX_ITEMS = 20;
typedef char menuoption [ITEM_LEN];

class menu      // class for a menu of up to MAX_ITEMS
{
    private:
        char menutitle[26];
        menuoption menuitems [MAX_ITEMS];   // array to hold the items
        int count;  // # of options in the menu

    public:
        menu (char [], menuoption [], int); // constructor
        void displaymenu (void);
        int chooseoption (void);
};
```

Listing B.12   menu.rsc

```
#include "menu.h"

menuoption maintitle = "MAIN MENU";
menuoption mainmenu [] = {"1. Manage drug information",
                          "2. Manage customer information",
                          "3. Manage prescriptions",
                          "9. Quit"};

int mainmenucount = 4;

const DRUGS = 1;
const CUSTOMERS = 2;
const PRESCRIPTS = 3;
const MAIN_QUIT = 9;

menuoption drugtitle = "DRUG MENU";
menuoption drugmenu [] = {"1. Enter a new drug",
                          "2. View all drugs",
                          "9. Return to main menu"};
```

Listing B.12 (Continued)   menu.rsc

```
int drugmenucount = 3;

const NEW_DRUG = 1;
const SEE_DRUGS = 2;
const DRUG_QUIT = 9;

menuoption custtitle = "CUSTOMER MENU";
menuoption custmenu [] = {"1. Enter a new customer",
                          "2. View all customers (mailing labels)",
                          "9. Return to main menu"};

int custmenucount = 3;

const NEW_CUST = 1;
const SEE_CUST = 2;
const CUST_QUIT = 9;

menuoption prescripttitle = "PRESCRIPTION MENU";
menuoption prescriptmenu [] = {"1. Enter a new prescription",
                               "2. Refill a prescription",
                               "9. Return to main menu"};

int prescriptmenucount = 3;

const NEW_PRESCRIPT = 1;
const REFILL = 2;
const PRESCRIPT_QUIT = 9;
```

Listing B.13   menu.cpp

```
#include <iostream.h>
#include <string.h>
#include "menu.h"

menu::menu (char * title, menuoption menutext[], int numbitems)
{
    strcpy (menutitle, title);
    count = numbitems;
    for (int i = 0; i <= count; i++)
        strcpy (menuitems[i], menutext[i]);
}

void menu::displaymenu ()
{
```

Listing B.13 (Continued)   menu.cpp

```cpp
    cout << endl;
    cout << "---------- " << menutitle << " ----------" << endl << endl;
    for (int i = 0; i <= count; i++)
        cout << menuitems[i] << endl;
    cout << endl;
}

int menu::chooseoption ()
{
    int choice;

    cout << "Enter an option: ";
    cin >> choice;
    return choice;
}
```

Listing B.14   main.cpp

```cpp
#include <iostream.h>
#include <fstream.h>
#include <ctype.h>
#include <string.h>
#include <stdio.h>
#include <strstrea.h>
#include "pharmacy.h"
#include "menu.rsc"
#include "list.h"
#include "array.h"
#include "tree.h"

void main()
{
    // Drug management functions
    void HandleDrugs (menu, drugArray *);
    void NewDrug (drugArray *);
    void ViewDrugs (drugArray *);
    void sortArray (string [], int);

    // Customer management functions
    void HandleCusts (menu,CustList *);
    void newCust (CustList *);
    void seeCust (CustList *);
    void DisplayLabel (Customer *);

    // Prescription management functions
```

Listing B.14 (Continued)   main.cpp

```cpp
void HandlePrescripts (menu, CustList *, drugArray *, PrescriptTree *);
void newPrescript (CustList *, drugArray *, PrescriptTree *);
void refillPrescript (PrescriptTree *);

char drugFile[10], CPFile[10];
char yes_no, dummy;
int chosenOption = 0, result, IFLAG;
int drugCount = -1, custCount = 0, lastPrescript_numb = 0,
    prescriptCount, i, j;
// holding area for pointers
Customer * currentCust, * previousCust, * firstCust;
Prescription * newPrescript;  // holding area for pointer
Drug * newDrug, * outDrug;  // holding area for pointers

// define & initialize menu objects
menu MainMenu (maintitle, mainmenu, mainmenucount),
    DrugMenu (drugtitle, drugmenu, drugmenucount),
    CustMenu (custtitle, custmenu, custmenucount),
    PrescriptMenu (prescripttitle, prescriptmenu, prescriptmenucount);

// data structure management objects
CustList * LinkedCusts;  // header object for list of customers
PrescriptList * PrescriptHeader;   // header object of one prescription list
drugArray * drugs;  // object to manage array of drug objects
PrescriptTree * tree;  // object to manage binary search tree of drugs

// read drugs in from file
cout << "Enter the name of the drug file: ";
cin >> drugFile;

ifstream drugIn (drugFile);
if (!drugIn)
{
    cout << "No drug file was found. Continue? ";
    cin >> yes_no;
    if (toupper(yes_no) == 'N')
        return;
    drugs = new drugArray();  // create object to manage drug array
}
else
{
    drugIn >> drugCount;
    drugs = new drugArray (drugCount); // create object to manage drug array
    for (int ind = 0; ind <= drugCount; ind++)
```

Listing B.14 (Continued)   main.cpp

```
    {
        newDrug = new Drug(drugIn);   // constructor reads the object
        drugs->fInsert (newDrug, ind); // insert drug into array by drug name
    }
    drugIn.close();
}


// read in customers and prescriptions, creating linked lists as you go
cout << "Enter the name of the customer and prescription file: ";
cin >> CPFile;

ifstream CPin (CPFile);
if (!CPin)
{
cout << "No file for customers and prescriptions was found. Continue? ";
    cin >> yes_no;
    if (toupper(yes_no) == 'N')
        return;
    LinkedCusts = new CustList (); // create list object with no customers
    tree = new PrescriptTree (); // create an empty prescription number tree
}
else
{
    CPin >> custCount;// number of customers
    CPin >> lastPrescript_numb; // last prescription #

    // create prescription number tree
    tree = new PrescriptTree (); // create an empty prescription number tree

    CPin.get (dummy); // space preceding first customer
    currentCust = new Customer (CPin); // get first customer

    // create object for linked list of customers including first customer
    LinkedCusts = new CustList (currentCust, custCount,
        lastPrescript_numb);
    int k = 1;
    while (k) // exit condition is within loop
    {
        LinkedCusts->Insert (currentCust, FALSE);
        // get address of prescription list object
        PrescriptHeader = currentCust->getPrescriptHeader();
        prescriptCount = PrescriptHeader->getPrescriptCount();
        for (j = 1; j <= prescriptCount; j++)
```

Listing B.14 (Continued)   main.cpp

```
        {
            newPrescript = new Prescription (CPin); // read prescription
            // insert into linked list
            PrescriptHeader->Insert (newPrescript, FALSE);
            tree->Insert (newPrescript,
                newPrescript->getPrescript_numb()); // insert into tree
        }
        // break out before attempting to read beyond end of file
        if (custCount == k++) break;
        currentCust = new Customer (CPin); // constructor reads a customer
    }
    CPin.close();
}


while (chosenOption != MAIN_QUIT)
{
    MainMenu.displaymenu();
    chosenOption = MainMenu.chooseoption();
    switch (chosenOption)
    {
        case DRUGS:
            HandleDrugs (DrugMenu, drugs);
            break;
        case CUSTOMERS:
            HandleCusts (CustMenu, LinkedCusts);
            break;
        case PRESCRIPTS:
            HandlePrescripts (PrescriptMenu, LinkedCusts, drugs, tree);
            break;
        case MAIN_QUIT:
            break;
        default:
            cout << "You've entered an unavailable option";
    }
}

ofstream drugOut (drugFile);
if (!drugOut)
{
    cout << "Troubling opening output file for drugs. Continue? ";
    cin >> yes_no;
    if (toupper(yes_no) == 'N')
        return;
}
else
```

Listing B.14 (Continued)   main.cpp

```
    {
        drugCount = drugs->getDrugCount();
        drugOut << drugCount << ' ';
        for (int i = 0; i <= drugCount; i++)
        {
            outDrug = drugs->getDrug(i);
            outDrug->writeDrug(drugOut);   // object writes itself to the file
        }
    }

    ofstream CPout (CPFile);
    if (!CPout)
    {
    cout << "Trouble opening output file for customers and prescriptions.
        Continue? ";
        cin >> yes_no;
        if (toupper(yes_no) == 'N')
            return;
    }
    else
    {
        custCount = LinkedCusts->getCount();
        CPout << custCount << ' ';
        CPout << LinkedCusts->getLastPrescript_numb() << ' ';
        currentCust = LinkedCusts->getFirst(); // start at beginning of list
        for (i = 1; i <= custCount; i++)
        {
            currentCust->writeCustomer (CPout);
            PrescriptHeader = currentCust->getPrescriptHeader();
            // get pointer to first prescription
            newPrescript = PrescriptHeader->getFirst();
            while (newPrescript != 0)
            {
                newPrescript->writePrescription (CPout);
                // get pointer to next prescription
                newPrescript = newPrescript->getNextPrescript();
            }

            // get pointer to next customer
            currentCust = currentCust->getNext();
        }
    }
}

void HandleDrugs (menu DrugMenu, drugArray * drugs)
{
    int drugoption;
```

Listing B.14 (Continued)   main.cpp

```cpp
    drugoption = 0;
    while (drugoption != DRUG_QUIT)
    {
        DrugMenu.displaymenu ();
        drugoption = DrugMenu.chooseoption ();
        switch (drugoption)
        {
            case NEW_DRUG:
                NewDrug (drugs);
                break;
            case SEE_DRUGS:
                ViewDrugs (drugs);
                break;
            case DRUG_QUIT:
                break;
            default:
                cout << "You've entered an unavailable option";
        }
    }
}

void NewDrug (drugArray * drugs)
{
    int idrug_numb, inumb_generics, inumb_conflicts, result;
    string igenerics[GENERICS], iconflicts[CONFLICTS];
    char idrug_name[81];
    Drug * Tdrug; // temporary pointer for sorting

    // drugCount is max array index (one less than max drug #)
    idrug_numb = drugs->getDrugCount() + 2;
    cout << "Drug #: " << idrug_numb << endl;
    cout << "Drug name: ";
    gets (idrug_name);
    cout << "\n\nType the names of generic equivalents. Press Enter on empty
        line to end." << endl;
    inumb_generics = 0;
    cout << "\nGeneric: ";
    gets (igenerics[0]);
    if (strlen (igenerics[0]) == 0) inumb_generics = -1; // none
    while (strlen (igenerics[inumb_generics++]) > 0)
    {
        cout << "\nGeneric: ";
        gets (igenerics[inumb_generics]);
    }
    if (inumb_generics >= 0) inumb_generics -= 2;
```

Listing B.14 (Continued)   main.cpp

```cpp
        sortArray(igenerics,inumb_generics);
        cout << "\n\nType the names of interacting drugs. Press Enter on empty line
            to end." << endl;
        inumb_conflicts = 0;
        cout << "\nConflicts: ";
        gets (iconflicts[0]);
        if (strlen (iconflicts[0]) == 0) inumb_conflicts = -1; // none
        while (strlen (iconflicts[inumb_conflicts++])  > 0)
        {
            cout << "\nConflicts: ";
            gets (iconflicts[inumb_conflicts]);
        }
        if (inumb_conflicts >= 0) inumb_conflicts -= 2;
        sortArray(iconflicts,inumb_conflicts);
        Tdrug = new Drug (idrug_numb, inumb_generics, inumb_conflicts, idrug_name,
            igenerics, iconflicts);
        drugs->iInsert (Tdrug); // insert into array
}

void sortArray (string source[], int count)
{
    int result, i;
    string temp;

    result = SWAP_MADE;
    while (result == SWAP_MADE)
    {
        result = NO_SWAP;
        for (i = 0; i < count; i++)
        {
            if (strcmp(source[i],source[i+1]) > 0)
            {
                strcpy(temp,source[i]);
                strcpy(source[i],source[i+1]);
                strcpy(source[i+1],temp);
                result = SWAP_MADE;
            }
        }
    }
}


void ViewDrugs (drugArray * drugs)
{
    int count, drugCount;
    char dummy[2];
    string  * holdingArray;
```

Listing B.14 (Continued)   main.cpp

```cpp
    Drug * Tdrug; // pointer for a drug object

    drugCount = drugs->getDrugCount();
    for (int i = 0; i <= drugCount; i++)
    {
        Tdrug = drugs->getDrug(i);
        cout << "#" << Tdrug->getDrug_numb() << ": " << Tdrug->getDrug_name()
            << endl;
        cout << "Generic equivalents:" << endl;
        holdingArray = Tdrug->getGenerics (&count);
        if (count >= 0)
            for (int y = 0; y <= count; y++)
                cout << "   " << holdingArray[y] << endl;
        cout << "Interacting drugs:" << endl;
        holdingArray = Tdrug->getConflicts (&count);
        if (count >= 0)
            for (int y = 0; y <= count; y++)
                cout << "   " << holdingArray[y] << endl;
        cout << "\nPress Enter to continue:";
        gets (dummy);
    }
}

void HandleCusts (menu CustMenu, CustList * LinkedCusts)
{
    int option;

    option = 0;
    while (option != CUST_QUIT)
    {
        CustMenu.displaymenu ();
        option = CustMenu.chooseoption ();
        switch (option)
        {
            case NEW_CUST:
                newCust (LinkedCusts);
                break;
            case SEE_CUST:
                seeCust (LinkedCusts);
                break;
            case CUST_QUIT:
                break;
            default:
                cout << "\nYou've entered an unavailable option" << endl;
        }
    }
}
```

Listing B.14 (Continued)   main.cpp

```cpp
void newCust (CustList * LinkedCusts)
{
    char ifname[16], ilname[16], istreet[31], icity [21], istate[3], izip[6],
        iphone [13];
    Customer * newCust;

    cout << "\nFirst name: ";
    gets (ifname);
    cout << "\nLast name: ";
    gets (ilname);
    cout << "\nStreet: ";
    gets (istreet);
    cout << "\nCity: ";
    gets (icity);
    cout << "\nState: ";
    gets (istate);
    cout << "\nZip: ";
    gets (izip);
    cout << "\nPhone: ";
    gets (iphone);
    newCust = new Customer (ifname, ilname, istreet, icity, istate, izip,
    iphone);
    LinkedCusts->Insert (newCust, TRUE); // insert new customer into list
}

void seeCust (CustList * LinkedCusts)
{
    Customer * currentCust;
    int i;
    char dummy[2];

    int Count = LinkedCusts->getCount();
    currentCust = LinkedCusts->getFirst();

    for (i = 1; i <= Count; i++)
    {
        DisplayLabel (currentCust);
        cout << " " << endl; // blank line between
        currentCust = currentCust->getNext();
    }
}

void DisplayLabel (Customer * currentCust)
{
    strstream label; // need to kill object and recreate each time because of freeze
```

Listing B.14 (Continued)   main.cpp

```cpp
        currentCust->mailingLabel (label);
        cout << label.str();
}

void HandlePrescripts (menu PrescriptMenu, CustList * LinkedCusts, drugArray *
    drugs, PrescriptTree * tree)
{
    int option;

    option = 0;
    while (option != PRESCRIPT_QUIT)
    {
        PrescriptMenu.displaymenu ();
        option = PrescriptMenu.chooseoption ();
        switch (option)
        {
            case NEW_PRESCRIPT:
                newPrescript (LinkedCusts, drugs, tree);
                break;
            case REFILL:
                refillPrescript (tree);
                break;
            case PRESCRIPT_QUIT:
                break;
            default:
                cout << "\nYou've entered an unavailable option" << endl;
        }
    }
}

void newPrescript (CustList * LinkedCusts, drugArray * drugs, PrescriptTree *
    tree)
{
    // memory stream for pill bottle/box label
    strstream label;

    int irefills, iFDA, numb_prescripts, OK;
    char iFName[16], iLName[16], idoctor[31], idoctor_phone[13];
    string idrug_name;
    date_string iprescript_date;
    Customer * whichCust;
    Drug * whichDrug;
    Prescription * newPrescript, * nextPrescript;
    PrescriptList * PrescriptHeader;

    // Locate the drug
```

Listing B.14 (Continued)   main.cpp

```cpp
cout << "\nEnter the name of the drug: ";
gets (idrug_name);
whichDrug = drugs->findDrug(idrug_name);
if (whichDrug == 0)
{
    cout << "We don't stock this drug" << endl;
    return;
}
```

```cpp
// Locate the customer
cout << "\nEnter the customer's first name: ";
gets (iFName);
cout << "\nEnter the customer's last name: ";
gets (iLName);
whichCust = LinkedCusts->findCust (iLName, iFName);
if (whichCust == 0)
{
    cout << "This customer isn't in the database. Please create a customer
        record" << endl;
    return;
}
```

```cpp
// Look for drug interactions
OK = whichCust->checkNewDrug (idrug_name, drugs);
if (!OK)
{
    cout << "An interaction exists with this drug. Check with the doctor."
        << endl;
    return;
}
```

```cpp
// Now get the rest of the prescription info and create the object
cout << "\nEnter the doctor's name: ";
gets (idoctor);
cout << "\nEnter the doctor's phone number: ";
gets (idoctor_phone);
cout << "\nEnter the doctor's FDA number: ";
cin >> iFDA;
cout << "\nEnter the prescription date: ";
gets (iprescript_date);
cout << "\nEnter the number of refills allowed: ";
cin >> irefills;
```

```cpp
// increment last prescription number
LinkedCusts->incLastPrescript_numb ();
```

Listing B.14 (Continued)   main.cpp

```cpp
    newPrescript = new Prescription (whichDrug->getDrug_numb(),
        LinkedCusts>getLastPrescript_numb(),irefills,iFDA,idoctor,
        idoctor_phone,iprescript_date)

    // now insert into customer's prescription list. New prescriptions are inserted at head
    // of list.
    PrescriptHeader->Insert (newPrescript, TRUE);

    // now insert into binary search tree by prescription number
    tree->Insert (newPrescript, newPrescript->getPrescript_numb());

    cout << flush; // flush I/O buffer before formatting label
    newPrescript->bottleLabel (whichCust,label,drugs);
    cout << label.str(); // display the formatted label stream
}


void refillPrescript (PrescriptTree * tree)
{
    int iPrescript_numb, OK;
    Prescription * whichPrescript;

    cout << "Enter the prescription number: ";
    cin >> iPrescript_numb;
    whichPrescript = tree->findPrescript (iPrescript_numb);
    if (whichPrescript == 0)
    {
        cout << "There's no prescription by that number." << endl;
        return;
    }
    OK = whichPrescript->refill();
    if (!OK)
    {
        cout << "No more refills are available." << endl;
        return;
    }
}
```

The Video Store

Listing B.15   video.h

```
const MAX_STARS = 20;
const MOVIE = 0;
const OTHER = 1;
const GAME = 2;

typedef char string[81];
typedef char date_string[9];
typedef char rate_string[6];

class Item_copy;
class MerchTree;
class CopyTree;

class Merchandise_Item
{
    protected:
        int Title_numb, Copy_count, Item_type;
        string Title;
        string Distributor;
        Merchandise_Item * Left, * Right; // binary search tree of titles
        Item_copy * First, * Last;   // linked list of items
    public:
        Merchandise_Item (int, string, string);
        Merchandise_Item (ifstream &);
        char * getTitle();
        int getCopy_count(); // return number of copies
        Merchandise_Item * getLeft();
        Merchandise_Item * getRight();
        void setLeft (Merchandise_Item *);
        void setRight (Merchandise_Item *);
        void Insert (Item_copy *);
        Item_copy * getLast ();
        int getItem_type ();
        int getTitle_numb();
        Item_copy * available (); // check to see if any copies are available
        virtual void write (ofstream &) = 0;

};

class Video : public Merchandise_Item
{
    protected:
```

Listing B.15 (Continued)   video.h

```
        string Director;
        string Producer;
        string Classification;
        int Length;
    public:
        Video (int, string, string, string, string, string, int);
        Video (ifstream &);
        virtual void write (ofstream &) = 0;
};

class Movie : public Video
{
    private:
        string Stars[MAX_STARS]; // array of strings for stars
        int numbStars;
        rate_string Rating;
    public:
        Movie (int, string, string, string, string, string, int, int,
            string [], rate_string, MerchTree *);
        Movie (ifstream &, MerchTree *);
        void write (ofstream &);
};

class Other : public Video
{
    public:
        Other (int, string, string, string, string, string, int, MerchTree *);
        Other (ifstream &, MerchTree *);
        void write (ofstream &);
};

class Game : public Merchandise_Item
{
    private:
        string System;
        rate_string Rating;
    public:
        Game (int, string, string, string, rate_string, MerchTree *);
        Game (ifstream &, MerchTree *);
        void write (ofstream &);
};

class Customer;

class Item_copy
{
    protected:
```

Listing B.15 (Continued)   video.h

```
            int Inventory_numb, Title_numb, Renter_numb;
            int In_stock; // boolean
            date_string Date_due;
            Item_copy * Next, * Right, * Left;
        public:
            Item_copy (int, int);
            Item_copy (ifstream &);
            void Rent (Customer *, date_string);
            void Return ();
            int getStatus();
            int getInventory_numb();
            Item_copy * getNext();
            void setNext (Item_copy *);
            void setRight (Item_copy *);
            void setLeft (Item_copy *);
            Item_copy * getRight ();
            Item_copy * getLeft ();
            virtual void write (ofstream &) = 0;
};

class Video_copy : public Item_copy
{
        private:
            string Media, Format;
            int Dolby, LBX; // these are all booleans
        public:
            Video_copy (int, int, string, string, int, int, Merchandise_Item *,
                CopyTree *);
            Video_copy (ifstream &, Merchandise_Item *, CopyTree *);
            void write (ofstream &);
};

class Game_copy : public Item_copy
{
        public:
            Game_copy (int, int, Merchandise_Item *, CopyTree *);
            Game_copy (ifstream &, Merchandise_Item *, CopyTree *);
            void write (ofstream &);
};

class CustTree;

class Customer
{
        private:
            int Renter_numb;
```

Listing B.15 (Continued)   video.h

```
        string fname, lname, street, CSZ, phone;
        string credit_card_numb;
        Customer * Right, * Left;
    public:
        Customer (int, string, string, string, string, string, string,
            CustTree *);
        Customer (ifstream &, CustTree *);
        int getRenter_numb();
        void setRight (Customer *);
        void setLeft (Customer *);
        Customer * getRight();
        Customer * getLeft();
        char * getLongname(); // note: lname + fname
        void write (ofstream &);
};
```

Listing B.16   base.cpp

```
#include <string.h>
#include <fstream.h>
#include "video.h"
#include "tree.h"

Merchandise_Item::Merchandise_Item (int iTnumb, string iTitle, string
    iDistributor)
{
    Title_numb = iTnumb;
    Copy_count = 0;
    strcpy (Title, iTitle);
    strcpy (Distributor, iDistributor);
    First = 0;
    Last = 0;
}

Merchandise_Item::Merchandise_Item (ifstream & fin)
{
    char dummy;

    fin >> Title_numb;
    fin >> Copy_count;
    fin.get (dummy);
    fin.getline (Title, 80, '\0');
    fin.getline (Distributor, 80, '\0');
    First = 0;
    Last = 0;
```

Listing B.16 (Continued)   base.cpp

```
}

char * Merchandise_Item::getTitle()
    { return Title; }

int Merchandise_Item::getCopy_count ()
    { return Copy_count; }

Merchandise_Item * Merchandise_Item::getLeft()
    { return Left; }

Merchandise_Item * Merchandise_Item::getRight()
    { return Right; }

void Merchandise_Item::setLeft (Merchandise_Item * newItem)
    { Left = newItem; }

void Merchandise_Item::setRight (Merchandise_Item * newItem)
    { Right = newItem; }

void Merchandise_Item::Insert (Item_copy * newCopy)
{
    if (First == 0)
    {
        First = newCopy;
        Last = newCopy;
    }
    else
    {
        Last->setNext (newCopy);
        Last = newCopy;
    }
}

Item_copy * Merchandise_Item::getLast ()
    { return Last;}

Item_copy * Merchandise_Item::available()
{
    Item_copy * current;

    current = First;
    while (current)
    {
        if (current->getStatus() == TRUE)
            return current;
        current = current->getNext();
```

Listing B.16 (Continued)   base.cpp

```
    }
    return 0; // no copies available
}

int Merchandise_Item::getItem_type()
    { return Item_type; }

int Merchandise_Item::getTitle_numb()
    { return Title_numb; }

Video::Video (int iTnumb, string iTitle, string iDistributor, string iDirector,
    string iProducer, string iClass, int iLength)
    : Merchandise_Item (iTnumb, iTitle, iDistributor) // call base class constructor
{
    strcpy (Director, iDirector);
    strcpy (Producer, iProducer);
    strcpy (Classification, iClass);
    Length = iLength;
    First = 0;
    Last = 0;
}

Video::Video (ifstream & fin)
    : Merchandise_Item (fin)
{
    char dummy;

    fin.getline (Director, 80, '\0');
    fin.getline (Producer, 80, '\0');
    fin.getline (Classification, 80, '\0');
    fin >> Length;
    fin.get (dummy);
}
```

Listing B.17   itembase.cpp

```
#include <string.h>
#include <fstream.h>
#include "video.h"

Item_copy::Item_copy (int iNumb, int iTnumb)
{
    Inventory_numb = iNumb;
    Title_numb = iTnumb;
    Renter_numb = 0;
```

Listing B.17 (Continued)   itembase.cpp

```
    In_stock = TRUE;
    strcpy (Date_due, "");
}

Item_copy::Item_copy (ifstream & fin)
{
    char dummy;
    fin >> Inventory_numb;
    fin >> Title_numb;
    fin >> Renter_numb;
    fin >> In_stock;
    fin.get (dummy);
    fin.getline (Date_due, 80, '\0');
}

void Item_copy::Rent (Customer * Renter, date_string Due)
{
    Renter_numb = Renter->getRenter_numb();
    strcpy (Date_due, Due);
    In_stock = FALSE;
}

void Item_copy::Return()
{
    Renter_numb = 0;
    strcpy (Date_due, "");
    In_stock = TRUE;
}

int Item_copy::getStatus()
    { return In_stock; }

int Item_copy::getInventory_numb()
    { return Inventory_numb; }

Item_copy * Item_copy::getNext()
    { return Next; }

void Item_copy::setNext (Item_copy * newCopy)
    { Next = newCopy; }

void Item_copy::setRight (Item_copy * newCopy)
    { Right = newCopy; }

void Item_copy::setLeft (Item_copy * newCopy)
    { Left = newCopy; }
```

Listing B.17 (Continued)   itembase.cpp

```
Item_copy * Item_copy::getRight()
    { return Right; }

Item_copy * Item_copy::getLeft()
    { return Left; }
```

Listing B.18   movie.cpp

```
#include <string.h>
#include <fstream.h>
#include "video.h"
#include "tree.h"

Movie::Movie (int iTnumb, string iTitle, string iDistributor, string iDirector,
    string iProducer, string iClass, int iLength, int inumbStars, string
    iStars[], rate_string iRating, MerchTree * Items)
    : Video (iTnumb, iTitle, iDistributor, iDirector, iProducer, iClass,
    iLength)
{
    numbStars = inumbStars;
    for (int i = 0; i <= numbStars; i++)
        strcpy (Stars[i], iStars[i]);
    strcpy (Rating, iRating);
    Left = 0;
    Right = 0;
    Item_type = MOVIE;
    Items->Insert (this, Title);
}

Movie::Movie (ifstream & fin, MerchTree * Items)
    : Video (fin)
{
    char dummy;

    fin >> numbStars;
    fin.get (dummy);
    for (int i = 0; i <= numbStars; i++)
        fin.getline (Stars[i], 80, '\0');
    fin.getline (Rating, 80, '\0');
    Item_type = MOVIE;
    Left = 0;
    Right = 0;
    Items->Insert (this, Title);
}
```

Listing B.18 (Continued)   movie.cpp

```cpp
void Movie::write (ofstream & fout)
{
    fout << Title_numb << ' ';
    fout << Copy_count << ' ';
    fout << Title << '\0';
    fout << Distributor << '\0';
    fout << Director << '\0';
    fout << Producer << '\0';
    fout << Classification << '\0';
    fout << Length << ' ' << numbStars << ' ';
    for (int i = 0; i <= numbStars; i++)
        fout << Stars[i] << '\0';
    fout << Rating << '\0';
}
```

Listing B.19   other.cpp

```cpp
#include <string.h>
#include <fstream.h>
#include "video.h"
#include "tree.h"

Other::Other (int iTnumb, string iTitle, string iDistributor, string iDirector,
    string iProducer, string iClass, int iLength, MerchTree * Items)
    : Video (iTnumb, iTitle, iDistributor, iDirector, iProducer, iClass,
    iLength)
{
    Left = 0;
    Right = 0;
    Item_type = OTHER;
    Items->Insert (this, Title);
}

Other::Other (ifstream & fin, MerchTree * Items)
    : Video (fin)
{
    // note: base class's constructor reads all data
    Right = 0;
    Left = 0;
    Items->Insert (this, Title);
    Item_type = OTHER;
}
```

Listing B.19 (Continued)   other.cpp

```
void Other::write (ofstream & fout)
{
    fout << Title_numb << ' ';
    fout << Copy_count << ' ';
    fout << Title << '\0';
    fout << Distributor << '\0';
    fout << Director << '\0';
    fout << Producer << '\0';
    fout << Classification << '\0';
    fout << Length << ' ';
}
```

Listing B.20   game.cpp

```
#include <string.h>
#include <fstream.h>
#include "video.h"
#include "tree.h"

Game::Game (int iTnumb, string iTitle, string iDistributor, string iSystem,
    rate_string iRating, MerchTree * Items)
    : Merchandise_Item (iTnumb, iTitle, iDistributor)
{
    strcpy (System, iSystem);
    strcpy (Rating, iRating);
    Item_type = GAME;
    Left = 0;
    Right = 0;
    Items->Insert (this, Title);
}

Game::Game (ifstream & fin, MerchTree * ItemTree)
    : Merchandise_Item (fin)
{
    fin.getline (System, 80, '\0');
    fin.getline (Rating, 80, '\0');
    Left = 0;
    Right = 0;
    ItemTree->Insert (this, Title);
    Item_type = GAME;
}

void Game::write (ofstream & fout)
{
```

Listing B.20 (Continued)   game.cpp

```
    fout << Title_numb << ' ';
    fout << Copy_count << ' ';
    fout << Title << '\0';
    fout << Distributor << '\0';
    fout << System << '\0';
    fout << Rating << '\0';
}
```

Listing B.21   copies.cpp

```
#include <string.h>
#include <fstream.h>
#include "video.h"
#include "tree.h"

Video_copy::Video_copy (int iNumb, int iTnumb, string iMedia, string iFormat,
    int iDolby, int iLBX, Merchandise_Item * Item, CopyTree * Copies)
    : Item_copy (iNumb, iTnumb)
{
    strcpy (Media, iMedia);
    strcpy (Format, iFormat);
    Dolby = iDolby;
    LBX = iLBX;
    Item->Insert (this);
    Copies->Insert (this, Inventory_numb);
}

Video_copy::Video_copy (ifstream & fin, Merchandise_Item * Item, CopyTree *
    Copies)
    : Item_copy (fin)
{
    char dummy;
    fin.getline (Media, 80, '\0');
    fin.getline (Format, 80, '\0');
    fin >> Dolby >> LBX;
    fin.get (dummy);
    Item->Insert (this);
    Copies->Insert (this, Inventory_numb);
}

void Video_copy::write (ofstream & fout)
{
    fout << Inventory_numb << ' ';
    fout << Title_numb << ' ';
```

Listing B.21 (Continued)   copies.cpp

```cpp
    fout << Renter_numb << ' ';
    fout << In_stock << ' ';
    fout << Date_due << '\0';
    fout << Media << '\0';
    fout << Format << '\0';
    fout << Dolby << ' ';
    fout << LBX << ' ';
}

Game_copy::Game_copy (int iNumb, int iTnumb, Merchandise_Item * Item, CopyTree
    * Copies)
    : Item_copy (iNumb, iTnumb)
{
    Next = 0;
    Item->Insert (this);
    Copies->Insert (this, Inventory_numb);
}

Game_copy::Game_copy (ifstream & fin, Merchandise_Item * Item, CopyTree *
    Copies)
    : Item_copy (fin)
{
    Item->Insert (this);
    Copies->Insert (this, Inventory_numb);
}

void Game_copy::write (ofstream & fout)
{
    fout << Inventory_numb << ' ';
    fout << Title_numb << ' ';
    fout << Renter_numb << ' ';
    fout << In_stock << ' ';
    fout << Date_due << '\0';
}
```

Listing B.22   customer.cpp

```cpp
#include <string.h>
#include <fstream.h>
#include "video.h"
#include "tree.h"

Customer::Customer (int iRnumb, string ifname, string ilname, string istreet,
    string iCSZ, string iphone, string iccn, CustTree * Renters)
{
```

Listing B.22 (Continued)   customer.cpp

```
        Renter_numb = iRnumb;
        strcpy (fname, ifname);
        strcpy (lname, ilname);
        strcpy (street, istreet);
        strcpy (CSZ, iCSZ);
        strcpy (phone, iphone);
        strcpy (credit_card_numb, iccn);
        Right = 0;
        Left = 0;
        Renters->Insert (this, fname, lname);  // insert into tree
}

Customer::Customer (ifstream & fin, CustTree * Renters)
{
        char dummy;

        fin >> Renter_numb;
        fin.get (dummy);
        fin.getline (fname, 80, '\0');
        fin.getline (lname, 80, '\0');
        fin.getline (street, 80, '\0');
        fin.getline (CSZ, 80, '\0');
        fin.getline (credit_card_numb, 80, '\0');
        Right = 0;
        Left = 0;
        Renters->Insert (this, fname, lname);  // insert directly into binary tree
}


int Customer::getRenter_numb()
        { return Renter_numb; }

void Customer::setRight (Customer * newCust)
        { Right = newCust; }

void Customer::setLeft (Customer * newCust)
        { Left = newCust; }

Customer * Customer::getRight ()
        { return Right; }

Customer * Customer::getLeft ()
        { return Left; }

char * Customer::getLongname()
{
```

Listing B.22 (Continued)   customer.cpp

```
    static string Tname;
    strcpy (Tname, lname);
    strcat (Tname, fname);
    return Tname;
}

void Customer::write (ofstream & fout)
{
    fout << Renter_numb << ' ';
    fout << fname << '\0';
    fout << lname << '\0';
    fout << street << '\0';
    fout << CSZ << '\0';
    fout << credit_card_numb << '\0';
}
```

Listing B.23   tree.h

```
// Can use a single tree to hold all merchandise items
// Alternatively, could define one tree from for each type of merchandise
// Base class pointer can hold pointers to any of the derived classes
class MerchTree
{
    private:
        Merchandise_Item * root;
        int Item_count, lastTitle_numb;
    public:
        MerchTree (int); // base constructor
        void Insert (Merchandise_Item *, string);
        Merchandise_Item * find (string); // find
        int getItem_count();
        void setItem_count (int);
        int getlastTitle_numb ();
        int inclastTitle_numb ();
        Merchandise_Item * getRoot();
};

class MerchItr
{
    private:
        Merchandise_Item * stack[25], * root;
        int stackPtr;
        void push (Merchandise_Item *); // push onto stack
        Merchandise_Item * pop (); // pop from stack
```

Listing B.23 (Continued)   tree.h

```
            void goLeft (Merchandise_Item *);
    public:
        MerchItr ();
        int Init (MerchTree *);
        int operator++ (); // find node
        int operator! (); // check for end of traversal
        Merchandise_Item * operator() (); // return pointer to current object
};


class MerchTree
{
    private:
        Customer * root;
        int Cust_count;
    public:
        CustTree (); // constructor
        CustTree (int);
        void Insert (Customer *, string, string);
        Customer * find (string, string);
        int getCust_count();
        Customer * getRoot();
};

class CustItr
{
    private:
        Customer * stack[25], * root;
        int stackPtr;
        void push (Customer *);
        Customer * pop ();
        void goLeft (Customer *);
    public:
        CustItr ();
        int Init (CustTree *);
        int operator++ (); // find nodes
        int operator! (); // check for end of traversal
        Customer * operator() (); // return pointer to current node
};

class CopyTree
{
    private:
        Item_copy * root;
        int lastCopy_numb;
```

Listing B.23 (Continued)   tree.h

```
public:
    CopyTree (int); // constructor
    void Insert (Item_copy *, int);
    Item_copy * find (int);
    int getlastCopy_numb ();
    int inclastCopy_numb ();
};
```

Listing B.24   tree.cpp

```
#include <string.h>
#include <fstream.h>
#include "video.h"
#include "tree.h"

MerchTree::MerchTree (int inumb)
{
    root = 0;
    Item_count = 0;
    lastTitle_numb = inumb;
}

void MerchTree::Insert (Merchandise_Item * newItem, string iTitle)
{
    Merchandise_Item * current, * child;

    if (root) // if root node exists
    {
        current = root;
        while (current) // keep going while there's a pointer
        {
            if (strcmp(current->getTitle(), iTitle) < 0)
            {
                // go down right side
                child = current->getRight();
                if (!child) // if no right child, insert
                {
                    current->setRight (newItem);
                    return;
                }
            }
            else
            {
```

Listing B.24 (Continued)   tree.cpp

```cpp
                        // go down left side
                        child = current->getLeft();
                        if (!child) // if no left child, insert
                        {
                        current->setLeft (newItem);
                        return;
                        }
                    }
                current = child;
            }
        }
    else
        root = newItem;
    Item_count++;
}

Merchandise_Item * MerchTree::find (string iTitle)
{
    Merchandise_Item * current;

    if (root) // make sure there is at least one node
    {
        current = root;
        while (current) // as long as there's a pointer
        {
            if (strcmp (current->getTitle(), iTitle) == 0)
                return current; // send back pointer to drug object
            // if less, go down right side
            if (strcmp (current->getTitle(), iTitle) < 0)
                current = current->getRight();
            // if greater, go down left side
            else
                current = current->getLeft();
        }
    }
    return 0; // not found
}


int MerchTree::getItem_count()
    { return Item_count; }

void MerchTree::setItem_count (int count)
    { Item_count = count; }
```

Listing B.24 (Continued) tree.cpp

```cpp
int MerchTree::getlastTitle_numb()
    { return lastTitle_numb; }

int MerchTree::inclastTitle_numb ()
{
    lastTitle_numb++;
    return lastTitle_numb;
}

Merchandise_Item * MerchTree::getRoot()
    { return root; }

MerchItr::MerchItr()
{
    stackPtr = 0;
    root = 0;
}

int MerchItr::Init (MerchTree * tree)
{
    stackPtr = -1; // set stack as empty
    root = tree->getRoot(); // initialize current node to root
    goLeft (root); // go down left side of tree
    return stackPtr >= 0; // is stack empty?
}

int MerchItr::operator++ ()
{
    Merchandise_Item * parent, * child;

    if (stackPtr >= 0)
    {
        parent = pop();
        child = parent->getRight();
        if (child)
            goLeft (child);
    }
    return stackPtr >= 0;
}

Merchandise_Item * MerchItr::operator() ()
    { return stack[stackPtr]; }  // current node is top of stack

void MerchItr::goLeft (Merchandise_Item * Item)
{
    while (Item)
```

Listing B.24 (Continued)   tree.cpp

```cpp
    {
        push (Item);
        Item = Item->getLeft();
    }
}

int MerchItr::operator! ()
    { return stackPtr >= 0; }   // check for end of traversal

void MerchItr::push (Merchandise_Item * Item)
    { stack[++stackPtr] = Item; }

Merchandise_Item * MerchItr::pop ()
    { return stack[stackPtr--]; }

CustTree::CustTree ()
{
    root = 0;
}

CustTree::CustTree (int count)
{
    root = 0;
    Cust_count = count;
}

void CustTree::Insert (Customer * newCust, string ifname, string ilname)
{
    Customer * current, * child;
    string iLongname;
    char * cLongname;

    strcpy (iLongname, ilname);
    strcat (iLongname, ifname);

    if (root)  // if root node exists
    {
        current = root;
        while (current)  // keep going while there's a pointer
        {
            cLongname = current->getLongname();
            if (strcmp(cLongname, iLongname) < 0)
            {
                // go down right side
                child = current->getRight();
                if (!child)  // if no right child, insert
```

Listing B.24 (Continued)   tree.cpp

```
                {
                    current->setRight (newCust);
                    return;
                }
            }
            else
            {
                // go down left side
                child = current->getLeft();
                if (!child) // if no left child, insert
                {
                    current->setLeft (newCust);
                    return;
                }
            }
            current = child;
        }
    }
    else
        root = newCust;
}

Customer * CustTree::find (string ifname, string ilname)
{
    Customer * current;
    string iLongname;
    char * cLongname;

    strcpy (iLongname, ilname);
    strcat (iLongname, ifname);

    if (root) // make sure there is at least one node
    {
        current = root;
        while (current) // as long as there's a pointer
        {
            cLongname = current->getLongname();
            if (strcmp (cLongname, iLongname) == 0)
                return current; // send back pointer to drug object
            // if less, go down right side
            if (strcmp (cLongname, iLongname) < 0)
                current = current->getRight();
            // if greater, go down left side
            else
                current = current->getLeft();
        .}
```

Listing B.24 (Continued)   tree.cpp

```cpp
    }
    return 0; // not found
}

int CustTree::getCust_count()
    { return Cust_count; }

Customer * CustTree::getRoot()
    { return root; }

CustItr::CustItr()
{
    stackPtr = 0;
    root = 0;
}

int CustItr::Init (CustTree * tree)
{
    stackPtr = -1; // set stack as empty
    root = tree->getRoot(); // initialize current node to root
    goLeft (root); // go down left side of tree
    return stackPtr >= 0; // is stack empty?
}

int CustItr::operator++ ()
{
    Customer * parent, * child;

    if (stackPtr >= 0)
    {
        parent = pop();
        child = parent->getRight();
        if (child)
            goLeft (child);
    }
    return stackPtr >= 0;
}

Customer * CustItr::operator() ()
    { return stack[stackPtr]; }   // current node is top of stack

void CustItr::goLeft (Customer * person)
{
    while (person)
    {
        push (person);
```

Listing B.24 (Continued)   tree.cpp

```cpp
        person = person->getLeft();
    }
}

int CustItr::operator! ()
    { return stackPtr >= 0; }  // check for end of traversal

void CustItr::push (Customer * person)
    { stack[++stackPtr] = person; }

Customer * CustItr::pop ()
    { return stack[stackPtr--]; }

CopyTree::CopyTree (int iCopies)
{
    root = 0;
    lastCopy_numb = iCopies;
}

void CopyTree::Insert (Item_copy * newCopy, int Inumb)
{
    Item_copy * current, * child;

    if (root)  // if root node exists
    {
        current = root;
        while (current)  // keep going while there's a pointer
        {
            if (current->getInventory_numb() < Inumb)
            {
                // go down right side
                child = current->getRight();
                if (!child)  // if no right child, insert
                {
                    current->setRight (newCopy);
                    return;
                }
            }
            else
            {
                // go down left side
                child = current->getLeft();
                if (!child)  // if no left child, insert
                {
                    current->setLeft (newCopy);
```

Listing B.24 (Continued)   tree.cpp

```
                    return;
                }
            }
            current = child;
        }
    }
    else
        root = newCopy;
}

Item_copy * CopyTree::find (int Inumb)
{
    Item_copy * current;

    if (root) // make sure there is at least one node
    {
        current = root;
        while (current) // as long as there's a pointer
        {
            if (current->getInventory_numb() == Inumb)
                return current; // send back pointer to drug object
            // if less, go down right side
            if (current->getInventory_numb() < Inumb)
                current = current->getRight();
            // if greater, go down left side
            else
                current = current->getLeft();
        }
    }
    return 0; // not found
}

int CopyTree::getlastCopy_numb()
    { return lastCopy_numb; }

int CopyTree::inclastCopy_numb()
    { return ++lastCopy_numb; }
```

Listing B.25   main.cpp

```
#include <iostream.h>
#include <fstream.h>
#include <string.h>
#include <stdio.h>
```

Listing B.25 (Continued)   main.cpp

```cpp
#include "video.h"
#include "tree.h"
#include "menu.rsc"

void main()
{
    // function prototypes
    int EnterMovie (MerchTree *, int);
    int EnterOther (MerchTree *, int);
    void EnterVideoCopy (MerchTree *, CopyTree *);
    int EnterGame (MerchTree *, int);
    void EnterGameCopy (MerchTree *, CopyTree *);
    int EnterCustomer (CustTree *, int);
    void Rent (MerchTree *, CustTree *);
    void Return (CopyTree *);


    // local variables
    menu MainMenu (maintitle, mainmenu, mainmenucount);
    MerchTree * Items; // alphabetical list of all titles
    CopyTree * Copies;
    CustTree * Customers;
    int choice = 0; // menu choice
    char yes_no, dummy;
    int Movie_count = 0, Other_count = 0 , Game_count = 0, Cust_count = 0, i, j;
    int lastTitle_numb, lastCopy_numb;
    Movie * newMovie;
    Other * newOther;
    Game * newGame;
    Video_copy * newVideo;
    Game_copy * newGC;
    Customer * newCust;

    ifstream MasterIn ("Master"); // master file
    if (!MasterIn)
    {
        cout << "Master file not found. Continue? (y/n)";
        cin >> yes_no;
        if (yes_no == 'n')
            return;
    }
    MasterIn >> lastTitle_numb >> lastCopy_numb;
    MasterIn.close();

    Items = new MerchTree(lastTitle_numb); // tree for all titles
```

Listing B.25 (Continued)   main.cpp

```cpp
Copies = new CopyTree (lastCopy_numb); // tree for copies by copy number

// read in movies
ifstream MovieIn ("Movies"); // movie file
if (!MovieIn)
{
    cout << "Movie file not found. Continue? (y/n)";
    cin >> yes_no;
    if (yes_no == 'n')
        return;
}
MovieIn >> Movie_count;
MovieIn.get (dummy);
for (i = 1; i <= Movie_count; i++)
{
    newMovie = new Movie (MovieIn, Items);
    for (j = 1; j <= newMovie->getCopy_count(); j++)
        newVideo = new Video_copy (MovieIn, newMovie, Copies);
}
MovieIn.close();

ifstream OtherIn ("Others"); // other videos file
if (!OtherIn)
{
    cout << "Other video file not found. Continue? (y/n)";
    cin >> yes_no;
    if (yes_no == 'n')
        return;
}
OtherIn >> Other_count;
OtherIn.get (dummy);
for (i = 1; i <= Other_count; i++)
{
    newOther = new Other (OtherIn, Items);
    for (j = 1; j <= newOther->getCopy_count(); j++)
        newVideo = new Video_copy (OtherIn, newOther, Copies);
}
OtherIn.close();

ifstream GamesIn ("Games"); // games file
if (!GamesIn)
{
    cout << "Games file not found. Continue? (y/n)";
    cin >> yes_no;
    if (yes_no == 'n')
        return;
```

Listing B.25 (Continued)   main.cpp

```cpp
}
GamesIn >> Game_count;
GamesIn.get (dummy);
for (i = 1; i <= Game_count; i++)
{
    newGame = new Game (GamesIn, Items);
    for (j = 1; j <= newGame->getCopy_count(); j++)
        newGC = new Game_copy (GamesIn, newGame, Copies);
}

Items->setItem_count (Movie_count + Other_count + Game_count);

ifstream CustIn ("Customers"); // customers file
if (!CustIn)
{
    cout << "Customers file not found. Continue? (y/n)";
    cin >> yes_no;
    if (yes_no == 'n')
        return;
    Customers = new CustTree (); // empty tree for customers
}
else
{
    CustIn >> Cust_count;
    CustIn.get (dummy);
    Customers = new CustTree (Cust_count);
    for (i = 1; i <= Cust_count; i++)
        newCust = new Customer (CustIn, Customers);
}
CustIn.close();

while (choice != 9)
{
    MainMenu.displaymenu();
    choice = MainMenu.chooseoption();
    switch (choice)
    {
        case NEW_MOV:
            Movie_count = EnterMovie (Items, Movie_count);
            break;
        case NEW_OTH:
            Other_count = EnterOther (Items, Other_count);
            break;
        case VID_COPY:
            EnterVideoCopy (Items, Copies);
            break;
```

Listing B.25 (Continued)   main.cpp

```cpp
            case NEW_GAM:
                Game_count = EnterGame (Items, Game_count);
                break;
            case GAM_COPY:
                EnterGameCopy (Items, Copies);
                break;
            case NEW_CUST:
                Cust_count = EnterCustomer (Customers, Cust_count);
                break;
            case RENT:
                Rent (Items, Customers);
                break;
            case RETURN:
                Return (Copies);
                break;
            case MAIN_QUIT:
                break;
            default:
                cout << "\nYou've entered an unavailable option." << endl;
        }
    }

    ofstream MasterOut ("Master");
    if (!MasterOut)
    {
        cout << "Couldn't open master file. No further data will be written.";
        return;
    }
    MasterOut << lastTitle_numb << ' ' << lastCopy_numb;

    ofstream CustOut ("Customers");
    if (!Customers)
        cout << "Couldn't open customers file.";
    else
    {
        CustOut << Cust_count << ' ';
        CustItr writer;
        for (writer.Init (Customers); !writer; ++writer)
        {
            Customer * currentCust;
            currentCust = writer();
            currentCust->write (CustOut);
        }
    }

    ofstream MovieOut ("Movies");
    ofstream OtherOut ("Others");
```

Listing B.25 (Continued)   main.cpp

```cpp
    ofstream GameOut ("Games");
    MerchItr traversal;
    for (traversal.Init (Items); !traversal; ++traversal)
    {
        int Type;
        Merchandise_Item * currentOne;
        currentOne = traversal();
        Type = currentOne->getItem_type();
        if (Type == MOVIE)
            currentOne->write (MovieOut);
        else if (Type == OTHER)
            currentOne->write (OtherOut);
        else
            currentOne->write (GameOut);
    }
}

int EnterMovie (MerchTree * Items, int Movie_count)
{
    Movie * newMovie;
    int Title_numb, iLen;
    string iTitle, iDistributor, iDirector, iProducer, iClass;
    int numb_stars = 0;
    string istars[MAX_STARS];
    rate_string iRating;

    Title_numb = Items->inclastTitle_numb();
    cout << "Title: ";
    gets (iTitle);
    cout << "Distributor: ";
    gets (iDistributor);
    cout << "Director: ";
    gets (iDirector);
    cout << "Producer: ";
    gets (iProducer);
    cout << "Classification: ";
    gets (iClass);
    cout << "Length in minutes: ";
    cin >> iLen;
    cout << "Star: ";
    gets (istars[numb_stars]);
    while (strlen (istars[numb_stars]) > 0)
    {
        cout << "Star: ";
        gets (istars[numb_stars]);
    }
    if (numb_stars >= 0) numb_stars -= 2;
```

Listing B.25 (Continued)   main.cpp

```cpp
    cout << "Rating: ";
    gets (iRating);
    newMovie = new Movie (Title_numb, iTitle, iDistributor, iDirector,
    iProducer, iClass, iLen, numb_stars, istars, iRating, Items);
    return ++Movie_count;
}

int EnterOther (MerchTree * Items, int Other_count)
{
    Other * newOther;
    int Title_numb, iLen;
    string iTitle, iDistributor, iDirector, iProducer, iClass;

    Title_numb = Items->inclastTitle_numb();
    cout << "Title: ";
    gets (iTitle);
    cout << "Distributor: ";
    gets (iDistributor);
    cout << "Director: ";
    gets (iDirector);
    cout << "Producer: ";
    gets (iProducer);
    cout << "Classification: ";
    gets (iClass);
    cout << "Length in minutes: ";
    cin >> iLen;
    newOther = new Other (Title_numb, iTitle, iDistributor, iDirector,
    iProducer, iClass, iLen, Items);
    return ++Other_count;
}

void EnterVideoCopy (MerchTree * Items, CopyTree * Copies)
{
    string iTitle, iMedia, iFormat;
    Merchandise_Item * Parent;
    int newCopy_numb, iDolby, iLBX, iTitle_numb;
    Video_copy * newCopy;

    cout << "Title: ";
    gets (iTitle);
    Parent = Items->find (iTitle);
    if (Parent == 0)
    {
        cout << "We don't stock that title.";
        return;
    }
    iTitle_numb = Parent->getTitle_numb();
```

Listing B.25 (Continued)   main.cpp

```cpp
    newCopy_numb = Copies->inclastCopy_numb();
    cout << "Give this copy inventory # " << newCopy_numb << endl;
    cout << "Media: ";
    gets (iMedia);
    cout << "Format: ";
    gets (iFormat);
    cout << "Dolby surround sound? (1 = yes, 0 = no) ";
    cin >> iDolby;
    cout << "Letterboxed? (1 = yes, 0 = no) ";
    cin >> iLBX;
    newCopy = new Video_copy (newCopy_numb, iTitle_numb, iMedia, iFormat,
    iDolby, iLBX, Parent, Copies);
}

int EnterGame (MerchTree * Items, int Game_count)
{
    Game * newGame;
    int Title_numb;
    string iTitle, iDistributor, iSystem;
    rate_string iRating;

    Title_numb = Items->inclastTitle_numb();
    cout << "Title: ";
    gets (iTitle);
    cout << "Distributor: ";
    gets (iDistributor);
    cout << "System: ";
    gets (iSystem);
    cout << "Rating: ";
    gets (iRating);
    newGame = new Game (Title_numb, iTitle, iDistributor, iSystem, iRating,
    Items);
    return ++Game_count;
}

void EnterGameCopy (MerchTree * Items, CopyTree * Copies)
{
    string iTitle;
    Merchandise_Item * Parent;
    int newCopy_numb, iTitle_numb;
    Game_copy * newCopy;

    cout << "Title: ";
    gets (iTitle);
    Parent = Items->find (iTitle);
    if (Parent == 0)
    {
```

Listing B.25 (Continued)   main.cpp

```cpp
        cout << "We don't stock that title.";
        return;
    }
    iTitle_numb = Parent->getTitle_numb();
    newCopy_numb = Copies->inclastCopy_numb();
    cout << "Give this copy inventory # " << newCopy_numb << endl;
    newCopy = new Game_copy (newCopy_numb, iTitle_numb, Parent, Copies);
}

int EnterCustomer (CustTree * Customers, int Cust_count)
{
    Customer * newCust;
    string ifname, ilname, istreet, iCSZ, iphone, iccn;

    Cust_count++;
    cout << "First name: ";
    gets (ifname);
    cout << "Last name: ";
    gets (ilname);
    cout << "Street: ";
    gets (istreet);
    cout << "City, State Zip: ";
    gets (iCSZ);
    cout << "Phone: ";
    gets (iphone);
    cout << "Credit card number: ";
    gets (iccn);
    newCust = new Customer (Cust_count, ifname, ilname, istreet, iCSZ, iphone,
    iccn, Customers);
    return Cust_count;
}

void Rent (MerchTree * Items, CustTree * Customers)
{
    string iTitle, ifname, ilname;
    Customer * renter;
    int cust_numb;
    Merchandise_Item * item;
    Item_copy * whichItem;
    date_string due;

    cout << "Customer's first name: ";
    gets (ifname);
    cout << "Customer's last name: ";
    gets (ilname);
    renter = Customers->find (ifname, ilname);
    if (renter == 0)
```

Listing B.25 (Continued)   main.cpp

```
        {
            cout << "That customer isn't on file.";
            return;
        }
        cout << "Title: ";
        gets (iTitle);
        item = Items->find (iTitle);
        if (item == 0)
        {
            cout << "We don't stock that title.";
            return;
        }
        whichItem = item->available();
        if (whichItem == 0)
        {
            cout << "No copies of " << iTitle << " are available.";
            return;
        }
        cout << "Date due: ";
        gets (due);
        whichItem->Rent (renter, due);
}

void Return (CopyTree * Copies)
{
        Item_copy * item;
        int copy_numb;

        cout << "Inventory #: ";
        cin >> copy_numb;
        item = Copies->find (copy_numb);
        if (item == 0)
        {
            cout << "That inventory number isn't in use.";
            return;
        }
        item->Return();
}
```

This program uses the same menu class as the pharmacy program. The two menu files are menu.h (Listing B.11) and menu.cpp (Listing B.13).

Listing B.26   menu.rsc

```
#include "menu.h"

menuoption maintitle = "MAIN MENU";
menuoption mainmenu [] = {"1. Enter a new movie",
                          "2. Enter a new miscellaneous video",
                          "3. Enter a copy of a video",
                "4. Enter a new game",
                "5. Enter a copy of a game",
                "6. Enter a new customer",
                "7. Rent a video or game",
                "8. Return a video or game",
                "9. Quit"};

int mainmenucount = 9;

const NEW_MOV = 1;
const NEW_OTH = 2;
const VID_COPY = 3;
const NEW_GAM = 4;
const GAM_COPY = 5;
const NEW_CUST = 6;
const RENT = 7;
const RETURN = 8;
const MAIN_QUIT = 9;
```

Glossary

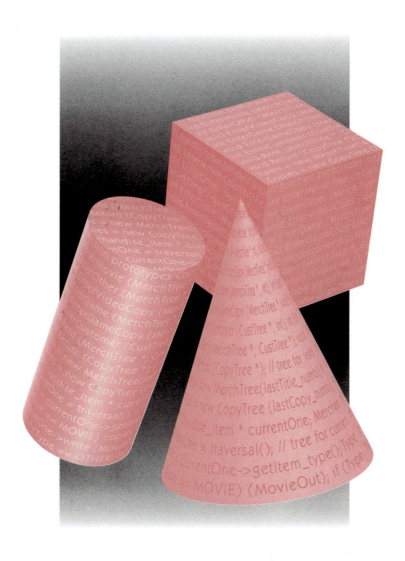

Abstract class: A class from which objects are never created; a class that contains at least one pure virtual function.

Access mode: A designation that determines the accessibility of the variables in a class by other functions.

Arrow operator: The operator used to reference a variable or member function of an object using dynamic binding.

Assignment operator: The operator used to assign a value to a variable; an equals sign.

Base class: A class from which other classes are derived; a parent class in a class hierarchy.

Binary file: A file that stores data as an unorganized stream of bits.

Binary search: A search technique that can be used on a random access, ordered data structure, based on the principle of eliminating half the values each time one value is examined.

Binary search tree: An ordered data structure in which each object has at most two child objects.

Binding: Linking an object to the member functions of its class.

Bit-wise AND operator: An operator (&) that performs a logical AND operation on pairs of bits in two storage locations.

Bit-wise OR operator: A C++ operator (|) that logically ORs the individual bits of two storage locations.

Bottom-up design: Designing a program beginning with detailed functional modules and assembling them into a complete program.

Bubble sort: A sorting algorithm that examines successive pairs of values and swaps them if they are in the wrong order. The sort makes repeated passes through the values until no swapping occurs, indicating that the values are in the correct order.

Child: In a tree data structure, an object pointed to by another object.

Class: A template from which objects are created, containing definitions of the data that describe an object along with the actions that the object knows how to perform.

Class library: A collection of previously compiled classes that can be used in an object-oriented program.

Compiler directive: An instruction to the compiler that is processed when a file is being compiled.

Concatenation: Creation of a longer string by combining two shorter strings, one on the end of the other.

Concrete class: A class from which objects can be created; a class that isn't an abstract class.

Constant: A variable whose contents can't be changed.

Constructor: A function that has the same name as its class. It is executed automatically whenever an object is created from the class.

Copy constructor: A constructor that initializes a new object with data copied from another object of the same class.

Dereference (a pointer): Access the location pointed to by the contents of a pointer variable.

Derived class: A class that is defined as a more specific instance of another class; a child class in a class hierarchy.

Direct memory access: The transfer of data directly between RAM and an I/O device, without the intervention of the CPU.

Dot operator: A period that indicates which object variables and/or member functions belong to.

Dynamic binding: Allocating space for objects while a program is running.

End-of-file: A condition that arises when a program attempts to read beyond the last data stored in a data file.

Escape character: A character used to send formatting information to an output device.

File system: An operating system's directory hierarchy, consisting of a tree of directories and files.

Formal parameter: A value that is passed into a function when the function is called by another function.

Forward reference: Naming a class in a header file, indicating that a definition will follow later.

Function: A self-contained module of code in a C or C++ program. C and C++ programs are made up of a collection of functions.

Function signature: The name of a function along with the number, type, and order of its parameters, used to uniquely identify a function.

Global variable: A variable defined so that it is accessible to an entire program.

Hard link: The path name of a file or directory in the same or other file system, used as a substitute for the physical file.

Header file: A file with a .h extension used by C and C++ to store constants and data structures.

In order traversal (of a tree): Processing the nodes of a tree in the order imposed by the tree.

Information hiding: Hiding the details of a class from other classes and/or programs.

Inline function: A member function whose body is defined with the class definition.

Instance (of a class): An object created from a class.

Instantiate (an object): Create an object from a class.

Interrupt-driven: An operating system that accords high priority to processes that handle I/O, which can interrupt the normal processing sequence of the CPU.

Iterator: A class designed to process all the nodes in a data structure (an array, list, or tree).

Kernel: The core of an operating system that contains the OS's fundamental functions, including functions that are hardware dependent.

Literal values: Values that are coded directly into a program, without placing them in main memory under a variable name.

Local variable: A variable defined within a function or compound statement (delimited by braces) that can be used only within the function or compound statement.

Make file: A file that lists source code files for compiling along with object code files and function libraries that need to be linked into an executable program.

Manipulators: Functions in the ios class hierarchy that format I/O stream output.

Member function: An action that an object knows how to perform.

Messsage: Information sent to an object to get it to perform some action.

Method: An action an object knows how to perform.

Mount (a file system): Make a file system available to an operating system.

Multiple inheritance: Deriving a class from more than one base class.

Navigational: A characteristic of a database in which access to data is through relationships explicitly defined in the database's schema.

Node: An object in a tree data structure.

Object: An entity in the data processing environment that has data that describe it and actions that it can perform.

Object-oriented programming: A paradigm for designing and developing application programs that encapsulate data and the actions data can perform into objects.

ODBMS: The abbreviation for object-oriented database management system.

OOP: The abbreviation for object-oriented programming.

Overloading: A technique for giving operators and functions more than one meaning so that they react differently to different messages.

Page: A block of data that is swapped between physical RAM and disk.

Page frame: A slot in RAM that is large enough to hold one page.

Paradigm: A theoretical model that can be used as a pattern for some activity.

Paradigm shift: A major change in the paradigm, or model, used as a pattern for some activity.

Parameter list: A definition of the values passed into a function.

Parameter passing: Sending data into a function through the function's parameter list.

Pass by reference: Including the address of a variable in a function's parameter list so that if the value is changed in the function, the modified value will be returned to the calling function.

Pass by value: Passing a value into a function so that if the value is changed in the function, the change isn't returned to the calling function.

Persistent object: An object that reads itself in from a file when it is created and saves itself to a file when it is destroyed.

Pointer: A main memory address, usually the location of data used by a program.

Pointer arithmetic: Any arithmetic operation performed on a main memory address.

Pointer variable: A variable that is declared to hold a pointer to some type of data storage.

Polymorphism: The ability to have classes in the same inheritance hierarchy respond differently to the same message.

Pop (off a stack): Remove one piece of data from the top of a stack.

Precompiler: A program that turns database manipulation statements embedded in an application program into calls to external library functions so that the source file can be compiled by a standard language compiler.

Project file: With most microcomputer C++ compilers, a file that lists the source code files that make up one program. The project file is used by the linker.

Pure function: A function that is declared but not defined in a class; a virtual function that is initialized with = 0.

Push (onto a stack): Place one piece of data on the top of a stack.

Resource: A program element, such as a window or menu, used by a program.

Resource file: A file containing resource specifications.

Root: The node at the top of a tree data structure.

Root directory: The directory at the top of a file system's directory tree.

Scope (of a variable): The portion of a program in which a variable is recognized.

Segment: A block of data that is swapped between physical RAM and disk.

Sequential search: A search that proceeds from the first element, to the second, and so on, visiting each element in turn until the desired element is found or all elements have been checked.

Set: In an object-oriented database, a group of objects of the same class.

Shell sort: A sorting method that recognizes when portions of a list are correctly sorted and limits the number of comparisons that need to be made during the sort by avoiding those portions that are already sorted.

Soft link: A pointer to a file or directory in the same file system, used as a substitute for the original file.

Software development life cycle: A set of procedures for developing success application software.

Stack: A data structure in which items are entered and removed only from the top (last in, first out).

Stack pointer: The top of a stack; a pointer to the last element added to a stack.

Static binding: Allocating space for objects when a program is compiled.

Storage class: A category (auto, static, register) that determines the placement and/or persistence of a variable in main memory.

Stream extraction operator: The operator (>>) that takes a value from an I/O stream and places it into a variable.

Stream I/O: Operations that view I/O as a stream of characters coming to or from some destination, such as the screen, keyboard, or a file.

Stream insertion operator: Two less than signs (<<) that insert a value into an I/O stream.

Structure member operator: A period that indicates which object variables and/or member functions belong to.

Structured programming: A programming paradigm in which programs are built from only three structures (simple sequence, iteration, selection).

System development life cycle: The process used by systems analysts to design and implement information systems.

Threads: Processes or parts of processes created for the same program that can run concurrently.

Top-down design: A process for designing a program in which the high-level design of the program is created first; the design is then fleshed out in detail.

Traversing (a tree): Accessing the nodes in a tree in order.

Virtual function: A function that will probably need to be called using a pointer so the program can determine exactly which function to use.

Virtual memory: Extending available main memory by using a disk file to simulate RAM that isn't physically installed in the computer.

Weak data typing: Minimal checking of the type of data assigned to variables.

Index

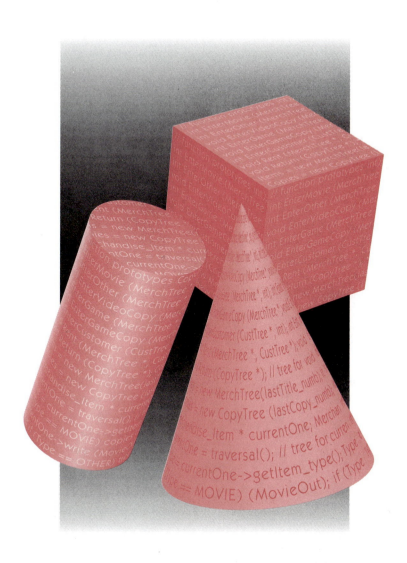